THE BROKEN PROMISES OF AMERICA AT HOME AND ABROAD, PAST AND PRESENT

AN ENCYCLOPEDIA FOR OUR TIMES

VOLUME 2

Douglas F. Dowd

Common Courage Press   Monroe, Maine

Library of Congress Cataloging-in-Publication Data is available
from the publisher on request.

ISBN 1-56751-314-x paper
ISBN 1-56751-315-8 cloth

Common Courage Press
Box 702
Monroe, ME 04951

(207) 525-0900; fax: (207) 525-3068
orders-info@commoncouragepress.com

See our website for e-versions of this book.
www.commoncouragepress.com

First Printing

Printed in Canada

This book is dedicated to Paul M. Sweezy (1910-2004). From the 1930s to the present, his works and generosity of spirit have been indispensable to those seeking to move our world toward decency, sanity, and safety. The book is also dedicated to the young of today and tomorrow who now and in the future will carry those efforts forward.

Contents

Volume 1

Volume 2

Abbreviations

AAA: Agricultural Adjustment Administration
AFL: American Federation of Labor
AP: Associated Press
BLS: Bureau of Labor Statistics
BW: *Business Week*
CA: *Covert Action*
CCC: Civilian Conservation Corps
CIO: Congress of Industrial Organizations
D&S: *Dollars & Sense*
EPA: Environmental Protection Agency
ERP: Economic Report of the President
FCC: Federal Communications Commission
FDIC: Federal Deposit Insurance Corporation
FEPC: Fair Employment Practices Commission
FM: *Fortune Magazine*
FTC: Federal Trade Commission
GAO: Government Accounting Office
GDP: Gross Domestic Product
GE: General Electric
GM: General Motors
GATT: General Agreement on Tariffs and Trade
HC: *Hartford Courant*
HMOs: Health Maintenance Organizations
HUAC: House Un-American Activities Committee
IBRD: International Bank for Reconstruction and Development ("World Bank")
IHT: *International Herald Tribune*
im: *il manifesto* (Italy)
IMF: International Monetary Fund
IRS: Internal Revenue Service
ITT: International Telephone and Telegraph
LAT: *Los Angeles Times*
LBO: *Left Business Observer*
MJ: *Mother Jones*
MM: *Multinational Monitor*
MNC: Multinational corporation
MR: *Monthly Review*

NAFTA: North American Free Trade Agreement
NATO: North Atlantic Treaty Organization
NRA: National Recovery Act
NSA: National Security Administration
NY: *New Yorker*
NYA: National Youth Administration
NYRB: *New York Review of Books*
OPEC: Organization of Petroleum Exporting Countries
OSHA: Office of Safety and Health Administration
OSS: Office of Special Services
PBS: Public Broadcasting System
PWA: Public Works Administration
S&L: Savings & Loan Banks
SEC: Securities and Exchange Commission
SFBG: *San Francisco Bay Guardian*
SFC: *San Francisco Chronicle*
TIPS: Terrorism Information and Prevention System
TN: *The Nation*
TVA: Tennessee Valley Authority
UN: United Nations
UNICEF: United Nations Childrens Fund
UNRRA: United Nations Relief and Rehabilitation Administration
USDA: U.S. Department of Agriculture
USDE: U.S. Department of Education
USGPO: U.S. Government Printing Office
USNWRP: U.S. NEWS & WORLD REPORT
USS: United States Steel Corporation
USSIC: U.S. Senate Intelligence Committee
USSR: Union of Soviet Socialist Republics
WHO: World Health Organization
WP: *Washington Post*
WPA: Works Progress Administration
WSJ: *Wall Street Journal*
WTO: World Trade Organization
ZM: *Z Magazine*

GATT (see IMF...)

GE

General Electric was among the first companies to see the need for and possibilities of **mergers and acquisitions (M&As)** when, already in 1892, it was born from the merger of Thomson-Hughson and Edison General Electric; by the 1920s, it had taken the lead among the major companies not only in **M&As** but in the political arena of the USA. In part that was because the electrical products industry, as with **GM** and **cars,** was at the cutting edge of something new; both could and had to develop novel business ways and means. As will be seen below, Gerald Swope, GE's chief in the 20s, added a special touch to those ways and means.

This is to say that GE was a frontrunner along the path toward the business, cultural, and political principles of what by the 1950s was emerging as **monopoly capitalism.** (BARAN/SWEEZY) Like GM, it was among the "inventors" of **consumerism**; unlike GM, it entered the political realm head first in the 1920s, marrying its fervent anti-unionism with the **Red Scare** of the 1920s. As an early adept in the budding field of **public relations**, GE became skilful at creating a benign image while behaving otherwise; notably in its ways of resisting unionization. The champions in that fight in mining, metals, and railroads were never reluctant to use any tactic at hand to prevent or break unions—hired killers, soldiers, the courts, labor spies, anything. (HUBERMAN, 1937)

GE, while publicly eschewing rough tactics, placed itself on the cutting edge of **spin**: while making it virtually impossible for a union to form or, if formed, to function, it made much of its presumed kindness to workers with inexpensive items such as recreation facilities while setting exploitative wages and working conditions and effectively holding off **unionization.** (Coincidentally, Mussolini was doing the same in Italy, with his "dopolavoro" gyms, etc.: Treat the workers kindly after work, squeeze them hard at work. Perhaps GE had someone in their PR department who knew Italian.)

GE's driving spirit in much of the interwar period was Gerald Swope; he would be called a **CEO** today. In 1931, he wrote a book advocating "self-government in business." His arguments served as the basis for what became the National Recovery Act (NRA) of

1933. Its rules, coming at the very pit of the worst depression in history, were just the opposite of what was needed, as well as being anti-democratic.

The NRA was a privately-controlled but government-backed system of laws requiring the business trade associations of over 800 industries to develop "industry codes" to which all their member companies had to adhere. The codes specified minimum—not maximum—prices and set required geographic market quotas, a close copy of the principles of Germany's long-standing "industrial cartels." In a depressed economy what is needed are lower prices and governmental stimuli (see **deficits and surpluses**). Companies not in compliance were punished by heavy fines imposed by federal courts.

The head of the NRA was the retired army General Hugh Johnson; the NRA symbol, displayed in all shop windows and business offices, was "The Blue Eagle," with lots of red, white, and blue. It is not beside the point to recall that, in 1934, Hitler dispatched a delegation to the USA to study the NRA. In 1935 the Supreme Court declared the NRA to be unconstitutional. (BRADY, 1937 and 1943)

After World War II, GE became the sponsor of what was a pretty good TV program—the General Electric Theater. Its host from 1954 to 1962 was Ronald **Reagan**. As part of that job he was also GE's regular and frequent spokesman at Rotary and Elks Clubs and other civic organizations.

Reagan's speeches, written for him by GE, were distinctly political, mixing entertainment and politics in ways then novel; now become our daily gruel. It was the combination of those activities for GE more than his film work that brought Reagan to public attention and, at the same time, shifted his politics away from his earlier New Deal position over to the Right. When the chips were down, Reagan could always bend far enough to scoop them up. (WILLS, 1988)

GE's radio and TV programs and the club speeches were a foretaste both of the potent power of today's cultural/political economy and of GE's position in its closed circle of power: GE is now one of the ten leading **media** giants in the world, owning NBC, AT&T, and TCI (cable) as well as "scores of other media enterprises." (MCCH-ESNEY, 1999) In its full-page ad in the NYT of 4-17-02, this is how GE proclaimed itself as the leading global businesses "in Medical Equipment, Aircraft Engines, Engineered Thermoplastics, Network Television, Power Generation, Locomotives, and Equipment

Leasing. /Plus/ A set of leading diversified financial services businesses and leading consumer businesses...." /And concluded:/ We bring good things to life.

That motto seems to have replaced what they had been saying since the 1920s: "Progress is our most important product"; now its most important product appears to be socioeconomic power and immodesty: One of the five largest U.S. companies, its sales—$134 billion in 2003 (FM, 4-5-04)—give it an income higher than all but about 20 countries in the world.

As indicated by its ad, GE's power is not only economic; it is a major player in the **infotainment** sphere (BARBER), in the **military-industrial complex**, in the razzle-dazzle of **consumerism** and in **financialization**. One of GE's many changes since Swope's time has been in the nature of its **CEO**. In the "new economy" of recent years, the role played by Swope for GE in the "new economy" of the 1920s was played by John F. Welch, Jr. Like him or not, Swope was a hard-working, hard-thinking kind of guy; Welch is something else. When he stepped down as CEO of GE as the 21st century began, he had assets of $500 million and a monthly income of $1.4 million. But it didn't end there; here are just some of the "perks" Welch gets from GE for the rest of his life:

> Floor level seats to NY Knicks games, courtside seats at the U.S. Open tennis matches, all costs associated with his Manhattan apartment (including food, wine, laundry, toiletries), newspapers, dining bills at the fancy restaurant in his apartment building, and... Not bad, especially considering his fortune is estimated to be from $400 to $800 million. ("Welches Reach Divorce Settlement," *NYT*, 7-4-03)

Glass-Steagall Banking Act

Passed in 1933, the law was designed to prevent the kinds of financial practices that carried the nation's banks to disaster, 1929-1933, resulting in their all having to be closed down in March, 1933. FDR declared the law to be essential "to prevent speculation with other people's money." In addition, the law set up the Federal Deposit Insurance Corporation (FDIC) to insure small depositors against bank failures.

The Act was repealed by Congress in 1998. How come? In the 15-20 years preceding that year, the financial hi-jinks going on were precisely what the Act was designed to prevent, such as the dike-breaking **S&L crisis** eased into being by **Reaganomics**. What was Glass-Steagall?

> ...The New Deal legislation was designed to ensure that publicly traded companies and the financial institutions that dealt with them would have to tell investors what and how their businesses were doing. Legal walls were built to separate functions—to make commercial banks specialize in short-term loans and investment banks in long-term ones, to insure saving deposits and to leave equity investments at risk—in the hopes of enforcing clarity.... (MAYER)

However, as the structure of profits and power shifted from industry to finance in the 80s and 90s (see **financialization**), the FIRE sector (finance, insurance, and real estate) quite sensibly (and predictably) used a good portion of its profits to boost its political clout:

> From relative peanuts in the early eighties, the money contributed to federal politics by the FIRE sector rose almost as fast as the money channeled to finance by /S&L/ federal bailouts and permissive regulation. .../T/he totals contributed rose from $109 million /in 1992/ to... $297 million /by 2000/..., by which point the FIRE sector was the largest giver.... In 1998 industry executives and lobbyists, led by Citigroup co-CEO Sanford Weill, succeeded in convincing Congress to effectively revoke the New Deal era Glass-Steagall Act which among other things separated banks and insurance companies. (PHILLIPS, 2002)

Some of the consequences of that set of corrupting processes were aptly summarized by the <u>NYT</u> in the summer of 2002:

> Regulators collaborated in finding ways around the law, and eventually Congress removed major restraints that had forbidden firms to mingle apples and oranges and to move important activities "off the balance sheet." Over the counter and behind closed doors, banks and investment banks "shifted their risks" by selling complicated partnerships and derivative instruments to mutual funds, pension funds and especially insurance companies.... Most of these scandalous activities were legal and many still are... The new legislation /of August, 2002/... improves disclosure in only one area... Congress and the president should stop patting themselves on the back and get to work restoring what is still viable in the intelligent protections put in place during the New Deal. (NYT, 8-25-02)

In the palmy New Deal days, however, there were at most but 5 percent of the number of **lobbyists** as now, plus a liberal majority in both houses of Congress, a population concerned with harsh realities rather than TV images, and in the White House was **FDR,** a president as different from **Bush II** as wine is from dishwater.

Glass-Steagall was repealed in 1998, Hardly a week goes by without some new revelation of corruption within and between the financial and other sectors; lots more is on its way. Regulation is for sissies.

globalization

Introduction. A starting-point for understanding this much overused and heavily loaded term is that it is the latest version of what has always been a necessity for **capitalism**; namely, the ability of capitalist economies to have an always expanding access to natural and human resources and markets beyond their own borders. The seeds of what would become industrial capitalism in the 19th century were planted in the medieval trading cities of Europe. Whether Venice, Florence, Genoa, and Bologna in southern Europe, or Leipzig, the Hanseatic League, London, Bruges, Paris in the North, the prosperity of those cities was dependent upon external trade with the other medieval cities of Europe and, over time, more distant regions.

What is usually termed "the early modern period" was modern by virtue of the economic and military strength of its emerging nation-states. By the 17th century, the city-based medieval trading relationships between European, Asia, and Africa and the Middle East gave way to **colonialism**, the establishment of regional monopolies by various nations, almost always facilitated by brute force against the colonized peoples—and to war amongst the colonizers: In the 17th century, there were only four years without war. (G.N. CLARK)

Trading that had long existed in terms of small quantities was transformed and expanded by improved navigation and ships—and firepower. Those processes were led first by the essentially pre-capitalist Portuguese and the Spanish at the turn of the 16th century; they were superseded by the business-minded Dutch in the 17th, and the Dutch by the French and the British in the 18th century. (BOXER; PARRY; BRAUDEL; HECKSCHER)

The nature and importance of that early set of national expansions were vividly described by MARX:

> The discovery of gold and silver in America, the extirpation, enslavement and entombment in mines of the aboriginal population, the beginnings of conquest and looting of the East Indies, the turning of Africa into a warren for the hunting of black-skins, signalized the rosy dawn of the era of capitalist production. Those idyllic proceedings are the chief momenta of primitive accumulation. (1867-1967)

Just as colonialism had supplanted medieval trading routes, so did **imperialism** push colonialism aside; and just as pre-industrial capitalist colonialism was made possible and necessary by technological change and nationalistic rivalries, so was industrial capitalist imperialism a product of further such changes, but with quantum leaps:

> Imperialism required, as the colonial system of earlier centuries did not, a large measure of political control over the internal relations and structure of the colonial economy. This it requires, not merely to "protect property" and to ensure that the profit of the investment is not offset by political risks, but actually to create the essential conditions for the profitable investment of capital. Among those conditions is the existence of a proletariat sufficient to provide a plentiful and cheap labour supply; and where this does not exist, suitable modifications of pre-existent social forms will need to be enforced (of which the reduction of tribal land-reserves and the introduction of differential taxation on the natives living in the tribal reserves of East and South Africa are examples.) Thus the political logic of imperialism is to graduate from "economic penetration" to "spheres of influence" to protectorates or indirect control, and from protectorates via military occupation to annexation. (DOBB, 1937)

Industrial capitalism in the 19th century is customarily seen as extending from 1815 (the end of the Napoleonic wars) to 1914, and the outbreak of World War I—made unavoidable by that same imperialism. The ensuing decades, embracing global depression, revolution and counter-revolution and World War II, left the USA standing alone as a strong nation.

The war also meant the end of the major European (and Japanese) ability to hold on to their chunks of empire. As the previously colonized areas over the globe sought to rid themselves of their foreign rulers, the USA some times assisted their struggles (as in Indonesia), some times assisted the rulers to hold on (as in Indochina), some times remained aloof (as in South Africa).

As the 1940s became the 1950s, U.S. aims and policies moved inexorably toward creating a new world economy and a new form of imperialism, both suited to the imperatives of the very different post-World War II era: taken together, by the 1980s the new world economy and the new imperialism had been baptized as "globalization" both by supporters and opponents. The French like to say (in French, of course) "the more things change, the more they stay the same." Is that so for the evolution from colonialism to imperialism to globalization? Not quite. What Dobb saw in the transformation of colonialism to imperialism was a set of <u>qualitatively</u> different institutions and processes producing a much worse world for the imperial<u>ized</u> also in <u>quantitative terms</u>: more different kinds of damage done to many more people with irreversible consequences. That has happened once more as globalization has taken over from imperialism: quantum jumps on quantum jumps, with permanently deleterious effects in every realm of social and physical existence for both the globalizers and with considerably greater destructive force, for the globalized.

The ideology of today's globalization has its theme song that "a rising tide lifts all boats." But the "boats" of the vast majority of the people of the non-rich societies have been the flora and fauna of their countries; those resources have been commandeered by giant **transnational corporations**, whether agribusinesses such as **Archer Daniels Midland** or by equally gigantic mineral and industrial companies: the "rising tide" for <u>billions</u> of people has been a tidal wave, drowning them, or sweeping them on to a barren shore.

In now discussing the various "realms" involved, and remembering that they are in constant interaction, they will be seen as 1) economic, 2) political, 3) cultural and social (education, etc.) 4) environmental, and 5) military.

In addition to the continuous and important interactions among and between all those categories are the usually invidious relationships between the strong and weak societies. Our delineation of consequences for both the strong and the weak will be confined mostly to the USA—with the understanding that a review of all others would not change the analysis.

1) Economic.

Note first that much of what is relevant here has been discussed at length, if from a slightly different standpoint, under **free trade** and **financialization**. The economic consequences of globalization have been positive for a few, and harmful for most, whether in the USA or in the relatively poor societies (often classified as "the South.")

a) For the USA.

In 1997, William GREIDER wrote a readable and comprehensive analysis of this matter with the title <u>One World, Ready or Not</u>. Except for its zealous propagators, the world was and is not "ready," for the "one world" of <u>this</u> globalization. (For the giant international corporations of the USA the processes of globalization could not be implanted soon enough; successive governments, whether controlled by Democrats or Republicans, did and do what they could and can to speed up and spread the processes—come what may.)

What came for the <u>corporations</u> was what they sought—easier access to the raw materials and markets and very cheap labor of other countries, subsidies and tax breaks where possible, and expanding sales and profits from both domestic and foreign markets—for a while (see below). The consequences for ordinary people have been positive for some, negative for some, disastrous for some.

The main negative processes in the USA were a result of "**downsizing and outsourcing**" What was sized down were good jobs in a whole string of industries—most notably, in electronics, cars, metallurgical and machinery products, and all forms of clothing.

Downsizing was the other side of outsourcing: U.S. companies relocating their high wage and benefits jobs from here to the opposite in the poorer countries, where wages are a small fraction of those in the USA: $2 a <u>day</u> is the <u>maximum</u> in Mexico or China for jobs paying $20 an <u>hour</u> here; then there are <u>no</u> benefits (health care, pensions, etc.) in the weaker countries, no 8-hour days, no sanitary provisions, no environmental costs: Back to the palmy days of the Industrial Revolution in Britain. (BLUESTONE & HARRISON, 1988; STIGLITZ /2002/)

Add to that the consequences for the US economy as a whole. To be sure, for the several decades since the new global economy after World War II took hold and then came to be called globalization, the US economy as a whole benefited. The benefits could be measured in fatter bottom lines for businesses both large and small, and—for a while—a rise in good jobs and more and more not so good jobs. As will be seen under **jobs**, a major "blowback" consequence of <u>our</u> globalization will be a modern repetition of Britain's more than a century ago; namely, as U.S. corporations place their manufacturing facilities where labor is cheapest, the manufacturing sector slowly but surely shrinks—with many associated consequences, none of them positive.

Thus, as the 1970s began, Japan had come to be seen as the major competitor of the USA in the "best" manufactured goods—in **cars** and the entire "electrical sector" (from TVs to computers). For ten years or more, Japan (and, subsequently Western Europe) ceased to run and began to limp; now China and India are the lively ones: <u>really</u> lively.

China's share of the world's output of goods and services has nearly doubled since 1991, to 12.7 percent, closing in on the EU's 15.7 percent and approaching America's 21 percent.... India has increased its share by 33 percent since 1991.... In Asia, China is supplanting the United States as the principal trading partner.... (Louis Uchitelle, "When the Chinese Consumer is King," <u>NYT</u>, 12-14-03)

The term "blowback" was used above because the "supplanting" is a direct and—it would have seemed—a predictable consequence of "**downsizing and outsourcing**": If the best **jobs** in the rich countries are sent to the poor countries (in order to increase profits), isn't it obvious that sooner or later those jobs will be gone forever? And, as is happening in China and Japan, not only be held by Chinese and Japanese workers but in Chinese- and Japanese-owned companies?

That process has already gone a long way; it has a long way to go and it is going there—as China's GDP increases at over 12 percent/year, with India's catching up. And note, their populations taken together equal more than one-third of the entire world's.

So is the USA not only following in the UK's path by becoming "financialized" but also in becoming dependent—ultimately—on stronger economic powers? Maybe no, probably yes; in any case a <u>very</u> large gamble to continue to pursue just so a few hundred giant companies can—or think they can—increase their profits. For a while.

Back to the 1970s. As is discussed under **financialization**, when those good times hit the "stagflation" road bump of the 1970s the stage was set for another transformation. It took the form of razzmatazz **mergers and acquisitions** on the one hand, with accompanying financialization, on the other, accompanied by the just-noted downsizing. As that razzmatazz merged with what was becoming "the new economy" of the 1980s and, especially, the 1990s, what was also developing was a degree of economic fragility for the U.S. economy and, therefore, the world economy.

It is worth repeating that the USA has been for two decades or so and remains the "consumer of last resort" for the world economy: almost <u>all</u> of the other economies depend in important degree upon to exports <u>to</u> us in excess of their imports <u>from</u> us for their own economies' wellbeing: The USA has, does, and must run a persistent—and always rising—deficit in its balance of payments with the rest of the world: $435 <u>billion</u> for 2002, $500 for 2003, the highest ever, and, necessarily, rising—the most dynamic element being our increasing indebtedness to China (which is taking the place of Japan in that as well as in trade).

For purposes of perspective, note that in its heyday at the end of the 19th century Great Britain also imported more than it exported, and lived well accordingly for a while. But its <u>balance of payments</u>—trade, plus or minus all other inflows and outflows—was always positive and very high: because it was the world's <u>lender</u> of last resort.

That was true for the USA also, up to the 1980s. When **Reagan** took over the White House in 1981, the USA was the world's largest creditor nation ever, the rest of the world owing us well in excess of $1 <u>trillion</u> dollars. When he left office eight years later, the figure had been reversed; we had become the world's largest <u>debtor</u> nation by about the same amount. Now it is six times that, and going up by a trillion every two years. (R. Du Boff, "U.S. Hegemony: Continuing Decline, Enduring Danger," <u>MR</u>, 12/2003)

The term "economic fragility" was used above. It refers to the fact that whenever the U.S. economy slows down (and it has been doing that for two years as this is written, with little expectation of changes for the better), our purchases from abroad also drop, as do, therefore, their purchases from us, and so it goes.

At the same time, keeping financialization in mind, and adding to foreign debt the mountains of internal debt (see **debt, financialization**), and one would have to believe in—and depend upon—the tooth fairy to be relaxed about the future, with or without war, with or without the 1920s economic policies of **Bush II**, with or without further socioeconomic surprises.

b) Poorer countries

Are not the workers in those countries now able to find jobs where none existed before? Are not their economies stronger, more stable? No.

Very bad jobs are now available to countless millions of people who once worked the land, or worked in country villages supplying those who did.

Take Mexico: one of the least poor of such nations—the hordes of desperate people working at the maquiladoras, directly or indirectly for U.S. companies, making car parts, etc., are there only because their alternative, illegally and dangerously, is to cross the border to work for dirt wages in the USA, or not work at all. Where did they come from?

They came from the agricultural lands of Mexico. On those lands—as was true of their unfortunate predecessors in the Britain of the early industrial revolution—they had not lived lives of luxury but they had lived very much better than now they do—not only in terms of food and clothing and shelter, but in terms of the quality of their lives (see 3, below).

What the earlier history of the 20th century did to Mexico's agricultural population—its largest part—was made considerably worse by one of the gems of globalization; namely, the U.S. constructed North American Free Trade Agreement (NAFTA). Its promises were many; its results, as CYPHER (2001) has detailed (see **IMF, NAFTA**, etc.), made an ongoing disaster into a catastrophe—for already poor Mexicans, that is.

The facts notwithstanding, NAFTA, which caused not only good jobs but some of all jobs to be lost in the USA, continues to have its praises sung by—of course—our government and our relevant giant corporations.

What is true of Mexico now did not begin with recent globalization, but it has been carried now to horrendous depths—as, meanwhile, globalization has been moving to the even cheaper labor in Asia. All of that is true as well for others of the countries of "the South"—whether moderately or terribly poor.

Only one more example, India, touted as a grand success: India's current travail began with the British colonization that destroyed with intent its previous balanced agricultural pre-modern industrial economy: how else wreck their cloth industry, help the British textile industry and, in the process, also have a desperate workforce in both Britain and India?

The Indians had lived off their land and, very much like their late 18th, early 19th century British counterparts, made cloth on the side. They lived very well indeed in comparison with the dread conditions of the lives of most Indians after the British brought progress to them, right up to now: Official estimates of unemployment in India in the 1990s showed that "while the total number of unemployed persons /was/ 336 million, the number of employed stood at only 306.7 million." (MESZAROS)

There are so many cruelties and injustices of this sort, for so many countries, and to the benefit of so few in the already relatively rich countries, that to go on with it would seem to verge on caricature. (see BARBER; GREIDER /1997/; KLEIN, 1999, 2002; STIGLITZ, /2002/)

As for their putative increases in strength and stability, just ask Thailand, or Argentina, or South Korea or Taiwan or Hong Kong or.... All those and more have discovered that at the slightest sign of troubles in their economies, far from their place at the table of globalization helping them it swiftly transforms trouble into disaster: The **IMF** and/or the World Bank come marching in with demands for cutting back this or that—or else. The "or else" has to do with cutting back financial support; and in that those two institutions are at the beck and call of the USA and, like the USA at home, practicing the economic policies of Calvin Coolidge and Herbert Hoover, the smaller countries always have a sword hanging over their heads which, when its supporting rope is cut, brings down the whole economy—as in Thailand; or, as in Korea, forces otherwise healthy companies to sell out at dirt cheap prices to eager "vulture capitalists," (HENWOOD)

2) *Political*

Although the once colonized/ imperialized societies are now formally independent, their "independence," like political democracy in the USA, provides a cover story for what in reality is subjection to the power of giant corporations and their political emissaries: in this case, the WTO, IMF, World Bank and, in the Western Hemisphere, NAFTA.

The tendencies toward what may be seen as imperialism in modern dress began to take hold as independence was achieved, that is, already in the 1950s; so much as to lead to the emergence of the new analytical school of "dependence and underdevelopment." (COCKROFT, et al.)

The "dependence" claiming attention in that analysis arose from the combination of indebtedness and subjection to outside companies' policies. Even though usually rich in natural resources, the ex-colonized countries were poor in capital and had to borrow in order to develop their own economies If—or, more accurately—and when their economies fell into recession or worse, they faced the need to borrow more and, at the same time, to shape and reshape their socioeconomic policies in accord with dicta from the IMF and the World Bank.

Stringent though outside controls may have been already in the Fifties and Sixties, they became even more so from the Seventies on; from then on (see **free trade** and **debt**), what had usually been governmental grants and low interest loans from the USA and others were transformed into loans from private finance in the strong countries—a consequence of the latters' inability to find sufficient demand for their capital at home in that decade of simultaneous rising prices-cum-rising unemployment called "stagflation."

The Seventies were crucial to what now exists, for both rich and poor nations. Not only was borrowing by the poorer countries increased dramatically, but its terms, especially as issuing from the USA, were altered so that a) interest rates would rise along with inflation, and b) oil payments—which virtually all countries had to make—were to be made in dollars.

If we step back and ask what kinds of circumstances were necessary if the "underdeveloped countries" were to develop economically within a positive political framework, it should be obvious that what was required for them was cooperation rather than coercion. The reality became and remains the national counterpart of worker exploitation: the poorer countries and of course, in the same processes, their peoples were used and abused to the interest of outsiders—who, moreover, when trouble developed, as it always did, hastened away and left the country to its own devices.

The IMF and World Bank were created by the USA in the last years of World War II; GATT just after the war. The **WTO** and **NAFTA** are creatures of the years after the 1970s. Taken together, these means of control have been euphemized as "transparency," the euphemistic kissin' cousin of the also euphemistic "free market." (BLOCK)

So it should not be surprising that the political lives of the previously colonized countries have been characterized more by ugly dictatorships and squalid corruption than by anything approximating democracy.

The costs of plutocracy in a rich country such as ours are high; for the poorer countries, they are deadly.

Adding insult to injury, the major powers, not least the USA, criticize the desperate nations for not behaving more responsibly: "Why can't they be like us?" Those major powers, all of which rose to economic well-being in small or large part because, for centuries, they were able to make great gains at the expense of the lesser nations, fail to recognize that the poorer countries have no poor countries to colonize, imperialize, and exploit: except their own. Injustice rules.

3) Cultural and social

Immense though the economic and political damage done to the people of societies once imperialized have been, it has been equaled by the virtual destruction of their cultures. Marx and Engels put it succinctly in the

Communist Manifesto, as colonialism was being replaced by imperialism and industrial capitalism was strengthening:

> Constant revolutionizing of production, uninterrupted distur-
> bance of all social conditions, ever-lasting uncertainty and agitation
> distinguish the bourgeois epoch from all earlier ones. All fixed, fast-
> frozen relations, with their train of ancient and venerable prejudices
> and opinions, are swept away, all new-formed ones become antiquated
> before they can ossify. All that is solid melts into air, all that is holy is
> profaned, and man is at last compelled to face with sober senses his real
> conditions of life and his relations with his kind. (1967) (1848)

That "uninterrupted disturbance of all social conditions" took on sensational dimensions in Britain's industrial revolution, and something like the same wherever capitalism took root; but what happened in what became the powerful nations was like the difference between a slow-motion film and a fast-forwarding VCR compared to the sociocultural tidal waves that overcame "all that /was/ solid…, all that /was/ holy" in Africa, Latin America, the vast area extending from China in the East to Persia in the West—and pre-colonial "America."

The Europeans—which here includes those who settled North America and became "Americans"—had undergone changing lives for millennia, but at a slow pace produced by largely internal developments; not so for the rest of the world. From the 16th century on, they had change imposed upon them—ruthlessly, and for the benefit of outsiders.

There never was and there is not yet any meaningful respect for the cultures and societies which, at an always-faster pace from the 16th century to today, were flattened, corrupted, distorted, enfeebled, ridiculed, scorned. What are now billions of people in those areas have lives that are now not only materially desperate, but whose cultures have been spun out of control, if they survive at all.

Those who wish to understand the whys and wherefores of Jihad vs. McWorld (the title of Barber's probing study) must begin with what began its vile career centuries ago—and which, given the always more potent technologies of transportation and communication, now penetrate all nooks and crannies of the lives of people—here in the USA, in France, in Japan, etc., to be sure; but not so devastatingly, yet, as for the peoples of the weaker nations: their health, their education, their shelter… their basic needs are so little met that at least 15 million children die of malnutrition every year.

4) Environmental

Under its own essay, much that is relevant here has been discussed. Here all that needs saying in addition is that, as with the political, cultural, and social damage wrought by the main institutions of the modern era, that done to Mother Nature in the "emerging economies" is so much greater in degree as to be different in kind.

If there have been any benefits accruing to the destruction of nature, they have accrued almost entirely to the people of the rich nations; whereas, for the rest of the people in the world, while there have been few if any benefits, damage is so great as to be beyond description—as regards the ruination of their water supplies, their flora and fauna; their lives. Our crimes, their punishment.

5) Military

Historians have long argued back and forth in answering the question "Which came first, the flag or trade; trade or the flag?" The answer is that they strode into the weaker areas hand-in-hand. The partnership was habit-forming, utilized from Columbus to the Puritans in "America" to Cecil Rhodes in Africa to Admiral Perry in Japan to General Tommy Franks in Iraq.

Given its long history, the militarization of economic efforts became not just a habit, but an addiction. Since World War II, the Europeans and the Japanese have finally learned to control their addiction. And we in the USA? We're the new kid swaggering around the block. We have suffered seriously from only one war, the one in which we fought against each other: Over 600,000 soldiers died in the Civil War—more than all of our foreign wars. Compare that with others' losses: In Europe, 60 million died in World War II alone; at least 30 million of the USSR, 4 million Germans, 500,000 Italians (with a population one-fifth of ours), 2 million Japanese, one million Polish soldiers, 5 million civilians (most of them Jews), China over 2 million... Those are deaths only; then there were the many millions wounded, and displaced, and... so on. Which says nothing of the economic, social and political destruction of the two world wars for all but us (and the Swedes, the Swiss, the Canadians and the Aussies).

Then, for us, tens of thousands died in Korea and in Vietnam, which meant, finally, all hell being raised at home. But even that affected a tiny percentage of U.S. families. And now **Iraq**, and....?.

In short and in sum, globalization is not only or, after all, mostly an economic phenomenon. It may be "just business" for businesses; it is not for those who are harmed here, let alone those abroad, where the harm has many dimensions and consequences whose end will probably never end.

That is the globalization we have. There is another globalization, the kind the "No Global" groups seek. It proposes what many of us thought the USA was going to work for after World War II; namely, a set of processes starting from the proposition that the welfare of one depends upon the wellbeing of all. That wars must never occur again. That a world economy based upon mutual interdependence rather than exploitation is not only the only ethical but the only safe path; and that done properly it would allow all of us, in both rich and poor nations to be better off then any of us has been before. Instead, perhaps 15 percent of the world's people are rolling in asinine luxuries and another 10 percent or so seeking madly to do likewise; meanwhile, the other 75 percent of the world's people, mostly but not only in the poor countries, writhes in increasingly unquiet desperation. Such a world will not, because it cannot, help but fall prey to one war after another, a process that will inevitably conclude with "the big one"; the last big one.

global warming (see environment)

GM

General Motors has been, so to speak, the **GE** of the automobile industry; however when compared to GE in terms of business innovation and politico-cultural influence it comes out as a stick-in-the-mud. That may be explained in part by the differences in their technologies—GM's in the stodgy realm of mechanics, GEs in the hip zones of physics and, from the start, **media.**

However, GM need bow to none if the focus is on the serious damages to nature and society; it has done the lion's share of **environmental** damage and **waste,** and its contributions to the destructive consequences to people and society of **consumerism,** household **debt** and behemoth capitalism would be hard to beat.

GM made its first move toward giantism just before World War I. It was then that Buick, Cadillac, and Oldsmobile (and some smaller companies) became General Motors, Inc.; Chevrolet and Pontiac were brought into the family later, as GMC also began to make buses and trucks. It became and remains the largest motor vehicle company in the world; until Wal-Mart shoved it aside it was the largest company of any kind in the world.

Not content to stick with **cars**, GM also makes earth-moving equipment, diesel locomotives, and even refrigerators and other household appliances—cheater, cheater, cries GE—plus aircraft engines and tanks, making it one of the major honchos of the plush **military-industrial complex.**

Finally (at least as of this moment), having led the parade into **consumerism** in the 1920s with its introduction of the annual model change, massive advertising, and consumer borrowing through its GMAC (General Motors Acceptance Corp.), GM also became a major player in what has now become the **financialization** of the economy.

Much of what GM has meant for our life and times is discussed under the headings noted just above; and, except for this, we'll leave it at that: after 1941, and until he became Defense Secretary under Eisenhower, GM's most influential and powerful **CEO** (as we now call the heads of companies), was Charles E.—Charlie—Wilson. Charlie was fond of <u>bon mots</u>; My favorite (as also noted elsewhere) was the way he narrowed down President Coolidge's famous "What's good for business is good for America." Charlie made that into "What's good for GM is good for America." Tell it to the **downsized.**

greed

The unholy family of the seven deadly sins is usually seen as composed of anger, avarice, envy, gluttony, lust, pride, and sloth. Four of those are greed's parents: avarice, envy, gluttony, and lust—with pride and anger serving as aunt and uncle, as first cousin sloth drags himself behind.

An honest self-scrutiny would reveal that all of us, some or much of the time, have had at least a passing acquaintance with all of those sins; scarce does a day pass, I wot, when most of us do not respond to one or more of them, whether with guilt, pain, pleasure, or shame: c'est la vie.

All or most of those excessive emotions and activities have their origins in our instinct for survival. They connect with essential qualities which can serve or disserve us and our society, Time and circumstance can make someone (if not just anyone) who might have spent his life laboring in the fields into, instead, a Beethoven (who also had an ugly side to him); could, indeed did, make a housepainter into, instead, a Hitler (who did <u>not</u> have a good side to him). And so on, ad infinitum.

Our genes are only the raw material of our lives; what kind of person we become with them depends upon whether the who, where, when and whats of our time and place and situation will bring out the best or the worst in us.

Unfortunately, <u>we</u> live in times and circumstances that discourage the best in us and encourage the worst: Where would **capitalism** and its **consumerism** and its **militarism**, to say nothing of its **racism**, be, had they not found the ways to feed and to titillate those deadly sins—to make us want MORE, MORE, MORE, always MORE!, for us and ours, and fuhgeddabout the rest?

Greed signifies wanting whatever is wanted beyond one's needs, even beyond one's pleasure. Once on its way, it cannot be satiated: It becomes addictive, irrational, often self-destructive.

The **advertising** industry and its **media** outlets and their **big business** paymasters depend upon pushing us to and through the wall of good sense, where greed awaits. Up to now those bozos are winning hands down—not only in the home of their first major triumphs, the USA, but pretty much all over the globe, in large or small degree. It's called "americanization."

A prime instance of the greed standard we have set for ourselves may be found among our **CEOs**. As noted and pursued at greater length under **HMOs** and **pharmaceuticals**, the latter's **CEOs** are well up in the race. The top nine of that industry's **CEOs** average $19 million a year in salary <u>and</u> between them own $900 million in unexercised stock options—awarded to them by boards of directors over whom they have considerable influence. What does this have to do with greed?

Well, let's suppose that each of them finds some things upon which to spend $1,000 <u>a day</u>, 365 days every year. Doing that for three years would add up to a bit over $1 million. At the end of those three years, assuming they hadn't invested the other $18 million or the incoming other two $19 millions—and hadn't yet cashed in their stock options—they would still have $56 million in the bank.

Note that these nine guys (they're all guys) are **CEOs** of drug companies, the industry whose profits are <u>four times</u> higher than the average of the other <u>Fortune 500</u> largest companies. The policies of those **CEOs** aim to and have succeeded in keeping prescription drug prices always rising (now in double-digits, annually) and in preventing lower-priced imports from abroad—aided and abetted by their 650+ **lobbyists** in D.C.

In doing so, they have contributed to numberless premature deaths and painfully desperate lives for <u>millions</u> of their fellow citizens.

Why would they commit such heinous social crimes? Because, like all too many other industries' **CEOs**, they are <u>greedy</u>, that's why; greedy for money, for power, for status, for something irrational and destructive, and let the Devil take the hindmost.

As such, by any reasonable standard, they are mentally and morally unbalanced. <u>And</u> they are among the most powerful people in our society.

Green Berets (see Asia....Vietnam)

Greenspan, Alan

<u>Pfui!</u> (and see **monetarism**)

Gulf War (see Middle East)

Gulf of Tonkin Resolution (see Asia....Vietnam)

guns

For a country that likes to be Numero Uno in everything, the gun industry is very pleased to announce that per capita ownership of deadly weapons is higher in the USA than anywhere else in the world; that, moreover, only a small minority of those guns are possessed for hunting purposes. (A point pursued at length by Michael Moore in his funny/horrifying film "Bowling for Columbine.")

Setting aside the question of how high "hunting purposes" would rank in a society both modern and sane, there is the larger question: Why do so many people, criminals excepted, have so many guns? Is it, for example, because we are such a dangerous society at home; or, rather, are we dangerous <u>because</u> of all those guns—or, more to the point, because of the socialized mentalities of those who cherish them?

Another question then: Why do we do so little to control and reverse that dangerous situation? The main reasons are found, as might be expected, both in the attitudes of the gun owners, and the political power they share with the gun makers: their National Rifle Association (NRA) is one of the very most effective political pressure groups with some the most effective of **lobbyists** —not, however, even coming close in expenditures or power to, say, **pharmaceuticals, oil, cars,** and others of the <u>Fortune 500</u>. (see **big business**)

First, attitudes. The popularity of guns in the USA is very clearly a product of our history as a gun-slinging nation, both in terms of how we came to be and how have behaved in the ensuing centuries. (See **buffalo, "Indians," militarism, Cold War,** and, not least, **media.**)

From childhood we—especially us guys—learned to see gunslingers as heroes, whether slaughtering "Indians" or others in their way in the fabled—and phony—West.

Skipping to the past 20 years or so, contemporary media in the entertainment sector have much enlarged that influence by the role given to violence in **TV** and films—where the good guys never lose and, when hurt, are always comforted by a beautiful loved one as they ride off in the sunset. Bang bang.

In 1939, the Supreme Court ruled that the Second Amendment to the Constitution protects <u>only</u> the right of state-organized militias to own firearms and that Congress and local governments have great freedom to regulate the possession and use of firearms by individuals.

Better than nothing; however, it gave lots of leeway for state governments such as that of—surprise!—Texas to look the other way about who had guns for what, or even to applaud gun owners. Thus, for example, "in 1999, the most recent year for which statistics are available, 28,874 Americans were killed with guns." ("More Guns for Everyone!", <u>NYT</u>, 5-8-02.)

Pshaw! says Attorney General **Ashcroft**. "Reversing decades of official government policy on the meaning of the Second Amendment, the Justice Department told the Supreme Court for the first time last Monday that the 'Constitution broadly protects the rights of individuals to own firearms.'" ("In Shift, Justice Dept. Tells Court Individuals Have a Right to Guns," <u>NYT</u>, 5-8-02) The article goes on to note that the National Rifle Association "calls Ashcroft 'a breath of fresh air to freedom-loving gun owners'" That the NRA has also been a major contributor to Ashcroft's campaigns is one of those coincidences difficult to explain in a few words.

Four months later, another headline: "Gun Industry Is Gaining Immunity From Suits." (<u>NYT</u>, 9-1-02)

The article begins by stating that "A spate of government litigation against the nation's gun companies has been stifled in 30 states which have passed laws granting the industry immunity from civil lawsuits."

All that has been too grim. Time now to relax and enjoy. On August 28, 2001, in an editorial entitled "Check Your Gun Here," the <u>NYT</u> reported, and I quote:

> Utah permits its residents to carry guns just about anywhere. It's a theory that the Bush administration should appreciate, since the /Bush II/ signed a bill permitting people to bring weapons into church or hospitals when he was governor of Texas. But at a recent Utah Republican convention where Vice President Cheney was to speak, the U.S. Secret Service insisted that handguns be checked at the door.... In a compromise between the agency and the delegates who felt naked without their weapons, state party officials decreed that guests could come to the convention armed as long as they checked their guns in lockers outside the hall during Mr. Cheney's appearance.
>
> The executive director of the Utah Gun Owners Alliance, who apparently regarded listening to the vice president under the watchful eye of the Secret Service as high risk, protested giving up her weapon. "Delegates are entitled to the same right to be safe as anybody else," she said.

Kalashnikov, anyone?

Haldeman, H.R.

H.R. "Bob" Haldeman was **Nixon**'s main advisor before his 1968 election and served as his Chief of Staff until Nixon's forced resignation in 1973. For that entire period he kept a daily diary, both in writing and in tapes. After his death in 1993, his wife had the diaries published as <u>The Haldeman Diaries:; Inside the Nixon White House</u>. They are probably the most revealing document ever written about the ways and wiles of any president, anywhere.

Such a book would be of interest even as regards a lackluster president—Gerald Ford, say—but Nixon had the "luster" of highly-polished brass, and was just as hard. Much bowed but never broken, Haldeman was as loyal to him as though he represented all that was good and just—even keeping his mouth shut and going to prison for what <u>Nixon</u> had done. Few of us could do that for even a really good guy; but for a Nixon? Wow.

Nixon's appetite for power was insatiable and his ways of gaining, increasing, and using it utterly ruthless. Haldeman very probably knew more about what preceded and accompanied "Watergate" than anyone other than Nixon himself (much, perhaps all of it, contained in the <u>Diaries</u>). Knowing what he did, by the summer of 1974 Haldeman advised Nixon to resign—and proposed that

> ...before you leave office you should exercise your Constitutional authority and grant pardons to all those who have been or may be charged with any crimes in connection with Watergate and at the same time to grant amnesty to the Vietnam war draft dodgers. (HALDEMAN)

That statement is provided in the book's "Afterword" by Nixon historian Stephen Ambrose. Ambrose goes on to provide Nixon's reaction: "He rejected the idea coldly. Amnesty for the draft dodgers was 'unthinkable,' while a blanket pardon for Watergate defendants could cause a 'hysterical' political reaction."

That was Nixon at his egomaniacal best. For when, on August 9, 1974, Nixon resigned he did so only after seeing to it that when Gerald Ford automatically assumed the presidency he would immediately pardon <u>him</u>; that is, just to be clear, Nixon. Ford dutifully did the dirty deed; subsequently Nixon "depicted himself as a man done in because he was 'too loyal' to his subordinates, blaming Haldeman, Ehrlichman, and Mitchell for the Watergate "coverup."

The coverup was covering Nixon, of course, not those who went to prison for a year or more. Too much, no? Nope, there is also this: as you may have noted, Tricky Dick found his way back to acceptance, even to praise. Justice, where is thy sting?

The <u>Diaries</u> are not entirely or even mostly concerned with Watergate: at the end of each day, Haldeman either wrote or dictated the day's events of over four years. And what events! How cunning was the 36th President of the USA! How bowing and scraping his Cabinet and advisors—even, perhaps especially, the guy who couldn't stand him: **Kissinger!**

Withal, he was a winner, sort of. If one were to read up on all of our presidents' histories, asking only this question: "What was there in the way of dishonesty, deception, ruthlessness, self-seeking ambition, and lack of scruple in those presidents' tenures," the competition would surely be fierce, but Nixon would win hands down. You don't believe that?

Read the <u>Diaries</u>.

health care

This book's discussions are replete with past and ongoing scandals in and by the USA, many of them deserving to be seen as social crimes; among the latter are those matters of life and death having do with the cruelly limited availability <u>and</u> high costs of health care for most of our people.

In support of that unhappy generalization, what follows will treat of the many dimensions of the complex structure of unmet health care needs in greater or lesser degree. Some aspects dealt with briefly here will be dealt with more fully in **HMOs** and **pharmaceuticals**.

I begin with a lengthy summary of a seemingly encouraging but ultimately disgusting Harvard Medical School study (HIMMEL-STEIN/WOOLHANDLER) published July 10, 2002 in the <u>Journal of Health Affairs</u>:

Government expenditures accounted for 59.8 percent of U.S. health care costs in 1999... At $2,604 per capita, government spending was the highest of any nation—including those with national health insurance.... (Estimated total for 2002 is $5,427 per capita, with government's share being $3.245).

The study analyzed data on spending for government health care programs like Medicare, Medicaid and the Veterans Administration ($548.7 billion in 1999), as well as two categories that have previously been overlooked in calculating government health costs: 1. Expenditures to buy private insurance for government employees (16 percent of the U.S. workforce—e.g., members of Congress, firemen and school teachers—of $65.6 billion in 1999; 2) tax subsidies for private coverage—$109.6 billion in 1999. Most of these tax subsidies go the wealthiest Americans. The study found that government's share of expenditures has nearly doubled since 1965, with tax subsidies and public employee benefit costs increasing fastest.

The hidden government health spending has a major impact on family budgets. In 1999, a family of four with average health costs spent $7,016 for their own health expenses and premiums (including what their employer paid). In addition, they paid $10,416 in health care taxes: $1,578 for tax subsidies, $943 for government workers' coverage, and $7,895 for government health programs like Medicare and Medicaid. Even many uninsured families pay thousands of dollars in taxes for the health care of others.

One of the study's authors (Dr. Woolhandler) commented that "We pay the world's highest health care taxes. But much of the money is squandered. The wealthy get tax breaks, and HMOs and drug companies pocket billions in profits at the taxpayers' expense. But politicians claim we cannot afford universal coverage. Every other developed nation has national health insurance. We already pay for it, but we don't get it." It adds up to "Public money, private control."

Another of the authors (Dr. Himmelstein) noted that "We spend over $209 billion each year on paperwork in insurance companies, hospitals and doctors' office—at least half of which could be saved through national health insurance. We spend $150 billion on medications, at prices 50% higher than Canadians pay for the same drugs. By slashing bureaucracy and drug prices we could save enough to cover all of the uninsured and improve coverage for the rest of us."

In the same arena: Have those who are covered by Medicare noticed that when you receive notices from Medicare, on the envelope it says "NHIC: National Heritage Insurance Company, A CMS Contracted Carrier." Ever wonder how much that raises our taxes?

So, while spending more overall and per capita than any other nation we nonetheless manage to provide the least coverage to the average citizen: From 15 to 20 percent of us are completely without coverage; among the other rich countries, the worst rate is under one percent—and all those other societies have higher longevities and lower infantile mortality rates than the USA. (RASSELL, D&S, 5-1993): Number 1 in wealth and power, we are Number #37 in terms of "overall performance" for health care systems. (France is first, Italy second; we are behind Chile, Colombia /!/, Saudi Arabia and Singapore. /WHO, 1997/)

Yet, the people of the USA are told—and all too many believe—that ours, because largely private, is the most efficient and the best health care system in the world: OK, the man-in-the-street sez, maybe we pay more, but we get more and better health care. The yawning gap between that belief and ugly reality is now explained.

The reasons are many and diverse, but all connect with the fact that in the USA medical care is portrayed as a **commodity**, not as an indispensable **need**; something to be bought and sold to the profit of the seller—as though it were a cabbage, a CD, a hamburger, a vacation to the Bahamas. Result? Regardless of your health, the richer you are, the more and better your health care. For those not <u>very</u> well-off, it is often a rocky road; and for at least half of our people life is nastier, more brutish, and shorter than it need be.

Our health care system will now be examined further under several headings:

> 1) its inequality, in terms of accessibility, patients' costs, and quality of treatment; 2) the special and unmet needs and problems of the aged, the disabled, and children; 3) work dangers and the worsening inadequacies of work-coverage; 4) high and always rising hospital costs; 5) the self-created shortage of nurses by hospitals; 6) the perverse role of medical technology; 7) the rising costs of prescription drugs and their associated problems; and under their own entries, HMOs and pharmaceuticals as aggravating all that has been and is increasingly wrong with the U.S. health care system.

1) Inequality of health care

If you are among the top 10 percent of income receivers in the USA, you are likely to receive the best overall health care in the world; if you are not that well off financially, you are likely someday, if not already, to be badly off if and when you need medical care.

Why so? The answer is all too simple: the **commodification** of health care in the USA: you get what you—or your insurance—pay(s) for. For those who have it, insurance has diverse sources: As noted above, the U.S. government insures those over 65 or officially poor (Medicare and Medicaid, respectively), and the military and other government employees; and/or you may have gained health care benefits as part of your job (of which, more later); and/or you may have purchased health insurance for yourself and your family on your own. Or, for about 60 million, you are likely to have no insurance part of the time or all of the time. ("New Study Finds 60

Million Uninsured During a Year," <u>NYT</u>, 5-13-03).

There are almost 300 million of us, so 60 million doesn't sound too bad—unless you are one of them. In which case, and especially if your family income is less than the median, you are likely to have more health problems than those better off. Nor is it unimportant to note that a quarter of the families without insurance have an income of $50,000 and over. ("Health insurance crisis quickly moves upscale," <u>NYT</u>, 11-26-02)

But what about those who <u>are</u> covered? That points to the need to go behind general statistics:

1)   Although it is seldom if ever pointed that not only is the "coverage" of most people generally partial but that the "partiality" tends to be critically inadequate.

2)   Even for the most fortunate among the non-very rich, the best insurance is still far from "free": Permit me to use myself as an example of those well-covered. I have both Medicare coverage and lifelong insurance from university teaching. That combination provides what is probably the most generous health coverage in the country (except for those granted to themselves by CEOs, and by Congress to itself and to the military).

The earlier-quoted Harvard study cited $7,016 for the average family of four to cover its own health expenses and premiums. In 2001, according to my tax returns, and despite my good coverage, I paid out $9,784 (for a family of two), just about half of which was for "supplements"—i.e., payments required of me without any treatments or medications. This does not include my share of "health care taxes" of the Harvard study quoted earlier; that is, however appalling their figures are, they are if anything an understatement.

The "average" can refer either to the family in the middle (half better off, half worse off) or "all families divided into the total." Taken either way, the "average family's" coverage is considerably weaker than mine.

3)   Their "health care taxes" would be pretty much the same as mine but their health care would be considerably less adequate.

4)   Then there are the poor who are not "poor enough" to have Medicaid; a family of four with an annual income of just over

the cruelly mindless poverty level of $17,000; or those old enough to have Medicare. At the tail of that melancholy list is that

5)   In recent years there has been a plague of private hospitals shutting down emergency rooms while, most grievously in Los Angeles, public hospitals close altogether—and doctors increasingly refuse to take Medicare or Medicaid patients. ("They don't pay enough." Wherefore art thou, Hippocrates?)

And in the other rich countries? In the USA we read of how inefficient or just plain awful the health care systems are in, say, Canada, or Italy, or the UK: so much time spent waiting in doctors' offices, long waits for surgery, incompetent medics.

Setting aside that we also spend quite some time waiting in doctors' offices (while, all too often, pharmaceutical reps waltz by us), and often wait a month or two for an appointment, etc. Ah! But we have choice.

We can always go to a different doctor—and wait for her or him the same way.

As regards those "long waits" in those other countries, one is reminded that when Britain initiated its National Health Service soon after World War II there were long lines at doctors' and dentists' offices. That led to much gossip about how all these people were cramming those offices just because it was free. Setting aside a few masochists and those otherwise peculiar, are there really that many people who would go to a doctor—let alone a dentist—just because it is free?

In Italy (where I have lived and worked half of every year for decades), one can and does go without an appointment to a doctor of one's choice (who is likely also to have "non-governmental" patients in other hours), wait no longer than in the States, be examined, sent to a specialist if warranted, given a prescription if needed, and that's that (although, if you are well off, you may have to pay ten percent of prescription's cost). My own experience with health care in Italy is revealing, especially when compared with an Italian's experience here. First, Italy: In recent years I have been hospitalized twice in Italy, once for a serious street accident, once for what was thought to be a heart condition. In both cases I went to Emergency; in both cases I was asked for identification (Calif. drivers' license).

For the brain/bone incident I was in emergency for four hours, for the heart for more than 12 hours, with many examinations for both, then and later. Cost to me? Zero. All they asked me for was identification: my California driver's license.

In contrast, when an Italian family visited us in San Francisco a while back and their son came down with a worrisome abdominal symptom we took them to Emergency. We were there for two hours. The family was billed for $1,700; and Germany, Austria, Sweden, and Holland are more generous than Italy.

Then consider this (as reported in the IHT, 3-9-01): In 1999, annual health care taxes in France and Britain were, respectively, $1,800 and $1,312. As noted earlier in my own case, even without any medical care or prescription drugs, the "supplements" to my much better than average health insurance plus "deductibles and co-payments" (administered through an HMO), were just under $10,000, with nothing special happening in that year. The IHT story goes on to note a particular patient who had previously complained about his taxes in France, stopped complaining when a serious illness, which would have cost hundreds of thousands of dollars without insurance, cost him only that yearly tax. And he didn't have to wait in line.

Postscript: As the European Union adopts "americanizing" policies, its member nations—Berlusconi's right-wing lurching Italy in the lead—are also finding themselves pushed downward toward our practices in the realm of health care, inter alia.

If not privatization and its cousins, how is a decent governmental program to be paid for? The way all such basic needs, including **social security**, should be paid for: through a progressive income tax; that is, by ability to pay. Health care should be determined by need, first and foremost; the making of a payment should be the exception not the rule. More of that in the Afterword.

In the 1960s it seemed that long strides ahead were underway, when **LBJ** had Congress pass Medicare (for the old and disabled) and Medicaid (for the poor). But Medicare covered only 90 days of hospital care; a payment "supplement" was required to take care (and then only partially) of doctors and drugs. (It started out as $3 a month; by 2002 it was $50.) Medicaid covered only half of the poor; the rest would have to be taken care of in steadily disappearing emergency rooms. (EHRENREICH, B.; D&S, 5/93)

From the early 1980s to now, the average worker's family has gone from bad to worse, an outcome of the interaction of declining union strength, a conservative shift in U.S. politics, the rising costs of physicians, hospitals and drugs, and the Scrooge-like **HMOs**.

All that deterioration was aided and abetted by the severe cut-back or ending of employer-funded plans.

Thus, according to a report from The Commonwealth Fund (C. KLEIN) in the years 1979-1998, this is what has happened to employer-sponsored health insurance benefits:

Item: On average, two thirds in the private sector had such coverage in 1979; in 1998, down to one-third.

Item: For workers in the lowest fifth of the wage scale, coverage fell from 42 to 26 percent.

Item: Of the top 20 percent of wage-earners, 80 percent received coverage, as compared with only 25 percent of those receiving less than $7.00/hr.

Item: In 1983, 45 percent of employers paid the full share of premiums; in 1998, only 26 percent.

And in the years since 1998, all that has deteriorated further—yielding, for the average family, a crushing process in which costs rise and benefits decline, and jobs are harder to find.

Item: Under the headline "Small employers severely cut health care" (NYT, 9-6-02) it was shown that despite an inflation rate that has steadily declined from 1989 to the present, health insurance premiums for the past 6 years have risen sharply, and in double-digits since 1999. The NYT is quoting the report of the Kaiser Family Foundation, which shows that "Workers are paying more of the costs, as higher premiums deductibles and co-payments for prescription drugs, doctor visits and hospital charges outpace wage increases." In that same report, it is shown that for small companies the normal situation now has become substantial increases in workers' payments for insurance alongside substantial decreases in services and drugs provided—with every prospect of much worse to come—including no insurance.

2) Special needs of the aged, disabled, and children.

Despite the strong emphasis on "family" by our politicians and in the media, the USA is stunningly indifferent to what happens to those who cannot pay for needed health care, food, or shelter (**homeless, hunger**).

There is something distinct as well as overlapping about these groupings; what they have in common is their existent or emerging helplessness.

But didn't Medicare meet the needs of the old and the disabled? Would that it were so. As is discussed in this section and **pharmaceuticals**, Medicare did not assist in the payments for prescription drugs (and the 2004 Medicare Act does more harm than good), and the number of Medicare patients whose **HMOs** have ceased to cover them—over 2 million in the past few years—and who often find it difficult or impossible to find another HMO in their locality is high and rising.

To repeat, among the richest countries we stand as uniquely and often heartlessly indifferent to the weak and the helpless. In Europe, considerably more often than not, to be old and/or disabled is either to remain "in the bosom of the family," and/or to be able to participate in the facilities for old people in numerous centers. More to the point, when old people are ill, they are taken care of in all the rich and some of the poor countries in ways which are not found in the USA (except when the left-behind family is able and/or inclined to set them up in a "home").

And our disabled? To the degree, and only to the degree, that they have constituted themselves as a political lobbying group, are they able to achieve even minimal improvements in their "rights."

A better word than "rights" would be "**needs**." In the *Afterword*, there will be a discussion of the desirability of thinking in political terms of the "basic needs" of our society's people—for food, clothing, shelter, education, and opportunity. Here, <u>need</u> as a basis for public policy is as "un-American" as <u>apfel strudel</u>; in no country is all done that could be; but the gap between needs and possibilities in our country makes those in others seem slim indeed.

Whatever our rhetoric concerning children, it is seldom realized in practice. The children of the top twenty percent of incomes in the USA have easy access to the basic needs just cited; but the other eighty percent? Certainly not for the millions of U.S. children who live in **poverty**; and as for those in between bottom and top, what then? It depends.

Depends upon what? Upon just how caught up in the hurly-burly of U.S. socioeconomic existence their parents are; how much real time the children have with their parents, as distinct from their TV's; just how attentive their parents are to their diets, their schooling, their health, to the needs and possibilities of their <u>being</u> children.

And that is a way of asking how attuned those parents have been and are to their own lives in those same terms, as distinct from the pressures of work, of shopping, of borrowing, of.... threading one's way through the socioeconomic jungles of **consumerism**, of the stresses of the job, of being—"an American."

3) Work dangers and coverage.

Until very recently the matter of injuries and ruined health on the job—where most of us spend almost half of our waking hours after we leave school—has been more neglected than studied. A recent scholarly study (LEIGH, 2000) has filled that partial vacuum. Here the data for 1992:

——There were over 6,000 job-related deaths, over 13 million non-fatal injuries, over 60,000 disease deaths, and over 1 million illnesses contracted at work.

——The total direct and indirect costs associated with those injuries and illnesses were estimated to be $155.5 billion, almost 3 percent of GDP.

——Direct costs included medical expenses for hospitals, physicians, and drugs, as well as health insurance administration costs, over $51 billion.

——Indirect costs included loss of wages, costs of fringe benefits and loss of home production (e.g., child care provided parent and home repairs), as well as employer retraining and workplace disruption costs, amounting to about $103 billion.

——Injuries were responsible for 85 percent and diseases for 15 percent of all costs.

——Workers compensation covered roughly 27 percent of all costs. Taxpayers paid approximately 18 percent of the costs, through Medicare, Medicaid, and Social Security.

——The foregoing costs were borne by injured workers and their families, by all other workers through lower wages, by firms through lower profits, and by consumers through higher prices.

——The Bureau of Labor Statistics is the most reliable source for non-fatal injuries, but it misses over half of job-related injuries.

And so? A major conclusion of LEIGH's study was that "despite the size of these costs and the fact that so many people pay them, occupational injuries and illnesses do not receive the attention they deserve...; in the course of four years of medical training, the typical U.S. doctor receives six hours of instruction in occupational safety and health."

In addition to more medical training, it also seems a good deal could be done to make the workplace safer; and bad as it was in the past (SINCLAIR, 1906) it is evidently still dangerous enough to have caused 4,600 injuries and 9 deaths in just one company, for reasons given in the headline of the story: "At a Texas pipe foundry, indifference to safety and life" (NYT, 1-1—03). The details verge on obscenity—as "profits soared."

The relevant company is Tyler Pipe, recently bought up by the McWane, Inc., "one of the world's largest manufacturers of cast-iron sewer and water pipe." After McWane bought Tyler, they "cut nearly two-thirds of the employees" while maintaining the same levels of production. How?

> McWane eliminated one of the three /8-hour/ shifts...; everyone would work one of two 12-hour shifts. At the end of a shift, supervisors often marched through yelling "Four more hours!" So employees worked 16-hour days, sometimes seven days a week.../and made/ double the profits of the preceding five-year period.

The NYT story goes on to detail how, after OSHA inspectors found hundreds of safety violations and filed reports, the company not only went on its deadly way, but managed to blame the workers when they were injured:

> In 2000 and 2001, the records show 350 workers were subjected to disciplinary actions after reporting injuries—"with the intent and purpose to teach," the plant's employee handbook explained.

The Times story is accompanied by a horrifying photo of the latest death in November, 2002 It shows the victim's dead body caught in an "aging conveyor belt," his head crushed, etc. And its report closes in this fashion:

> Last summer /before the death noted above/, Tyler plead-
> ed guilty in federal court... to deliberately ignoring safety rules...,
> and reached a settlement with the OSHA.... /However:/ A
> recently completed internal safety audit found 1,219 hazards.

Withal, in April of 2002, **Bush II** "unveiled a new workplace
safety policy that calls for no mandatory steps by industry and
instead relies on <u>voluntary</u> actions by companies to reduce injuries
from repetitive notions on the job.... /of which/ there are more than
1.8 million injuries... that result from repetitive motions like lifting,
bending and typing." (<u>NYT</u>, 4-6-02)

The next section is concerned with skyrocketing hospital costs.
Among the many meanings of that is one that is well-concealed
from view; namely what that means for workers' compensation:
Rather than pay the rising costs of insurance, companies are laying
off workers.

In the article "Cost of Insurance for Work Injuries Soars across
U.S." (<u>NYT</u>, 6-23-3) we learn 1) that 127 million workers are covered by workers' compensation insurance, 2) that "the average cost
of workers' compensation insurance has risen 50 percent in the last
three years... because of rising medical and legal costs..., and a significant amount of fraud," 3) that the insurance is mandatory, and
that businesses cannot trim their workers' compensation coverage to
save money; 4) so, "the <u>only</u> way to reduce your cost is to reduce
your payroll" (quoting the president of the California Chamber of
Commerce). (my emphasis)

4) High and rising hospital costs.

As noted earlier, both as a percentage of GDP (15) and per
capita ($4,000), the USA has the most costly health care system in
the world, but it provides the least coverage for the average inhabi-
tant. The reason for this extraordinary gap between cost and benefits is in a real sense a mirror image of the inequalities, extravagance,
and **waste** marking our entire socio-economic system. Here some of
the bare elements of that explanation:

<u>Item</u>: U.S. doctors' incomes are the highest in the world by far,
averaging $200,000: twice those of Canada and Germany, three
times those in Japan and the UK (DOWD, 1997b). Evidently that
was not enough for one graduate of Harvard Med. School, an ortho-
pedic surgeon "Who Left an Operation to Run an Errand" (<u>NYT</u>, 8-

9-02). With the surgery only partially done, he left surgery to deposit his just-arrived paycheck (delivered to him in surgery, yet) "because he had to get the check to his bank because he was in a financial crisis and had to pay his bills." Next time you have to be operated on, best to ask the surgeon if his credit cards are maxed out.

Item: Hospital staffs are bloated with non-patient care and financial and billing employees. There are at least one thousand five hundred separate for-profit health insurers in the USA. Their administrative costs are sky high and amount to 25-35 percent of total health costs.

In contrast, Canada has only one insurer (the government), with fewer administrators and costs than one company in one state: Blue Cross system, Massachusetts (which covers only 3 million people). In 1991, according to the U.S. General Accounting Office (GAO), administrative costs were $67 billion more than would have been required under the Canadian system. (WHITE) In that same year—and remember, the subsequent decade took matters from bad to worse—the inefficiency exploded. According to a Harvard Medical School Study,

> On an average day in 1968, American hospitals employed 435,100 managers and clerks while caring for 1,378,000 patients. By 1990, the average daily number of patients had fallen to 853,000, but the number of administrative personnel had grown to 1,291,600. (NYT, 8-5-93)

Think of that while you are cursing your way through the many letters you get from your insurance system: "This is not a bill" or "This is a bill" or "....." All that annoying paper they see as essential for their profits. None of it does anything for your health, and may harm it. And mind you, we are told, over and over and over, a for-profit system—in health care, in education, in everything—is the high road to efficiency. Bah humbug.

5) The shortage of nurses.

Having spent time in hospitals as both a patient and as an orderly in surgery (for two years), I have learned that however important doctors may be in critical moments, the nurses are the mainstay of a successful stay in a hospital, and are also vital at critical moments, with or without a doctor present.

As with the military, the doctors are the general staff, the nurses are the lower orders of officer and the ranked enlisted personnel. The higher-ups devise the strategy—for better or for worse—and the rest do the fighting, the hard work, and often have to revise misguided strategies on the spot. But also, as with the military, the prestige, the power, and the incomes go to those on high. So what else is new?

When we read that there is now a dire shortage of nurses—12 percent of the total needed—it would be serious enough if that shortage were due to the lack of interest in such difficult work by sufficient numbers; but that is not the reason. Rather, as the health care system shifted toward managed care, hospitals merged, and nurses were laid off to cut costs. Those who remained found themselves working longer hours and caring for more patients.... and many nurses moved to work in other fields or other non-hospital jobs...(NYT, 5-28-02)

So what? Well, in a study in The New England Journal of Medicine, it was estimated that "hundreds or, perhaps, thousands of deaths each year are due to low staffing"; that "nurses are the eyes and the ears of the hospital for judging whether a patient is recovering normally...; that problems cannot be spotted if nurses do not have time to observe their patients." (NYT, 5-30-02) A sorry confirmation: In "Patient Deaths Tied to Lack of Nurses," (NYT, 8-8-2) we are informed that "the national organization that accredits hospitals reported today that the lack /of nurses/ contributed to nearly a quarter of the unanticipated problems that result in death or injury to hospital patients."

That present shortage will be very hard to resolve. Even though hospitals are now in a "bidding war" to gain more nurses, it is not only that they are in competition for a pool that will not be sufficiently refilled for some years, it is that the mere increase of nurses' salaries will not change the larger fact that nurses are now treated like workers on an assembly line; that is, the "eyes and ears" of the hospital will still have too little time to pay due attention.

It probable that it is the most conscientious nurses who have left the hospitals; it seems reasonable to assume that if ever hospitals were to return to the mission we have all assumed was theirs—namely, the care and cure of the sick—then those best nurses would return. It isn't up to them; the system has to become sane first.

In this and all the other elements of our wrong-headed health care system, there is an ineradicable conflict between providing sufficient health care and making sufficient profits; worse, we now move in exactly the wrong direction, and at high speed.

As will be discussed under **HMOs**, since they and their managed care system began to take firm hold in the 1990s, that gap has widened at an accelerating rate, producing a major crisis. The crisis is the result of the interaction of unnecessarily rising costs whose managed care "solution" is to provide always less satisfactory health care. "Unnecessarily"? Yes, for the costs have little to do with health service, and almost everything to do with profits.

As matters now stand, our health care crisis cannot be resolved, because in this country an alternative system—whether along the diverse lines of Italy, or Germany, or Japan, et al.—ceased even to be discussed during or after the disastrous episode of the "Clinton Health Care Plan." (CHP)

In 1993, As some will remember, with great flourish and tomes of information and data the Clintons (with Hillary Clinton in charge), initiated an interminable discussion of new directions for health care in the USA. The trouble began at the beginning; the Clintons evidently made a strategic decision that even though their goal was universal coverage, a national health insurance plan (NHI)— first recommended, by Truman in 1945, incidentally— could not be passed, so it was totally ruled out by them as even discussible. Right on. What was discussed was "employer mandate," "individual mandate," and "no mandate." In just those words; period.

The "employer mandate" became the CHP; but in that it required that all be covered and that "the employer had to pay all the premiums," it quite simply could not be accepted by the employers, so it was therefore "dead on arrival." There was no point in discussing the "individual" and "no" mandates; they were what we have for most. (GORDON, C.; STARR, P.)

All countries have problems of one sort or another with their health care systems, to one degree or another; but only ours has a self-induced crisis that inexorably worsens by the day.

6) The perverse role of medical technology.

In the health care sector, as elsewhere, technological change can be for better and for worse. Its negative role in the ongoing health care crisis may be seen as arising from the two main types of technological invention at work there: 1) "genuine improvements in the invention of new technologies for existing maladies, and 2) technologies invented to "solve" equally invented problems." (KEANEY, 2002) In both cases, costs <u>rise</u> disproportionately to the contribution to improved health.

In the case of "genuine improvements," the main tendency is for them to be available only to those with the very best coverage (and usually the highest incomes), where need is not the main criterion nor success the common effect. Rather, the hospitals or clinics dispense such technologies where payment and profits are assured, and hope for the best.

In such cases at least a real need might be met. But in the case of "invented technologies for invented problems," <u>only</u> the profits (to patent holder and hospital) are at issue; not health: "Two-thirds of the drugs approved from 1989 to 2000 were modified versions of existing drugs or even identical to those already on the market.... Some of the reformulated prescription drugs are now among the most heavily advertised." (<u>NYT</u>, "Patents challenged...," 5-29-02)

Evidently, a major reason for these "reformulations" is that a patent on an existing drug will expire: so Sarafem, the same drug as Prozac, comes out with a new name and differently colored capsules—and a higher price, accompanied by lots of **advertising**. (The industry spends $2.5 <u>billion</u> yearly on ads.) The report on which the <u>NYT</u> article was based is from the National Institute for Health Care Management, which concluded stating that "**pharmaceutical** companies are turning more into marketing companies."

Thus, and like so much else in our socioeconomy, medical technology is driven more by "the main chance" than by any social or human use it might have. Occasionally, of course, such a use has existed; more often (see **technology**) there is no beneficial effect, or harm has been done.

7) High and rising prices of prescription drugs.

What has just been noted about false "invention" and drugs is unfortunately not the worst element regarding such drugs; that honor goes to the problems created by extortionately high drug prices for those who are not rich; that is, at least 80 percent of the population, hitting the old among them hardest.

The problem is great for at least half of the U.S. people, and greatest of all for those who might seem to be "covered," but are not; namely, those dependent upon Medicare and Medicaid, the old, disabled, and the poor.

In a recent <u>NYT</u> op-ed essay by Senator Zell Miller (Dem., Georgia), he pointed out that "If Medicare were being invented today, no one would think of starting it without a prescription drug benefit...." (NYT, 6-1-02)

The good Senator was wrong even—or especially—about "today." Congress has passed the Medicare bill that is touted as covering cover prescription drug costs for the old and disabled. That the Bush administration pushed hard for passage should have made everyone suspicious. The following very lengthy quote shows why:

> Although the government must provide drugs to 40 million people, it may not negotiate a bulk discount; it must pay whatever price the manufacturer sets or asks—prices that in recent years have been rising at a rate of 12 percent a year. The legislation forbids the importing of less expensive drugs from Canada, prohibits beneficiaries from buying supplemental insurance for drugs unacknowledged by Medicare, reduces or eliminates payments to as many as 6 million people for whom Medicaid now defrays at least some of their costs, declares a suspension of payment at precisely the point when most people might need the most help. An annual premium of $420 covers 75 percent of drug expenditures up to $2,250; from that point upward the beneficiary must pay, with his or her own money, 100 percent of the next $3,600 in costs; once the expenditures reach a total of $5,850, the government pays 95 percent of the subsequent bill.... As a further means of implementing the shift of the nation's health-care burden from the public to the private sector, the legislation offers various inducements to the life-enhancing profit motive:

> A. A $12 billion slush fund from which, over the next 10 years, the secretary of health and human services may pay out bribes to HMOs otherwise reluctant to accept patients whose illnesses cannot be preempted for a quick and certain gain.

> B. A windfall of $70 billion, also over the next 10 years, to those corporations willing to continue prescription-drug coverage for their retired employees, the money to be paid in the

form of both tax-deductions and tax-free subsidies.

C. The guarantee of "maximum flexibility" to the private enti-
    ties seeking to recruit customers from the general population
    now served by Medicare. The private entity may exercise the
    right to "cherry pick"—i.e., to offer services only to those
    individuals not likely to require expensive treatment....

D. The legislation's reliance on the drug companies and the pri-
    vate insurers to curtail spending and control costs, /which/
    serves a dual purpose/:/ the eventual destruction of the entire
    Medicare apparatus, and to relieve the government of any
    responsibility for what will be reported as an act of God.
    Even the dimmest of Republican congressmen knows that
    the government doesn't have the $400 billion that the drug
    prescription benefit presumably will cost over the next 10
    years..., which could easily become an invoice presented for
    $1 trillion. (Lewis LAPHAM, Harper's Magazine, February,
    2004)

Lapham goes on to point out that the family of Bill Frist, the
Senate's majority leader, established Hospital Corporation of
America (HCA), the nation's largest consortium of "for-profit hospitals" (an official title that should in itself make all of us sick)—the
company which, just two days before Bill became the Senate leader,
having admitted to defrauding the government, had to pay over
$1,600,000 in fines to the government.

That the drug industry has 635 **lobbyists** in D.C., and are
among the highest bribers—'scuse me, contributors—to election
campaigns goes a long way toward explaining such disgraceful
behavior. They've spent wisely.

As will be seen in the examination of **pharmaceutical** companies, the **CEOs** of the nine biggest companies receive an average of
$19 million annually (not counting stock options, etc.), and their
industry (according to Fortune), is not only the most profitable of all
industries, but its profits margins are nearly four times the average of
the profits of the Fortune 500 largest U.S. companies. (MM, 9/2001)

> If the U.S. were to adopt Canada's single-payer system, it
> would save approximately $286 billion a year (just) in adminis-
> trative costs ($982 per capita). The thorny problem of 43 mil-
> lion Americans without health insurance—whom it would cost
> only about $69 billion a year to insure—could be eliminated,
> with money to spare. ("Let's not get tangled up in America's red

tape." Andre Picard, <u>Globe and Mail</u>, 6-10-04)

Enough said? Not yet. See **HMOs, pharmaceuticals**.

hegemony (see globalization, Bush II, milex)

Hiroshima/Nagasaki

On August 6, 1945, the atomic bomb was dropped on Hiroshima. Of a population of about 350,000, at least 70,000 people died instantly, 60,000 within three months, and an additional 70,000 from radiation not long after. On August 9, three days later, the second atomic bomb was dropped on Nagasaki, killing another 70,000 people instantly, with subsequently the same number dying from radiation. For the horror of it as viewed shortly after the bombing, read John Hersey's <u>Hiroshima</u> (1946).

The slaughter was all too tragic taken by itself; apart from other considerations, it must be seen as obscene when we understand the following:

1) There was no <u>military</u> justification for it as regards the war with Japan. Months before, Japan's ability to resist militarily had dwindled to almost the vanishing point. As one of those entrusted with air-sea rescue missions for my bomb group in that area, I <u>know</u> that already by July our planes were receiving little or no resistance from either Japanese fighters or anti-aircraft; they had run out of oil, among other problems. (And see SHERWIN.)

I could understand my underling's word might not be convincing, but it does not stand alone: the judgment of the vast majority of top American military leaders was that the bombings were unnecessary—including Generals Eisenhower, MacArthur, LeMay and Arnold (ALPEROVITZ) and Admiral William D. Leahy, head of the Navy in the Pacific during the war. And this is what the Admiral said (as quoted in WEALE):

> The use of this barbarous weapon at Hiroshima and Nagasaki was of no material assistance in our war against Japan. The Japanese were already defeated and ready to surrender because of the effective sea blockade and the successful bombing with conventional weapons....My own feeling was that in being the first to use it, we had adopted an ethical standard common to the barbarians of the dark ages. I was not taught to

make war in that fashion and wars cannot be won by destroying women and children. One of the professors associated with the Manhattan Project told me that he hoped the bomb wouldn't work. I wish he had been right.

2) Even had there been continuing resistance, as soon as Emperor Hirohito learned of the nature and magnitude of the attack on Hiroshima, "... he instructed his Foreign Minister Togo to 'Tell Suzuki that the war must be ended as soon as possible on the basis of the Potsdam Proclamation.'" (TAKAKI)

3) The second bomb, originally scheduled to be dropped on August 11, was instead dropped on August 9, and not on the planned target (Kokura), which was clouded over, but on Nagasaki.

4) All this as, meanwhile, Hirohito was continuing to seek an end to the war, an effort begun well before Hiroshima. As discussed under **Cold War**, through contact with our then ally the USSR—as it prepared to enter the Pacific war in August—Japan had sought to begin peace talks—refused flatly by President Truman unless preceded by Hirohito's stepping down. (ALPEROVITZ) About two weeks after the bombing, the peace treaty was signed and Japan was occupied by the USA: Hirohito remained on the throne until 1989, to be succeeded by his son Akihito.

So: If the war was soon to be won without atomic bombs, if Japan was seeking peace well before that, and if Hirohito stayed on the throne another 44 years, why the bombing? The answer to that question has many dimensions that ruled out the less catastrophic options. Those "dimensions" included the mentality of the military and of **Truman** himself; most important, however, was the emerging political strategy of the **Cold War**—the **preemption** of its time,

1. Truman as president and as a person is examined more fully under that entry; suffice it to note here his comments a) when informed the bomb had been dropped and b) his response to criticism afterward:

(a) In August, on his way home from the Potsdam conference on the USS Augusta: "This is the greatest thing that ever happened." (WEALE) (b) And after criticism:

> Nobody is more disturbed over the use of atomic bombs than I am but I was greatly disturbed over the unwarranted attack by the Japanese on Pearl Harbor and their murder of our prisoners of war. The only language they seem to understand is

the one we have used to bombard them. When you have to deal with a beast you have to treat him as a beast. It is most regrettable but nevertheless true. (quoted in SHERWIN)

2) So <u>that's</u> where **Bush II** learned his lines!

In that war, as subsequently in Korea, Vietnam and, most recently, **Iraq**, that militarist's mentality won out—with, as noted above, reservations from a few generals and an admiral, after the fact.

3) But the most compelling reason, embraced by both Truman and the military (among others) was integrally connected to the patterns of global economic, military, and political domination whose core came to be called the **Cold War**: As ALPEROVITZ has said, "It was the first shot of the Cold War": Soviet Union, watch out!

As with so many of the USA's "warnings" and aggressive actions, whether military or socioeconomic, there have been unintended as well as intended consequences. Among the intended were 1) that the USSR would get caught up in an arms race—a race which would benefit the U.S. economy and harm the Soviet's to the point where its whole system could not but fail—and let the "collateral damage" fall it where it might: 2) that a nuclear arms race would commence not only in the Soviet Union but elsewhere, in countries rich and poor, large and small: the UK and France and China, North Korea, Iran, Israel and Pakistan—again with consequences whose nature, dimensions and manifold threats to wellbeing, even survival, are as potent as they are immeasurable.

Since Hiroshima there have been many attempts by scientists, politicians, and other simply sane people to ban the very existence of nuclear weapons and, as well, nuclear energy. (see **nukes**) The USA has been the main resistant force to those efforts; "successfully" so.

So just who is the "beast" Mr. Truman had in mind?

Hiss, Alger

Along with the **Rosenbergs**, Alger Hiss was a prime victim of the many injustices and the hysteria produced by the **Cold War** and its bedmate **McCarthyism**. The fate of Hiss was to be imprisoned for five years; among his principal prosecutors was Representative Richard **Nixon**: his role in the **House Un-American Activities**

Committee's (HUAC) "trial" of Hiss, it is generally agreed, served to launch him into, first, the public eye and, later, the White House.

From 1936 until 1947 Hiss was with the State Department, often serving as adviser at international conferences, most notably and importantly at the conference in San Francisco that birthed the United Nations. In 1947 he left the State Department to become President of the Carnegie Endowment for International Peace.

Not quite the stuff one normally associates with being a secret agent of a designated enemy power. So how and why did he become a federal prisoner for five years? What had he done to deserve such a fate? Well, he was accused of having been a member of the Communist Party and of having passed over secret documents to his accuser. And who was his accuser?

It was Whittaker Chambers, a former member of the Communist Party and, at the time of his accusation, a senior editor at Time Magazine. Time, along with Fortune and other periodicals, was then the private property of Henry Luce, a flamboyant and very successful media capitalist, the Rupert Murdoch of his time: a vigorous, politically ambitious, nationalistic right-winger, not known for having scrupled at anything.

Mr. Chambers, on the other hand, was something out of a Coen brothers film: physically unpleasant to view, heavy drinker, giving every appearance of being emotionally and psychologically at risk; and a clever writer.

Chambers claimed that Hiss had furnished him with 200 secret documents—and here we enter the theater of the absurd—leaving the documents for him in a pumpkin somewhere (presumably a very large pumpkin, if it held 200 documents). There ensued the ignoble spectacle of a public "trial" before HUAC, starring the bizarre trio of Chambers, Hiss, and Nixon.

Hiss denied everything, including any ability to remember even knowing Chambers. He was charged with perjury—on the grounds that Chambers said Yes and Hiss said No.

It is relevant to note that Hiss was as reputable in character as Chambers was not: During the hearings, Hiss was stated as being of high character and decency not only by Adlai Stevenson (twice-failed presidential candidate vs. Eisenhower) but, as well, by John Foster Dulles, one of the most warlike of cold warriors, and Ike's Secretary of State.

The following personal note may not count for much, but it is one of many matters that persuaded me of the injustice of the "Hiss Case." While I was teaching at Cornell in the Sixties I was in Manhattan one day for a <u>Monthly Review</u> luncheon where I had been permitted to raise money for a Cornell civil rights project. I was then a pipe smoker. Sitting across me at the dining table was a pleasant-looking man; both he and I were smoking our pipes. He asked me what tobacco I was smoking, and we fell into that kind of discussion. I introduced myself, as did he; he, of course, was Alger Hiss. (Why else would I be telling this story?)

Subsequently, we saw each other a few times, not just to speak about pipes, etc., but because I found him to be a very good person to know. I am not alone in taking the position that if one has to choose between believing a thug like Chambers or a fine man like Hiss, there could be no question at all—except in a period of social lunacy. Does my trusting Hiss more than Chambers signify that I am but another gullible country boy—like John Foster Dulles and Adlai Stevenson—easy to fool by city slickers?

Maybe not: On October 29, 1992, the <u>NYT</u>, in the article "Laughing Last?" reported that "newly-opened archives in Russia clear Alger Hiss of accusations of ever having spied for the Soviet Union.... When notified of this, Mr. Hiss said he had been waiting 44 years for that news." Me too. (And see Tony HISS, <u>The View from Alger's Window: A Son's Memoir</u>.)

HMOs

The HMOs and their managed care systems—first supported in the 1970s—ballooned from a headache to a plague beginning about ten years ago. Their pitch was that <u>they</u> would end the inefficiencies of the past. However, the period in which they have come to dominate the health care system is precisely that in which its costs—and its inefficiency—began the acceleration that continues.

Some of the rising costs were due to factors other than the HMOs, as was noted earlier, not least the gouging prices set by the **pharmaceutical** giants. OK, but all of them are part and parcel of the "for-profit health care system." But the HMOs have done at least their share in bringing about today's mountainous costs. What started out as annual one-digit overall cost increases became two-digit as the 1980s ended, rising to 15.3 percent for 2002 (over $1.5 <u>trillion</u>). Two years ago (6-5-02) the <u>NYT</u> reports that "Health maintenance organizations are demanding rate increases of 22 percent in their ongoing negotiations with employers for 2003... which will be passed on to consumers." They surely were.

As this tendency of always-higher costs and prices has gone on, it needs repeating that the provision of **health care** to the average person has decreased both quantitatively and qualitatively. What is it about the HMOs that such is the case?

What was the system which they presumed to replace with great savings to all, and profits to them? It was called the "fee-for-service" system: Other than those covered by Medicare and Medicaid, those who had health insurance had paid for it themselves or through their employer, the latter true for about two-thirds of workers (as noted under **health care**).

As the numbers of insured rose from the 1950s on, so did doctors' incomes: the insured could choose their own doctors and the doctors soon realized that the more treatments they gave the better off they—but not necessarily their patients—were. "American doctors performed invasive tests and procedures at rates far exceeding international norms.... Caesarian sections, surgerized ulcers, hysterectomies and tonsillectomies far above the rates in other countries, etc." (FRANK, <u>D&S</u>, 5/6, 2001) In addition was (and is) the **corruption** between doctors and labs, and drug companies. The happy consequence for doctors was that their incomes rose two to three times faster than the nation's, 1960-1990, bringing them up to a lovely $200,000 annual average.

One might think that such an evolution—or, better, devolution— would have led everyone but the doctors and labs and drug companies to open their minds to a national health service/single-payer system. But that overlooks certain large facts: 1) Employers as a whole tend to have a knee-jerk negative reaction against anything to do with government (unless it is in the nature of a subsidy for themselves), and just as "instinctive" a response in favor of "private enterprise," which is what HMOs are; 2) the average citizen lives in the same society, and has been taught to think in much the same way, if not for the same reasons; 3) the major insurance companies have always been opposed to <u>any</u> form of <u>social</u> insurance—beginning with their adamant fight against **social security** from 1935 to the present; and 4) this created a new industry for

lobbyists, who have been very successful indeed in their efforts on behalf of the "Big Five" insurance companies (Aetna, Cigna, Metropolitan, Prudential and Travelers) and related managed care companies—which, taken together, now "cover" 90 percent of those receiving care. Here FRANK's lucid and crisp summary review of what brought us to our present state, and how it happened:

> The early 1990s saw a wave of mergers and acquisitions among health insurers that left large regions of the country with only two or three competing health plans. Their superior bargaining power allowed insurers to negotiate sharp reductions in fees, which were passed on to employers in the form of lower premiums. In 1994 the average health-insurance premium /paid by employers/ fell for the first time in years; premiums increased at or below the inflation rate for the rest of the 1990s.
>
> Hospitals, facing lower reimbursement rates, cut staff and beds for traditional inpatient care while expanding facilities for expensive services like outpatient surgery. Still, hospitals throughout the country suffered operating losses. Large urban hospitals in low-income areas were especially hard hit.../some like that of Los Angeles, closing entirely/. For-profit hospital chains moved in quickly, buying ups cores of non-profit community hospitals. (FRANK, ibid.)

So, with patients and providers (doctors, labs, and hospitals) getting the dirty end of the stick, that leaves the HMOs, drug companies, and top insurance companies getting the sweet end—their owners, their **CEOs** and their countless **lobbyists**, that is.

Then there is this: (9-10-02), <u>NYT</u>), "HMOs For 200,000 Pulling Out Of Medicare." That by itself isn't a great number, but the 2.5 <u>million</u> of those dropped by HMOs from 1998 to the present is; and that number accelerates. Plus, "Medicare patients can expect 'major changes—that is, reductions of—benefits, even if they are still enrolled: cutbacks in drug coverage /already cruelly inadequate/, and increases in premiums and co-payments." (ibid.)

So there we are. Or are we? Although there is a rising tide of anger, frustration, and worry among our people at the costs of medical care in the USA, with some emerging movement toward universal coverage, most still see the U.S. system, though costly, as the best.

The best is none too good: "According to a recent study of the

Institute of Medicine, medical errors in hospitals <u>kill</u> up to 98,000 patients yearly, while injuring perhaps a million more." (<u>WP</u>, Editorial, "America's medical scandal," 12-10-02). Such deaths and injuries are called "iatrogenic"; that is, caused by the docs themselves.

That was a few years ago. Now, as the USA's entire health care system becomes always more **privatized** and always more expensive to those needing it, those years are coming to look like paradise lost; and we ain't seen nothin' yet.

Hoover, J. Edgar

The **FBI** was created just after World War I. Hoover went to work for it in 1921, became its Director in 1924, and, by hook and by crook (including much blackmail of members of Congress), was Director for 48 years (!), until his death in 1972.

Hoover very much resembled an angry bullfrog; except that they only <u>look</u> dangerous; Hoover was dangerous; very. He was instrumental in heating up the Red Scare of the 1920s, was a main feeder for the "Un-American activities" persecutions of the 1930s, and was the Godfather of the **McCarthyism** of 1940s and since (now called **Ashcroft**ism). (CAUTE)

The FBI's mandate was to investigate interstate crimes. Except for a few much-ballyhooed criminal chases, such as Bonnie and Clyde and Al Capone, Hoover's FBI pursued only his sociopolitical passions. These centered upon a select group he just plain hated: blacks (notably, Martin Luther King), Jews, homosexuals, and, last but by no means least, those he deemed to be dangerous lefties. He would have been at home with the Gestapo: he made the FBI into the Federal Bureau of Inquisition. (HACK)

Hoover did not confine his villainy to politics; he knowingly allowed more than one innocent person to be imprisoned for murder Hoover <u>knew</u> he had not committed; which had indeed been committed by gangsters working with the FBI. Documents released by the House Committee on Government Reform show

> that officials at F.B.I. headquarters, apparently including Mr. Hoover, knew as long ago as 1965 that Boston agents were employing killers and gang leaders as informers and were protecting them from prosecution—while allowing four known-to-be innocent men to be imprisoned, one for 30 years, two of whom died while in prison. ("Hoover's F.B.I. and the Mafia..."

(NYT, 8-25-02)

To probe Hoover's dark depths would require the combined talents of Shakespeare and Freud. Here we settle for a few questions: How did he select his victims? What dubious means did he use to do them in? How much of his famous blackmailing was for himself; was any of it for the nation?

Also, given that we know that the Mafia blackmailed him, (MILLER, SUMMERS) what did they have on him? It is known that the Mafia possessed a film in which hater of homosexuals Hoover was engaged in a "compromising position" with another (highly-placed FBI) man. When it also came out that J. Edgar was a practiced cross- dresser, John Updike wrote a sweet parody in the New Yorker (3/1/93), entitled "Glad Rags." In it, all the male members (no pun intended) of the Eisenhower administration and our hero party in fancy dresses, while engaged in hilarious conversations. Worth digging out of your local library.

But there was never anything amusing about J. Edgar Hoover. He wrecked the lives of numberless people. Through blackmail he used his office to enlarge his power and used that power so as greatly to damage both his victims and our/his country. In the process, he did much to accustom the USA to a set of assumptions and ways and means which, far from withering away after his death, continue to cripple our abilities as a nation to ever become a truly good—as distinct from great—society. Despite—or because?—of all that, Hoover's very long entry in Who's Who in America is taken up largely by a listing of dozens of "honorary degrees" from all sorts of civic and other groups, including universities (!).

May he rot in Hell.

House Un-American Activities Committee (see McCarthyism)

housing/homeless

In his 1933 inaugural address, **FDR** famously deplored the desperation of "one-third of a nation, ill-clothed, ill-fed, and ill housed." It was a fine sentiment, but his facts were wrong: according to H. MILLER, a U.S. Bureau of the Census statistician for 30 years, using contemporary measures of **poverty**, over half of the nation was in that fix.

Be that as it may, then as now those who find themselves in one of those categories usually find themselves in all three—and, as well, badly need **health care**.

When FDR spoke, the USA and much of the world were deep in history's worst depression ever; in contrast, the 1990s encompassed the most prosperous years ever—if, that is, you were on the top layers in the USA or the other rich countries.

If, on the other hand, you were among the 4 <u>billion</u> or more living in poverty in the rest of the world, the 1990s were likely to have been harder on you than the 1980s, and they harder than the 1970s, and so backward <u>ad infinitum</u>. Thus have the blessings of **colonialism, imperialism**, and **globalization** been distributed.

The focus here will be on the large number of homeless in the USA. Disgracefully high though those numbers are here, they are both absolutely and relatively puny when set against the plight of billions of desperately poor people elsewhere. In no case, however, neither for the suffering people in the USA nor in rest of the world are such conditions due to natural calamity; they have been "manmade" or, more accurately, are a consequence of economic policies combining **greed**, callousness, ruthlessness, and ignorance: There are explanations but no acceptable excuses for such human misery; especially in the USA.

<u>Uncle Scrooge</u>. When confronted with those who live badly it is common for those who live well to "blame the victim" and, of course, to assume that the speaker's wellbeing is the consequence of some combination of ability and hard work; that being so, clearly the harsh conditions of the badly-off are due to their lack of ability and/or laziness: a comforting position for the comfortable, of course; but wrong analytically, to say nothing of ethically. (RYAN)

More often than not the homeless are viewed with scorn and rage when seen in the streets, and with anger when proposals are made to alleviate their numbers and condition; that condition, when not taken to be a result of laziness and stupidity, is seen as one of self-indulgence—in drugs, liquor, gambling; or something.

The facts are disturbingly different: The homeless of the USA are in that condition for one of several and usually overlapping reasons: they are physically and/or psychiatrically disabled, either or both cases requiring not just a shelter but special facilities; and/or they have problems with alcohol and/or drugs; and/or they are "normal" people (often families) who work full-time and cannot find an affordable dwelling; and/or they are (all too many) women who, alone or with their children, have fled from a dangerously abusive father.

Those among us whose attitudes toward the homeless are prompted by disgust, fear, racism, attitudes of superiority or some mixture of those and other forms of prejudice—and they seem to constitute a high percentage of the people of the USA and of our legislators—should be ashamed of themselves rather than scornful of the victims.

In fact, at least a third of the homeless are veterans of the war in **Vietnam**. The injuries of those veterans were by no means confined to bodily wounds, numerous and damaging though they were; in addition, or instead, they are due to the psycho-emotional damage done by participation in a devastating, murderous, and insane war entailing the large-scale and indiscriminate killing of civilians. If you have done that and can come out of it inwardly unharmed, there may well be something wrong with you. (YOUNG)

Whatever problems those in the streets have as individuals, they have been deepened by the "reforms" of the **Reagan** era (worsened by Clinton), which deposited them there, in the name of one artifice or another, including "benign neglect"—the vicious term coined by much-admired "liberal" Democratic Senator (and adviser to Pres. **Nixon**), Daniel Moynihan.

In California alone it is estimated by the State Department of Housing and Community Development that more than 500,000 people are homeless; that at least a third of them are families, most with children; that about 50,000 of those sleeping on the streets are seriously mentally ill; that nearly 4,000 young people "graduated" from foster-homes are without skills, adequate education, financial security, or morale. (SFC, "Homelessness is our problem," 5/8/02) In the Los Angeles area, still rising **unemployment** has caused the number of working families without homes to rise from a third to more than half in shelters: "The breadwinners can't find jobs, so they're losing their housing." (NYT, Op-ed, "Now Work, No Homes," 8-14-03)

Then there is the high percentage of homeless individuals and families with jobs, but with such low incomes they cannot find affordable housing. Add to that the steadily rising numbers of jobless people who quite simply cannot find a job, plus those who now work part-time and need the full-time job they lost through recession and/or **downsizing**, plus the cruel inadequacy of the "minimum-wage": what was always an inadequate wage and becomes more so pushes a fully-employed recipient <u>below</u> the official (itself under-stated) **poverty** level. But doesn't the federal government provide assistance in the way of public housing or housing subsidies for those who need it? It did; or, rather, once it almost did.

When the New Deal programs for public housing and subsidies took hold in the 1930s and were improved by the Federal Housing Act of 1949, they created livable rental units for poor and working-class people.

That legislation was deliberately undone in the 1980s, "...when the **Reagan** administration cut funding for the construction of low- and moderate-income housing and revised the tax structure in a way that made affordable multi-family units less attractive for investors to build." (<u>NYT</u>, Editorial: "Facing up the housing crisis," 7/-5/02) (and see HARTMAN)

Nowadays such assistance as there is goes mostly to those who are happy to <u>get</u> it but who don't <u>need</u> it: the National Low Income Housing Coalition, taking its figures from the 2001 Budget of the U.S. Government, found that <u>62</u> percent of all housing subsidies go to households earning more than $100,000 (!) a year.

So those with under $100,000 at least get the other 38 percent? Sure, but neither in terms of nor in order of need. Consider these data:

Item: The California Association of Realtors showed that in 2002 only 29 percent of all Californians are able to afford a home at all, and only 12 percent a median-priced home.

Item: The U.S. Conference of Mayors, after surveying the 27 major cities of the USA, listed the leading cause of home-lessness as the lack of affordable housing.

Item: In California, more than 500,000 are on the affordable hous-ing waiting lists.

Item: Presently, more than 70,000 affordable low income rental units, like so many thousands before them, are "at risk of conversion to market rate units, driving low income families into homelessness." (SFC, "Myths about the homeless delay solutions." /7/5/02/)

Much of the foregoing relates to California; but rather than thus being misleading, it is therefore a large understatement of what exists in the rest of the country: California is one of the richest states, and its local and state governments are among the least conservative.

At the other end of the country, here is how Mayor Bloomberg has been handling the problem of the homeless:

> On /August 11, 2002/ the Bloomberg administration reopened an old jail in the Bronx as a temporary shelter for homeless families, who have been crowding the city's Emergency Assistance Unit in record numbers over the last year.... On /that night alone/ a record 8,458 families /my emphasis/ received shelter from the Department of Homeless Services. (NYT, 8-13-02, "Testing the Mayor.")

About a month later, a young woman (now a senior at Cornell University) wrote a piece for the Op-ed page of the NYT concerning her family's treatment when homeless. During her childhood she had lived in "four or five different homeless shelters in New York City." She recounts some of her experiences, some of her feelings:

> Living in those shelters... helped me to see that the biggest cause of homelessness is not lack of money to pay rent. There were a lot of broken families in these shelters: broken by drugs, alcohol abuse, divorce, AIDS, early pregnancy, lack of education and, most important, lack of information about how to get out of these troubles.... Sure having a bed to sleep on is better than having no bed at all. But sleeping on a bed in a shelter that was once a jail doesn't help ease the psychological burden of being homeless in the first place... A line for food, cramped space, no privacy... sounds a lot like a prison to me. (8-18-02)

Meanwhile, the Bush White House had the Department of Housing and Urban Development issue "new guidelines to the country's 2,500 public housing agencies declaring that it would no longer pay the full cost of housing vouchers but would cap the federal contribution at the level of August, 2003..., which will force housing officials to raise rents or evict tenants." (NYT Editorial, "Killing off housing for the poor," 5-4-04). Same day, same NYT, the following story: "House Approves $447 Billion for Military."

Meanwhile, also, agricultural surpluses continue to pile up; countless thousands seek handouts who would much rather line up for jobs doing something useful.

hunger

If the Rev. Thomas MALTHUS were alive and kicking today, he would be jumping up and down with pride; even, perhaps joy; not because his "theory" was right, but that now his harsh policies are being put in place. Over two centuries ago he argued against what today is called "welfare" for the poor—then meaning the unemployed—with his "theory of population growth": He said it didn't help the "poor," but did hurt taxpayers like him and his landed gentry family; doing good did bad. How come?

Because, he pronounced confidently, populations inexorably rise more rapidly than food supplies; therefore, do <u>nothing</u> to help the poor; to help them now means to have more of them around in misery later—to their own and everyone else's harm.

Moreover, Malthus went on, in addition to proposing that the poor be left to wallow in their desperation, steps should be taken to <u>force</u> them to live under unsanitary conditions, so as to increase the death rates among them. (See the fuller discussion in **environment**.)

There are many sensible and decent reasons to seek to lower global rates of population growth, not least because most of it takes place among people who are poor and uneducated, and as a consequence of coercive sex for socially powerless women. Those causes <u>can</u> be alleviated, but only by pursuing socioeconomic measures <u>opposed</u> by Malthus and his present followers, not least in the **Bush II** administration.

The historical and contemporary facts of food supply fly in the fact of Malthusian "theory": Since he wrote (1798), food supplies in the world have <u>always</u> increased more rapidly than population; over the past 35 years—years in which more people starved to death than ever—global food production has outstripped population growth by a good 16 percent, "enough to supply every person on the earth with 4.2 lbs. of food every day." (LAPPE).

In sum, as the Nobel economist-philosopher Amartya SEN has pointed out,

> Starvation is the characteristic of some people not having enough to eat. It is not the characteristic of there not being enough food to eat.

Indeed, one of the major political disputes in this era of **globalization** is that the **free trade** advocated by the richest economies—the USA, not least—is violated by all of them with their practices of encouraged and rewarded <u>restriction</u> of production which, despite all, leaves immense surpluses which are maintained by subsidies and "dumping," practices. (see **farmers**) Such policies became common in the 1930s, the years of deepest privation of modern times (up to then): more than symbolized by the "bonfires" of oranges in California and coffee in Brazil.

The intermittent "famines" of the present find their counterparts in the many "famines" of the past, best known of which was Ireland's in the mid-19th century. The quotation marks around famine are meant to point to an ugly fact: While at least one million Irish died from malnutrition and starvation 1846-49, Ireland was <u>exporting</u> food to England; as usual. How could that be?

It was made not only possible but probable by the brutal colonization of Ireland from the 17th century on. Among its other social crimes, colonization meant that the best lands were taken over by English (and, later, Scottish) landowners, the hard work on the land was done by destitute Irish, producing agricultural products for export at a profit to the oppressors.

The lands left for the Irish themselves were the worst—the so-called "peat bogs." The bogs produced potatoes, period. Thus, when in 1846 the potato blight took hold (and continued for several years), the average Irish family was left to starve—or, as in the case of my own family, to emigrate. Ireland's population fell from nine to less than five million over those years, and it stays there.

In addition one must add the religious persecution extending for over two centuries: The Irish were almost entirely Catholic in religion, the invaders and their imported successors almost entirely Protestant. In consequence, the Irish suffered not only from harsh expropriation of their lands and exploitation of their bodies but severe religious oppression: The mere practice of Catholicism was punished, and its priests executed. (One of the other consequences, not as funny as it seems, is that 85 percent of the Irish population dropped the identifying "O'" of their names (my own family included), not to be put back until after 1916. (CAHILL; DELANY; WOODHAM-SMITH)

And in the USA? In its <u>Advanced Report on Household Food</u>

<u>Security</u> (1999), the USDA found approximately 36 million people without adequate access to food and, worse, about 20 percent of children from 5-18 living in "hungry homes" in the ebullient good years of the late 1990s. (<u>CA</u>, Spring/Summer, 2000)

At the same time, also in the USA, studies found that 55 percent of U.S. adults are overweight, and 23 percent are obese. Worldwide, a <u>billion people are overweight</u>, while several <u>billion</u> are malnourished, with at least 15 <u>million</u> children dying from lack of adequate food every year. (<u>SFC</u>, "Bodily Harm," 4-23-00)

Serious though that problem is in the USA, however, it is dwarfed by the catastrophic food shortages for at least two-thirds of the world's people. As discussed elsewhere (**ADM, farmers, globalization, imperialism**) the main cause of always greater and more deadly hunger in the poorer countries in the world is quite simply that their lands have been stolen out from under them—their lands, their water, their cultures and, it must be added, their dignity.

The USA, as the richest and most powerful nation in all history, has the main responsibility for this ongoing catastrophe. That is made always more evident in the cumulative reports of how the USA stalls and obstructs proposed reforms put forth, however limited, by our fellow culprits in rich Europe or the victimized countries of Asia, Africa and Latin America. (MAGDOFF, et al.; GEORGE /1976; LAPPE'; KLEIN /2002/)

The realities of death-dealing hunger have been haunting most of the world's people now for a century; in recent years (mostly through the United Nations) well-publicized programs for alleviating that hunger have been announced and, once in a while, efforts have been made to put them into effect. Meanwhile the problem worsens and even those limited efforts decrease. In the article "U.N. Official Urges Food Aid For the Poor As a Priority," (<u>NYT</u>, 6-9-02), we learn that

> With about 810 million people going to sleep hungry, the head of the UN Food and Agricultural Organization says that development experts mesmerized by international trade and high technology need to tackle poverty first.
> "We /the FAO/ say, before /the G-8/ goes to discuss the digital divide, you need to look at the three elements you need to live, which is to breathe, to drink and to eat... Among

those living in perpetual hunger are 200 million children under age 5.... Because of big subsidies to farmers in richer nations, at a cost of more than $1 billion a day there are huge stocks of food in developed countries... Yet there are still 800 million people who don't have enough money to buy the food they need." Over one billion live on a $1 day.

Although hunger is literally a life-and-death issue for at least a billion people and a life-and-misery matter for billions more, decent people in the USA are kept from doing the decent thing about it by ignorance and confusion. Those weaknesses are fed by those such as **ADM** who profit from it. Meanwhile, through the media, bought and paid for politicians, and the difficulties for a decent public to know the realities, our policies continue to make a horrifying situation always more so. Those who wish to combat that horror with knowledge may do easily with a powerful and readable book, put together by the Institute for Food and Development Policy: World Hunger: 12 Myths, by Francis Moore Lappe', et al. Here is a mere listing of those myths, many of them treated in this book:

1. There is not enough food. 2. Nature is to blame. 3. Too many mouths to feed. 4. Food vs. the environment. 5. The Green Revolution is the answer. 6. Justice vs. production. 7. The free market can end hunger. 8. Free trade is the answer. 9. Too hungry to revolt. 10. Foreign aid. 11. We benefit. 12. Food vs. freedom.

That bare listing indicates the many complexities and, thus, the many barriers to clarity for even well-intentioned people; all the more reason to get to work to break through those barriers, to save countless lives.

(See fuller discussions in see FINNEGAN; FOLBRE, et al.; GANS; PIVEN & CLOWARD.)

IMF/IBRD/GATT/WTO/NAFTA

First, so you don't have to check the Abbreviations, what do all those initials stand for? Then, what are they supposed to do and what, instead, have they done?

IMF (1944): International Monetary Fund, often called "the Fund." IBRD: International Bank for Reconstruction and Development, or World Bank. GATT: General Agreement on

Tariffs and Trade (1947); replaced, modified, and renamed WTO (1995): World Trade Organization. All those were designed to be global in function; NAFTA (1992): North American Free Trade Agreement is limited to Canada, Mexico, and the USA. Praise the Lord.

Although the IMF and IBRD began with intentions different from those of their offspring, they have come to use much the same means for much the same ends: the means are the abolition of restrictions on trade in goods and services and investment; the ends are to enhance the profits and power of the richest countries and their largest companies. All this is supported, natcherly, by a rhetoric promising benefits for all, everywhere through universal economic growth and development, portrayed as a "rising tide that lifts all boats." **Spin** at work.

The Fund and the World Bank were importantly different in their initial intent and functioning for perhaps two decades after World War II; at least in some degree. The original intentions and their subsequent transformation have to do with when and why they came into existence and the ways in which the world has changed: The Fund and the World Bank were created by the USA and Britain in the midst of World War II, where Keynes proposed several admirable policies which, ultimately, were given short shrift.

The starting-point for the war-born organizations was 1) the long-standing global economic chaos and depression preceding World War II and 2) the prospect that left to itself the postwar world economy would verge toward considerably deeper disaster because of the extraordinary destructiveness of the war.

GATT was created in 1947 by the USA as the **Cold War** was making its first public statements; it gave the first hint of what is now the established behavior of all these institutions. Just as the Marshall Plan facilitated **NATO**—to be a member of the former required being a member of the latter—the Cold War served to assist the purpose of GATT; namely, to "institutionalize" and "lubricate" U.S. dominance over the world economy within the framework of presumed "**free trade**." It was thus a major step of the several designed to carry the USA to the position occupied by the British in the 19th century—and then some.

The global political atmosphere in 1944 and still in 1947 was sharply different from that which began to emerge in the 1970s —to say nothing of the 80s and 90s: <u>Economically</u>, by the 70s the major nations were more than "reconstructed"; they (especially Germany and Japan) had become potent competitors of the USA; <u>politically</u>, both within the major nations and the USA itself, dissent from left of center was diminishing toward what by the late 1980s would become a mere whimper—consequent upon a combination of rising real income for majorities and, especially in the USA, upon an effective weakening of the power of unions and the stifling of serious political argument; <u>socially</u>, the populations of all the major and an increasing number of smaller countries had become addicts of **consumerism**, their attention diverted from social to individual concerns, learning "to want what they don't need and not to want what they do." (BARAN/1969/)

Accompanying and facilitating those changes was an accelerating shift toward an always-increasing concentration of socioeconomic **power** in the hands of the few. In addition to what is discussed under that heading, here a few generalizations.

As might be expected in a capitalist society, the accretion of power was mostly by **big business**. It had gained from war-achieved and always new technologies and their interaction with the rapidly growing <u>postwar</u> **military-industrial complex**; through their **lobbyists** they in turn were able to delegate the "paper work" of power to a coterie of legislators on all levels, increasing long-standing **corruption**.

The late sociologist C. Wright MILLS saw the materialization of a triangular pattern early on in his <u>The Power Elite</u> (1951), a book still worth reading for its prescience. The monster Mills was able to perceive was disturbing, but a fledgling compared to the colossus of power today: As commented upon in **big business**, the ability and will to decide the direction and quality of the main elements of social existence today is in the hands of not more than 10-2000 people—or, probably, many fewer. (see CYPHER, 1/2 and 7/8, 2002)

The core source of that power is the domination over production, markets and, thus, profits by only several <u>hundred</u> giant firms—the <u>Fortune</u> "Global 500"—which in turn effectively control their national economies and the global economy—and take in about two-thirds of all non-financial corporations' profits.

Their power is in turn enhanced by and utilizes the power granted to our alphabetic friends IMF, IBRD, NAFTA, and WTO, themselves controlled indirectly by the same companies through their uncontested power in making their appointments and their decisions—with the USA the "first among equals."

To the mainstream economists, as to most of the **media** and politicians, the position I have taken above would be seen as stuff and nonsense. Until recently, spurred on by the anti-**globalization** movement, there had been virtually no significant criticism of the functioning of the institutions discussed here nor on globalization as such. Now there is much, and much more is needed.

IMF et al.: Benefactors or Malefactors?

When the resistance began and could no longer be ignored, the critics of globalization and the IMF (et al.) were portrayed as ignorant fools, even as dangerous; as the ugly realities pile up the tables are turning, helped along by the literature and demonstrations of an always growing and spreading "No-Global" movement.

Thus it is that in addition to the critiques of left of center critics, the attentive citizen now may find confirming information from, as the saying goes, "the horse's mouth." There is more than one such "horse"—e.g., Herman DALY, often noted in this book—was with the World Bank for many years, but is now a penetrating critic; Stiglitz, the economist now to be quoted, worked on the very highest level, and received a Nobel prize along the way.

Joseph E. STIGLITZ was head of the Council of Economic Advisers under Clinton and Chief Economist and Senior Vice President of the World Bank from 1997 until 2000 when he "left" the Bank; one of those polite resignations masking the simultaneous strong intent of the boss to fire and of the firee to leave before the stink became unbearable.

Stiglitz therefore knows very well whereof he speaks and is one of those rarities whose function as a leading economist has not robbed him of his decency; still, welcome though his critique is, it needs adding that as someone who was invited to and willingly agreed to participate on those high levels <u>when</u> he did (that is, in the 1990s, when the damage had been underway for decades), he makes one wonder why it took so long for him to get the point. What point?

It is that **free markets** can be trusted to do no harm, let alone do some good, <u>only</u> when its business participants are small and economically powerless and, politically, no more powerful than any other citizen. Even more, as non-mainstream economist Samuel BOWLES has pointed out,

> Markets not only allocate resources and distribute income, they also shape our culture, foster or thwart desirable forms of human development and support a well-defined structure of power. Markets are as much political and cultural institutions as they are economic.

Adam SMITH, the icon of "free markets," knew that and expressed it: the free market can be free only when no firm is big enough to control a market (or anything else) but is, instead controlled by it. Tell that to the leading companies producing **cars, pharmaceuticals,** chemicals, **oil, tobacco,** or, among almost all others, the leading **media** companies.

By the 1960s we had already arrived in the era of "the multinational corporation" (**MNCs**), now called "transnational companies" (**TNCs**). In **big business** the market power of fewer than 500 companies in the USA (and, as noted above, in the world economy) is virtually total; and that power infiltrates deeply into all realms of our existence.

Stiglitz knows those facts as least well as I do; but he sees what has "gone wrong" as problems of "mismanagement" (as he puts it)—something like believing that with a little therapy Jack the Ripper could be trusted to take your daughter to the dance.

Be that as it may, Stiglitz has much that is important to say and he says it well. Here are some selections from the introduction of his deservedly popular Globalization and its Discontents; there he shows what the IMF and the IBRD were meant to do and, as well, the ways in which they have strayed from or acted against their original intent:

> Over the years since its inception, the IMF has changed markedly. Founded on the belief that markets often worked badly, it now champions market supremacy with ideological fervor. Founded on the belief that there is need for international pressure on countries to have more expansionary economic policies—such as increasing expenditures, reducing taxes, or lower interest rates to simulate the economy—today /it/ typically provides funds only if countries engage in poli-

cies like cutting deficits, raising taxes, or raising rates that lead to a contraction of the economy.

/In/ the era when Ronald Reagan and Margaret Thatcher preached free market ideology in the United States and the United Kingdom, the IMF and the World Bank became the new missionary institutions through which these ideas were pushed on the reluctant poor countries that badly needed their loans and grants. In the early 1980s, a purge occurred inside the World Bank. /Whereas/ before...the Bank had focused on how markets failed in developing countries and what governments could do to improve markets and reduce poverty, /the new team/ saw government as the problem...; free markets the solution.... It was at this time that activities of the IMF and IBRD became intertwined /instead of, as before/, distinct... But the IMF took a rather imperialistic view of the matter...; it viewed almost everything within its domain /of a strict monetary policy/.

A half-century after its founding, it is clear that the IMF has failed in its mission. It has not done what it was supposed to do—provide funds for countries facing an economic downturn, to enable the country to restore itself to close to full employment.... Many of /its/ policies, in particular, premature capital market liberalization, have contributed to global instability. And once a country was in crisis, IMF funds and programs not only failed to stabilize the situation but in many cases actually made matters worse, especially for the poor.

Stiglitz then moves toward description and explanation of the mini- and major disasters of the USA and world economies in recent decades. His analysis of the East Asian crisis of the late 90s is painful to read, even in retrospect; and his characterization of it is apt: "How IMF policies brought the world to the verge of a global meltdown."

East Asia may have been able to find its way back in important degree, despite the IMF; the same cannot be said for Russia. In the West, and for some in the ex-Soviet Union, there were high hopes that the end of Stalinism might well mean the beginning of a better life for the people. It has not; indeed, Russia may be seen as a malign caricature of capitalism: It is often and accurately dubbed "mafia capitalism."

The blame for all this may be apportioned to structures and

habits of mind left over from the Soviet decades; but the injection of unbending free market policies—facilitated by the usual IMF carrots and sticks—transformed difficulty into impossibility and opened wide the gates for gangsterism: For the Russian people as a whole, "incomes are markedly lower than they were a decade ago, and poverty is much higher." (ibid.)

Meanwhile, the top ten percent have money to burn, spent on furs, limousines, diamonds, and villas, as the average person, once provided with free health care cannot now afford any health care; housing is a disaster except for rich and the lucky. The rich in Russia make the corporate crooks of the USA who were recently (and are still being) caught with their hands in the till look like crooked Boy Scouts.

Topping it off (unmentioned by Stiglitz) is that if one ominous consequence of the IMF's idiot policies has been to cripple the possibilities of a decent economy for Russia, another and connected consequence has been to create political anger and desperation: The most potent and growingly popular political movements in Russia are those that 1) seek to bring back Communism or 2) to move toward fascism. With its unemployment at levels much like those of Germany in 1930 and its income and social inequalities always widening, Russia seems ripe for a very large disaster indeed. (see BARBER)

Before turning to the consequences of the IMF, et al., a closing word on the fairly common tendency of those we may call "liberal" mainstream economists—where "liberal" in the USA refers to what may be seen as a modernized New Deal position. (In Europe it means "free marketeer.")

They see that something is terribly wrong, whether within a narrowly economic and/or in a social, political, even military focus. But they see this as something that has gone wrong; not as systemic but something like an infection, curable by—what? Thus, and only as one important example with two sides, Stiglitz makes it crystal clear 1) that IMF policies are made in terms set by the most powerful companies in the financial community, and 2) that the USA has an effective veto over all IMF policies. He may know, but he does not state that the USA itself is also dominated by those same powerful companies. (**financialization, globalization. big business**).

His closing chapter, "The Way Ahead," is chock full of reforms, ranging from improved governance to more safety nets, more bank regulation; and so on. Just how such reforms are to get on the floor, let alone be passed by, a bought and paid for Congress (with counterparts on the local and state levels) and a judiciary tilting always more away from its normal conservatism and toward the right is not mentioned.

All this in a society where elections are bought and sold, and **lobbyists** not only fill the halls of legislatures, but often sit in the offices writing the proposed laws, while the legislators are out raising money for the next election.

The concluding note of his book is almost heart-wrenching; it is a call for more multilateralism on the part of the USA and its kept IMF, IBRD, WTO, and NAFTA institutions. Asking and perhaps expecting that in this day and age is akin to asking Godzilla to pause to brush his teeth before plunging ahead. Now some details.

NAFTA The complexities of the global economy are numberless, and the functions of the IMF, et al., equally so. A useful shortcut through the maze is to examine the origins, nature, and consequences of just one of the gang; namely, NAFTA.

It was designed by and for the USA and "sold" with the usual promised carrots and sticks to Mexico (first) and then Canada. It has functioned as its U.S. corporate proponents desired. Its functioning for well over a decade now allows us to draw some conclusions.

Although the NAFTA legislation was not formally signed and sealed until 1993, many of its provisions had begun to function while negotiations were ongoing. Thus, by 2001 James CYPHER's study of its accumulated experience was able to show to whose benefit and to whose harm it worked; in doing so, he also illuminated the meaning of the larger GATT/WTO agreements. What follows depends upon Cypher's work, whether or not directly quoted. As with the IMF and World Bank, NAFTA paved its road to hell with good intentions:

> The momentum to pass NAFTA was propelled by four primary myths. Beginning as a bilateral trade agreement between the USA and Mexico, 1) it would be a trade agreement, not a project to shift production to Mexico; 2) it was a binational search for efficiency, not a government/corporate-led strategy to regain the steady loss of U.S. economic dominance from the 1980 on; 3) it would reduce consumer prices in the USA; 4) it would quickly create 170-200,000 jobs in the USA, as a result of balanced trade. (CYPHER, 2001)

As regards (1), Mexico's trade tariffs had never been a major concern of U.S. capital, but its restrictive <u>investment</u> laws were. In the negotiations that began in 1986 and were concluded in 1990, the key problem was to free up Mexico for U.S. capital. In 1987, **Reagan** signed the "Bilateral Framework Agreement on Trade and Investment"; a bit more than a year later, Mexico provided a foreign investment law to U.S. liking; in 1990, Mexico's President Salinas provided his support for a "Free Trade Agreement"—which, although not mentioning "investment" in its title, was in fact all about investment: It eliminated <u>all</u> "barriers" to the movement of U.S. capital into and out of Mexico; which, as Cypher points out, "is at the core of NAFTA."

It is pertinent to add at least this: The "eliminated barriers" had to do with wages and working conditions and/or environmental protection. In all the "free trade" bargaining between nations in recent years, however intense they have been over subsidies, tariffs, and the like, they have been most intensive of all as regards installation of U.S. productive facilities in countries of very cheap labor and environmental "freedom."

The only major defeat the U.S. has suffered is revealing: that of the Multilateral Agreement on Investment (MAI). When its provisions became known to local populations, the resistance was such that it had to be indefinitely set aside. In Italy, the point was made not only with a great effort by the unions, but also with a nice touch: In protestors' marches, they carried placards and banners saying: MAI? Mai!! (<u>Mai</u> in Italian means "never.")

2) "In the late 1980s and early 1990s /before the agreement was signed/, the U.S. auto parts industry proceeded to make heavy investment commitments in Mexico, confidently premised on passage of NAFTA... The impact on Mexico of the NAFTA project was overwhelmingly large years before final passage /or tariff changes/."

3) As for the promised reduction of consumer prices in the USA, "roughly 85 percent of all imports from Mexico are manufactured goods and roughly 25 percent of these goods are auto-related products. **GM** became a main element in that: In 1994 it moved 50 percent of its "Suburban" production to Mexico, "cutting wages from $19 an hour to $1.54." By 1996, with Mexico generating one-half the output, their average price had <u>risen</u> by 20 percent—while the general auto price index for all vehicles sold in the USA rose by

only 5.4 percent.

4) So what happened with **jobs**? "The employment effects on the USA have been consistently negative, with NAFTA's structure responsible for employment losses of approximately 316,000 jobs in 1999, due to both trade effects and investment shift effects."

In that realm, moreover, something of a "Ricardian effect" was promised: because of increased efficiency in both countries, real wages would rise for both also. However: "Far from producing a mutual wage increase, Mexican wages have stagnated throughout the industrial structure. Current wages are approximately 25-30 percent below manufacturing wages realized in the early 1980s..., with also lowered wages for U.S. production workers."

"Finally, NAFTA has deepened the maquiladorization effect whereby Mexico, far from developing its industrial base, has become an assembly site for (primarily) U.S. corporations, which thrive on a workforce whose worklife averages ten years. (emphasis added) NAFTA has created roughly 753,000 new maquila jobs from 1993-2000, at an average wage-per-hour level of roughly $1." (See the article for details.)

Postscript: Since the CYPHER essay, the continuing devastation of agriculture that has provided the foreign-owned factories with cheap labor has in turn been followed by the "outsourcing" from maquiladoras to the even cheaper labor of China. (D. BACON, "Maquiladora Bosses Play the China Card," D&S, 9-10/2003)

All those processes under the name of **globalization**, have been swelling since the end of World War II, spreading and deepening over the earth at an always accelerating rate. As they have done so, although there has often (but not always) been what is called prosperity for a significant portion of those in the rich industrialized countries, in the rest of the world there has been increasing poverty, hundreds of millions dying prematurely from malnutrition (including 12-15 million children dead from malnutrition every year), their lives dominated and ruined by that "rising tide that raises all boats." Sure, if you've got a good boat; but most in the world have never had a boat at all, or, when they have, have seen them washed away by a tidal wave.

Despite all, the econ profession has served as cheerleaders all along the way—just as it did in the 19th century. Ricardo (see **eco-**

nomics) put forth the shaping "theory" for today's free traders/IMF-ers way back in 1817; it was <u>after</u> that, when the industrial revolution took hold, that the disasters accruing to ordinary people in the <u>preceding</u> century began to deepen and spread, producing what the poet Blake called "dark satanic mills" in the early 19th century, and much worse than that as it moved toward its end.

Well, there are many <u>hundreds of millions</u> more living desperately, with "nasty, brutish and shortened lives." As discussed elsewhere in these pages, their earlier lives, whatever their great shortcomings as regards education, health, and housing, were demonstrably better than today—with a future threatening worse to come. (see MANDER /1991/; WRIGHT/; BARBER)

The IMF and its university cohorts cannot be blamed for all of that history; for the decades of the past half century, however, they <u>can</u> be blamed for greasing the skids that have sped up "the race to the bottom" for most of the world's people. Shame on them.

imperialism

Much that is relevant and important concerning this vital matter has been said in the preceding discussion and, as well, because it has infiltrated so much of the social process, in several others, including **anti-colonial imperialism, capitalism, globalization, Cold War,** and many of the entries within the regional discussions—**Africa,** et al.).

Here the analysis will take place on the "generic" analytical level. Imperialism will be seen for what it has been and remains, "organically" intrinsic to capitalism, very much as are private ownership of the means of production, the national state, expansion, exploitation, and oligarchic rule—"organic" in much the same sense that the relationships between the heart, the lungs, and bloodstream function organically, interdependently, for all mammals.

There were empires before there was capitalism as there was also, of course, exploitation. But there has been and can be no capitalism <u>without</u> imperialism and exploitation. Thus both capitalism and imperialism came into existence when and where they did as they fed and were fed by the coming into being of the other elements: <u>in</u>dependently and <u>inter</u>-dependently.

All these critical elements grew out of complex sets of relationships dependent upon their particular histories. Thus, British capitalism and German capitalist history differ greatly from that of the USA, from their birthing processes on; and all have had very different (as well as similar) consequences.

Along with its functional relationship with capitalism, imperialism also had a functional/historical relationship with colonialism. It is useful initially to remember that the two countries giving birth to modern colonialism were Portugal and Spain—neither of which became meaningfully capitalist societies until two to three centuries later, when, so to speak, it was thrust upon them as they became economic colonies of Great Britain. (PARRY)

Colonialism, that is, was one of several pre-conditions for the emergence of capitalism; whatever the colonizers' intentions—spreading Christianity, the search for gold or, with the Portuguese, for the mythical Prester John. After colonialism took hold through the Portuguese and Spanish, it spread at the hands of the Dutch, the French, and the British; over time, colonialism itself became transformed as it in turn transformed the colonizers and the colonized societies. Colonialism's main effect (for present purposes) was to provide the two most modern countries of the 17th-18th centuries, the Dutch and the British, with a source of capital. (BOXER) That capital's basis was not production but colonial trade, a euphemism for large-scale thievery. Marx called it "primitive accumulation." The quote to follow appears elsewhere in the book; it is useful to repeat it here:

> The discovery of gold and silver in America, the extirpation, enslavement and entombment in mines of the aboriginal population, the beginnings of the conquest and looting of the East Indies, the turning of Africa into a warren for the hunting of black-skins, signalized the rosy dawn of the era of capitalist production. These idyllic proceedings are the chief momenta of primitive accumulation. (MARX, 1867-1967)

The "loot" thus obtained by what were becoming, and by the 18th century had become, the most powerful nations in the world, constituted an "economic surplus." Whatever else that would come to mean, it was then a means for transforming and strengthening an economy through industrialization. Such a surplus, up through and beyond the 18th century, could be and was used by "non-modern" societies like the Spanish and Portuguese and French to feed the pleasures of their Courts and their sycophants; not so, or, more accurately, less so, for the Dutch and the British.

The Dutch used the surplus to produce a larger surplus over time, by developing the first modern shipbuilding industry in the world and using it to dominate trade utterly in the 17th century—thus increasing the surplus. Their tiny population and lack of land resources kept them from advancing further toward industrialization; so they used it for finance.

In the 18th century, the Dutch surplus was being borrowed by, among others and mostly, the British. Even more crucial for the British by mid-18th century was their ability—deliberately or not—to create a propertyless, powerless working class. This was accomplished through the "enclosure movement." (see **capitalism**)

Legally and illegally, those hundreds of thousands of families who had been the "proud yeomanry" of England were pushed or sucked off the land; by mid-19th century that land was owned by fewer than 3,000 families; those who had once farmed the lands became destitute, unable to survive except on the terms of the new capitalists—although "survive" is a euphemism: As discussed further under **capitalism**, the life-span of the average worker fell by 20 percent, 1821-1851. (HOBSBAWM, 1968)

Nowhere else were the conditions so ripe for capitalism as in Britain—except that the USA would be close behind, once it gained its independence, using a slave-based agriculture as the initial basis for its early capital accumulation. (see **slavery**)

With the gains from its always-spreading colonies, and with an easily exploitable working force, Britain was poised both to create and thrive from the first steps toward an industrial society. They were the first to put together the newly-emerging technological changes, critically the steam engine, both for factories and for rail and sea transportation (it had been used in coal mines for pumping out water much earlier (SWEEZY, 1938).

Britain became the first genuinely capitalist and imperialist and industrial nation; thus equipped, it set out to preach Ricardo's "free trade" for the rest of the world, to lend to them out of its enormous riches; and to get very much richer—for a while. (HOBSON)

"For a while," because in both prodding and unwittingly assisting other nations to go and do likewise, Britain was also making it possible for those others, especially the USA and Germany, not only to industrialize but ultimately to become stronger than Britain itself. VEBLEN (1915) ironized the process as "the penalty of taking the lead and the advantages of borrowing." Now our **globalization** is doing that with China.

Britain's great lead over all others in terms both of industrialization and empire placed enormous pressure on those nation-states to catch up, to speed industrialization and, at same time, to chase frantically to meet their own resource and strategic needs elsewhere in what after World War II came to be called "the third world" (now called "the South").

That calamitous effort came to be symbolized as the "scramble for Africa" by the Dutch, British, French, Germans and Italians of the 19th and early 20th centuries. (ASHWORTH; BOWDEN, et al.) Taken together, or even separately, the consequences for the imperialized societies were quite simply horrendous.

The "scramble" was not confined to Africa, nor were its horrors begun in the 19th century. Africa's ancient slave trade was targeted in the 16th century; so was Asia, when the Spanish took the Philippines; then in the 17th, the Dutch took over "the Dutch East Indies" and managed to be the only nation to gain entrance to Japan. (until the USA in the 1850s) Japan itself joined the race as the 19th century ended, by taking over what was called Formosa (Taiwan) and Korea. (ALLEN, G.)

Similarly for Latin America and the Caribbean: The earlier colonial conquests of Spain and Portugal, spreading from Mexico to South America's southern tip, were altered formally or informally by the British, Dutch, French, and the USA, through treaties or wars.

The USA, in an early version of its contemporary **arrogance**, provided itself with the Monroe Doctrine (1823). It claimed an inherent territorial right over the entire Western Hemisphere. Thus did we open the door for ourselves, a right whose full expression in practice began with the 1898 war in **Cuba**. (see **Latin America....**)

Nor did the **Middle East** escape imperialism. The struggle for control over that region by Europeans of course dates back at least to the Crusades. Its modern conflicts—before the age of **oil**—were provoked by its location, a means of circumventing the need to go around southern Africa to get to Asia. Britain quite naturally triumphed in that struggle in the 19th century, culminating in its construction and control over the Suez Canal and Egypt.

The conflicts among and between the Europeans, especially over Africa and the Middle East and adjacent lands (such as "Yugoslavia")—and there are always "adjacent lands"—became increasingly heated. A war among and between the major and minor European powers became inexorable; it was triggered by a young man's assassination of a comic opera archduke at Sarajevo.

The ten million + who died in that war were merely the opening act of the scenario created by what, up to about 1910, had been called "the century of peace"—where what was called peace by the major powers was their euphemism for exploitative wars against weaker societies. (VEBLEN /1917/)

And the USA? Although it is seldom recognized—especially by ourselves—already before the 19th century ended the USA had become the most successful of <u>all</u> imperial powers. Then, as since, we sought to dignify our imperializing efforts with precocious spins, such as "westward expansion"; or, after having invaded and defeated Mexico in the 1840s, with "We take nothing by conquest... Thank God." (ZINN /2000/

Later, when we conquered the **Philippines** at the turn of the century, President McKinley went that one better; as we slaughtered hundreds of thousands of Filipinos who thought they had been freed from the Spanish, McKinley proclaimed that we were doing for the Filipinos what they could not do for themselves. From there to our "liberation and democratization" of **Iraq** is not too much of a leap.

It is important to note that the main element of the U.S. empire until the 20th century was not overseas, but the lands between the Atlantic and Pacific Oceans and between Mexico and what became Canada. Our non-empire encompassed more and richer agricultural and mineral and water resources than all of Europe's put together; they became "ours" almost, but not quite, effortlessly. (WILLIAMS, W.A. /1980/)

In order for us to press ever "westward the course of empire" the USA took it as essential to repress and destroy the peoples who had inhabited those vast spaces for millennia. The latter called their quite diverse societies Cherokee, and Seneca, and Mohawk, and Seminole, and Paiute, and Choctaw, and Creek, and....; we lumped them together in one cruelly stupid name: **"Indians"**—cruel, because while stealing their names we also stole their identity and their culture, their livelihood, and countless lives; stupid (or at least ignorant), because Columbus (among other early conquerors) was seeking a passage to India, and thought he had found it. (WRIGHT; MANDER /1992/)

Not content to control the world's greatest natural resources within our achieved boundaries, as the 19th century ended we too jumped into the "scramble": We took over **Cuba** and **Puerto Rico** in the Caribbean, then Hawaii, Wake Island, Guam and the **Philippines** in the Pacific; thence to our forceful creation of **Panama** (sliced out of Colombia) and the beginnings of our move upwards into Central America: **Nicaragua** and then **Guatemala**, for starters. (MAGDOFF /1968/; WILLIAMS, W.A. /1969/; ZINN /2000/)

As the 20th century opened, the USA was already close to being one of the three or four strongest economies in the world; it had ceased to be just an entrancing new nation. That was slow to be acknowledged in Europe; indeed, as late as 1926, a leading British economic history text characterized the USA an "agricultural society", although by then the USA was already the world's strongest industrial economy.

The leading slogan for Woodrow Wilson's re-election campaign of 1916 was "He Kept Us Out of War"; in that same year, the emerging PR champ Edward L. Bernays was hired by Wilson to work up popular agitation for us to <u>enter</u> the war—to protect Belgian nurses or French children or...something, anything. (TYE) **Spin** had been born; Edith Wharton's "age of innocence" was over, even as an irony.

War was not the only appalling outcome of capitalism <u>cum</u> imperialism; already by the time the "guns of August" were being fired in Europe the lands and cultures, economies and politics of most of the imperialized societies had long been trapped in a process of being stolen from and destroyed, processes from which they are still desperately seeking to recover while, at the same time, they are again intensified by **globalization**.

In brutalizing, however and as always, the conquering peoples have also had their own lives and societies brutalized and distorted, much as **racism** and gender oppression damage the perpetrators and their own societies as well as they do their victims—if also in ways less bitter and usually less destructive.

The consequences of that first world war were many: a further devastation of most economies, already themselves distorted for decades by the combined effects of capitalism/imperialism/nationalism/militarism; and the war's aftermath took the world toward and into the even more destructive second world war. (BOWDEN, et al.; LEWIS, W.A.)

World War II could have and should have brought the world to its senses; it did not. More accurately, it was not allowed to do so. (see **Cold War**) From the vantage point of the half century or more following World War II, it may be said that the peoples of all the participant nations except the USA had finally discovered the need to do everything possible to avoid war. In losing more than 60 million people 1939-1945, and with at least that many having been seriously damaged, plus personal and/or family harm and losses, the Europeans had learned to hate war; and the Japanese are not likely ever to forget **Hiroshima/Nagasaki** or fire-bombed Tokyo.

Unlike the peoples of all other major powers, however, the people of the USA have not learned to hate war enough. Indeed, through the economic "benefits" of the Cold War all too many of us—unconsciously, for most—found the militarization of our economy and resulting domination of the world to be a positive development: It was and is effectively portrayed as having created jobs, as having saved the world from a totalitarian takeover, as a triumph of "America!"

And even though the war in **Vietnam** brought many of us to an awakening, that it killed "only" about 60 thousand GIs (with little interest in the millions of Indochinese killed and badly-damaged), even that had faded into memory by the time that **preemptive** war became an accepted policy for the USA.

Imperialism as such faded or was shoved away after World War II; over 150 countries have become politically independent since the 1940s—but by no means independent economically. But without even the semblance of economic independence almost all of their "political independence" is terminological rather than substantial. The processes of taking that subservience into the economic realm were already well advanced by the late 1960s. (See COCKROFT/ FRANK/JOHNSON, Dependence and Underdevelopment); the **globalization** and **financialization** of recent decades have turned "dependency" into a combined economic and political nightmare for dozens of countries; sent into deep crises by the flick of an **IMF** finger. Moreover, all too many small and larger wars have added terrible bloodshed to economic desperation. (BARBER)

The response of the U.S. government and what appears to be a majority of our people combines indifference with a generally uncritical acquiescence in militaristic resolutions. At least part of that must be attributed to our seeing our "star wars" weapons of mass destruction as killing others, with only a handful of casualties for "our boys." Any other nation behaving as we do in these respects would receive—and deserve—our contempt.

As one who has lived and taught in Europe for half of more than 20 years, I feel impelled to add this note. When I first began to teach in Italy, almost 40 years ago, it was very clear to me that the Italians (and Europeans generally) looked upon the USA with admiration and affection; they saw us as being somewhat peculiar, vulgar, and callow, but did so with amiability and admiration.

Not now. U.S. bullying over economic matters—our tariffs are OK, theirs are not; our genetically modified foods must be accepted, etc.—and our disdainful arrogance regarding multilateral treaties such as the Kyoto treaty for protecting the **environment**, or the International Court of Justice, or the **WHO** treaty on **tobacco**, or the UN treaty on land-mines.... have steadily worn away their goodwill.

The proverbial straw that has broken their back was our attempt to shove—and to bribe—the UN toward war. When all that failed, our go-it-alone tactics were too much for the Europeans.

They know that war is hell, and must and can be avoided; they fear that what the USA does cannot help but damage all, themselves more than the USA, and that they are helpless in the face of what they now see: The USA as the "rogue nation." They cannot control us. They are right. The more important question is "can we?" And if not, what then?

income distribution (see inequality)

"Indians"/"Indian removal"

The quotation marks around those words are a way of seeking not to continue one of those matters that have gone wrong with "America!" from the start. In addition to other injustices we have imposed upon various peoples, one has been to take their names away from them.

Ronald WRIGHT is a profound historian of the original peoples of this hemisphere as they were 500 years ago compared with the present. After apologizing for the use of "Native American," "Amerindian," "aboriginal," and "indigenous" he goes on to say,

> These are not the only loaded words. An entire vocabulary is tainted with prejudice and condescension: whites are soldiers, Indians are warriors; whites live in towns, Indians in villages; whites have kings and generals, Indians have chiefs; whites have states, Indians have tribes.... /And he quotes an "Indian" leader as telling the Mayor of Chicago in 1927/: "...School histories are unjust to the life of our people.... They call all white victories, battles, and all Indian victories, massacres.... White men who rose to protect their property are called patriots—Indians who do the same are called murderers."

That usage is so natural to us it may seem sheer nitpicking to make a point of it; it has not seemed so to the many peoples oppressed by **racism** and, along with that, taunted by what they rightly see as insults; very much as women become angry (if, often, silently so) when they are referred to as "girls" by men of the same age (or younger).

In the <u>Foreword</u> I specified the dominating characteristics that have fouled the American dream; racism was of one them. When Wright (as above) notes words as being "loaded," he means they are like bullets: always harmful, sometimes deadly.

Racism contaminates our society like an oil spill; we cannot cleanse ourselves of it unless we <u>at least</u> stop and think before we use insulting words to refer to other human beings; and then stop using them and, one day, stop thinking them. I shall continue to place quotation marks around the words noted above.

Now a word about two very important and insightful books useful for breaking our habituation, from grade school on of feeling and thinking in deeply racist terms, not least as regards "Indians."

First is Wright's book. It is absorbing and gratifying reading for those who would gain understanding of what the Europeans (ourselves included) have done to <u>all</u> the peoples of this hemisphere. His book concerns itself with five societies: the Aztec, the Maya, the Inca and, in North America, the Cherokee and the Iroquois.

The differences Wright found and explored for all are profound and, shockingly, they redound in favor of those living 500 years ago.

Those centuries of "progress" were the opposite for them.

Second is the book by Jerry MANDER, <u>In the Absence of the Sacred</u>. (1991) His focus is both similar and very different, as suggested by his subtitle: "The Failure of Technology & the Survival of the Indian Nations." His geographic scope is limited to the USA; in addition to showing just how murderously we have treated the "Indians" over the centuries and up to today he also demonstrates how badly we have "treated" ourselves—in his caustic appraisal of how we live and what we have lost.

Mander does not idealize the lives of the original peoples but, in bringing their socioeconomy and cultures back to life, he allows us to think more clearly about the insanities and inanities of our contemporary "way of life." Nor does it hurt that Mander writes well. Beginning on the first page his "Indians Shmindians" tells us of the struggle he had with the publisher over the term "Indian." Now to the elements of that history.

<u>Holocaust USA</u>. As discussed under **racism** and **slavery**, when Columbus arrived in 1492,

> there were approximately 100 million Native Americans—a fifth, more or less, of the human race. Within decades... most of those people were dead and their world barbarously sacked by Europeans. The plunderers settled in America, and it was they, not the original people, who became known as Americans.... Unlike Asia and Africa, America never saw its colonizers leave. (WRIGHT)

A century later, their numbers had fallen by 90 percent. What happened? The two most frequent answers given by historians are derogatory as well as stupid:

1) "The native peoples were primitive and weak." That, in spite of the fact that from Alaska to Terra del Fuoco they had survived for millennia; and, as their numbers and locations multiplied, had developed a multitude of diverse cultures. 2) "They died not from being murdered but from disease." Indeed they did die from disease(s)—smallpox, measles, influenza, bubonic plague, yellow fever, cholera and malaria—none of which, however, had existed in the Western Hemisphere before the Europeans arrived. The number who died was staggering:

> The great death raged for more than a century /after 1492/. By 1600, after some twenty waves of pestilence had swept

through the Americas, less than a tenth of the original population remained. Perhaps 90 million died, the equivalent, in today's terms, to the loss of a billion.

Those who survived in **Latin America** remained under the control of Europeans (and, later, the USA) through the ensuing centuries, some gaining independence of a sort in the 18th century, some in the 19th and 20th, some not yet. Because "the colonizers" in the USA never left, the life of the "Indians" in both past and present has combined poverty with degradation, misery, and humiliation; it is a national disgrace.

Only a few of us view it that way; rather, if that tragedy is thought of at all, it is viewed as a burden <u>we</u> carry; even as a triumph of civilization over barbarism: the opposite of the truth. (MANDER)

The components of that created social disaster are many: 1) "Indian removal"; 2) the portrayal of the native peoples as vicious savages and our cowboys and soldiers as heroes in children's and adults' books and in films; 3) the perfidy and violation of treaties which, in any case, were initially unjust; 4) the institutionalized inability of those peoples ever to return to their historic lands; 5) the forced need to remain on "reservations" where their ability to survive hangs by a thread—unless they create gambling casinos (which attract gangsters, their latest exploiters).

All of that cannot be dealt with here; even what will be discussed will be desperately brief. I begin with "Indian removal," for its means and ends foretold the future all too well.

<u>Uncle Sam's Concentration Camps</u>. Such words are very "un-American": How dare I? The better question is how could "America!" sink as low as it did with the "Indians," and then, centuries later, do it again with the Japanese—mostly U.S. citizens—interned during World War II?

The answer is that it came easy; as discussed at some length under **slavery**, our existence as a slave-holding society and as oppressors and killers of "Indians" took hold in tandem: As settlement in New England was increasing and deepening, so was slave-holding; by the 17th century the South had become the productive center of the colonies, with production by African slaves at its core. (NORD-HOLDT)

When U.S. slavery is thought of in critical terms the focus is usually confined to the southern plantation owners. However, their slaves, brought first to the Caribbean and then to New England, were sold to the planters by New England merchants. New England, the first commercial center of the colonies, had its basis in the trading between Africa, the Caribbean, New England, and Britain. In order of importance, the trade was in slaves, sugar, rum, and tobacco: Just what the doctor ordered. As VEBLEN put it (quoted more fully under **slavery**), thus

> were laid the foundations of some very reputable fortunes at that focus of commercial enterprise that presently became the center of American culture, and so gave rise to some of the country's Best People. At least, so they say.

The simultaneity of slavery and the taking over of the lands of "Indians" interacted to make the treatment of both always harsher—and to establish a firm basis for an always-broader **racism**. Until Independence, the colonists, led by the British (and opposed by the French and the "Indians" in what became the war of that name) continually expanded inward from the coasts, as well as north and south.

Even before the successful struggle for independence, colonists had been pushing westward; after the USA was born the push became explosive: the beckoning lands, rich with resources and promise were, of course, occupied; the solution was simple;

> Indian Removal, as it has been politely called, cleared the land for white occupancy between the Appalachians and the Mississippi, cleared it for cotton in the South and grain in the North, for expansion, immigration, canals, railroads, new cities, and the building of a huge continental empire clear across to the Pacific Ocean. The cost in human life cannot be accurately measured, in suffering not even roughly measured. Most of the history books given to children pass quickly over it. (ZINN, 2000)

After all is said and done, after counting the dead and the maimed, the lands lost, the cultures ruined, the demoralization of subsequent generations—after all that and more—if such an accounting were done and its results known, what would be the response of our people?

Sorrow? Shame? Indifference? Satisfaction? What has it been as regards slavery?

We have condemned the invasions of China by the Japanese

from the 1930s on, and those of Hitler over Western and then Eastern Europe, among others. We do not see ourselves historically as a people who <u>invaded</u> this (or any other) hemisphere; we settled it and improved it. It would be pleasant to be wrong about that; if it is, instead, an accurate guess, it points to our frequent recourse to a **double standard** on such matters.

Be that as it may, there is something else fundamental. When the Europeans first arrived and subsequently entered new territories on the continent, they were universally received in a friendly and a cooperative manner—beginning with Columbus. ZINN, in his opening page provides a revealing quote from Columbus himself:

> They brought us parrots and balls of cotton and spears and many other things, which they exchanged for the glass beads and hawks' bells. They willingly traded everything they owned.... They were well-built, with good bodies and handsome features... They do not bear arms, and do not know them, for I showed them a sword, they took it by the edge and cut themselves out of ignorance. They have no iron. Their spears are made of cane... They would make fine servants. With fifty men we could subjugate them all and make them do whatever we want.

The subsequent behavior of Columbus would have him condemned in an international tribunal today; it was common then and subsequently. Most famously and effectively was that so with Andrew Jackson, oft portrayed as a paragon of democracy. Revealingly, when he was portrayed as such in Arthur Schlesinger's <u>Age of Jackson</u>, it won the author the Pulitzer Prize—despite that Jackson was "a land speculator, merchant, slave trader, and the most aggressive enemy of the Indians in early American history." He was Number One among the "removers," both in quantities and maltreatment and killing, from the War of 1812 through his presidency in the 1830s. (ZINN, 2000)

This section's heading notes "concentration camps." The "Native Americans" were not placed in such camps, as the 110,000 Japanese were in the 1940s, but they were forced onto "reservations." Those lands were of course <u>not</u> in or near their historic lands; nor were they the better lands where to which they were "removed." Quite the opposite, and cruelly so.

The lives of virtually all of the tribal societies had a harmony and a wholeness to them that brought together human and natural needs and possibilities—perforce, it might be said; as such, it was an adaptation well-suited to the needs and possibilities of those people then and there. Not only were the "Indians" at home with nature, they viewed it with awe and love. Set against our accelerating destruction of the natural world that created and sustains us, it would seem fair to portray ourselves as savages, them as civilized. (MANDER) The USA has colonized the native peoples as much as the British did the Indians (of India), the Spanish did the Mexicans, the Japanese did the Koreans; and we still do. Those who have visited "Indian reservations," whether on the plains of Montana or the mountains of the Four Corners (Utah, Colorado, New Mexico and Arizona) must have noted the air of demoralization and hopelessness characterizing many of their "villages": women selling trinkets, men sitting nearby (or unseen), an artificial and deadening life for a people whose past was very much the opposite: lively, creative, dignified and, more often than ours, peaceable.

The only means by which any of this can be accepted is by our remaining ignorant of it; we allow ourselves to be so through our **arrogance** and our **dehumanization**.

inequality

Introduction. Before moving into the complex issues of inequality, it is pertinent to discuss what is and is not meant by equality, at least here.

The "equality" held up as a standard here takes as its starting-point that 1) at birth we are essentially equal in terms of needs, 2) in a given society all such needs should be met equally—from "cradle to grave", and 3) all should have equal opportunity to work toward the fulfillment of their possibilities.

The USA prides itself on the principle of one "man" one vote while, at the same time, the structure and functioning of **power** insure that our votes are largely for people selected by those at the top of that same structure. A society dedicated to equality would strive to see that in addition to the vote, each person have the same amount of **power**, necessary if all people's needs and possibilities are to have equal claims on the society's resources.

The reality in all societies, of course, is that inequalities are the rule regarding needs, possibilities, and power; needs and possibilities are met or not met to one degree or another dependent upon where and when we are born, our gender and "color," and the income, wealth and social standing of our parents; the structure of power is always triangular, in varying degrees of steepness, depending upon which society, and when. A probing and readable study of inequality, especially as regards gender and color, is recommended here: ALBELDA, DRAGO, AND SHULMAN, Unlevel Playing Fields.

In the USA, in the past and still today, gender and color and parentage have established the very definition of both our needs and our possibilities, and the associated structure of power determines who makes the definition. In what ways?

Begin with something simple (which does not mean non-controversial). Do black children have the same educational needs as white children? Girls the same as boys? Or, do the children of poor white parents have the same educational needs as those of rich white parents? Girls the same as boys? Such questions, if raised, will be answered in the negative by people accustomed to taking racial and gender oppression for granted, and who have learned to "blame the victim." (RYAN) The result has been and remains a bottomless tragedy. Recall scientist Stephen Jay GOULD's comment under **education** on "Einstein's brain":

> I am less interested in the weight and convolutions of Einstein's brain than I am in the near certainty that people of equal talent have lived and died in cotton fields and sweatshops.

The questions raised about education may be asked about nutrition, health, and shelter—which, along with education and, especially in the poor countries (up to now), water, constitute what STREETEN and SEN have called our "basic needs.

The USA is far from being unique in such matters. As we continue to pride ourselves on being the free and equal people of the world, we remain the world's leader in **racism**. That is so whether as measured by the broad variety of those discriminated against and the length and depths of their mistreatment (to the point of genocide for the **"Indians"**). Also, in comparison with the other rich economies, of which we are the richest, there is our shameful treatment of children, the disabled, the old, and the poor, along with at least the average degree of discrimination against women found in all the "advanced" societies.

The proverbial "man from Mars" (especially if "he" were "non-white" and a woman) would find it difficult to equate our national smugness with our behavior. There have of course been notable changes for the better in the last century or so: women and blacks have gotten the vote; blacks can <u>legally</u> live and eat and relieve themselves where once they could not; a significant percentage has gotten much better jobs and can hold public office; through **affirmative action**," people of color" and women have greater access to equal education in significant numbers. All that and more is true.
However. Keeping in mind the standard of equality and its relationship to the meeting of basic needs and possibilities, it is important to note (as will be pursued further below) that 1) the numbers of those benefiting from the reforms of the early post-World War II decades are now a declining <u>percentage</u> of their groups; although many are now less poor and even well off, there are many <u>more</u> now than ever who are poor (and poorer) than ever: blacks and Hispanics able to enter universities are in decline, poverty is rising, health care and housing are worsening; and, 2) the political processes and legislation enabling those reforms, already weakened since the 80s, now face an even bleaker future.

> <u>Item</u>: "The number of black Americans under 18 years old who live in extreme poverty /i.e., at less than <u>half</u> the official poverty level/ has risen sharply since 2000 and is now at its highest level since 1980 /when the government began to collect such data/.' (<u>NYT</u>, "Report Finds Deep Poverty On the Rise." /4-30-03/)
>
> <u>Item</u>: Also in April, it was reported that the number of black men behind bars rose to 2.3 million, the highest ever (and the highest in the world—except, perhaps, for China, whose population is more than four times ours. (see **crime and punishment**)

The persistence of discrimination and oppression on racial, gender, and income grounds assures that any talk of equality is more rhetoric than reality. (See **racism** and **boys and girls/men and women, jobs**, and **poverty** for a fuller statement on matters pursued here.)

Now we proceed to examine inequality as a condition and consequence of **capitalism** "narrowly-defined"—as principally an <u>economic</u>, rather than as a <u>socio</u>-economic system; that is, the impact of other realms of discrimination and oppression will be taken as given (until later).

Inequality and capitalism. The relationship has many elements to it, but at its center sits what may be seen as a fact: capitalism depends upon inequality; bluntly, no inequality, no capitalism. The reference here is not to the "ideal equality" noted earlier: one person, one unit of power. The inequality of capitalism is structural, is defined in terms of classes, not individuals. Put differently, although it is feasible to imagine some societies in which that "ideal equality" could be seen as a useful goal (as distinct from ongoing reality), that is not so for capitalism: its defining institution is the ownership and control of the means of production by a class, the work done by another class. (see YATES)

In practice, capitalist inequality has varied over time and place, but it has always been decisively present, its different depths a response to culture and history, time and place. We now examine inequality's essentiality to capitalism and some of the history relating to its beneficiaries.

The economic inequality initially referred to here is that regarding two different but closely-related phenomena: the patterns of wealth and income. Economists often portray wealth as being like a lake and income like a stream that flows into and out of that lake; or, "wealth is a stock, income a flow."

That is a suggestive but insufficiently dynamic metaphor; wealth both results from and creates income, and income can both come from and create wealth. Moreover, those from wealthy families, even though they may not inherit their families' wealth, are very likely to have lives providing them with high incomes (via privileged education, good jobs as gifts, contacts, etc.). There are all too many instances of very wealthy and powerful men—even U.S. presidents—who have been mentally weak. Now a closer look.

Wealth. There have many useful studies of wealth and income, some of which have been referred to in other entries, others that will be. The most useful authors to consult for recent and ongoing statistical data are Edward WOLFF for wealth, and MISHEL et al., for income and wealth. Also, the latest most comprehensive and readable historical and analytical study of income and wealth (among other important matters), is that of PHILLIPS (2002), also noted many times in this work.

Phillips pays careful attention to one <u>very</u> important source of wealth: <u>inheritance</u>. His numerous tables and charts from the 18th century up to the present are excellent in showing its importance. Phillips denotes the wealthiest families (and the origins of their wealth: oil, railroads, cars, chemicals, etc.) at seven points: 1901-14, 1928, the 1930s, 1957, 1968, 1982 and 1992. Those are but a few of dozens and dozens of tables and charts concerning income and wealth (among other matters).

"Shirtsleeves to shirtsleeves in three generations"? Nope. The Rockefeller, Du Pont, Ford, Morgan, Hearst (and **Bush**) kids (among dozens of others) didn't have to be, and most were not, smart or hard-working; they just had to show up. Phillips draws the unavoidable conclusion: The USA, never a full-fledged democracy, had a short flirtation with that possibility sometime after the middle of the 19th century; since **big business** came to be the rule, we have become an always tighter "plutocracy."

Given the immense amount of technological and related changes of the past century, it is not surprising that the membership in the "rich man's club" has changed markedly since 1914; impressively, however, it has also retained a hard core of virtually permanent members: "Wealth creates wealth."

For capitalism, the initial wealth, as noted under **colonialism**, derived from trade in slaves, "spices," cloth, etc. It provided the "seed corn" for capitalist development in what became the first handful of industrial nations, via trade with distant societies, and <u>their</u> pre-industrial production.

<u>Given</u> the accumulating gains from centuries of that trade, what enabled young industrial capitalism to function and to expand was the **exploitation** of labor and the farming land **commodified** by the enclosure movement—the original source in Britain of the commodification of human beings.

Swept off the land as though by a hurricane, those who had worked the land were transformed into laborers; those who had worked "for themselves" on their own and nature's terms, then had no alternative but to labor for others—the when, where, how long, how, and why decided by the purposes of those "others."

In our era, we no longer distinguish between "worker" and "laborer"; 'twas not always thus. In the precapitalist world of the ancient Greeks, those who "labored" were slaves; those who "worked" were free; in modern times, workers became "wage slaves." (HAMMONDs)

Ask where the equipment of a textile factory comes from; it must be created, for which "capital" is required. The very first factory was a cotton mill in England 1815. It involved a steam engine, spinning and weaving machines, and a building. They did not fall from the skies; they themselves had to be "produced" and paid for; financed.

Whence that capital? It came from the "economic surplus"— that is, from what the economy had produced but not consumed; economists call that "savings." Savings (or borrowing) thus defined are essential for "real investment" (i.e., additions to productive capacity). (BARAN, 1957)

The "economic surplus" may be seen as the measure of an economy's possibilities for change and growth. How it will be used is decided in a capitalist society by those who possess the capital—ultimately, the means of production. And the means of production are the means of life. (ibid.)

In the days of the incipient industrial revolution, the wealthy were the merchants and financiers of Britain (many of whom became, also, "the landed gentry"). Their wealth had accrued from colonialism abroad and the land at home—the latter, especially, from the profitable agriculture associated with the enclosures of the 18th century.

When the first factory was built in 1815 (and for decades afterward) there were no "corporations" as we mean the term; that is, would-be industrial companies could not sell shares in their projects; their factories had to come out of their (and/or their "partner's") savings and wealth. (The modern corporate form awaited the mid-1850s, simultaneously in the UK and the USA, to meet the needs of mass-production.)

Given that as a beginning, the always more rapidly accumulating wealth of industrial capitalism came from the "unpaid labor" of the working class—the income they had earned but did not receive. Some elaboration is in order.

The production process may be viewed as having two kinds of personnel involved, owners and workers. The owners had the "capital" to "invest" in the engines, etc.; the workers did the work. If the workers did the work, that is, the production, and if they were paid in terms of the value of what they had produced, whence the **profits** and, thus, capital accumulation?

The answer was provided from the beginning, by SMITH and RICARDO, the main theorists (and proponents) of industrial capitalism from 1776 into 1850s. It is found in their variations on the "labor theory of value"—the theory that Marx adopted and adapted, which begins on Page 1 of Marx's <u>Capital</u> (1867), under "Commodities."

All three agreed that the workers did <u>not</u> receive a return equal to their production (their "use value"); rather, they received a money wage equal to their <u>subsistence</u> needs (their "exchange value"); just enough to keep them alive. (But, as pointed out elsewhere, in the decades of early industrialization, 1821-1850, the average worker's life span in fact <u>decreased</u> markedly: i.e., wages were less than subsistence. /HOBSBAWM, 1968)

Marx carried the logic of the labor theory of value to its full meaning. The profits of business were equal to the "surplus value" of workers, the difference between the value of what they produced and what they received. <u>This</u> was the source of capitalist wealth and, more importantly, of the capital for use in further investment: capital accumulation. <u>"Accumulate! Accumulate! That is Moses and the Prophets!</u> said Marx.

> (Here a side comment, but an important one in its bearing upon **economics**: Neither Smith nor Ricardo was stupid; very much the opposite. But they, like all "theorists" (including Marx and other social thinkers), naturally focused upon what concerned them most. (ROGIN) In Smith's case, that meant encouraging industrialization; in Ricardo's encouraging **free trade**; in Marx's, encouraging the overthrow of capitalism. It isn't that Smith didn't know or care about **exploitation** (indeed he <u>hoped</u> it would lessen over time (GINZBERG); nor that Ricardo was indifferent; he believed that everyone—despite all—would be better off this way than any other; lesser of two evils, and all that. And Marx? Marx hated what capitalism did to humanity. (see **dehumanization/ alienation**)

But didn't things change once industrialization deepened and spread, and corporations were born, and democracy, and…, so on? Things did indeed change, for better <u>and</u> for worse; what also changed was what we have learned to <u>mean</u> by "better" and by "worse"—and who and what belongs in which category.

After this long discourse, in whose midst we still are, it is useful to remind the reader that the subject here is **inequality**. Let's look at "the better" first.

Certainly, studying only the past century (and what it inherited), the societies that are now industrial and capitalist have been able to provide much to many of their citizens that was available to very few (or nobody) in earlier periods, as regards health care, housing, education, and diets, not least—and political democracy, with all its seeming possibilities. And there has been what may be called "democratized culture," bringing the reality and possibility of intellectual and aesthetic pleasures to great numbers of people previously excluded from or unaware of such possibilities. I could go on.

But two large points: 1. It needs reminding that access to all of the above has been highly unequal, both within and, even more, outside the rich nations—and that the riches of rich people and rich nations <u>depend</u> in important part on just that. As Paul BARAN put it in his <u>Political Economy of Growth</u>, "It is precisely the relationships between the poor and the rich peoples of the world that keeps both the poor <u>and</u> the rich that way." (1957)

That was said in the 1950s; Baran had in mind the horrific history of what capitalism <u>had done</u> to the peoples both of their own and other nations and what it was on its way to <u>doing</u> as the postwar era unfolded. Baran expected all hell to break loose but, if anything, he underestimated what subsequent decades would bring—both at home and abroad. Which takes us to a closer look at "the better," beginning with the USA.

Whatever is meant by "better" within the USA, access to it has of course been highly lopsided, no matter what its definition. For a moment, however, assume equal access to whatever "better" means. What <u>does</u> it mean, and to what does it apply? To be brief, we refer to a higher level of material wellbeing, its "basket of goods" including food, clothing, shelter, consumer durables, health care, transportation, shorter working day, vacations, pensions..., and there is more.

Food? Of course people today are generally able to eat more and better than ever before in history; we do eat more, on average, but do we eat better in our "fast food nation"? Not if we take into account that over half the U.S. population is considered to be overweight and more than a fifth obese. (see **health care, hunger**)

Shelter? There are more families seeking and unable to find

affordable or any housing (**homeless/ housing**) now than ever before (including the 1930s)—many of them (stereotypes notwithstanding) with full-time jobs, many mentally-ill—not least from service in Vietnam—many more unemployed.

Consumer durables? We are afloat in them, dominated by them, indebted to—and for—them: kitchen things (stoves, dishwashers, microwaves, fridges, toasters,), **TV**s, DVDs, VCRs, computers, radios, washers/dryers, furniture, and not least, most of all, **cars** and houses. Who could get along without all that? But do we really "get along" <u>with</u> it?

Some reading this had become more or less adult by, let's say, the 1950s. Life was different in those earlier years, to be sure. Was it better or worse? More or less tense? More or less demanding? More or less banal? Easier or harder to get around? Better or worse for kids? Was there more or less <u>pleasure</u>? (SCITOVSKY)

The younger one is, the greater the "more" answers; the older, the more the "less." Part of the reason for that is, surely, that if one has no contrasting experience, what is "now" is of course "natural" and what is "natural" is... well, normal or OK, or something.

Maybe so. Except when it comes to objective measures, like what is happening to traffic, to the air, to your indebtedness, to children and teens, to your health care bills, to your <u>own</u> weight and girth. Etc. (see **health care, cars, environment, consumerism**)

And then we drop the assumption of equality for this "basket of goods and services" and paid vacations and pensions and just about everything else. A good half of our people are partially or wholly fenced out from all that bounty; 60 percent of us work full-time for <u>less</u> than a "living wage." (**jobs**)

Although this consumeristic life may be tinged with negativity, it <u>is</u> the way one is s'posed to live in this promised land; it may drive you crazy, but you're crazy if you don't go for it. For those who work very hard for very low wages—especially if they have kids—it is surely very hard to be fenced out, especially in the **TV** era of continuous display.

A final word on the <u>distribution</u> of wealth, which will help to explain the distribution of income: If wealth were equally distributed, each one percent of us would have one percent of the nation's wealth. Instead, the Top One Percent in 2000 owned more than 40 percent of <u>all</u> assets (including homes and financial investments).

The most unequal distribution of wealth since—guess when?—the 1920s. (PHILLIPS) And there's more:

The bottom 80 percent hold only 17 percent of national wealth. The ownership of stocks, much touted these days as being "democratic," is quite the opposite: The Top One Percent of stock owners hold almost half (47.7 percent) of all stocks, while the bottom 80 percent own just 4.1 percent of all stock holdings. (MISHEL)

Since "them what has, gits," that takes us into the other half of the economics of capitalist inequality.

Income. The distribution of income is not just a table or a chart; it is best seen as answering a long list of different and overlapping questions concerning different groups, time periods, and processes, all of them important in their way. What follows will refer principally to matters of inequality as revealed by the levels and movement of family incomes, wages, and jobs. (Much that is relevant in these and related matters is also treated under **jobs, poverty,** and **racism.**) Unless otherwise indicated, all data are from MISHEL /2003/).

Census data show that since the mid-1980s the share of the national income going to the top 20 percent of families has risen; however,

> it's not simply that the top 20 percent of families had bigger percentage gains than families near the middle; the top 5 percent have done better than the next 15, the top 1 percent better than the next 4, and so on up to Bill Gates. In turn, 60 percent of the gains of that top 1 percent went to 0.1 (its top ten) percent, those with incomes of more than $790,000 /in 1998/. And almost half of those gains went to a mere 13,000 taxpayers, the top 0.01 percent, who had an income of at least $3.6 million and an average income of $17 million. (KRUGMAN)

And, as will be seen under **taxes,** as **Bush II** has his way the top 0.1 to 0.01 percent can sit back and watch their after-tax incomes balloon even more. **Greed** is king; or, rather, is President, 'cuz he's in the top 1 percent.

OK, already, it might be said; even if the other 80 percent aren't getting as big a slice of the pie as the those in the catbird seat, still, the 90s gave them more jobs, higher wages, and a higher income than ever, no? Yes and no. Yes for a while, but now the absolute and relative amounts (for the fully-employed) are shrinking—a return to the trend that began about 30 years ago. The late 1990s were not a reversal of that trend, but a hiccough:

> Between 1947 and 1973 real median family income grew 2.8 percent annually, then dropped to 0.4 percent from 1973 to 1995. In the boom of late 1990s, it sped up again to 2.2 percent annually. But when recession took hold in 2001, the median family income decreased at an annual rate of 1.4 percent (equal to $741 in 2001 dollars)—and it has been falling more rapidly since then, as recession has continued and unemployment has risen. (MISHEL)

Two further comments: Among the bottom 80 percent, those who gained most relatively were the normal objects of discrimination: blacks and Hispanics and women. The boom meant a sharp drop in unemployment, and business bidding for workers. What was good for that bottom percent was good for the other 60 percent as well, for the key to workers' incomes is the level of unemployment.

But there was another element, not entirely positive: The 90s also saw a step-up in the employment not just of more women, but of more married women (see **jobs**), and this was just as much a consequence of need as of opportunity, where the need arose from the mountains of **debt** incurred by the average family—which now faces a monthly debt (credit cards plus mortgage debt) exceeding monthly average household income.

Again, MISHEL: As the long-term convergence of wages for men and women stalled, the gap between them at the end of the 1990s was as wide as at their beginning—as health care and pension benefits declined in the late 1990s. However,

> As wages fell for the typical worker, executive pay soared. From 1980 to 2000, the wage of the typical (i.e. median) chief executive grew 79 percent, and average compensation grew 342 percent. In 1965, CEOs made 26 times more than a typical worker; this ratio had risen to 72-to-1 by 1989 and to 310-to-1 by 2000. U.S. CEOs make about three times as much as their counterparts abroad. (ibid., my emphasis)

A recurring theme in PHILLIPS is the similarity between the 1920s and the 1990s, in more ways than one: The control over the economy by a very small and very greedy bunch of industrialists and financiers, with the eager cooperation of governments, both state and federal; the fragility of the U.S. economy, due to the financial shenanigans dominating it in the late 20s and the growing weakness of a good majority of the rest of the economy at home—and abroad; weakness in the agricultural sector, in much of industry and construction and, not least, in the condition of **poverty** of a good half of the population—as calculated by H. MILLER, a long-time U.S. Census official.

These are not the 'Twenties. As other parts of this book suggest, our economic/political/social/military world may well be teetering on the edge of something which, although very different, may be just as worrisome as the 'Twenties should have been, but were not. Or much worse.

infotainment (see TV, media)

"investors" (see also "earnings")

Investors used to be those who invested, that is, those who took their (and others' borrowed from-) savings to build or expand a company, or those who bought stocks and bonds to hold for a lengthy period of time on the expectation that they would get more than they put in because of the success of the company (or the wellbeing of the bond issuer). Not now.

Now an "investor" is anyone who plays the 24/7 game, buying and selling in the same week, day, hour. The "investor" of today is what used to be called a "speculator." There's nothing "wrong" with **speculation** as such; it is only when it becomes a typhoon force that both economy and speculator are likely to be thrown up hard against a wall at some time.

That was what happened 1929-33; after which it was seen necessary to legislate the **Glass-Steagall Act**, as a means of controlling a Wall Street that had become a gambling casino, and the **SEC**. Glass-Steagall was repealed in the 90s, and the SEC does more wobbling than regulating. See **deregulation;** then fasten your seat belts.

Israel (see Middle East)

jobs

Most of us spend more time at our job, and talking/ thinking/ worrying about it than anything else in our lives; for better or worse, like it or not, in this society, jobs "identify" us—to each other and ourselves.

For most, it's for worse. The lucky some of us like our jobs, a lot or at least a little; it's fair to say that the great majority—and that includes "housewives"—like their jobs very little, even hate them. It shouldn't be hard to see why; if it <u>is</u> hard for you to see why, read TERKEL, <u>Working...</u>, SCHOR, <u>The Overworked American</u>, and EHRENREICH, <u>Nickel and Dimed</u>.

Reading the experiences noted in those books, and pondering the lives of most jobs you have known or seen, you will also see why historically there has been a sharp distinction made between "work" and "labor." It goes back to the Ancient Greeks. For them "work" meant doing something useful under one's own direction, if also because of necessity; "labor" meant doing something under another's direction—bending to <u>their</u> decisions as to the when, where, how, and why.

Ancient Greece was a slave society: those who "labored" were slaves; those who "worked" were free. In both the Latin and Germanic languages—from the combination of which English is almost entirely derived—that distinction has continued: but you'd never know it, least of all in the USA.

What may be seen as a "good job" is one that carries with it some combination of good income and status, some challenge and enjoyment, and at least some power and dignity: it is "work." In turn, such jobs depend upon a certain level of skills and training. But who gets the skills, training and the good jobs and who does not?

That takes good luck: where and when you were born, your "color" and gender, whether your parents were rich or poor (and what their "jobs" were), the socioeconomic and political values of your society, and how they affect job opportunities and rewards. In short, whether you can ever <u>get</u> such a "good job" does not mostly depend upon how hard you work or how smart you might be.

Many who read those words would find them reasonable; most

in our society would not. Rather, our tendency is to start from the other end: those whose jobs give them a good income, status, and the like, are seen as having <u>deserved</u> them; more to the point, those who do <u>not</u> have good jobs are seen as getting what <u>they</u> deserve: they don't work hard enough, aren't smart enough, lack the proper temperament; something is lacking in <u>them</u>. (But recall the comment by Stephen Jay Gould regarding Einstein, in **education**.)

When teaching introductory economics, I usually began with the distribution of income and wealth and power, asking "What determines those distributions? Why are so many poor and so few rich; so many powerless and so few powerful?" And I would ask the students to imagine that I, with a comfortable income and a good job and a certain amount of power (if only over <u>them</u>), instead of having been born a boy in San Francisco in the early 20th century to a middle-class "white" family, let's suppose I had been born a girl in rural Mississippi to a black family—is it likely that I could ever have been standing in front of a university economics class asking this—or any—question?

Set the foregoing questions aside, and ask another: Why is it that some jobs carry with them a relatively high income and some power and status and others carry the opposite; and why are those good jobs the most satisfying and least unpleasant, regardless of the pay? In Ancient Greece, Plato asked such questions (in his <u>Republic</u>). Although in many ways deeply conservative, Plato answered such questions in a revolutionary way. In putting forth his answer in a sentence or two, the intent is not suggest that his principle is one that has any chance at all of being applied here and now (or even much later, elsewhere), but because it is thought-provoking.

Those who have the worst, least satisfying jobs, Plato argued, should receive the highest incomes. Because their jobs give them no satisfaction they should at least be able to live well and comfortably. And he added that those whose jobs provide pleasure, challenge, and/or status and power should have the lower incomes.

Sound crazy? Think: Would <u>you</u> prefer to be a professor/doctor/actor/writer/executive with a low (though sufficient) income, or collect garbage, work in a coal mine, sweep the streets, clean out the toilets in a hospital, work in a slaughterhouse with a high income? All this is another way of saying several things: 1) every effort should be made to eliminate the most unpleasant/dangerous/brainless/-

humiliating jobs through appropriate technologies and 2) when that cannot be done, to raise the pay of those doing those jobs so they have an income that provides a generously defined "living wage" (see below) with equally generous benefits (health care, pensions, vacations), 3) and that everything be done, also, to alter our educational system to see to it that those from the poorest families be provided with an **education** designed to narrow the gap between them and the lucky ones who already have the "good jobs."

Such a statement made a century or more ago would have been fundamentally impractical, undoable; today it is politically "impractical," but economically easy; and it would be rewarding for all. The times have changed in innumerable ways since Plato's Greece; the principle stands.

In the past few decades, the major changes affecting the nature, conditions and rewards from jobs have changed fundamentally and, for those in the bottom two-thirds of the population, very much for the worse in all those regards. Just looking at the top and bottom 10 percents in terms of wages speaks volumes: Between 1970 and 2000, the top 10 percent of full-time male workers had a 30 percent increase in their real earnings; the bottom 20 percent (20 million workers) in 2003 earned $8.23/hour or less; "adjusted for inflation, that is only 9 percent higher than the $7.55 they earned 30 years ago. (Louis Uchitelle, "A Way to Break the Cycle of Servitude," NYT, 8-31-03). The bottom ten percent's real earnings fell by 20 percent or more. ("Blunt Portrait... of U.S. Work Force," NYT, 8-30-02)

Those at the bottom were not only paid much less but worked at jobs you would not wish upon your worst enemy, combining dirt with servility, insult and boredom and uncertainty and no benefits, no job security—jobs vividly etched by EHRENREICH. Here a few of her observations (all documented in the book):

Item: Quoting the NYT, and in discussing the very low wages ($6-8/hr.) and long hours (including unpaid overtime at, among other companies, Wal-Mart), she points to the common practice of "Employers /who/ offer almost anything—free meals, subsidized transportation, discounts, etc.—rather than raise wages, for such 'extras can be shed more easily' as one employer put it." Item: The non-living wage of U.S. workers: "The Economic Policy Institute estimates that a living wage for a family with one adult and two children would be $14 an hour ($30,000/year). That would pay for health insurance, a telephone, child care at a licensed center, and the like, but no dining out, video rentals, wine, liquor, cigarettes, lottery tickets or even much meat." Note: 60 percent of U.S. workers earn less than $14/hour.

To compensate, most families require at least two wage-earners (great for the kids and family life in general), live in dangerously bad **housing**, need food stamps, and so on. Most small businessmen claim that they would fail if they paid such a wage. (EHRENREICH)

If, as is likely, that is often true, it seems that either a) we acquiesce in a very large number of workers having to live badly so the rest of us can get the stuff those small businesses provide, or b) businesses that cannot provide a living wage should be made illegal, or c) through progressive **taxes**, the government should provide universal health insurance, subsidize adequate **housing** (which was done in the past but is no longer), child care centers, and other necessities. Or else we must learn to redefine the word "necessity." (Ibid.) (See **housing/homeless, poverty, health care**, and **welfare**.)

For reasons difficult to admire, there is a general disinterest on the part of comfortable to very rich top fifth of the population for what is happening to the bottom four-fifths; but what happens to them can be, and has become, part of a general contagion.

In an article headed "As Companies Reduce Costs, Pay Is Falling Top to Bottom," (NYT, 4-26-03) we learn that

> ... the weekly pay of more than nine-tenths of all workers fell 1.4 percent over the last year.... The inflation-adjusted weekly pay of the median worker—half made more, half made less—fell 1.5 percent..., according to the Labor Department; the biggest drop since the mid-1990s. After more than two years of canceling investments in new equipment and laying off workers, many companies are turning to the pay of remaining employees.... The weak labor market, which has lost 2.6 million jobs in the last two years, is allowing them to restrain pay without fear of losing workers, executive say. /and see **unemployment**/

All that is bad enough; worse is on its way. As noted in **big business** and **globalization**, a major characteristic of both has been the combined process of "**downsizing and outsourcing**." The casualties of that are many, as noted in those discussions; not least on **jobs**, and especially for good jobs. There has been another, more abstract casualty; namely, the inter-related domestic and global strengths of the U.S. economy. Consider these facts:

> More than half of the manufactured goods that Americans
> buy are made abroad, up from 31 percent in 1987.... The exodus
> continues; the proportion of the work force employed in manu-
> facturing has fallen to 11 percent from 30 percent in the
> 1960s...; the share of manufacturing in GDP to between 16 and
> 17 percent.... The growing volume of imported merchandise
> /implies growing foreign debt/; as this debt balloons, foreigners
> will lose confidence in the United States as a place to put their
> money...; their demand for dollars will drop off, and so will the
> dollar's value. (Louis Uchitelle, "As Factories Move Abroad, So
> Does U.S. Power," NYT, 8-17-3)

That is a gloomy forecast; the only thing wrong with it is that
the writer's fears have been realized: As discussed in **financialization**,
the U.S. economy is for the first time in its history dominated by the
financial sector; it in turn is dominated by speculation; and since
2002 the dollar lost over a third of its value against the Euro.

Businesses in this country, especially the giant ones, have never
found it easy to understand that in today's consumption-based economy, if the majority of the people are doing badly, hey! It gets hard
to sell things to them. As noted above, as globalization has been
swinging, the <u>best</u> jobs are disappearing—not just for manufactures
but also, now, the good jobs in "Silicon Valley." Those jobs are now
in China, in India, in Indonesia. If you live in a city like San
Francisco or New York, you may have noticed a certain kind of now
common Chinese shop: "Everything 99 cents!"

But it isn't just cheap manufactures, it is those and some pretty
good stuff; more ominously, it is not just manufacturing jobs that the
USA is losing, it is some of the best jobs in the service sector. Some
examples:

> The dearth of jobs /today/ stems from factors signaling a
> sea change in today's business world; namely, higher productiv-
> ity, altered management and hiring practices, and the flight of
> both blue- and white-collar jobs overseas. Many of the changes
> in the labor market are structural, not cyclical. "It's similar to
> what we saw 50 years ago when people began leaving farms....
> The message to nation's 9.1 million unemployed is: Don't hold
> your breath." /Speaker: N. Gregory Mankiw, Bush II's top econ-
> omist. Good for him—except, as will be seen under **unemploy-
> ment**, it's not 9.1 but closer to 16 million unemployed./

A rapidly growing number of firms are moving entire divisions to locales like India and China, where costs from wages to real estate are vastly below U.S. norms, "Over the next five years, U.S. banks, insurers, and other financial services firms plan to ship more than 500,000 jobs abroad...; a leaked IBM conference call made public that the firm plans to move highly skilled jobs offshore...: 'Our competitors are going to do it, and we have to do it...' said an IBM director in the call. (U.S. News & World Report," The New Job Reality," 8-11-03)

If the foregoing sets of information are unsettling, an examination of rapidly emerging trends is frightening. Cited individually they are worrisome enough; when woven together they constitute a deep crises in the making:

> Item: Consider the following data provided by Jeremy Rifkin in his article "As Technology Devours Jobs at an Increasing Rate, the Conflict at the Heart of the Market Economy is Becoming Unreconcilable." (Guardian (UK), 3-2-04): The US has lost 12% of its factory jobs since 1998..., the UK 14%...; in China (!!) 15 million factory jobs were lost in the world's 20 largest economies, 1995-2002; industry observers expect the decline in white-collar jobs to shadow the decline in manufacturing jobs in the next 40 years; the US steel industry is typical of these trends—in the past 20 years, steel production rose by one-third while the number of US steel workers declined from 289,000 to 74,000
>
> Item: In the NYT, 5-11-04, the article "surge in Jobs Mostly Bypasses the Factory Floor," it is pointed out that "manufacturing employment is down nearly 3 million in the last 44 months;...of the 700,000 recent increase in jobs, only 37,000 were in manufacturing.

That is, there is an enormous problem unfolding, with every reason to believe 1) that it will deepen and spread, and 2) that neither our nor any other government seems in any way prepared to act in an appropriate manner. (see the "Jobs Crunch" issue of Monthly Review, April, 2004, for several relevant and probing essays.)

The foregoing melancholy conditions affecting so many of our and other people occur, it should be noted, as **technology** would seem to be promising something better for most people; as usual, the cream goes to those on the very the top.

That unjust process is aided and abetted by a system of **education** that systematically denies even a mediocre education to the bottom two-thirds of the people—not least because schools, funded mostly on the local and state levels, are paid for by **taxes**, and since the 1980s those who vote have been those taxpayers who don't wish to pay taxes for public schools. One of many vicious circles.

Plato would be downright disgusted; so should we be.

Johnson, Lyndon Baines (LBJ)

Like **Bush II**, LBJ came out of Texas. There the resemblance ends, and not only because, for better or for worse, LBJ was a real Texan and that Bush II is a wannabe. Both also became president without having been elected: LBJ because **JFK** was assassinated, Bush II because the Supreme Court unlocked the door so he could steal an election (which JFK may also have done in 1960, the door opened by Chicago's ultra-corrupt Mayor Daley). Bush II, rich as Croesus, has never worked a day in his life; he just showed up—as a playboy student at Andover, Yale, or Harvard (despising all three for their virtues, not their defects); as the functionless **CEO** of a loopy Texas oil company and Santa Claus-ed owner of the Texas Rangers; as an assisted avoider of service in Vietnam; functionless again as governor of Texas; ending up as the most muscle-flexing president ever. (see **Bush II**; also, IVINS).

LBJ, on the other hand, although never really as poor as he portrayed himself, did have to work his way through college just as the depression began, was elected to Congress (House) in 1937, did serve in the Navy during World War II, was elected to the Senate in 1948 to and become one of its most powerful leaders ever.

However. Those who went through the **Vietnam** days singing "Hey, hey, LBJ, how many kids didja kill today?" were doing so against a president who, although he hadn't started the war—that was done by **Truman** (see **Cold War, Vietnam**) and escalated by JFK—could have ended it any time from his inauguration through his second term: His bitter departure from the White House could have been triumphant.

However, as pointed out in the Vietnam discussions, LBJ was controlled by his fear of being accused of "being held responsible" for the humiliation of the USA; and he allowed that fear to lead him to self-betrayal. He ran for re-election in 1964 with the slogan "We seek no wider war." Soon after, in order to get Congress to pass the Tonkin Gulf Resolution in 1965, he lied to his old buddy and ally

Senator Fulbright (see **Vietnam** for details); even worse, he justified this to himself on the principle of "lest a worse fate befall"—in this case, the election of his (weak) opponent Senator Goldwater.

It would be easy to feel sorry for LBJ; but not if you were among the millions of those Indochinese and tens of thousands of U.S. dead, wounded, and demoralized while he was president. Still, LBJ inherited the Vietnam war; Bush inherited a fortune and has shown himself to be a war lover: "Bring 'em on!"—he hoots, just so long as he can do his hooting in Crawford, Texas.

LBJ, whether in Congress of the White House, natcherly indulged in at least his share of **corruption**; it goes with the territory. In addition to which he could be brutal and vulgar, sometimes imaginatively and simultaneously so—for example, when he would give press interviews while having a bowel movement in the Oval Room toilet, door open. (SHERRILL).

The foregoing leaves out the important social contributions made by LBJ, in sharp contrast to quasi-fellow Texan Bush II's ravaging of same. LBJ famously worked to make the USA into what he called a "Great Society." It didn't even become a "good society," but he at least helped to make it into a better one.

JFK was killed in November, 1963. Already in early 1964, LBJ began to press for and achieve reform legislation to support civil rights, education, health care, and public housing. (GOODWIN)

LBJ was done in by Vietnam, and rightly so. In his years, not only did U.S. troops fighting in Vietnam rise from the tens of thousands to an annual average of half a million, but the devastation by bombing and chemical agents with our "weapons of mass destruction" against Vietnamese civilians, North and South, caused at least a million additional deaths and countless serious injuries—and cemented both his and USA's "humiliation."

Warts and all, LBJ remained a good person. He was only 65 when he died; it is thought that his health had deteriorated at least as much from psychological/ emotional as from purely physical problems. His life, combined hard work with good luck, decency with indecency, splendor with tragedy. Tragedy won out.

(LBJ's career has attracted many "biographers." The most critical of them is journalist SHERRILL, The Accidental President; in her Lyndon Johnson and the American Dream, Doris Kearns Goodwin combines good history with a certain amount of flattery;

understandably, given that hers is the "authorized biography. Then, for the compulsive reader (which I am not, in this case) there is the ongoing multi-volume work of Robert A. Caro on LBJ.)

junk bonds (see financialization)

Kennedy, John F./Robert

Because he was a charmer and, at least as much, that he was so young when assassinated, JFK will go down in history as one our most beloved presidents. Criticisms of him are appropriate but seldom heard; all the more reason to put some forth here and now.

As I have written earlier (1997a), when the Sixties began and JFK pointed to "new frontiers" for the USA, it was not expected that they would be at the Bay of Pigs in Cuba (1961). That ill-fated invasion and the associated missile crisis of 1962 took the world closer to a nuclear war than anything before or—so far—since.

Nor was it expected (or known) then that at the same time we were establishing other new frontiers, in Indochina: by the end of 1962, although we did not declare war until 1965, JFK had sent 22,000 GIs (mostly "Green Berets") there. To advise. We were told. Later.

JFK himself cannot be blamed for all of that; as with **LBJ**, he inherited ongoing dirty policies. But his administration and its comfort with **Cold War** ways deserve a large cut of the blame.

His aides came to be called "the best and the brightest" and the White House their "Camelot." What they were "best" at was misinterpreting the realities of Cuba and Indochina, aided and abetted by a close to witless **CIA** and an entranced and pliant **media**. (YOUNG; POWERS /2002)

One of JFK's best and brightest was Robert McNamara, his Secretary of Defense. Because he was also one of the more vigorous "hawks" of the administration, it is more than revealing—and frightening—to learn from him just how insanely close a nuclear war was in 1962. "Insanely"? Yep. As the Cold War was drawing to a close in the 80s, someone not so stupid called together five meetings of representatives from the three powers involved: Cuba, the Soviet Union, and the USA. McNamara, present at the meetings for the USA, had this to say, in his Introduction to a 1992 book on the crisis:

By the conclusion of the third meeting in January 1989, it had become clear that the decisions of each of the three nations immediately before and during the crisis had been distorted by misinformation, miscalculation, and misunderstanding. (CHANG/KORNBLUH)

JFK is usually viewed as having been a "liberal Democrat," but it is difficult to find legislation that might be called "liberal" supported by him, except as regards "free markets"—but that is not the U.S. New Deal's version of "liberal" but the European term for **free markets.**" It is difficult to identify <u>any</u> legislation receiving sustained attention and support from JFK except in the realm of what is now called **globalization.**

He became president at a critical turning point in post-World War II economic history; namely, when what had been the other major powers <u>before</u> World War II, were beginning, by 1960, to become major <u>again</u>—after 15 years of so of various forms of assistance from the USA. By then, the economies of Western Europe and Japan <u>had</u> to have easier access to U.S. markets for their exports if they were to continue to grow. At the same time, U.S. industry and agriculture felt the need to make <u>their</u> way more easily into the foreigners' markets.

It was these pressures that led JFK to have his advisers work up and press for passage of the Trade Expansion Act of 1962. It was based on the realistic premise that the only way for all to be accommodated was for the <u>global</u> economy to expand.

The Act never passed, but what it had sought was "achieved"—or, better, "happened." It happened not because of an act of legislation but because the emerging new Cold War economy and its "military Keynesianism" (see **milex**) most stimulated the three largest economies in the world: Germany, Japan, and the USA.

As is discussed in **milex**, with the industries and agriculture of those economies all expanding, so too did much of the rest of the world—too much so, for by the mid-1970s the expanding economy moved into a global crisis of excess capacities, as both unemployment <u>and</u> inflation were rising pretty much everywhere.

It was those developments that produced what, from the 80s on, yielded **financialization, downsizing/ outsourcing** and conscious attempts to <u>assure</u> and control an expanding economy through old and new institutions such as **IMF/World Bank/NAFTA/WTO.**

JFK did not fill out his first term; now we can never know what he might have done had he lived. What we do know is that in his years as president, he left no mark on the major <u>domestic</u> issues facing the USA, and merely continued Cold War foreign and military policies. It was his younger brother **Bobby Kennedy** who, probably seeking to honor JFK, worked hard and with effect to institute something of a liberal tinge in U.S. domestic policy—especially as regards civil rights.

While JFK was alive, there were few if any signs of any but token support for the civil rights struggle going on in the South or, in its different way, in the North. As the 1960s opened, already in the South blacks had been struggling for some years to gain, quite simply, the right to vote—something guaranteed in the Constitution and in the 14th and 15th Amendments, of course. And then there had been the Civil Rights Acts of 1957 and 1960 (of Ike) and of 1964 (LBJ) but.... But if you were black in the South and tried even to <u>register</u> to vote, you were in trouble; sometimes, deadly trouble.

The "hot summer" of the Deep South was in 1964. The local whites seem never to have heard of the Act passed in July of that year, and didn't want to. In that summer (for which I was present), the beatings, jailings, and killings were simply ignored by the local **FBI** office..., until <u>after</u> the killings.

Bobby Kennedy was instrumental in that "awakening." I was in the South, present and witness to the first positive steps by the federal government. I can say that the FBI never lifted a finger to assist or prevent harm or injustice—the outrageously FBI-enshrining film "Mississippi Burning" to the contrary notwithstanding.

What <u>was</u> done by the federal government, inadequate though it was, was done by federal marshals at the instance of Bobby Kennedy's office; secretly. In at least one instance in which I was involved, it kept local whites from beating up or killing civil rights workers. (DOWD, 1965)

By 1967 and 1968, Bobby Kennedy had become a public figure in his own person. His stand was always liberal, for decency, peace, and freedom. His murder was sheer tragedy, the loss of one who might well have been a major figure in mitigating the rising injustices of what has become today's USA. (PALERMO)

Kissinger, Henry

Ugh. From the late 1960s through the 1980s, Kissinger was in the news all the time; nowadays he pops up only once in a while, proffering his hard-nosed opinions on foreign policy, piling up riches on riches from his consulting business, and occasionally dusting off his Nobel Peace Prize. In a sequence that leaves satire in ashes, Kissinger was awarded that prize for his "peacemaking" in the **Vietnam** war in the very year in which he was a major participant in U.S.-sponsored and financed overthrow of the democratically-elected government of Chile. Some details of his contributions to both of those tragedies are provided below.

For those to whom Henry the K. is merely a name, get the DVD/VCR for the 1964 film "Dr. Strangelove," an eerie preview of what was to come. Kissinger was a (relatively) harmless academic in 1964; by the 1970s he had become the Second Coming of Dr. Strangelove. (Come to think of it, maybe that's where he got some of his foul ideas.)

Kissinger began to become a household name—or epithet—after and because of his service as **Nixon**'s <u>secret</u> advisor in the 1968 election campaign—"secret" because he allowed the Humphrey campaigners to believe he was advising <u>them</u>. What great fun that must have been for Henry the Specialist in playing both sides against the middle as he raked in the chips. (HERSH, 1983)

What he was doing then, all of it now fully documented (see HERSH and later references) may or may not have been technically criminal, but it was certainly obscene: it had to do with the ongoing **Vietnam** peace talks in Paris in the early fall of 1968, the November election right around the corner.

Kissinger, although a Democrat, had been an advisor to Republican Nelson Rockefeller's failed attempt to get the GOP nomination; through that he had become known to GOP insiders, particular Richard Allen, Nixon's foreign policy advisor.

The 1968 Paris peace talks were seen by **LBJ** as the last chance for him to get us out of the bloody "quagmire." Democratic foreign policy bignik Kissinger had covert access to what was going on at the peace talks as the USA and the North Vietnamese sought to forge an agreement which, in ending the war, would also substantially lift the trailing Humphrey's presidential chances. (If there were other—

shall we say, nobler—considerations, they are not known.)

Kissinger privately encouraged both the Demos and the GOP to think he was in their camp, and the GOP to think they were alone in receiving his information about the evolving peace agreement. At some point he made the decision to go with Nixon, doubtless because he was sure Nixon would go with <u>him</u> (as Nixon did, making Henry his National Security Chief). As is shown below, Nixon used Kissinger's information to paralyze the peace talks; and the war continued for another five years. Before it ended the USA had dropped at least three times as many bombs on Vietnam as the <u>total</u> tonnage of World War II. Killing and maiming how many?

However, taking advantage of professional friendships while also betraying Democrats with whom he had worked on the still-secret Vietnam negotiating efforts did not suffice for Henry Kissinger. At the same time he was telling colleagues at Harvard and New York about his contempt for Nixon while offering the Humphrey camp information that discredited Nixon—such as making Rockefeller's private files on Nixon available (which came to be known as the Nixon "shit files." /HERSH, ibid./) Hell, Henry might have thought, "If I don't do it, somebody else would; and after all,...."

The upshot of all this (and more) was that Nixon, seeking to <u>prevent a peace agreement</u> by LBJ/Humphrey secretly (of course) promised then President Thieu of South Vietnam a "better deal" if Thieu would <u>not</u> go along with the peace deal before November. Thieu didn't, the peace talks flopped, Nixon won, the war descended to always more horrendous depths of devastation—and voila'! Dr. Strangelove was in the White House as National Security Advisor (and, later, as Secretary of State). No academic punk, our Henry.

The word "obscene" was used above; the reference was to KIssinger's shiftiness but, even more, to his key role in destroying the real possibility that the war neither LBJ nor Ho Chi Minh wanted could have been ended had it not been for Kissinger's double dealing.

The peace talks having failed, the war went on and on. President Thieu stayed in charge long enough to block <u>all</u> further attempts at an agreement which would have meant his downfall; and then we got rid of him. (see Vietnam and **Cold War**). It should not be forgotten that it was <u>after</u> 1968 that Laos and Cambodia were brought into the war, and that the largest number of Indochinese <u>and</u> U.S. casualties occurred. Obscene? No, <u>criminal</u>, as in "war crime."

As will be seen below, that crime led to one rivaling it; namely the <u>secret</u> bombing of **Cambodia**. That bombing began at Kissinger's behest and Nixon's orders almost immediately after his inauguration in 1969, a <u>created</u> tragedy, indescribable in its horrors then and since.

Kissinger utilized his inclination for doing serious harm in one country after another, large and small. Here I have limited myself to the devastation he helped to wreak only in Indochina and in the overthrow of the democratically-elected Allende government of Chile. In all those countries his touch had the same effect: at a time or in a situation in which <u>without</u> his intervention, peace could have been made or (as in the case of Chile) democracy could have continued, the policies Kissinger aggressively and successfully put forth brought about <u>millions</u> of deaths and distorted the social process for long periods—perhaps, in the case of Cambodia, forever.

Because of the gravity of those assertions, and their seeming unlikelihood when set against popular opinion, I note here only two books, both fully documented and beyond dispute in their conclusions: HERSH, <u>The Price of Power: Kissinger in the Nixon White House</u>, and SHAWCROSS, <u>Side-Show: Kissinger, Nixon and the Destruction of Cambodia</u>. I seek to do no more than provide some highlights.

As you read along note also that both Kissinger and Nixon remain highly-regarded and respected; despite all. Is it because "we 'Americans'" cannot abide the thought that any of our high officials might be, have been, <u>are</u>, monsters?

First, Indochina. It comprises Cambodia, Laos, and Vietnam (all of them also discussed separately under **Asia** and **Cold War**). The area, called "Indo-China" by the French, was invaded by the them early in the 19th century; within 50 years or so they had solidified control and, first and especially in Vietnam, had begun their deep exploitation of the people and resources. Then they took over Cambodia and, later, Laos—more because they were "there" than for deep exploitation; otherwise the British would have taken over (as they did with Thailand).

When the Japanese conquered the whole of the East Asia area in 1940, the Vichy French government was allowed to continue its rule over Indochina—until Japan was on the edge of defeat in the summer of 1945.

Between the 1830s and the 1940s, the French had managed to

destroy a venerable, attractive, and, in Vietnam, democratic society. (see KAHIN) From 1945 on, the USA participated in its further destruction, going well beyond the French in the havoc wrought upon the land, the people, the society.

It is relevant here to note that neither the people nor the government of the USA have ever found their way to acknowledge our vicious and baseless destruction in Indochina—as, for example, the Germans have in at least some degree, as regards the Holocaust. It is as though—well, we went there to help them be free, and..., and..., well, we left. Or something.

Cambodia. Vietnam and Laos have both been treated at some length under **Asia**... and **Cold War**; here we focus only upon Cambodia, for two reasons: 1) because, although the U.S. role in Indochina was under way well before Nixon took office, the catastrophe that became Cambodia from 1969 on was due entirely to Kissinger/Nixon decisions. Because of them, ultimately, over two million Cambodians were cruelly displaced, with many imprisoned and tortured and mistreated, and at least one million killed; and what Cambodia had been was destroyed forever.

Certain things must be known to understand the dimensions of the crime against Cambodia: 1. When Prince Norodom Sihanouk came to the throne there in 1947, he issued a constitution promising to replace a monarchy with a democratic government. 2. Two years later, the French granted Cambodia independence within the French Union and agreement to a constitutional monarchy entirely free of France by 1955. 3. When the Vietnam war began to heat up from 1946 on (see **Cold War** and **Vietnam**) and especially after the French defeat at Diembienphu in 1954 and the susequent always rising presence of the USA, Sihanouk did everything possible to keep Cambodia out of any involvement whatsoever. He didn't have a chance.

That France was inclined to grant Cambodia its freedom was due almost entirely to its post-World War II weakness and that Cambodia had few resources of value (to the French). That the French were in any way able and inclined to contest Vietnamese independence after the war was due almost entirely to the USA's interference and financing; see **Vietnam, Cold War**.

As the USA increasingly involved itself after 1954—politically, militarily and covertly—Sihanouk correctly anticipated that nothing but harm could come from any involvement of Cambodia with either side.

The main U.S. rationale for its ultimate bombing of Cambodia was that Sihanouk had allowed the North Vietnamese to use "the Parrot's Beak" in the NE corner of Cambodia as a path for transporting troops and materiel, and that the area was a combination of a headquarters and a vast munitions dump for the Viet Minh. When, after the devastation, those claims were found to be either totally untrue or only minimally true—like the "weapons of mass destruction" raison d'etre for Iraq—the damage had been done, the arguments forgotten. (SHAWCROSS)

So this is what we did, and how we did it; its grisly details are recounted jot and tittle in SHAWCROSS, from reckless beginning to terrible end—if indeed the end is yet in sight.

Initially, our onslaught on Cambodia took the form of bombing; as time went on, the catastrophe was a consequence of our politicking. First, the bombing.

It is vital to note that when the bombing began Cambodia was a neutral nation;, therefore, to bomb it would be illegal in U.S. law. For that reason, it was kept secret even from the pilots doing the bombing (see below).

The bombing began on March 17, 1969. By the time it ended, 14 months later, 3,630 bombing raids—raids not flights—had been carried out by flights of 50 or so 8-engined B-52s flying mostly from Guam or **Okinawa**.

When the planes took off the pilots had been given "legitimate" targets in Vietnam; as they reached Vietnam, they were given new coordinates by radio: in Cambodia. We know that from the sworn testimony of one of the pilots. (SHAWCROSS)

Each plane carried dozens of 750-lb. bombs: **carpet bombs**. The planes dropping them were 30,000 + feet above the target, safe from any danger from below or nearby, and unable even to imagine what or who they were hitting, burning, killing.

All of that is disgusting in itself; the way in which the targets were named by Kissinger and Nixon turns disgust into revulsion: The overall name of our leaders' murderous plans for Cambodia was "Menu," with the progression of targets named "Breakfast," "Lunch," "Snack," "Dinner," "Dessert," and "Supper." (SHAWCROSS)

In 1970, while Sihanouk was away from Cambodia, a U.S.-

organized coup put Lon Nol into power. He was immediately recognized by the USA; our troops invaded, and the bombing was stepped up (leaving almost a third of the population without shelter). Then, after a long string of related disasters, the Khmer Rouge came to power.

In 1970, the Khmer Rouge's numbers were in the 100s; in the ensuing social chaos accompanying the heavy bombing and Sihanouk's removal, traditional Cambodian society simply dissolved and the Khmer Rouge's numbers multiplied. As covertly as possible the USA supported the Khmer Rouge throughout its devastating rule over Cambodia; in doing so, its principal ally in that regard—which if not so tragic, would be funny—was China. Like the USA, China saw the North Vietnamese as the enemy. Be reminded that one of our reasons for going to war in Vietnam was because, as we put it, if the Viet Minh of the North were to win, they would link up with their Red Chinese ally and... the dominoes would fall all the way to the Mediterranean.

In fact, as everyone but the USA seems to have known, the Chinese and the Vietnamese of the North had been enemies for at least 1,000 years. (YOUNG) Details, details, Henry the K could say; bombs away!

Once in full power, the Khmer Rouge wrought sheer disaster on their own people and the venerable society of Cambodia. It is impossible to find any official (or unofficial) statements from the USA during or since the Nixon years that might constitute even the beginnings of an admission of what we did, anything like, even, an apology; nor have we done anything significant toward finding ways of undoing the vast harm we have done to those people—people who never did and never could have done any harm whatsoever to the United States of America. The blame falls most directly on the Nixon White House and, within it, to its main strategist, Kissinger.

Having achieved all that, Kissinger went on from one nasty maneuver to another; now we now turn to one of the most flagrant, accomplished, as noted earlier, in the very year in which he won that Nobel Peace Prize. Depths below depths.

Chile. In terms of political democracy and modern capitalism, Chile may be seen as the most advanced of all the Latin American nations; but political democracy does not equal socioeconomic democracy; that has never been more than mildly approximated in a few western and northern European nations and considerably less so in the USA—which also did its very best in Western **Europe** to hold it back (most intensely in **Italy**), and went beyond that in **Latin America....**

Kissinger's energies were not entirely used up in Cambodia; as that continued in 1973, he found time also to play a monstrous role in Chile. From the mid-1970s on, that role was heavily documented in, among other works, two 1975 Reports by the U.S. Senate Intelligence Committee (USSIC), the biography of CIA Chief Helms by Cord MEYER, the book by Chilean UN official Armando URIBE, and in the comprehensive work on Kissinger and Nixon by Seymour HERSH (1983).

Chile is a country blessed—or cursed—by its rich deposits of copper and nitrates. They have long attracted foreign investment, most of all from giant U.S. mining companies such as Guggenheim (for nitrates), and Anaconda and Kennecott for copper. Before and after World War II other companies jumped on the wagon: Grace Airways, **GE**. ITT, Pepsi-Cola. Standard Oil....

They and other U.S. companies have never been able to leave Chile's domestic policies alone, least of all those having to do with unions and recurring moves to nationalize resources. Going back to at least the 1920s, attempts to organize labor and move toward social democracy or socialism in Chile were common; such attempts made headway and then fell back. Not until 1970 was a left coalition candidate ever elected to be president.

That was Salvador Allende, a medical doctor and a moderate Marxist. He was criticized from the right and the center for his Marxism and from the Communist left for his insistence upon seeking to move toward socialism within the functioning framework of democracy.

Even before his election, the **CIA** was doing what it could to keep him and left-leaning activities down. After the election?

> Declassified documents show that the Nixon administration, which had tried to block Mr. Allende's inauguration, began plotting to bring him down just 72 hours after he took office. (Editorial, NYT, 9-11-03, "The Other Sept. 11.")

Then the CIA stepped-up its efforts, with the distinct aim of having him overthrown by any means at hand, including assassination (USSIC, Nov. 1975)—with financial assistance from U.S. companies.

With or without U.S. intervention, Allende faced opposition from his left (which saw him as too moderate) and from the Chilean business world; but that came to be broadened, deepened, and organized: covert CIA activities, including the siphoning of U.S. corporate "contributions" to the opposition: buying up or buying out elements of the media, arranging and financing demonstrations and strikes and transport shutdowns against Allende's policies, not least. (USSIC, Dec. 1975)

Allende became president in a free election, with every reason to expect free elections to follow. Given that Chile was a political democracy, on the surface it might seem that the USA and foreign capitalists should have had little to fear. Not so, thought the CIA and the White House; they saw the situation as distinctly threatening. Why?

The other two-thirds of Chile were dominated by the Christian Democrats (led by Eduardo Frei) and the Communists. But for Nixon, even Frei was a danger: Had he not recognized Castro's Cuba in the 1960s? And, by 1970, had he not supported nationalization of copper? What's this nationalization stuff? The arithmetic for the USA as the 70s began was that the conservatives + the fascists equaled only a third of the electorate.

In a nutshell, free elections in Chile over time were veering to the left toward policies seen as harmful not just to U.S. interests there, but as setting in place another scary example for the rest of Latin America: one Cuba was already too much; the only hope was to find a way to bring a centrist/fascist government into power.

U.S. CIA and business activities—echoing those of **Italy** in the decade or so after World War II—contributed to ongoing economic crises which were easily transformed into a social crisis. The tactics included transport and other strikes, punitive actions by U.S. companies against left workers, and **media** campaigns financed by the CIA. (URIBE, HERSH)

As the 1970 election approached, the USA withdrew support for Frei, moving instead to support the campaign of Jorge Alessandri, a long-time campaigner for office—archconservative, and very friendly to foreign investors.

> Thousands of newsletters were mailed, booklets printed, posters distributed, walls painted—under the aegis of the CIA that equated Allende's election with the Soviet invasion of Prague... Until election day, the CIA confidently predicted a huge Alessandri victory.

Oops! Allende won the popular election in September. Customarily, it had to be affirmed by congressional vote, on October 14. Between the September victory and the congressional affirmation, the CIA was involved in a complex of economic and media efforts to have the election reversed, up to and including support for a military coup before the congressional vote in October.

That in turn required "proper" control of the Chilean army. However, General Rene Schneider, its Commander in Chief "was viewed as the only man capable of stopping a faction of right-wing officers from staging a coup to prevent Allende's /confirmation/" (HERSH) Two days before the October 24th election, Schneider was kidnapped and assassinated. All's fair....

Notwithstanding all that, Allende won. Time for Act Two; Enter right, Nixon and Kissinger. From before the 1970 election until the day Allende was overthrown and killed—along with 3,000 others (more than on our 9/11)—the USA and its CIA covertly spent at least $11 million, used every trick in the book, had its own agents doing some of the work, and paid the Chileans doing the rest, beginning with the attempt to wreck the Chilean economy, as pronounced in "National Security Decision Memorandum (NSDM) No. 93:

> Within the context of a publicly cool and correct posture toward Chile... /the Nixon administration will/ undertake vigorous efforts to assure that other governments in Latin America understand fully that the United States opposes consolidation of a Communist state in Chile hostile to the United States and other hemisphere nations, and to the extent possible encourages them to adopt a similar posture. (quoted in HERSH)

Such as? 1. Guarantees of private investments in Chile. 2. Study which existing guarantees and financing can be terminated. 3. Bringing maximum feasible influence to bear in international financial institutions to limit credit or other financial assistance.

In addition were the continuing efforts to promote discontent through the media and production sabotage and transport obstructions, as well as the expansion of hooligan activities reminiscent of Berlin in the early 1930s.

It all culminated in the military overthrow of the Allende government, the arrest, torture, imprisonment, and murder of at least 40,000 Chilean citizens, and the imposition of General Pinochet's fascist government. (see URIBE, HERSH, MEYER)

Henry the K wasn't responsible for all of this, of course; he was "just doing his job"; that is, encouraging and doing the bidding of Nixon. **Nixon** was a <u>hater</u>, and he very much hated Allende and all he stood for:

> President Nixon took /Allende's/ election as an affront—
> 'it's too much the fashion to kick us around..." (NYT, ibid.), not
> least his friendly attitude toward Cuba.

If ever there was a marriage made in Hell, it was that of Kissinger and Nixon. As HALDEMAN makes explicit, the two men circled each other like panthers; a gilded Mafia brotherhood of hate creating or exacerbating death and destruction. If you wish to be brought to some combination of laughter and tears, see HALDEMAN's rendering of the moment in the early 70s when, in the Oval Office, they <u>knelt</u> together to pray—for what and to whom, exactly, who knows. Whee!

Before Nixon's hasty exit from the White House he had made Kissinger Secretary of State; he continued in that office (while continuing to rule over National Security, of course) when Gerald Ford inherited the presidency. Ford, as noted under **Nixon**, was hapless; **LBJ** had wonderfully characterized him as a guy who "couldn't chew gum and cross the street at the same time."

Although Henry has continued to enrich himself and harm others through his consulting company, he has happily lost any significant say over our foreign affairs—or has he? In May, 2003, in **Iraq**, General Garner was replaced as Chief of the New Iraqi Order by one L. Paul Bremer III, ex-CIA, ex-Assistant to—guess who?—Henry Kissinger.

Nor is it utterly wild to speculate that Kisssinger—secretly, of course—is behind the USA's continuing refusal to join the International Court of Justice unless it exempts our guys from indictments. That is meant to protect many U.S. personnel who have done shady or deadly acts. But surely at the very top of that list one would find the name Henry Kissinger. He has already been singled out for trial in Chile for his role in the overthrow of Allende and the installation of General Pinochet (whose murderous government, incidentally, lasted for 17 years).

The only indictment and conviction for a war crime in our history was that of Lt. William Calley. He was held responsible for the cold-blooded slaughter of civilians, very young to very old, at My Lai 4. Calley was a Boy Scout compared to Kissinger; Henry is not up to Hitler, of course, but more than the equal of Milosevic.

OK, Dr. Kissinger? No? Sue me.

Kyoto Treaty (see environment)

land mines (see collateral damage)

Latin America and the Caribbean

The long-accepted principle for U.S. behavior in this hemisphere was put forth in 1823, with the Monroe Doctrine. It had four provisions: 1) the "American continents" were closed to further European colonization (the initial basis for **"anti-colonial-imperialism"**); 2) the USA would oppose any attempts to extend the European system of monarchy in its existing colonies; 3) the USA would not interfere with existing colonies; 4) the USA would not meddle in the affairs of any European country. In that relatively innocent era, nobody had ever thought of anything like the School of the Americas (of which. see below); they didn't have to, it emerged as a logical outgrowth of the doctrine.

The USA effectively lived up to points (1) and (2); that is, we almost entirely kept the Europeans at ocean-length; but we did not live up to point (3) for the countries discussed below, nor (4) as regards (for example) **Italy** and **Greece** (see **Europe**). Pace, President Monroe, half a loaf is better than none.

Certain countries of the region will not be examined, but that does not mean the USA has left them alone or has had entirely positive relationships with them. Thus, the Puerto Ricans (taken over in our first years as an overseas imperialist) hold many resentments against us, and with reason—only the latest of which is our use of their territory for bombing practice; or the Colombians, who have had their country used and stupidly misused in our futile attempts to contain drug use; or Argentina, whose current economic and associated political crises, whatever their domestic sources, may be laid squarely at the door of the **IMF, et al.**—that is, at <u>our</u> door; or Ecuador, or.... Put it this way: Is there a country in Latin America or the Caribbean that has <u>not</u> been harmed by us? The answer is, yes, there are several; they have been under the rule of the British, the Dutch, or the French; it has been <u>their</u> right to do the harm. (COCKCROFT, et al.)

Here we examine the countries that have suffered most grievously and, usually, militarily from us, turning first to some of the Central American countries: Panama first, then Guatemala, El Salvador and Nicaragua.

Central America extends from Guatemala south through Panama. We begin with the latter; that's where we began our serious interference in Central America. (See WILLIAMS, W., 1969 and 1980 for the overall history)

Panama

As discussed under **imperialism**, the main empire of the USA was that which spread over the enormous part of North America bordered by Mexico and Canada and extending from the Atlantic to the Pacific (with a bow north for Alaska). That <u>internal</u> empire was completed by the 1890s; before the decade was over we began to accumulate an overseas empire in the Caribbean and in the Pacific more or less simultaneously.

Our first appearance in Central America was within the northern extremity of Colombia that we took from them and called Panama. It is over 150 miles in length but its "isthmian" middle is less than 40 miles in width: just right for a canal and, in that raging era of global lusts and conflicts, a priceless gem of a location for both economic and military purposes.

Colombia, then as still, was powerless to oppose the will of the giant USA, led then by Teddy Roosevelt. A promoter of what he called the "doctrine of the strenuous life," Teddy had much enjoyed his "Rough Rider" years and their charges up hills during the Spanish-Cuban-American war.

Teddy didn't hesitate to use what he liked to call "the big stick" to pave our way toward gaining control over the isthmus. He sent warships to Colombian waters while, at the same time, the USA helped to create and then supported a "separatist" movement and a coup d'etat against Colombian rule of the area. The result was the Republic of Panama.

The new republic immediately "leased" to the USA a ten-mile deep chunk of land cutting across the isthmus; it came to be called the Canal Zone. The digging of the canal began a few years later, and was completed in August 1914, just as World War I began.

Exploitation and corruption were the dominant political characteristics of Panama from 1903 on, and the USA was its de facto ruler; a variation of our achievement in Cuba under our man Batista years later.

After World War II, as was occurring elsewhere in the imperialized world, agitation for independence became serious in Panama; in 1963 Panama broke off diplomatic relations with the USA. By the 1970s, its then president Omar Torrijos managed to convince President Carter to grant gradual independence to Panama; that is, over a period of 22 years. Torrijos died in a mysterious plane crash in 1981; it was plausibly seen as having been arranged by the **CIA** (NAYLOR).

Our man in Panama as the 1980s began was General Antonio Noriega. In 1983 he led the coup that rid Panama of whatever democracy Torrijos had managed to sustain. Both before and after 1983 Noriega worked for the USA, as a conduit for smuggling illegal weapons to our "contras" in Nicaragua (the "Iran-contra scandal; see **Reagan**)—for which he was granted freedom to control the drug trade of the region. Dirty hands galore. (NAYLOR)

Evidently Noriega's delegated power went to his head, leading him to become a nuisance to the USA. So, of course, the **Bush I** government mounted an invasion of Panama. Its pretext was the shooting of an off-duty U.S. Naval officer one evening who was partying in a forbidden zone. The military operation entailed the invasion of Panama by 24,000 U.S. GIs, and the hellish bombing of Panama City in the effort to locate Noriega. He was found, tried in a U.S. court on drug charges, and stuck in prison. He will not exit except in a coffin painted with the slogan: Don't fool with Uncle Sam!

You will have noticed that we give Hollywood-style names to our military invasions these days. That for Panama was called OPERATION JUST CAUSE; some cynic suggested it be changed to OPERATION JUST BECAUSE.

Guatemala

Like most of Latin America and all of Central America, Guatemala became a colony of Spain in the 16th century. As the 19th century began, still very ummodern Spain had begun to lose its colonies, one by one; all had been lost in Central America by 1821. From this emerged an independent federation (1823), called the United Provinces of America, with Guatemala as capital.

Under substantial local and European pressures, the federation disintegrated in 1838. Guatemala remained independent, but it was more than a century before it could move toward democracy; in the interim it was ruled over by one military junta or another. (For the detailed earlier and subsequent history, see JONAS)

When there was not iron rule there was turbulence seeking to get rid of it; none of that succeeded until late in World War II. Then, in 1944, the military dictator Ubico was overthrown. And Guatemala had its first free election.

They elected a professor named Arevalo; his politics were what today would be called "social democratic." The U.S. government was preoccupied with World War II then and looked the other way—much to the discomfort of the main U.S. presence in Guatemala; namely, the United Fruit Company (UFC).

In 1947, with the war over, President Truman initiated the first step of what would become Guatemala's continuing tragedy. It did so in response to the Arevalo government's attempt to develop "a work code affirming the right of /plantation/ workers to organize and strike." What nerve! It was the plantations of the UFC on which those workers toiled; and the UFC didn't like that at all. So, neither did the USA.

Conflict grew and spread and in the free election of 1950 Jacobo Arbenz Guzman was elected. Arbenz wished to go beyond workers' rights; like Lumumba in the **Congo**, Arbenz sought the redistribution of <u>unused</u> land. About 234,000 acres were turned over to the peasants, with payment to the UFC equal to the values they themselves posited on their tax forms. (HERMAN, 2003)

That was too much for the UFC. By the time Eisenhower had entered the White House, UFC, through "managed tours" and a media barrage predating what has since become customary, the giant fruit/coffee company had convinced the two Dulles brothers, John Foster (Secretary of State) and Allen (CIA chief), to mount a coup against Arbenz. It was called "OPERATION SUCCESS."

> Perhaps the most far-reaching U.S. intervention in Central America was the CIA's 1954 coup against President Jacobo Arbenz Guzman. That coup ended Guatemala's 10-year old experiment with democracy, which the Eisenhower administration feared would give Marxism a beachhead in the Western Hemisphere. Though a short-term success from the American point of view, it set off a decades-long paroxysm of war and terror that took hundreds of thousands of lives and shattered an entire nation. (NYT, 'U.S. and Central America: Too Close for Comfort?" 7-28-02)

The USA then installed "the CIA's man in Guatemala," Carlos Castillo Armas. He promptly gave the land back to United Fruit, abolished the tax on interest and dividends to foreign investors, eliminated the secret ballot, and jailed thousands of political critics. (ZINN, 2000).

The icing on the cake for the USA was that the CIA used Guatemala as its training-ground for the anti-Castro Cubans who landed at the Bay of Pigs. In a technique made common throughout the Cold War, attractive euphemisms were the stated purposes of the USA's unremitting support for the fruit company:

> The proclaimed objective... was neither protection of the UFC nor the desirability of getting rid of a social democratic government that allowed unions—it was the threat of "international communism: and "Soviet expansionism.... (ibid. And see COOK)

So maybe there <u>was</u> a Soviet threat? In 2003, the State Department—after half a century—released a collection of previously classified documents on the CIA's role in the 1954 coup. As you read some excerpts from those documents, be reminded that they are all quotations from telegrams and memoranda relating to a plot to overthrow a freely-elected government; USA not USSR documents. The plot's code was PBSUCCESS; the source for what follows is "The C.I.A.'s Cover Has Been Blown? Just Make Up

Something About U.F.O.'s," NYT, 7-6-03)

9-18-53. CIA's Deputy Director concurs in approval of general plan, but feels budget estimate should be raised to $3 million to provide more adequately for contingencies. Mr. Dulles agreed.

9-25-53. Tasks for Chief of Station: Controlled "penetrations" in major Communist and anti-Communist organizations; in the armed forces; of agents with high-level Guatemalan government political propaganda planning;

10-29-53: Initial shipment of approximately 15 tons of arms and ammunition... to Colonel Armas /in Nicaragua/.

1-30-54. White Paper issued by Guatemalan government has effectively exposed PBSUCCESS. If possible, fabricate big human interest story, like flying saucers, birth of sextuplets in remote areas, to take play away.

6-13-54: Rumors combining fact and fiction which ought to be circulated, may include... A group of Soviet commissars, officers and political advisers... have landed; the government has issued an order devaluating the quetzal at the rate of 1:10, so use your money to buy food and durable goods; the Communists will introduce labor conscription; food rationing is about to be introduced; Arbenz has already left the country; add rumors of your own...

6-24-54: We are now prepared to authorize specific bombing targets in Guatemala City... most effective move to achieve success... and have desired effect on army and regime morale with minimum political cost to the United States.

6-30-54: Heartiest congratulations upon outcome developments past 48 hours. A great victory has been won.

There was never anything resembling a "Communist threat" in Guatemala; the threat was to the United Fruit Company. (see SCHLESINGER/KINZER) No matter; Arbenz was overthrown in 1954. In the ensuing decades at least 200,000 Guatemalans were killed, with countless others injured, tortured, displaced, their lives ruined. That brings us to the present.

On May 24, 2003, we learn that "Guatemala's ruling party is preparing to nominate as its presidential candidate a former president who is remembered for massacres of civilians during his first presidency two decades ago." (SFC, "Guatemalan coup leader re-emerges.") He was nominated.

"Re-emerges" is not quite accurate. The "former president" referred to is General Efrain Rios Montt, who seized power in a coup in 1982 and proceeded to massacre Mayans in the thousands. He is currently president of the Guatemalan Congress. A Guatemalan truth commission's inquiry concluded that during his Presidency, "agents of the state committed acts of genocide against Mayan people." (ibid.)

Not to worry. If the General starts doing genocide again why, we brought about one regime change there in 1954, we can do it again. Si?

Nicaragua

Poor Nicaragua was "discovered" by Columbus ten years after he thought he had found a short route to India. Like Guatemala, it was freed from Spain in 1821. It soon fell prey to Mexico, then to the Central American Federation, then to the British—and then the real trouble began: In 1912, the USA invaded and occupied Nicaragua until 1933. Led by Sandino, the Nicaraguans had a brief moment of democracy; so the USA arranged a coup in 1937, led by one of history's worst brutes, Somoza.

Somoza and his appointees mistreated and murdered and exploited their own people until the revolution of 1979, which brought the "Sandinistas" to power.

The stage was set for the USA to worsen its already rotten record in Nicaragua, facilitated by **Reagan**'s ascension to the White House. What ensued from 1981 on constituted one of the lowest and bloodiest betrayals of whatever most of us would like to think our country stands for. This long quote from LAFEBER sums it up:

> In 1981 Reagan signed the secret National Security Decision Directive 17, which authorized the CIA to spend millions to train and to equip Nicaraguan exiles, or "contras," who would fight the Sandinistas. In clear violation of U.S. neutrality laws, the CIA trained contras in the southern United States, then shipped them through Honduras to fight in Nicaragua. The Sandinistas, however, responded by building a force of 65,000 troops.... By 1983, the contras' failures led the CIA to take over operations that destroyed oil refineries, mined NIcaraguan harbors, and aimed at assassinating Nicaraguan officials. A stunned U.S. Congress discovered these secret CIA mis-

sions, cut off military aid to the contras, and received support
from a large majority of Americans /including/ U.S. military
leaders /who/ wanted no policy that might force them to fight
an unpopular war in Nicaragua.... Reagan's economic sanctions
proved more effective, /making/ Nicaragua an economic basket
case that lacked many necessities and by 1989 suffered an unbe-
lievable 33,000 percent inflation rate. The Sandinistas nevertheless held power.... until 1990, when peaceful elections voted
them out of office.

They were voted out understandably. Nicaragua's population
was only about 4 million in those dreadful years; they had lived in
deep poverty for decades under Somoza, conditions worsened by the
long years of the U.S.-contra killings and totally destroyed economy.
Against a relentless giant, it was clear that to go on was national suicide. We won. Three cheers?

But, as is shown in the discussion in **Middle East... Iran**, the
story of the "contras" and the CIA didn't stop there: the "Iran-contra" affair, a deliberate attempt to bypass congressional resolutions
meant to stop our military intervention in Nicaragua had and continues to have larger consequences.

The obscenely tragic and destructive story of our intervention
in Nicaragua took place in tandem with processes at least as destructive in El Salvador. There was one great difference between them, at
least on the surface. The USA sought to overthrow a democratically-elected government in Nicaragua; in El Salvador it sought to prevent one from coming into being.

El Salvador

Its history is that of Central America, a shared and prolonged
tragedy—deepened in the last decades of the 20th century by the
malign activities of the USA. And for the usual justification: as with
Cuba, Nicaragua, and Guatemala, we had to keep this hemisphere
free from Soviet control. If there was ever a moment or an area
where that was a plausible threat, Central America in the 1980s was
not it; even setting aside that the USSR was wobbling badly as that
decade began.

In 1980 (LAFEBER points out), "with one of the most
inequitable societies and brutal militaries in the hemisphere, El
Salvador was ripe for revolution." The group that came into existence to achieve that desirable end was the Farabundo Marti

National Liberation Front (FMLN).

It spoke directly to the needs and the desires of the largely peasant, terribly oppressed, and exploited people. It would have had no need of help from any foreign source to get rid of the vicious government—except that the government was the recipient of substantial help from the U.S. government.

But the FMLN did get help, from Nicaragua and, probably, Cuba. That was described as foreign intervention in the U.S. **media**, whereas U.S. intervention—as in Vietnam—was seen as benign (until the Iran-contra scandal). Nor is it unimportant that what aid the FMLN (or the Sandinistas) got from outside was confined to rifles, machine-guns, and grenades, whereas that from the USA included aircraft and bombs and artillery.

The situation in El Salvador received little attention in the States until a string of killings: of Archbishop Romero, of four U.S. Catholic nuns and six Jesuit priests, and the head of the Salvadoran land agency and two U.S. aides; all in downtown San Salvador. But the worst case of all, El Salvador's My Lai 4, took place in the tiny village of El Mozote. In 1980, the entire population of that village and some from a surrounding province—900 men, women, babies, and old people—were lined up and machine-gunned to death.

News of the slaughter began to trickle out. U.S. reporters and a photographer got enough of the story to cause trouble, but faced effective obstacles from both the U.S. Embassy and their U.S. media companies. Raymond BONNER of the NYT was removed from the story, and the photographers dismissed as unreliable.

The news of the massacre was suppressed successfully—until more than ten years later. Then, in a long essay in The New Yorker (12-6-93, later a book), Mark DANNER told it all. He showed that the action was devised and led by Lt. Colonel Domingo Monterrosa, Commander of the elite Atlacatl Battalion—U.S. trained at the School of the Americas, equipped by us, and, as one embassy person put it, "that rare thing, a pure, one-hundred percent soldier, a natural leader, a born military man." (DANNER)

> Newsflash: The School of the Americas having gotten a bad name throughout its history, we shut it down; oops! No, that's wrong: we changed its name. Now it is called The Western Hemisphere Institution for Security Cooperation.

Had all the foregoing and innumerable other atrocities been done by the FMLN, why then of course our President, our State Department, and the media would have given it Super Bowl attention. It's called the **double standard**.

Chile (see Kissinger)

Cuba

Our tortured and torturing relationship with Cuba began just a year before President Monroe issued his warning to the European colonizers: In 1822 our armed forces set foot on Cuban/Spanish soil four times, in search of something or other. We returned in 1899, when we "supported" their struggle for independence against the Spanish. For reasons best left undiscussed, we took it upon ourselves to "police" Cuba from 1899 to 1902.

We stopped that after a provision—the Platt Amendment—was inserted into the Cuban constitution "confirming" the right of the USA right to intervene militarily if the political situation "deteriorated."

In 1934 that "amendment" was abrogated in favor of a trade agreement. In the interim, U.S. Marines "intervened militarily" four times—in 1906, 1912-13, 1917, and 1933. As all that unrolled, we also laid claim to Guantanamo—of recent infame. On what basis other than sheer force we did so has been left unspecified. Ah, yes; we have a "lease"; by whom it was written, holding what weapon, escapes my memory.

Be all that as it may, it became and remains a strategic U.S. military base; and if Castro doesn't like it, well.... Now, of course, it is the home for Camp X-Ray, seen by some as our smallest, most recent, and best-behaved state; concerning which, a separate comment will conclude the ensuing discussion of Cuba.

As a newly-independent society, much burdened by slavery throughout its history, after 1900 Cuba quite naturally became home to political struggles aimed at democracy. For the U.S. democracy is something best confined to voting; however, in that the great majority of Cubans were very poor meant that they came to have a broader and deeper view of democracy in mind; a socioeconomic, not just a political democracy.

Thus there was intermittent turmoil. To put an end to that, the

USA installed Army Sgt. Fulgencio Batista. He ruled with an iron fist, torture, and a bulging pocketbook from 1933 through 1944. Distracted by World War II and its clarion calls for democracy, from 1944 through 1952 two less ferocious governments were allowed; our nervousness led the USA to re-install Batista.

If Batista had taken any lessons in politics, they were from Hitler and Mussolini; more likely, his natural viciousness and greed served as his guidebook. He was so vile that in 1957 the USA 1) cut off its normal supply of arms to Cuba and, get this, 2) encouraged the resistance movement of one Fidel Castro. A few words about Castro himself, before going on.

Son of a comfortable middle class family, by the early 1950s he was thinking and acting very much as many young people would in the 1960s in the USA and Europe. He was just 25 when he led an assault on the Moncada Barracks in 1953. Before going off to prison for two years Castro gave his "Speech to the Court."

It is a justly famous, humanistic and, for many, an inspiring document. Reflecting on his words in that speech, and on the needs and possibilities of Cuba after the successful revolution of 1959, one cannot help but wonder how uniquely wonderful Cuba would almost certainly have become had the USA not done every damned thing it could to bring back the glorious days of Fulgencio Batista.

The conventional critique of Castro's Cuba is that in "turning toward the Soviet Union and China" he was also becoming a threat to the Western Hemisphere, and not only as a proxy military base for the Soviets and Mao.

Turn toward them he did, and in doing so, necessarily, he also developed friendly political relationships with them. But the original impetus came from the USA, not from Cuba. As with the new Soviet Union after World War I and the new Red China after World War II, the USA responded to the new Cuba with economic, military, and political hostility.

The first move was when Cuba's sugar exports to the USA—its prime, almost its only, source of income—were blocked, first and foremost at the instance of U.S. sugar growers. Along with that, the U.S. began the embargo that endures still against Cuban imports and exports—with strong pressures to participate on our allies. From that point on, one thing followed another, most dramatically (at first), the Bay of Pigs invasion.

It was a spectacular flop, and was blamed on **JFK**. The blame that should have fallen on him was that he did not cancel an invasion organized by **Nixon**, then V.P. of the recently departed Eisenhower administration.

Cuba was one of many stinking roses in the **CIA**'s very large bouquet. True to form, the CIA had assured Ike and then JFK that if we armed and trained the Cuban opposition to Castro (which was done in **Guatemala**), then on the basis of CIA intelligence, a relatively small invasion at the appropriately-named Bay of Pigs would be followed by spontaneous uprisings against Castro, and then.... Hearty congratulations! As for Guatemala?

Nothing of the sort happened. Why not? First, we now know that those the CIA questioned were among that minority of relatively well-off Cubans (still in Cuba or in Miami) who were dead set against Castro, no matter what. Next, already by the April 1961 invasion the revolution was popular, and its popularity was to increase for many years afterword—despite, as will be noted, reasons for dissent. Again, why?

Because the Cuban Revolution promised and soon began to deliver a better life to the overwhelming majority of Cubans in terms of clothing, food, shelter, education, and health care; in terms of dignity and hope.

Castro rules as autocrat, to be sure, and one who has treated at least a small number of Cubans badly—to the point, recently, of executions. From his first public appearances, it was clear that Castro had a compelling ego; in recent decades what was once compelling may now be seen as manic. But two points:

1) Certainly in material and probably in many "non-material" realms, the Cuban people are having far better lives than any prior Cuban generation or, than most of the people in the world; all that despite living in a small country with limited resources and under embargo; 2) the USA will have to answer this question: Had we left Cuba alone—to say nothing of, had we assisted them—who can say with reasoned arguments that the Castro of 1959 rather than the Castro of 2004 would not have prevailed; it is not so much Castro himself but the treatment of Cuba by the USA that has produced the Castro of today. (For an excellent and balanced summary of Cuba since 1960, see the articles in MR, January, 2004: "Cuba! 45 Years of Revolution.")

Camp X-Ray. For those who can get away with it, resort to the **double standard** is "normal." The entire history of U.S.-Cuban relations, if viewed "objectively," can be seen as a series of outrageous mistreatments, with variations. Given the history noted above, our behavior regarding Cuba's Guantánamo Bay then would rank high on any list of imperialist excess.

That an enormously rich powerhouse of a country would stoop to demanding of a newly-independent and very small nation such as Cuba that it must allow the giant to occupy and use a valuable portion of its land in perpetuity or take the military consequences was, is, would always be, outrageous.

It would be interesting to poll the people of the USA on this question: "The Spanish have demanded that the USA relinquish a piece of Florida for a naval station"; or, "The British have demanded we relinquish a portion for a military outpost on Long Island." Mr. and Mrs. America, what say you?

What our government has said is measured by what it has done; and our people's silence is our answer, with only now and then a dissent such as the following:

> For a year and a half, the United States has held hundreds of people captured during the war in Afghanistan as prisoners in Guantanamo Bay without access to family, lawyers or any semblance of due process.... The Department of Defense has held more than 600 male prisoners, some as young as 13, and of 42 different nationalities, including citizens of our closest allies, in a concentration camp. They have been declared "unlawful combatants" in order to deny them the protections of the Geneva Convention..., incarcerated at a naval base in Cuba, over which Cuba has no control, to put them beyond the reach of the law. The military set no limit on their detention, and it declared that if they were brought to trial, the proceedings would be before special military tribunal, which can act in secret, and their only appeal would be to the president—who stripped them of their rights in the first place. ("The Guantánamo Scandal," Editorial, NYT, 5-15-03)

Grenada

In October of 1983, the USA invaded Grenada. Most needed to be told where it was then, let alone why we invaded them. And now? Quick! Where is Grenada? Although "only" 87 were killed in the process (18 of them GIs), you can go to the electric chair for killing only <u>one</u>. So what was the good reason?

Reagan knew the reason why: it was Lebanon. That's right, we invaded Grenada because of Lebanon—a few thousand miles away. What had Lebanon to do with Grenada? Reagan's reasons were lousy for almost everything he did; for this they were worse than mere lousy. (And, of course, as always, he got away with it.)

As noted in **Middle East... Israel/Palestine**, the USA has been heavily involved in that corner of the world since at least 1948, when it took its first steps to help the Israelis get rid of the British (and their power over both oil and that strategic location). And we're at it still.

In 1982 Lebanon suffered one of the great horrors of the Israeli-Palestinian conflict. It was then that now Prime Minister of Israel General Sharon invaded Lebanon to destroy Syrian missiles and PLO positions. In the same process, with the help of Lebanese Christians, Israeli forces also massacred many hundreds of helpless Palestinians living in Israeli-controlled concentration camps.

In April of 1983, in retaliation, the U.S. Embassy in Beirut was bombed, and several lives were lost. Earlier, Reagan had sent 2,000 troops to Beirut, their mission never publicly stated. On October 23, 1983, a terrorist bomb killed 239 U.S. soldiers in their barracks. Reagan then declared that keeping our troops in Lebanon is "now central to our credibility on a global scale"—but, soon after, quietly <u>withdrew</u> those remaining. (LAFEBER)

It is generally recognized that therein lay <u>the</u> reason for invading Grenada. In his subsequent State of the Union Address a few months after Grenada, this is what Reagan said: "Our days of weakness are over. Our military forces are back on their feet and standing tall."

Reagan's closest and most trusted advisor, Michael Deaver, after denying that he had anything to do with the invasion of Grenada, went on to say that he had wholeheartedly supported it,

> because it was obvious to me that it had a very good chance of being successful and would be a good story. Asked whether he did not fear that attacking such a weak and tiny country would in fact expose the President to ridicule, Deaver replied, "No, because I think this country was so hungry for a victory, I don't care what the size of it was, we were going to beat

the shit out of it. You know, two little natives someplace, if we'd staked the American flag down and said, 'It's ours, by God,' it would have been a success." (HERTSGAARD)

The awful truth is, he might just have been right.

Mexico (see NAFTA)

lobbyists/campaign finance (L/CF)

In U.S. politics, lobbyism and what we now mean by campaign financing have only been significant for about a century; lobbying is called that because in the bad old days those who wanted to create, eliminate, or modify governmental policies hung out in the lobbies of Congress and state legislatures, waiting to buttonhole those with open minds and pockets to induce them to vote yes no or maybe; campaigns then were not dependent upon the **media**; except for the downright and common purchase of votes, campaigns were effectively costless.

Initially, we'll distinguish between the **L/** and the **CF**. In elections the two are interdependent so the distinction has steadily lost its meaning; for influencing or controlling legislation they remain connected but less tightly.

Lobbyists. Sitting in the lobby is now becoming a thing of the past, except for drug company reps who wait around in doctor's offices; the business—and it is a business—is more efficient now, no need to waste time hanging around. The result, as KUTTNER put it the title of his book is Everything for Sale (which I suggest be extended to Everything and Everyone for Sale).

Most shamelessly, doctors and pharmacists are repeatedly invited to "conventions" at a summer or winter resort where the presentations are for particular medications: the beach or ski slope is "the lobby."

Perhaps we should be grateful; that means we get to see the docs a bit faster in trade for being told to use a particular medication for reasons whose basis is at least partially bribery; on second thought, we should be angry because we are paying higher prices than are necessary due to the always more successful lobbying by the **pharmaceutical** industry to maintain patents (among other white collar crimes).

But the lobbyists' successes go well beyond such matters into at least as important areas: for the oil companies, whether as regards yes or no to drilling offshore or in the Arctic; or matters that can lead to wars, past and present. **Oil, cars,** steel, trees, fish, chemicals, **HMO**s, **taxes, milex, media, guns,** credit cards, subsidies..., if it's an industry or a law or anything where there's lots of money to be gained or lost—voila'! There you will find lobbyists.

Thousands and thousands of them: In his penetrating study of political corruption—Arrogant Capital (1994)—PHILLIPS points out that already in 1991, an academic study showed that in Washington D.C. alone there were over 90,000 lobbyists—many of whom are ex-legislators—with an additional 50,000 putting the pressure on at the local and state levels; and that was more than a decade ago. Since then? Let your imagination (plus more to be added below) fill in the details.

Campaign Finance. This has to do with the money directly raised by candidates on all geographic levels for all offices—including judges. There are now upper limits for contributions from any one person for any one candidate, as—perhaps—there will be for the critical "soft money" raised by a political party when it is used to support a particular candidate "indirectly." Except that in practice the only difference—and it is a big one—is that the soft money is greater than the legal contributions.

It is necessary to add that though it is illegal, a common and continuing practice in many businesses is to ask their employees to contribute to a particular campaign. And it works: one doesn't have to have a great imagination to assume that a very high percentage of employees would find it wise to make such contributions in their individual names—with some, surely, being given the money to do so, directly or indirectly, by the boss.

Campaign financing as generally understood has two legs to stand on, "hard" money given directly and "legally" and the "soft" (as a thief in the night) money indirectly and soon to be illegal; sort of. The amounts are great: Just in the first quarter of 2002, the Democrats had taken in almost $50 million and the Republicans almost $70 million, with nine months to go. ("Democrats continue to rely.... NYT 4-17-03) Plus,

individuals, organizations, and companies gave a total of

nearly $3 billion to national campaigns in 1999 and 2000...
/However/, organizations spend 10 times as much on lobbying as
on direct campaign contributions, and they spend undisclosed
millions more to establish special-interest research institutes, or
so-called think tanks, which do not legally count as lobbying
activities but are intended to manipulate public opinion and
public policy. ("Lobbying by businesses overwhelms their campaign contributions," Alan B. Krueger, NYT, 9-19-02)

Setting aside further ugly details of **L/CF** momentarily, two
questions: 1) How is it, as noted earlier, that **L/CF** awaited the opening of the 20th century? 2) And how did we get from their humble
beginnings to today's gimme, gimme, gimme! politics?

1. Initially, of course that **L/CF** didn't come into being until the
turn of the century is <u>not</u> to say that politics were "clean" up until
then. Take the U.S. Senate: It wasn't until the 1890s that U.S.
Senators were popularly elected; up to then, they were "elected" in
the legislatures of their separate states; and those legislatures, in
turn, were usually directly or indirectly controlled by the leading
economic interests of their states—oil companies, farmers, railroads.... House members <u>were</u> directly elected from the nation's
birth, but in virtually all of the cities and towns there was some
degree of political control from the top: 1) by the notorious but
nonetheless powerful "machines" of New York, Chicago, San
Francisco, Kansas City, New Orleans...., or 2) in the nation's towns,
by the "respectable" cabals of businessmen portrayed in Sinclair
Lewis's <u>Main Street</u>.

"Democracy" was then as now more "plutocratic" than "democratic," if with greater "fluidity" then than now, Now, as pointed out
in **big business**, we are confronted with a clubby few <u>hundred</u> giant
companies, their **media** allies, two political parties whose differences
are more of degree than kind, and a population bewitched, bothered,
and bewildered by **consumerism**.

Whatever the limitations of democracy a century or so ago,
there were at least intermittently democratic intervals on the local,
state, or even—as with the "Populist" movement of the late 19th
century, regional levels: lobbyists and organized campaign financing
were irrelevant and unnecessary.

Both came to be born as the 20th century came into being for
at least two overlapping reasons: 1) the emergence of the federal

government as an always more essential agency to influence the overall direction and health of the economy at home and abroad; 2) the growth and emerging dominance of **big business** and **finance**. Thus, around 1900, there were a few really big companies dominating the major businesses of their era: railroads, meatpacking, oil, finance, steel, finance. None of them were yet close to what they would become; least of all, and colossus though it already was, **oil**, for **cars** then were few and far between, either a rich man's toy or a farmer's "tool."

Already by 1910 the quantum leap between then and now had begun. It overarched all sectors of the economy and intersected with both domestic and international politics. The USA and the other capitalist powers were "growing up"—but, as subsequent developments revealed, growing up like adolescents (and remaining that way): in muscle, but not in brain.

It was the era in which a strong national state became imperative, if continually precarious situations were not to become worse. In the USA, Woodrow Wilson won the election of 1912. In his campaign, more than once he proclaimed that "When government becomes important, it becomes important to control the government." He didn't have to tell that to the business world; if anything, they had informed him.

On the surface of things, those same years—say, the first quarter of the 20th century—gave every outward appearance of promising that Wilson's "control" could be, even would be, control through an informed electorate: Education had taken its own leap in response first to the need for a literate workforce in modern economies; with literacy becoming widespread, so too would (or at least could) information and understanding.

For just those reasons, that era also produced the modern **media**, **advertising**, and public relations, all of which were from their beginnings more inclined to sell and manipulate than to "inform." However, the inclination to control in the pre-World War II era was paltry by comparison with what has occurred since then. The 20th century was made to order for rule by money, facilitated not just by the enhanced techniques of "mind management" and "infotainment," but as well by important accessory assistance of well-paid lobbyists and heavily-financed candidates at all levels—many more of the very rich today than earlier using their many millions—and it takes <u>many</u> millions—to buy an office—most recently Mayor Bloomberg, Governor Schwarznegger, the Presidents **Bush**.

So maybe there's something rotten here; but how about Denmark, and all those other countries? Isn't it like that all over? Not quite.

Things are far from ideal in Europe, but their <u>elections</u> aren't bought and sold. Take Italy (which I have observed while living there half of every year for many years): In Italy <u>nobody</u> has to or can buy "time" on radio or TV, or run ads in the newspapers: It is <u>illegal</u>. Apart from giving talks here and there, political campaigning is restricted to small billboards along some (not all) streets, in the few weeks before an election: "Small"? That means about 5 feet high by three feet wide. Such rules are not universal in Europe, but they are common. Candidates appear on TV, but at the same time, in contention with each other; no money changing hands. Dull.

But, those who know today's Italy might well say, "What about this guy Berlusconi?" Didn't he get to be Italy's Prime Minister through the media? Right, and he couldn't have gotten there <u>without</u> the media. How come? Well, he is the richest man in Italy, he <u>owns</u> five TV stations (there are only 7 private ones), a couple of newspapers and a radio station and, importantly in Europe, a soccer team. He does not and cannot campaign in the media, but his stations' news programs can indirectly campaign for him, with Berlusconi this and Berlusconi that. Once he was elected (along with members of his coalition), the parliamentary opposition sought to prevent a politician from owning in the media. They lost. And now Berlusconi effectively controls the three public TV stations.

Back to the USA. In the realm of **CF** and "soft money" the possibilities are infinite. Take the example of House majority leader Tom DeLay (also a leader of the rightwing in the GOP). As reported in the <u>NYT</u> (4-15-03), De Lay was "inviting wealthy donors to give as much as $500,000 to spend time with him... during the 2004 Republican convention..., and to have part of the money go to help abused and neglected children." Although Tom said through his staff that the entire effort was /for the children/...aides acknowledged that part /teensy?/ will go toward convention parties, a luxury suite during President Bush's speech at Madison Square Garden, and yacht cruises...., and other lawmakers may follow DeLay's lead. ("Bush ally mixes charity and politics.")

The article then provides some details for those interested. What you get for 500 grand was noted above (except dinner before and after the convention with Mr. and Mrs. DeLay. For $250,000 you can have pretty much the same deal, without the dinners. For $100,000 you get the yacht cruise, plus 12 tickets to an event with Congress members. Getting down to $10,000 (for the likes of you and me), you get the yacht cruise, but only with "a VIP," not with DeLay. I dunno; who's the VIP?

Quite apart from the **corruption** involved, there's something just plain disgusting about how many $$$$ these folks have and the contracts they'll get, and who would want to have dinner with <u>Tom DeLay</u>? On a boat, yet.

Those who pay for most of the lobbyists and most of both the "hard and the soft" campaign financing have effectively spread the notion that...well, after all, what about the unions, the Greens, the teachers...?

Good question; to answer it, here some excerpts from a well-documented study in the bimonthly <u>Dollars and Sense</u>, "How Money in Politics Hurts You," (July/August, 2000):

> Most of the money flows to the politicians serving on the congressional committees that oversee each industry. For example, most banking-industry money goes to members of the finance committees, regardless of party.../etc./
>
> Business interests outgave labor interests by a factor of 11-to-one in the 1997-98 election cycle.... Dirty industries—oil and gas, mining electric utilities, automobiles—outspent greens: spent more than 40 times than environmental groups.
>
> Only one-quarter of one percent of the population makes contributions in excess of $200; only 170,000 people contribute $1,000 or more; 80 percent of all donors make more than $100,000 a year.

Them what has gits. Money talks. Loudly. But we don't have to worry; the **Bush II** administration is the most moralistic in memory and so.... Oops! This just in: "Bush Names Lobbyist As Leader of G.O.P." (<u>NYT</u>, 6-17-03). His name is Edward Gillespie. "Mr. Gillespie said he would retain his stake in his lobbying firm..., but would do no work for the firm and collect no salary as long as he is a party official."

Sure. However, the article goes on to state,

> In the long term, Mr. Gillespie's lobbying business will hardly suffer from his run as party chairman.... He will closely consult with the White House and Congress on policy matters and electoral strategy. Such inside information would be invaluable to his clients and partners at Quinn Gillespie & Associates.... "That firm is going to be sitting pretty, and his stake is going to become more valuable; the clients of that firm are going to be in hog heaven," said the Director of the Center for Public Integrity.

Hog hell is where they belong.

loyalty oaths (see McCarthyism)

Lumumba, Patrice (see Africa... Congo)

MacArthur, Douglas

General MacArthur is singled out for discussion because he so well represents the group of much-lauded "Americans" who deserve at least as much scorn as the praise that has been heaped upon them. (A few others of that ilk have been discussed in other essays: Andrew Jackson /in **"Indians"**/, **Reagan**, and **Kissinger**, for example).

MacArthur first became nationally famous in 1932 for deeds that should have made him infamous. In that year the depression of the 30s was sinking toward its 1933 bottom. The ongoing "hard times" prompted the march of "the Bonus Army" of World War I veterans. (TERKEL, 1982)

The vets had been awarded "bonus certificates" which, however, were not to be cashed in for many years in the future; in 1932 many thousands of homeless and desperate veterans needed something to live on then.

Their effort went on for weeks, in a series of accumulating disasters. There was no **TV** then, so outrage did not make the splash it might today; less understandably, most historians have neglected it. Both the need for the march and its bloody outcome were important for what they revealed about MacArthur and about the USA and its much-praised but much-neglected war veterans—the World War II vets only a partial exception. Item: As **Iraq** moved toward quagmire in the summer of 2003—six months <u>after</u> the war had presumably ended—the Bush II guys cut GIs pay $150-$250 a month until the ensuing clamor gave them second—first?—thoughts. Back to the Bonus March:

> So /the veterans/ began to move to Washington from all over the country, with wives and children or alone.... More than 20,000 came. Most camped /on the ground/ across the Potomac River from the Capitol on Anacostia Flats.... The bill to pay off on the bonus passed the House, but was defeated in the Senate. /Some veterans left, but/ most stayed—some encamped in government buildings..., and President Hoover ordered the army to evict them....
>
> Commanding four troops of cavalry, four companies of infantry, a machine gun squadron, and six tanks, MacArthur led his troops down Pennsylvania Avenue, used tear gas to clear the veterans out of the old buildings, and set the buildings on fire.... Thousands of veterans, wives, children, began to run as the tear gas spread... Soon the whole encampment was ablaze. When it was all over, two veterans had been shot to death, an eleven-week-old baby had died, an eight-year-old boy was partially blinded by gas, two police had fractured skulls, and a thousand veterans were injured by gas. (ZINN, 2000)

MacArthur, Chief of Staff of the U.S. Army 1930-35, soon went from that triumph to the Philippines, to oversee U.S. interests in the region. He was there when the Japanese bombed Pearl Harbor; he then served as Supreme Allied Commander (his real title; probably his idea, too) for the war in the Southwest Pacific.

I was in the same area for about three years during the war, serving with both the infantry and the Air Force. It was in a three-month stretch with the infantry in 1943 that my scorn for him mounted toward new heights. Nor was mine a minority opinion: the GIs always referred to him as "Dugout Doug," dating back to his behavior in the war in the Philippines right after Pearl Harbor.

MacArthur came to be celebrated as a military genius. A representative opinion is that which is found in the entry for him in "<u>The Penguin Dictionary of Twentieth Century History</u> (PALMER): As Supreme Allied Commander... "he developed a strategy of throwing the Japanese back by 'island hopping' from Papua and Guadalcanal to Luzon, Iwo Jima and Okinawa..."

Well, we won the war, of course, and our armies did go from Papua up to **Okinawa**. I was part of one of those "island hops"; I note first something of his character, then his presumed strategic capabilities. First, MacArthur the media cheat.

Easterly across a broad channel from New Guinea is the island of New Britain, sticking out like an arm about 400 miles from west to east. The infantry outfit I was with was anachronistically called the 112th Cavalry, although we had no horses or even tanks. We were to make a "diversionary landing" at Arawe, a tiny spot 200 miles to the east of New Guinea.

We were a tiny little group for a landing; only about 3,000 of us—Rifleman Norman Mailer /!/ one of them. (The Naked and the Dead is dedicated to the 112th). At the eastern end of New Britain was a Japanese naval and airbase; at its western tip was Finschaven, an important Japanese military base. The landing at Arawe was meant to "divert" the attention and to draw troops and airpower toward us, so as to weaken them by the time (some months later) the USA would invade Finschaven. In brief, we were sacrificial goats.

Here an explanation: I was a pilot with the 309th Bomb Group at the time. What was a pilot doing with such a project? The answer has to do with "friendly fire." The war in New Guinea was jungle warfare; because there are no clearly demarcated lines between friend and foe in the jungle, our planes often bombed our troops and our troops often fired on our planes. Especially was this true of my part of the bomb group: low-level attack bombers.

I was sent along on the landing with eight radiomen, probably because I wasn't much of a pilot. Our task was to "talk" the A-20s in, to lay smoke around the target, and to tell the grunts not to shoot.

It worked, but not very well: We still shot down one of our planes, our planes still bombed us; one of my men was killed, one badly-injured, and one lost his mind; ultimately (as expected), we were pushed back into the sea. We knew we were supposed to "divert"; we didn't know we were supposed to lose. But all's fair in love and war, no?

Be all that is it may; the morning came when the 3,000 of us got into our tiny rectangular landing crafts (about 25 x 10 feet) to embark over 200 miles of open sea, thence to land at Arawe. As we were preparing to embark from New Guinea, MacArthur and a few aides-de-camp appeared, dressed for the occasion and all a-bustle. They got into one of little landing crafts; it then backed off for about

30 yards, reversed gears, and came back toward the beach. The ramp went down, and MacArthur debarked—cameras popping all the while. We who were getting set to go on a rolling sea trip (which would shortly have us wallowing around in vomit for 12 hours or more) were too worried and scared to give a damn about all that; but one could not help but notice. A few months later it all came back to me when I saw an old copy of Life magazine. On its cover was General Douglas MacArthur emerging from that selfsame craft—as though at Arawe, where he was not—along with a story touting his heroic participation in a risky invasion.

The whole thing was not quite as professionally done as **Bush II**'s phony landing on the aircraft carrier U.S.S. Abraham Lincoln in 2003, but in 1943 the craft of **public relations** was still in its infancy. Forgive them. So alright already, an ego freak and dishonest, but still...he was a great strategist, yes? Not quite. I was around for the rest of the war and its other "island hops." Our (planned) failure was not, so far as I know, repeated; but there were at least two landings I know well that were unnecessary, the bloodiest of which was Biak (the larger focus of Mailer's book). How so?

The land battles from Papua to the north depleted Japanese strength, but what brought them to their knees were the always more constraining naval blockades and always heavier aerial bombardments. Taken together they denied Japan of vital resources, ultimately requiring their own planes to resort to kamikaze, that is commit suicide, a tactic of the militarily weak—processes that began a year before the war's end. (see **Hiroshima**) Which brings up another "first-hand" note, this regarding MacArthur and our aerial bombing. As Supreme Commander, he could poke into bombing plans. As noted under **Cold War**, when our bomb group was flying out of the Philippines, we received a telegraphic order from MacArthur (which I saw): "Burn Taegu to the ground." Taegu was the second largest city in Formosa (now Taiwan), then a Japanese colony. We did what we were told, but we were "burning" mostly civilians— long-standing victims of Japanese colonization. Taegu was a precursor of fire-bombed Dresden and Tokyo—and of **Hiroshima/ Nagasaki**.

After his triumphs against Japan, and while ruling over the Occupation, MacArthur became Commander-in-Chief of the U.S. organized UN forces in **Korea**. There, praised to the skies for his "old strategic skills" (PALMER), he did himself in. He was dead set on having the USA bomb Manchuria and launch a full-scale ground and aerial war against China. President **Truman** was no angel, but sometimes he could see <u>utter</u> folly when it stared him in the face—especially when, as had become clear, it was a man with presidential ambitions who continued to propose war with China after told by Truman to shut up. So he was brought home in the spring of 1951 in what might be seen as disgrace. Not MacArthur; he was given a hero's welcoming parade <u>and</u> a rousing welcome by the Congress, wherein he made a speech that was a pitch for the presidency. Polls showed that despite—or because?—of all, he was still immensely popular with the public; nonetheless, the GOP pros gave him the cold shoulder. They had a different general in mind: Ike. After all, MacArthur was bogged down in an ugly war; Ike had <u>won</u> "the good war." (TERKEL, 1984)

Justice was never done, but at least MacArthur was finally disempowered. He died in 1962, followed by many sentimental tributes to a great hero.

maquiladoras (see free trade, globalization)

Marshall Plan

General George Marshall had a very long military career, from World War I through World War II; for the latter he was Chief of Staff of the U.S. Army. After being sent to China in 1946 to try, futilely, to end its civil war, in 1947 he became Truman's Secretary of State. In that same year at a Harvard commencement he gave the speech outlining his proposal for what became the Marshall Plan and the European Recovery Program (in 1948).

As noted under **Cold War**, all of Europe had been devastated by what for them was a six-year war: 60 million dead, three times that number wounded, countless millions displaced, jobless, homeless, desperate; <u>all</u> the economies of Europe were flat on their backs, their transportation systems broken, their factories bombed out or feeble from overuse, their agriculture in dire straits.

Put all that together and the result was not only a human catastrophe, but one that contained in it a set of political threats unmatched in history. Threats to whom, to what?

The answer to those questions has many dimensions, all circling around one set of realities: The prewar socioeconomic system and its leaders—who else?—had created or allowed the conditions that had taken Western Europe to calamitous wars twice in 25 years. Now, in the chaos of postwar Europe, they and what they stood for were unlikely to be able or trusted to take their nations out of such a deep and broad socioeconomic crisis.

As discussed at length under **Cold War** and **USSR**, the threat facing Europe was not a military invasion by the Soviet Union, but an effective acceptance of the need to work toward a new and different socioeconomic system—ranging from social democracy through socialism to communism, depending upon each nation's conditions.

Recognition of the looming crisis emerged as early as 1943, with UNRRA (the United Nations Relief and Rehabilitation Administration) before there <u>was</u> a United Nations—which, when created in 1945, may be seen as an outgrowth of the UNRRA. Its "relief and rehabilitation" efforts began in 1943 and extended up to 1949, spending up to $600 million (most of it provided by the USA) to relieve starvation in Italy, Greece, Poland, Yugoslavia and Albania as war receded; and then seeking to aid in reconstruction of industrial and agricultural facilities.

Such steps were vital stopgaps against sheer catastrophe; but if Europe was to become politically stable and, more to the point for the USA, to resume its role in the capitalist world economy, more was necessary. Some of that "more" was begun by the USA in 1943-44 with the creation of the **IMF/IBRD**; but they were neither designed nor able to deal with Europe's crisis.

The Marshall Plan was meant to bring the Western European economy (including Greece and Turkey) back to life by financing the building and rebuilding of productive capacities in industry and agriculture. Once begun, it was administered through the Economic Cooperation Administration (ECA). Over its life, 1948-1952, the USA provided $17 billion of financial aid; over 70 percent of that amount was spent on U.S. goods.

The program was sold to a reluctant Congress as "a means of rolling back the tide of Communism." For the people of the USA, still full of good spirit from the recently-ended "good war," the Plan was sold as U.S. generosity to people in need, the milk of human kindness. Maybe so; if so, it was skim milk.

A closer look suggests that it was more **oil** than milk. The most astute study of the oil industry in the post-World War II world summarized the relationships of oil to the Plan thus:

> Since war-torn Europe and Japan were heavily dependent upon U.S. assistance for reconstruction, the /U.S./ oil companies and the U.S. government used this opportunity to virtually ram American-controlled oil down the throats of the world to replace coal. Thus Walter Levy, head of the Marshall Plan's oil division, and previously an economist for Mobil, noted in 1949 that "without the ECA, American oil business in Europe would already have been shot to pieces" and commented that "ECA does not believe that Europe should save dollars... by driving American oil from the European market." /More than 15 percent/ of total Marshall Plan assistance... was for oil imports, while the Plan blocked projects for European crude oil production, and helped American oil companies to gain control of Europe's refineries. (TANZER, 1974)

The Marshall Plan was neither only nor mainly economic in intent: it is generally agreed that Congress gave its support in the name of "rolling back Communism": Within a year the North Atlantic Treaty Organization (NATO) was in existence. Soon it became apparent that to become a beneficiary of the Marshall Plan also meant to become a member of NATO, the military alliance.

When the Plan was first announced and all European nations were invited to join, the Soviet Union—the most devastated of all the European nations by the war—applied. After much haggling, they were made unwelcome. In that NATO was the exact military counterpart of the Marshall plan, and aimed at the Soviet Union, it would have been odd had they been allowed in. (BLOCK)

In sum, the Marshall Plan, which looked like something good and, up to a point, was, could have been much better; in any case, it turned out to be an important part of something really bad: the **Cold War**.

McCarthy, Joe/McCarthyism

When World War II ended there was an eruption of joy and good feeling in the USA whose nature is almost incomprehensible in the fearful and spiteful present. Innumerable street parties celebrated the end of a very long and destructive war; but more than that was in the air, and remained there. For a while.

Not just relief, but good feeling toward others was in that air, "others" both at home and elsewhere. There would be "war no more"; there would be "one world" of peace and plenty for all, somehow—with the abundant help of the one remaining rich power in the world. During the war we had all been "in the same boat"; we still are, will always be. Sounds almost icky today, no?

Slowly but surely and then always faster the atmosphere changed; more to the point, it was <u>changed</u>—by the newly-created foreign policy dubbed **Cold War,** its economic blood brother **military Keynesianism**, and the toxic domestic policy that came to be called McCarthyism: militarism, jobs, and repression marching hand in hand, a potent force hard to beat (ZINN, 1973, 2000)

Senator Joe McCarthy died of cirrhosis of the liver in 1957 but his spirit lives on; in one variation or another McCarth<u>yism</u> endured well beyond his death, now in the form of "anti-terrorism." McCarthy—a liar, a drunk, and a brute—became for a terrible moment the most powerful man in the USA, leaving behind a macabre legacy of loyalty oaths, political firings, congressional and state legislative investigating committees and resulting prison sentences, some suicides and, among other tragedies, executions (see **Rosenbergs**; NAVASKY)

How could that happen in the land of the free and the home of the brave? If it could happen once, could it happen again? It is now; this is how it happened then.

Joe McCarthy was first elected to the U.S. Senate in 1946, from Wisconsin. He was politically without experience and, at first, unknown. He became effectively "popular" with two issues: An imagined military experience as "Tail Gunner Joe" (which he had not been) and—he was "one-fourth German"—this appeal to the large German population of Wisconsin: "The Holocaust never happened." (MORISON; ROVERE) Clever guy, Joe.

The Senate term is six years. Thus, in 1950, Joe had to think about the election of 1952. Cynic that Joe was, so were his advisers. By 1950, the Cold War was well under way; Joe's advisers proposed that he begin to pound away on "Communists in the **Truman** White House." It is testimony to just how much mind damage the Cold

War had already accomplished that such a ludicrous charge could even be made, let alone "sell." (GRIFFITH)

Joe began to sell it as follows: "During twenty years of treason," he said, **FDR** and Truman had "conspired" to deliver America to the Reds. His proof was given at a talk in West Virginia:

> I have here in my hand a list of 205 /employees/ that were made known to the Secretary of State /Dean Acheson, of Wall St. fame/ as being members of the Communist Party and who nevertheless are still working and shaping policy. (FREELAND)

It mattered not then, and evidently it matters not still, that <u>no</u> person on that list—which over time and under questioning became shorter and shorter—was ever in fact <u>named</u>, let alone shown to be "guilty."

However, what matters a great deal is that our society was being changed in such fashion that an irresponsible brute such as he could gain enormous and intimidating power simply by climbing a ladder made of innuendo, lies, and threats.

Joe was brought down by his own stupidity when in 1954, always on the hunt for new targets, he goofed by accusing the U.S. Army of harboring Communists at the very highest levels. Its spine stiffened by an outraged Pentagon, the U.S. Senate in 1954 voted to criticize McCarthy for "bringing dishonor and disrepute" to that august body—something like carrying coals to Newcastle, it was remarked at the time.

So McCarthy was "censured." Even then, whether from fear of Joe or of the already large percentage of our people who had gone along with him, 22 Senators voted against censure. Can't be too careful.

Having been re-elected in 1952, Joe still had four years to go in the Senate. He didn't last; his always heavy drinking got heavier, and his liver brought him down in 1957, largely unlamented.

However, both during and after his death, the consequences of McCarthyism took on a life of their own: in the universities, in Hollywood, in Congress, in trade unions, in the media, in our hearts and minds. (ZAAROULIS/SULLIVAN).

I had started my teaching career in 1950 as a Lecturer at the University of California (Berkeley), where McCarthyism had a precocious takeoff. In that year, the first loyalty oath in the country was initiated by the U.C. Regents (the board of control). Everyone on the payroll—profs, teaching assistants, janitors, clerks—had to sign an oath stating "I am not now, nor have I ever been, a member of the Communist Party of the United States."

There was a great outcry against with about the same degree of acquiescence and a large middle of indifference. The Faculty Senate met to discuss it. As head of the junior faculty group fighting the oath I was allowed to be present (if I kept my mouth shut.) Robert A. BRADY, who had written what is still the best book on German fascism, proposed a strike, giving good reasons. Loud acclaim. However, when a pad was passed for signatures another prof said it was dangerous to sign that: "What are we signing?" In the ensuing angels on the head of a pin professorial debate the strike was abandoned.

The Governor of California then was Earl Warren. With his support, the State Supreme Court later ruled the oath unconstitutional; soon after a referendum to change the constitution was put on the ballot. It passed 2 to 1; bad enough.

But even worse, the oath was now for all state employees, not just those at the university. Soon after, I accepted a job at Cornell. When I arrived the chair said he was sorry to inform me that the N.Y. legislature had just passed a loyalty oath requirement. You can run but you can't hide.

Also this: While I was still at Berkeley, there was a California State Un-American Activities Committee, with its own hearings and, as well, an annual booklet containing a list of the leading Communists in California. Number 1 on the list was a good friend of mine, a local radio broadcaster for the waterfront union (ILWU); I was listed as Number 2. My friend and I were both somewhere left of center, with two other characteristics in common: 1. In our frequent personal discussions we privately agreed that the CP was wrong-headed on many issues. 2. Both of us refused to join any anti-Communist hullabaloo. Countless others, fearing loss of jobs, or worse, did join it.

McCarthyism was a snowball rolling down the hill; it did so faster and faster when the elections of 1952 turned control over the Senate to the GOP. Joe was then made chair of the Senate investigations committee. It had held only six executive (or closed) sessions in 1942; with Joe in charge that leapt up to 117, and it was more than a quantitative jump.

The transcripts of those secret hearings were sealed in the National Archives until 2001; in May of 2003 they were made public. The Senate's historian in charge of the documents spent the intervening two years reviewing what became five volumes. This was his comment to the press:

> You get to watch McCarthy trying to build his case. He's convinced he's going to find subversion and espionage. He just has to keep digging far enough. (NYT, "Transcripts Detail Secret Questioning....," 5-06-03)

Sounds like Rumsfeld et al. as they search for the fabled "weapons of mass destruction" in **Iraq**. The snowball that McCarthy helped to roll down the hill is once again picking up speed, helped along by 9/11 and Iraq. It has not yet reached its bottom. Although for many years the universities have been anything but hotbeds for dissent, even the beginnings of some revival regarding **globalization** and Iraq have led to heavy pressures being brought to stifle it. (see **Bush II... Ashcroft, terrorism**). Our sordid experience with McCarthyism should be a warning; let these bums have an inch and they'll go the whole way.

Congratulations, Joe.

media

When George ORWELL (1903-1950) wrote <u>1984</u> his focus was on the social shaping and pollution of what during the **Vietnam** war came to be called "hearts and minds." His main concerns were "doublethink" and "doublespeak." Reviewers tended to see the book as a critical satire whose target was the Soviet Union. That <u>was</u> one of his targets but it was not his main concern.

Orwell was a passionate believer in freedom and full-fledged democracy; he backed those beliefs by fighting against the fascists in Spain (<u>Homage to Catalonia</u>, 1938/1962), with <u>Animal Farm</u> (1946), and with <u>1984</u> (1949/2003.)

The latter two books were prompted by Europe's recent and ongoing totalitarian states, but also by tendencies in the official democracies (including his native Britain); he saw them as edging heedlessly toward thought control. Orwell never showed explicit concern with the USA; but the **Cold War** and its running mate

McCarthyism, which began to flourish just as Orwell died, fitted his concerns all too well.

So, what is "doublethink"? Early in the book we come to know Winston Smith (the book's "hero") as

> his mind slid away into the labyrinthine world of double-think. To know and not to know, to be conscious of complete truthfulness while telling carefully constructed lies, to hold simultaneously two opinions which cancelled out, knowing them to be contradictory and believing in both of them, to use logic against logic, to repudiate morality while laying claim to it, to believe that democracy was impossible and that the Party was the guardian of democracy, to forget whatever it was necessary to forget, then to draw it back into memory again at the moment when it was needed, and then promptly to forget it again, and above all, to apply the same process to the process itself—that was the ultimate subtlety: consciously to induce unconsciousness, and then, once again, to become unconscious of the act of hypnosis you had just performed. Even to under-stand the word "doublethink" involved use of doublethink.

Doublethink and doublespeak in their setting of "Oceania" are partially represented by the titles of its main "Ministries": Peace, Truth, and Love. Their functions are diammetrically opposite to their names. But, as Thomas Pynchon points out in his Foreword to the 2003 "Centennial Edition" honoring Orwell,

> If all this seems unreasonably perverse, recall that in the present-day United States, few have any problem with a war-making apparatus named "Department of Defense," /changed in 1947 from Department of War/ any more than we have saying "Department of Justice" with a straight face, despite well-docu-mented abuses of human and constitutional rights by its most formidable arm, the **FBI** /before Attorney General Ashcroft/. Our nominally free news media are required to present "bal-anced" coverage.... Every day public opinion is the target of rewritten history, official amnesia and outright lying, all of which is benevolently termed "**spin,**" as if it were no more harm-ful than a ride on the merry-go-round. We know better than they tell us, yet hope otherwise. We believe and doubt at the same time—it seems a condition of political thought in a mod-ern superstate to be permanently of at least two minds on most issues...; of inestimable use to those in power who wish to remain there. (ORWELL /1949/ 2003/, **bold** added)

The "doublethink" that now blends with the "doublespeak"

and "nonthink" that have spread and deepened over the past century are not products merely of the media (defined as newspapers, magazines, radio, **TV**, and film); our **education** in those arts begins as informal education begins: at our parents' knees, as theirs did, at home; in kindergarten through high school and college; in the office, the factory, the playing fields; from politicians; all of it shuffled and ingeniously reshuffled by the media.

The socialization process is a many-headed thing. In that process the media have become always more powerful and intrusive in all realms of life—considerably more so than Orwell feared, for they have used the techniques of **advertising** rather than jackboots and whips.

A ruthless "Party" was the root source of Orwell's totalitarian society; such a "Party" and its accompanying means of punishment are no longer necessary (which does not mean they will never be used): Doublethink/speak is the polluted social air we breathe, daily and "freely," as we as we are conveyed toward an effectively totalitarian society by an effectively one-party system, both in sheep's clothing—with us, however, as the sheep.

If all this were a humorous, the cream of the jest in the USA would be that as we have moved from **LBJ**'s "Great Society" to **Reagan**'s "Supply-Side Economics," to Clinton's "It's the bond market, stupid!", to **Bush II**'s "compassionate conservatism," we have complimented ourselves on being the most democratic society of all time. The media are not the only source of that evolution; but it couldn't have been done without them.

In their several components the media perform three overlapping social functions: entertainment, information, and advertising. The content and intent of what we see and hear serve the ends of the media's business and political clients; the means are devised by the experienced "mind managers" (SCHILLER /1973/) of the overlapping advertising and public relations worlds.

All these elements intermingle and interact—business with politics, profits with power, form with content; in doing so, they have provided a new word to our vocabulary: "infotainment." (BARBER)

An amusing word, that; but fearsome in its consequences. To assist in comprehending those consequences and their reasons, what follows will examine 1) how the media came to be what they are, 2) what they have helped to bring about, and 3) their present structures of ownership and control.

Each of these is in itself a bundle of complexities. They began to become a noticeable problem in the USA about a century ago, leading to Upton SINCLAIR's scathing attack on newspaper corruption, The Brass Check (1920). But the major analytical developments for this realm occurred with the brash potency displayed by the media in the early Cold War years—well-noted by I.F. STONE's Hidden History of the Korean War (1952) and his later collection of essays, Time of Torment (1967), and by LIEBLING's The Press (1961), CIRINO's Don't Blame the People, (1971), ARONSON's The Press and the Cold War (1970), ENSENZBERGER's The Consciousness Industry, and the first of several powerful studies by the late Herbert SCHILLER, beginning with his Mass Communications and American Empire (1971).

Because of the overriding importance of the media in our time, and in addition to the books above and yet to be noted in the text, at the end of this essay I append a list of references on other important books. All may be seen as "required reading" for those who recognize the need to grapple seriously with this ominous development. Now to its three main elements.

1. A brief history. A century ago the word "media" as now understood was not used; had it been, it would have referred only to newspapers and magazines. Newspapers were influential in the political realm on the local and regional level, but considerably less so for national issues; magazines were only influential in limited circles, mostly in matters of taste and culture. It was they, however, who gave birth to the modest beginnings of modern advertising.

The first significant jump in the USA toward the modern media took place as World War I was edging over the horizon, both because of its technology and its lift to incomes. In those same years **cars** became a consumer product (as distinct from a rich man's toy or a farmer's tool), and silent films opened the gate toward what would become Hollywood. Cars led to billboards before the war; after it cars, cigarettes, and soap were the major stimuli for really modern advertising—that is, the advertising that "teaches people to want what they don't need, and not to want what they do." (BARAN, 1969)

Radio was critical in those developments; as with so many other technological jumps, it was born as a military product; it became a consumer product in the early 1920s. By the end of that decade and through the 1930s, the impact of radio on public tastes and attitudes—whether frivolous or serious—became always more substantial; but in comparison with the monster TV has become, radio was a pygmy. (Note: TV was invented in the 1920s, but could not become a commercial product until the 1950s—when incomes had risen sufficiently to provide its mass market.)

More recently, the computer has come to be a member of the media, used as it is for both information, advertising, entertainment—and politics. In short, the media world has been utterly transformed in the past century, and at an always accelerating rate: What had only slightly influenced the average person's life in 1900 had in a real sense come to dominate social existence by 2000.

"Dominate" has been used pointedly; the media are no longer "products" but shaping forces in society. The evolution toward their present role was not, it may be said, intentional from the beginning. In recent years, however, it needs saying that it is becoming so—has in many instances already become so.

2. What the media have done to us. As one who was a boy in the 1920s and was eligible for the draft by 1940, I am struck by the sea change in the role of the media today, as compared with the pre-World War II years.

Even as late as the 1950s, when TV began to be common by comparison with today, the media were merely a now and then "presence"; today they are "in our face." Whether we are conscious of it or not, and mostly we are not, there are few indeed of our thoughts, our feelings, our inclinations, our behavior patterns which, for the young and not so young are not shaped or directed in significant degree by the media.

Business knows that, politicians know it; most of us know it. Yet almost all who know it also "make believe" that what is true is not; that what is not true, is: doublethink.

In a recent essay—"The Numbing of the Mind"—the author put it in a nutshell:

> Our minds are the product of a total immersion in a daily experience saturated with fabrications to a degree unprecedented in human history. People have never had to cope with so much stuff, so many choices in kind and number. (DE ZENGOTITA)

The process is what CHOMSKY & HERMAN called "manufacturing consent." It is not difficult to find instances of these phenomena; quite the opposite. Because what is happening in the **Bush
II** administration is so worrisome, here we take our examples from
its manipulative media tactics, beginning with three episodes: 1) at
Mount Rushmore, 2) at the Statue of Liberty, and 3) on the carrier
Abraham Lincoln. All three were discussed in an excellent (and
scary) article by Elisabeth Bumiller (<u>NYT</u>, 5-16-03), "Keepers of the
Bush Image Lift Stagecraft to New Heights.") What follows are
direct quotes:

1.   The White House positioned the best platform for the TV
     crews off to one side, not head on as other White Houses
     have done, so that the cameras caught Mr. Bush in profile,
     his face perfectly aligned with the four presidents carved in
     stone.

2.   The White House rented three barges of giant Musco lights,
     the kind used to illuminate sports stadiums and rock con-
     certs, sent them across New York Harbor, tethered them in
     the water around the base of the Statue of Liberty and then
     blasted them upward to illuminate all 305 feet of America's
     symbol of freedom. It was the ultimate patriotic backdrop for
     Mr. Bush, who spoke from Ellis Island.

3.   Mr. Bush's speech aboard the Abraham Lincoln announcing
     the end of major combat in Iraq /was/ the most elaborate
     event... White House officials say that a variety of people,
     including the president, came up with the idea, and that Mr.
     Sforza /the director/ embedded himself on the carrier to make
     preparations days before Mr. Bush's landing in a flight suit....
     Mr. Sforza and his aides choreographed every aspect of the
     event, even down to the members of the Lincoln crew
     arrayed in coordinated shirt colors over Mr. Bush's right
     shoulder and the "Mission Accomplished" banner placed to
     perfectly capture the president and the celebratory words in
     a single shot....

Although the <u>NYT</u> reporter was courageous enough to note
that the carrier was only a few miles off shore and thus easily accessible by helicopter, she and/or her editors were too polite to note
that not only was Bush II wildly over-equipped for a few minutes'
flight, but that his crotch bulged out as though he were Sylvester

Stallone. Go, man. Go.

If ever there were instances of doublethink, those and what followed must be among them. There cannot be many who watched those TV appearances who did not <u>know</u> or sense that they were being beguiled—make that deceived—by "staging" accomplished by highly-paid experts from the ad agencies and Hollywood—Mr. Sforza the most notable among them. What they may not have noted is that we, with our **taxes**, paid for these cunning deceptions: "The President's image makers... work within a budget for White House travel and events allotted by Congress; for fiscal 2003 it was $3.7 million." (ibid.)

After each such event, the polls have shown a significant rise in Bush's popularity. As P.T. Barnum said more than a century ago, "There's a sucker born every minute." He had it right for his time; nowadays innumerable suckers are <u>created</u> every nanosecond.

All that is important, but is a small part of the larger problem constituted by the pervasive and deep-seated **corruption** of the media. It has always been thus in some degree, of course (see SINCLAIR's <u>Brass Check</u> of a century ago); after all, newspapers, radio, and TV depend for their profits upon satisfying their advertising clients, upon whose toes they will seek not to step. Bidness is bidness, as they say in Texas.

But the differences between, say, newspapers a century ago and themselves and the media as a whole today are not merely those of degree; there has been a shift in kind. In turn, that is not "simply" a matter of money from advertisers; the big media companies and **big business** dine at the same table. (I was going to say they eat at the same trough, but that would be rude.) As will be seen below, not least among the reasons for those shared interests is that many of the media giants also own and control, or are owned and controlled by, non-media giants: **GE**, a pioneer in using its economic strength to gain non-economic power, was also the first to take that giant step when, in 1986, the **Reagan** administration made legal what had been illegal.

Given the business roots of the media, it is not surprising that they are—putting it politely—"cautious" in their presentation of controversial subjects that touch upon business interests; in addition, they (like almost all others) tend to be "naturally" **nationalistic**. Since the inception of the **Cold War** and **McCarthyism**, that natural tendency has led them (like almost all others) to be more hesitant than ever about criticizing U.S. aggressive policies abroad or repressive policies at home. The more aggressive and repressive such policies become, the greater the hesitancy—to say nothing of the numerous media owners who are enthusiastic supporters of such policies, and help to feed them.

Yet, you may have noted that a good share of the critical information found in this work has come from that selfsame media—most frequently from the New York Times. Does that contradict the foregoing assertions? Yes and no.

The NYT, the most influential of all U.S. newspapers and seen as our newspaper of record, is an "exception that proves the rule," with only a handful of others coming close: the Los Angeles Times and the Washington Post and the Boston Globe, perhaps the San Francisco Chronicle and the St. Louis Post Dispatch, and... I hope there are others. Taken together they—plus a small number of local papers with restricted readership—reach a very small percentage of all readers: cautiously and politely. (MCCHESNEY/FOSTER; ALTERMAN)

Momentarily setting aside the largest problem of the media, that which centers upon TV, the manner in which even the best newspapers curtsey to the powerful is subtle, rather than manifest; not always, but too often, it is done so as to permit them to believe they have indeed printed "All the News That's Fit to Print" (the NYT's claim for itself).

The problem arises as to who defines "fit." Commenting on a much-publicized firing by the NYT of a reporter for numerous minor falsifications, Edward HERMAN, in "Little Versus Big Lies (and Structures of Lies)," states the problem succinctly:

> But the New York Times itself, both as a media institution and the product that is delivered in its name on a daily basis, is built and thrives on structures of disinformation and selective information that constitute Big Lies. These structures do involve occasional direct lies, but far more important is their base in the conduiting of lies issued by official sources, lies by implication, and lies that are institutionalized by repetition and the refusal to admit contradictory evidence. It is possible to institutionalize a very big lie without actually telling a direct lie, although one can usually find them represented as well. (Z-Commentary, 5-19-03. Emphasis added.)

There are so many instances of this it is difficult to know where to begin—except, most recently, with **Iraq** and the elusive "weapons of mass destruction" that were said to be our <u>casus belli</u>. The list is very long; in his essay, HERMAN selects the Cold War era shooting of the Pope which, we were told over and over again by the **CIA** was done by the KGB and/or the Bulgarians—even though, <u>after</u> the **USSR** dissolved, a CIA official testified to Congress that the CIA <u>knew</u> that was a lie. Herman also notes the endless lies about the USSR's military capabilities (whether in the **JFK**, or **Reagan** years); and the decade of thoroughly "institutionalized lies" about why we were in **Vietnam** and what was happening there ("light at the end of the tunnel")...and so on,

> <u>Newsflash</u>: To its credit—at last—on its editorial page (5-26-04) the <u>NYT</u>, with its "The Times and Iraq," took a small bite of humble pie: "...we have found a number of instances of coverage that was not as rigorous as it should have been"; and promised "agressive reporting aimed at setting the record straight." Better late than never. Better still would have been a 5-course dinner of <u>mea culpa</u> with all the trimmings. Still, in today's media world, unless we do something to change it, we get what we pay for. And who knows? Maybe now that our good grey newspaper of record has 'fessed up to the 24/7 slanted news coming from on high, perhaps it will join the many who have known that for a <u>very</u> long time? And... what? Put CHOMSKY, HERMAN, MCCHESNEY, CONASON, Molly IVINS, and Michael MOORE on their payroll?

The foregoing focus has been on the <u>NYT</u>. All that said, given the dangerously deplorable state of most other newspapers, of TV—where most get their "information"—and the rest of media, the <u>Times</u> and the few others mentioned serve a vital function. Beggars can't be choosers. Indeed, given the latest development in military reporting, the news on the wars we probably face in the future will make some of that on Iraq and earlier seem worthy of the Nobel Peace Prize. That latest development is **embedding**—which see. Would that it were the beginning and the end of the media's "bending on knee." (HERTSGAARD) The problems of our time, in and outside of the USA, surely include U.S. aggression abroad and repression at home, but they are only the most dramatic of many other problems—also at home and abroad, from **health care** to **globalization**.

Only one set of examples: In August of 2002, the <u>San Francisco Bay Guardian</u> (a free and often reliable/ scurrilous paper), under the heading <u>CENSORED!</u> Listed 20 "big stories the mainstream media ignored in 2001." They ranged from important **privatization** policies and the revival of **nukes** being pushed in Washington to the harms done by **NAFTA** to a national housing crisis. Clearly the <u>Guardian</u> would have been unable to have written those 20 stories without sources; those and their documentation are provided, but they are not easily accessible to the average newspaper reader—who, to make matters worse, has been socialized in our darkened living rooms <u>not</u> to seek such information.

The reference, of course, is to the boob tube. **TV**'s importance is such that it has its own essay in this work; suffice it here to note that average adults watch TV an average of 4 hours a day, and their children watch it for 6 hours. If or when the news is watched, it comes in sound bites or as "infotainment" rather than substantial and informative statements, except—sometimes—on PBS. (BAGDIKIAN, POSTMAN)

That leaves a momentous task for even the most searching and uninhibited of newspapers, magazines, and books to fulfill as the sources for understanding what's going on. The "momentousness" of that task slides into irrelevancy, however, once we recognize that those who own and control the media are always fewer in numbers and that those few are proportionately huge in power. To that power we now turn.

3. <u>The Consciousness Industry</u>. The media "industry" with which Ensenzberger was concerned, like <u>all</u> of modern industry, is mostly owned and virtually controlled by a few big giants; not <u>every</u> newspaper, radio or TV station, just yet; but <u>most</u> of them. As pointed out by HERMAN/MCCHESNEY, already by 1997, the media world was presided over by

> ten or so integrated media conglomerates, most of which are based in the United States ...; /along/ with another thirty or forty supporting firms.... They compete vigorously on a non-price basis, but their competition is softened not only by common interests..., but also by a vast array of joint ventures, strategic alliances, and cross-ownership... /with their/ financial underpinnings in advertising and its thoroughgoing commercialism.

The five largest of these giants in 1997 were, in order, Time

Warner /Now AOL Time Warner/, Disney, Bertelsmann, Viacom, and News Corporation. Among the others control emanates from <u>outside</u> the media, as with Sony, Seagram, and **GE**.

The major honcho in media **mergers and acquisitions (M&As)** of the past 20 years or so has been Rupert Murdoch (News Corporation/Fox). He tersely expressed what underlies the structures and processes of today's concentrated ownership (as quoted in <u>BW</u>, 3-25-96): "We can join forces now, or we can kill each other and then join forces." They decided to join forces. Caution: this will make you dizzy:

> All six major broadcast networks are owned mostly by giant media companies... GE bought NBC... right after Disney failed in a bid to do the same thing. Ten years later Disney got its network when it bought Capital Cities, which then owned ABC..., the same year Westinghouse bought CBS..., and that UPN was begun by United Television/Chris-Craft Industries and Paramount Television/Viacom. Four years later... after some other media mergers, Vicaom bought CBS. That means Viacom owns CBS and UPN. As for the remaining networks, Fox, which is owned by Rupert Murdoch's News Corp, was started in 1986 the product of a media conglomerate, and the WB, begun in 1995, is owned by Warner Bros. (HERMAN/MCCHESNEY)

Advertising has always been central for both the birth and the strengthening of the media, and becomes always more so. As might be expected in the era of giant this and giant that, advertising too is now dominated by 500 or so global giants (**TNCs**).

> It is TNC advertising that has fueled the rise of commercial television across the world, accounting, for example, for over one-half the advertising on the ABN-CNBC Asia network, which is co-owned by Dow Jones and General Electric... In 1999, the United States still accounted for nearly one-half of the world's... advertising. Even in the developed markets of western Europe most nations still spend no more than one-half the U.S. amount on advertising per capita and /its/ 2.1 to 2.4 percent of GDP going toward advertising... /But/ European commercial television is growing at more than a 10 percent annual rate, twice the U.S. average. (MCCHESNEY, 1999)

McChesney goes on to point out that "the top ten global advertisers /Nike, Procter & Gamble, **GM**, **Phillip Morris**, et al./ alone accounted for 75 percent of the $36 billion spend by the one hundred largest global marketeers in 1997."

Bigness had become characteristic of the media before World War II, but the NBC's and <u>NYT</u>'s (et al.) of that era were teensy compared with what began to take hold after the war in the various realms of the media. The decades from 1950 to the present must be divided into three chunks: from 1950 up to the 1980s, from then until yesterday, and what is emerging now.

As with other sectors of the economy long regulated by the state and federal authorities, such as utilities and finance, so it was with the realm of what we now call... what? Let's call if **infotainment**.

As noted under **big business**, in recent decades the boundaries both within and between industries, sectors, and nations have become muddied; that has been true for the media, as well. Once upon a time, though, before the 1970s ended, there were quaint rules whose aim was to prevent centralized control over the sources and dissemination of "infotainment." For example:

> From 1953 into the Reagan years ownership limits were fixed by the 7-7-7 rule (7 AM, 7 FM and 7 TV stations per owner), and cross-ownership of newspapers and broadcasting stations within the same market was barred (although over a hundred exceptions were grandfathered). These limits were raised to 12-12-12 in 1985, with TV station owners allowed to reach up to 25 percent of the national population. The ownership limits for radio were raised to 24-24-24 in 1992 and owners were given the right to acquire multiple stations in each market. The 1996 Telecommunications Reform Act removed the national ceiling on radio station ownership and allowed as many as eight stations to be acquired by a single owner in the largest market. The ceiling on TV ownership was raised to allow a single owner to reach 35 percent of the national audience. (HERMAN, 1999

To some of us old-fashioned folks, 7-7-7 sounds like a lot, and 12-12-12 like a lot too much. But the greed for profits and power has no bottom; the foregoing shows they know how to get what they want—which is: MORE. Does what they already have gotten sound ominous? Before long it will sound like widely-dispersed ownership and wide-open competition. These were the good old days.

Already humongous companies can't wait to get more so. They have been salivating since the 1950s, taking every available opportunity to pile up money both from making the mergers and operating them—while lobbying to get rid of remaining constraints. The FCC ruling of June 2, 2002 gives them what they want. Hang on to your hats.

GE's first giant step in buying NBC in 1986 was a regression from the 1967 decision that prevented International Telephone and Telegraph from buying ABC on grounds of serious potential conflict of interest between ITT's international business interests and the objective performance of the media.

After that it was anything goes, where the anythings included the creation of media conglomerates such as AOL Time Warner, News Corporation, and Disney—with their simultaneous ownership of book publishing, magazines, TV show production, stations, cable, and networks, and movie production and amusement parks. (MCCHESNEY, 1999)

With the FCC decision of June, 2003, from now on it will be everything goes:

Item: "New Rules Give Big Media Chance to Get Even Bigger":

> As consumer advocates deplored yesterday's changes to media ownership rules as a blow to democracy, investors bought up shares of the biggest media companies. Both advocates and investors agree that the latest rule changes are likely to let media leviathans like /Murdoch's/ News Corporation and Viacom fortify their positions while increasing the odds against newcomers and small fry. (NYT, 6-4-03)

How come? The answer for the media is the same as that for the rest of the economy, whether as regards **pharmaceuticals** or **military expenditures**: In what has become our bought-and-paid-for democracy, political candidates have become almost entirely beholden to **campaign finance** (with strings attached, of course); once in office, they are besieged, bothered and, if good little boys and girls, rewarded by **lobbyists**. Which is what happened with the FCC switch. The Independent Center for Public Integrity

> examined the travel records of FCC employees and found that over the last eight years, commissioners and staff members have taken 2,500 trips costing $2.8 million that were "primarily" paid for by members of the telecommunications and broadcast industries.... "The top destination was Las Vegas, with 330 trips..." /with many others for New York, New Orleans, San

Francisco, Palm Spring, Buenos Aires.... (NYT, Op-ed, "Cozy
With the F.C.C.," 6-5-03)

Lots of communications to worry about in Las Vegas.... But
that's only part of the story. The FCC presumbly represents the
People; however, the Center

> reported that there were more than 70 closed-door meet-
> ings in recent months with FCC officials and representatives of
> the nation's top broadcasters /mostly with CEOs/, to discuss the
> relaxation of media ownership restrictions. /But/ the two major
> groups that represented the public... Consumers Union and the
> Media Access Project... met just five times with the FCC. (ibid)

The NYT piece closes with this report: "... a survey of 500,000
comments of the FCC web site showed that more than 97 percent
"were opposed to the new rules." Hey! Don't we have to pay attention to that other three percent? Isn't that what democracy is all
about? (my emphasis)

OK already; what's to worry? Everyone knows the media are
"liberal," no? So they say, but.... It's a very big but, enough to make
one die laughing. Indeed a few newspapers and magazines, and some
public radio and TV stations are, by comparison with the other 95
percent, relatively honest and, some, well-intentioned. As suggested
earlier, however, even they are more often than not purveying the
conventional wisdom and giving short shrift. As an example, I give
the best possible example to support the Myth of the Liberal Media
(HERMAN's 1999 book): Public TV. The best is none too good:

I rarely miss the Jim Lehrer News Hour, although I try to shut
my eyes and ears at the "announcements" of their big sponsors—not
least **Archer Daniels Midland**, the giant agribusiness whose main
business is pushing up prices (while claiming to feed the world's
poor). The News Hour at least takes a strong pass at presenting more
than sound bites and cheap drama. But when a major issue is under
discussion, and a "roundtable" of 2-4 is organized, almost invariably
there will be two conservatives and one reactionary and, maybe, one
liberal—whether the issue is health care, taxes, Iraq..., whatever.

There is a discussion, and it is not as vulgarly one-sided as on
other shows, or a mere shouting match. But only rarely is a seriously dissenting voice heard, and even then it barely gets a tenth of the
time. And PBS is the best available on the national level.

There is much much more to say on that on other matters concerning the media (and everything else); on the "liberal" issue, see HERMAN (1999) and the more recent book of Eric ALTERMAN: What Liberal Media?

The troubled hero of Orwell's 1984 was Winston Smith; the villain was represented on the ubiquitous posters stating "Big Brother is Watching YOU."

That was crude stuff; nowadays we are moving toward a situation where WE will be watching Big Brother: homogeneous newscasts, razzmatazz entertainment shows up to their necks in blaring sound, blaring violence, blaring sex, and exquisitely-staged pronouncements of our political leaders.

That will be hard to stop, and impossible to do so without understanding the nature of the problem. The following list is meant to assist in that understanding. All will also be found in the Bibliography), and some have already been noted above:

Ben Bagdikian, The Media Monopoly.
Edward L. Bernays, Public Relations.
Alex Carey, Taking the Risk Out of Democracy.
Noam Chomsky and Edward Herman, Manufacturing Consent: The Political Economy of the Mass Media.
Hans Magnus Ensenzberger, The Consciousness Industry.
Stuart Ewen, Advertising and the Social Roots of the Consumer Culture.
William Greider, Who Will Tell the People?
Edward S. Herman and Robert McChesney, The Global Media: The New Missionaries of Global Capitalism.
Aldous Huxley, Brave New World.
Frank Kofsky, Harry S. Truman and the War Scare of 1948.
Robert McChesney, Rich Media, Poor Democracy: Communication Politics in Dubious Times.
_____, The Problem of the Media: U.S. Communication Politics in the Twenty-First Century.
Neil Postman, Amusing Ourselves to Death: Public Discourse in the Age of Show Business.
Herbert Schiller, The Mind Managers; Communications and Cultural Domination; Culture, Inc.
Larry Tye, The Father of Spin: Edward L. Bernays and the Birth of Public Relations.

mergers and acquisitions (M&As)
(see big business)

Middle East

The term itself is a western conceit; the peoples of that region do not see themselves as "middle" anything; nor does China, which has long seen itself as "the center of the world," see itself as being in "the Far East." Be that as it may, the Middle East has been wracked by conflict, invasions, and manifold disasters since history began, and very probably in the prehistoric era as well. Western civilization as we define the term began in the Middle East; that it did so is testimony to the physical advantages of the region. The people of the area—what became Mesopotamia (now Iraq), and spreading from there—were able not merely to survive, but to produce an economic surplus in addition to survival needs. In turn, that gave rise to the ability for human beings to make technological gains and improve their relationships with nature in always more productive (and destructive) ways: It was in the Middle East that organized militarism, organized religion, and a distinct class system first came into being. Two cheers? (CHILDE)

It was also in the Middle East that the first western empires arose. They did so out of the virtually incessant warfare among and between Phoenicians, Egyptians, Persians, Greeks, Romans, et al. In the medieval era, those were supplanted by the Crusades; and they in turn were supplanted by the Ottoman Empire.

The Ottoman's doom was signaled as the 20th century approached, in consequence of the conflicts arising from the emergence and rise to power of industrial **capitalism** and its close associate **imperialism**.

The conflicts were numerous and ubiquitous, not least in the Middle East; there the main participants were the British, the French, Germans, and the decaying Austro-Hungarian Empire. Each sought to dominate this or that society in the Middle East; conflicts repeated in the most recent of the many layers of violent history, fraught still with religious, political, economic, cultural, and military conflict.

As the most powerful industrial nation in the 19th and in the first years of the 20th century, Britain took most of the prizes in the region. From the time of Marco Polo, the Middle East had been a magnet for control, as the shortest path to China. Britain's campaign to control Egypt and its building of the Suez Canal had that at its center. The UK's ability thus to have a trade route through the Red Sea to South and East Asia placed pressure on the two other main powers, France and Germany, to "catch up."

As the 20th century began, **oil** was becoming <u>the</u> prized resource. Already in 1901, Britain had managed a deal with Persia (now **Iran**) resulting in the Anglo-Persian Oil Company; it was taken over entirely in 1914 by the British. (EVEREST)

By that time, oil was becoming obsessional for all industrial countries because of always rising industrial and private uses. Those developments led squarely to Britain's 1917 invasion of Mesopotamia (**Iraq**) and, as World War II began, its occupation of Persia (**Iran**). Over those same years, France gained control over Syria and Lebanon. (BOWDEN, et al.; PALMER)

As was generally true after World War II, what had been colonies in the Middle East became politically independent in one degree or another. But, and again as was and remains true for almost all ex-colonies, the newly-freed societies were too weak to fend for themselves economically or to achieve political stability without repression. In one way or another, outsiders made their way into positions of control. From the 1950s on that almost always meant the USA, strongest of all by far.

In the medieval and early modern periods, as suggested earlier, the Middle East was prized not for its natural resources but for its sheer location. For the USA after World War II, given that the **USSR** borders the Middle East, strategic location was vital, but it was the mixture of that with the aim of controlling the region's vast **oil** resources that made for our deep and permanent involvement.

As noted in **Israel/Palestine**, both location and oil were vital in accelerating the U.S. entry into that locale in 1948. It is now largely forgotten, but in the first half of the 20th century the USA was seen as the world's leading oil producer; now we are the world's largest importer of oil. How we went so rapidly from world supplier to world buyer is a complicated story, but one element stands out: the means by which oil was taken from the ground.

Everywhere but in the USA the method used for oil extraction is the so-called "unified field." When an area is found to have oil underground, the pumping facilities are designed and placed so as to maximize the flow from a particular field—which is usually measured in many square miles. Not so in the USA: Here 1) the oil field was discovered, 2) the land was sold to the highest bidder(s), 3) the drilling began—with oil wells at least as numerous as the land buyers.

So: whereas in Saudi Arabia, for example, there might be 10 wells in a given area, in Oklahoma there might be as many as 500— each pumping as fast and as much as possible, in order to get the oil out before the other owners. The result was not only overpumping but, for engineering reasons, destructive pumping. Add to that our destructive addiction to **cars**, and the result was just plain crazy, man. (ENGLER, TANZER)

Thus, as U.S. domestic oil reserves have move toward insignificance and oil has become the most precious of resources for both production and consumption, the Middle East's (and Central Asia's) location and oil have fused as the main spur for our foreign policies. (BLAIR, ENGLER, SAMPSON, TANZER)

Our first move consisted of our support for the Zionists' (they were not yet Israelis) attempts to kick the British out of Palestine, discussed in the relevant essay. The next major move was in **Iran** in the 1950s, when we deposed its first democratically-elected leader—most revealing as to both means and ends. Our history in Iran repeated itself in terms of means and ends in the 1970s and 1980s, managing to make us the eternal enemy of Iran, with **Reagan**'s "Iran/contra" murderous hijinks for the low point it reached. (see EVEREST)

Since then, it's been two wars in **Iraq**, and ongoing tragedies in **Israel/Palestine** and for the **Kurds**, in all of which the USA has been harmfully intrusive. We look at them separately.

Gulf War. see Iraq

Iran.

After the decades of turbulence both preceding and following World War I, one Colonel Reza Khan managed a coup in 1925, installed himself as Shah, changed Persia's name to Iran, and ruled until 1941, when he dubbed his son Mohammed Shah-in-shah of Iran.

While Hitler was strengthening his power in the 1930s, Reza Khan found his ways and means admirable; indeed, "Iran" when translated into English is "Aryan." It was such leanings (and, just maybe, oil) that led to a joint Anglo-Soviet /!/ invasion of Iran in the early stages of World War II (fall of 1941). Their joint occupation lasted until 1946.

Both Britain and the USSR were utterly weak by 1946; as they exited Iran the stage was set for the entrance of the USA. We examine only two of the USA's aggressive acts against Iran, one in the 1950s, the other a quarter of a century later.

Oil. The young Shah was in power; like his father, he was autocratic. Despite and because of an always more restive population—to the point of assassinations—Iran held an election in 1951. It was generally deemed to be fair; it was won by the understandably popular Mohammed Mossadegh; his political goal was the overthrow of the Shah and his economic goal the nationalization of Iran's oil resources. Depending upon where one sat, that was either an excellent or plain awful set of ideas. The USA, unsurprisingly, took the latter position.

The USA was quick to provide assistance to the Shah to put an end to that nonsense and the **CIA** began its plottings. In 1953 a four-day military coup enabled the young Mohammed Reza Shah to arrest and jail Mossadegh (in a preview of **the Congo** and Lumumba in 1961), and the young ruler turned the screws to prevent anything like that ever happening again. God was in His Heaven and all was right with the world—except that from that point on the USA became "the great Satan," and not only for the Iranians. (DRAPER; KINZER; KORNBUHL/BYRNE)

As the Shah-in-shah worked closely and happily with the USA in Iran, he, those close to him, and U.S. companies all gained from what were called "modernizing" projects as, meanwhile, the lot of most Persians steadily worsened. Poverty and illiteracy and repression were rampant and, in ways that have been reproduced in many of the poorer countries since the 1970s, all hell regularly broke loose. In the 1970s the most effectively organized hell was that of the zealous Ayatollah Khomeini. Thus it was that in 1979,

> The Shah of Iran was deposed, overthrown by a popular revolt fueled by nationalism, anti-American sentiment, and fundamentalist Islamic rhetoric.... During the coup, the

American embassy was overrun by insurgents, and the American diplomats within were taken hostage. For 440 days they were held, bound and blindfolded to be paraded before cameras broadcasting the humiliation of America around the world...., assuring continuing enmity between Iran and America, and was the central factor in the electoral defeat of President Carter by Reagan in 1980. (PITT/RITTER)

In that same year, the dirty work got dirtier. **Reagan** was and remains much loved and admired by a large majority of the people in the USA, despite all. In that "all" must be included the means of getting elected and of defeating democracy in **Nicaragua**; there the Reagan forces pulled off the second of two of our really rotten acts. They were twinned, and called Iran-contra.

The just-noted hostage problem coincided with the ongoing 1980 U.S. election campaign. President Carter was pushed to send rescue helicopters in a badly failed mission. At the same time, Reagan representatives made a—necessarily—covert deal with the Ayatollah to secure the release of the hostages after the election— in exchange for the second part of the deal; namely, for the sale of U.S. weaponry to Iran—including 1,000 TOW missiles (used against Iraq in their 1980s war) the proceeds to be given secretly to the Nicaraguan Contras by Reagan (who were seeking to overthrow the elected government). All of that although our Congress had expressly prohibited any and all actions in assistance of the Contra insurrection. (DRAPER)

As this came to light in the Congressional Iran-contra inquiry and Reagan was confronted with it, this is what he said:

> I told the American people I did not trade arms for hostages. My heart and my best intention still tell me that is true, but the facts and the evidence tell me it is not. (WILLS, 1988)

ORWELL's "doublethink" in his 1984 had the people being watched, intimidated, and bewitched by "Big Brother." What occurred during that series of events was the President of the USA bewitching himself—or just plain lying. Most of us do something like that now and then, and most of us also find it very difficult to criticize our country, the more so the greater the offense. So in that case, as was generally true with Vietnam, we look the other way, or find excuses..., or something. That's bad enough in personal matters;

when it entails war and slaughter, is done to steal an election, and happens again and again, it needs to be seen as considerably worse. Which takes us to:

Iraq

I began to write this book in the summer of 2001; that is, before 9/11. It is difficult to believe now, but at that time **Bush II** and his administration—to use a favored expression of his Daddy—were "in deep doo-doo": The scandal surrounding his stolen election was still in the air, the economy had already begun to falter, his emerging and definitely non-compassionate positions on social policy were under attack and, seen as an ignoramus in general and especially on foreign policy, Bush II and his chums were decidedly unpopular.

Understandably, the human tragedy and the nature of the 9/11 attacks changed all that, opening the doors wide for grief, heroism and fear—and, at the same time for the cynical manipulation of all three. Within weeks the crusade against terrorism had become the mantra of the Bush Administration, providing it with the means to implement a rightwing domestic and aggressive foreign agenda—a vulgar application of the "wag-the-dog" formula. Madison Avenue and Hollywood types that his closest advisers are, they may well have gotten the idea from, may even have helped to write the script for, the film of that name. It's a filthy game, and an old one.

Critics of the **Cold War** have proposed that had Stalin not existed, the USA would have invented him; the same may be said for Saddam Hussein; nor does the similarity end there: Unquestionably, both were monsters, and both wrought much harm on their own people. But there is one more fundamental similarity: The Cold War was premised on Stalin's **USSR** being a <u>military</u> threat to Europe and Saddam's Iraq a military threat to the Middle East; also, both were described as a threat to the USA, the USSR directing conspiracies directly or indirectly threatening us, Iraq as a key element of Al Qaeda terrorism.

Heinous though Stalin and Saddam were, that was not the issue in either case for the USA, anymore than was the wellbeing of their countries' peoples; had such been our concern, as noted in other entries, there were and are all too many other leaders and nations eligible for "regime change" who, however, have had our support (and/or whom we have installed): Mobutu in the **Congo**, Pinochet in **Chile**, Batista in **Cuba**, Synghan Rhee in **Korea**... and (unfortunately) so on.

The arguments in the UN and at home for war against Iraq were based on two charges: 1) Iraq possessed "weapons of mass destruction" (WMD) and 2) Iraq assisted and supported Osama bin Laden's terrorist network. However, as 2003 evolved and 2004 appeared, not only did both charges come to be seen as baseless, but both were also mumbled away by the administration—as one lump of evidence and another was dropped in front of the world. My telling of this sordid tale will touch only on its highlights; for a definitive, comprehensive, and readable treatment of the background and ongoing realities of the war in Iraq, readers are advised to read EVEREST, Oil, Power and Empire: Iraq and the U.S. Global Agenda.

So—and why not?—the justification for all the mayhem and anarchy had to be changed. He had 'em and destroyed 'em before we got there. And anyway, hey!: freedom and democracy for all is our job. And we had to get rid of the monster Saddam Hussein (whom we supported and armed with WMD's in a now scrubbed out past). And so it goes as, meanwhile, a disturbingly large percentage of the U.S. population, when polled, shows little interest in the whole thing.

The "main fighting" in Iraq in 2003 was over in a few weeks; or so they say; in our first war against Iraq, the "main fighting" began in January of 1991 and presumably ended with a mutual cease-fire in February—which, however was broken in March by U.S. destruction of thousands of Iraqi ground forces, an early "preemptive" strike to eliminate Saddam's Republican Guard.

A considerably larger disaster ensued between the "end" of that war and the beginning of the second one—especially if one is concerned with the people of Iraq: death by economic sanctions (accompanied by regular U.S. bombings in the name of one thing or another): It is widely-agreed that up to a million Iraqi civilians—at least half of them children—died as a consequence of the shortages of food, water, and medical supplies brought about by those sanctions.

The sanctions were imposed by the UN, of course, the first Iraq war having formally been a UN action. But, although the sanctions were lifted by the request of the USA because of the present war, they had been imposed at the behest of the USA in the 1991 Gulf war: a replay and variation of the U.S. invocation of a global embargo on exports to **Cuba** after 1960.

The rationale for the 2003 war depended upon UN legalities regarding WMD and fears regarding further terrorist attacks on the USA and other western nations—with Iraq proclaimed as linked to Al Qaeda. We examine the two arguments in turn.

WMD. The phrase "weapons of mass destruction" was and is used so repetitively in the USA and Britain as to numb the senses, all too reminiscent of ads for breakfast cereals, soaps, and cell phones. As weeks of debate in the UN rolled on in the face of always declining support for the USA/UK position, Cheney did his part with the blunt assertion "Simply stated there is no doubt that Saddam Hussein now has weapons of mass destruction." (NYT, 8-26-02)

Despite and because of growing opposition, U.S. accusations became ever more forceful, culminating in the last-ditch "Positive proof" speech (plus maps) of Colin **Powell**—our "good cop"—before the UN Security Council, as the USA sought UN support for a new resolution to invade Iraq. However, "many of his gravest findings have been upended by David Kay, who until Jan. 23 was the chief weapons inspector for Iraq." ("Harsh light is shined on Powell's war logic," NYT, 2-2-04)

In some sense, even worse was Powell's position after this information came to light.

> The saddest spectacle was Powell, who had argued the case for using force against Iraq before the UN.... Powell said he was not sure that he would have recommended an invasion had he known that Iraq did not have stockpiles of banned weapons. /But/,,, the next day, in remarks coordinated with the White House, he quickly retreated and said, "The president made the right decision." (NYT Editorial, 2-7-04)

Wait a minute now! We went to war because of WMD; but if they didn't exist the president made the right decision, anyhoo? OK, no WMD, but how about us having to knock Saddam down because he was in on 9/11 with his buddy Osama bin Laden and the Al Qaeda? Well, that's what Bush said in the weeks leading up to the invasion. Now? "Bush Reports No Evidence of Hussein Tie to 9/11," (NYT, 9-18-03.) And besides Bush's pal Tony Blair was absolutely sure that "within 45 minutes" those WMD would go bang, and that's why, and... so on. Bushwa.

As this dirge goes on, it is important to remind that this was not just somebody's mistake; it was an invasion, a war. For its casualties up to now it has been much more than a mistake. Close to a thousand GIs are dead with many more wounded with, as well, many (at least 21) suicides and breakdowns (3-400 IHT, 1-15-04); thousands of Iraqi children and adults are dead and wounded, with a chaotic present and an ominous future lurking in the wings. As stated under **double standard**, had any other nation done what we have done in Iraq we would have—as we have—condemned it as barbaric.

Because Iraq is not the first time we have invaded a country on the presumed basis of sufficient "intelligence" (**Cuba** and the "Bay of Pigs" spring to mind), and will very probably not be the last time, it is important to look at the nature of the "unbiased providers" of presumably solid information used for justification.

For Iraq, we now know, that included 1) a 10-year old report from a disgruntled Iraqi, exile Ahmad Chalabi (see below) who—surprise!—was our first choice to preside over postwar Iraq (to general Iraqi distaste) and, among other delicacies; 2) the now famous forged Niger documents regarding their presumed sales of uranium to Iraq (the signature on one of them that of a minister out of office for more than a decade; plus 3) the Bush administration having "investigated the documents over a year ago and been told that they were bogus." ("Blind Spots: The Impossible Task for America's Spies," NYT, 5-11-03)

First, M. Chalabi. He left Iraq when still a boy and didn't return until we took him there. He studied econ and finance at M.I.T. and became a banker in Jordan. Their his bank was caught in embezzlement and had to pay $300 million fine. Chalabi was convicted and sentenced to 22 years of hard labor; by that time he was a fugitive in London. Subsequently he became a fellow at the U.S. rightwing American Enterprise Institute. That is one helluva curriculum vitae. He is our Number One buddy in Iraq until late May, 2004. Then he was dumped, accused of being a spy for **Iran**; More likely was that the intelligence he provided us with was backfiring.

The other "providers" included the bogus "official" informer from Niger and his bogus "information" about uranium and all that, plus the stuff that Powell took so seriously about the famous "trailers":

Months after the invasion, amidst ongoing skepticism about WMD, "Powell argued today that the accuracy of the prewar assessments was proven by the discovery of two Iraqi trailers that the CIA and the Pentagon have concluded were designed to produce deadly germs." Nope, said the substantial <u>NYT</u> article of 6-7-03, "Some Analysts of Iraq Trailers Reject Germ Use." In it, WMD experts voice their opinions and the Administration responds. First, the experts:

> American and British intelligence analysts with direct access to the evidence are disputing claims that the mysterious trailers found in Iraq were for making deadly germs...; /that/ the mobile units were more likely intended for other purposes and charged that the evaluation process had been damaged by a rush to judgment.... "I have no great confidence that it's a fermenter," a senior analyst with long experience in unconventional arms said of a tank for multiplying seed germs into lethal swarms. The government's public report, he added, was a rushed job and looks political." /Other/ skeptical experts said the mobile plants lacked gear for steam sterilization, normally a prerequisite for any kind of biological production, peaceful or otherwise.

By July the WMD tanks having been established as having an embarrassingly banal function, the subject ceased to be discussed after one of the experts stated: "It's not built and designed as a standard fermenter... Certainly, if you modify it enough you could use it. But that's true of any tin can." (ibid.) <u>Any</u> tin can? Yep. Despite all, Powell and Condoleezza Rice as late as June 8, 2003 were standing strong; sort of:

> ... the arguments that they put forward varied somewhat from the explanations that senior officials offered to reporters a few weeks ago and appeared to open the possibility that, in the end, American forces <u>might</u> find that Mr. Hussein had several development programs under way, but few or no weapons ready for use. ("Bush Aides Deny Effort to Slant Data on Iraq Arms," NYT. Emphasis added.)

Lotsa tin cans in Iraq, still. Maybe we oughta invade them again? Not if Henry Waxman, the ranking Democrat on the House Committee on Government Reform, has his way: On June 10, 2003, he sent a formal letter to Condoleezza Rice which, after summarizing the various elements of deception concerning Iraq, and detailing the documented evidence that the White House <u>knew</u> they were using evidence at best weak and at worst downright false to justify a war, and asking that she provide answers to those questions, Rep. Waxman concludes thusly:

> What I want to know is the answer to a simple question. Why did the President use forged evidence in his State of the Union Address? This is a question that bears directly on the credibility of the United States, and it should be answered in a prompt and forthright manner, with full disclosure of all the relevant facts. (See the Committee's Web site for the full letter.)

As we hold our breath in anticipation of an answer, we may examine the case of Tony Blair, whose acquiescence in the Iraq buildup led him to be called "Bush's Poodle." Also on June 8, 2003, the NYT reported that "Iraq Arms Report Mishandled, Blair Aide Concedes in Letter": Blair's director of communications "conceded that the government's presentation of a report on Iraq arms—/45 minutes.../—was mishandled and promised that 'far greater care' would be taken with files in the future so as not to discredit the spy agency's work..." "Mishandled" is a "veddy British" euphemism for what in fact happened, as had been reported earlier:

> Presented as the work of the intelligence services, the 19-page report had in fact been cobbled together from other sources by junior aides at Downing Street. Long passages were copied verbatim—and sometimes exaggerated—from a paper written by a Ph.D. student in California. Other information came from Jane's Intelligence Review. ("Blair Denies Britain Distorted Reports on Iraqi Weapons," NYT, 5-31-03)

Footnote: "An official British investigation into two trailers found in northern Iraq has concluded they are not mobile germ warfare labs, as was claimed by Tony Blair and President Bush, but were for the production of hydrogen to fill military balloons, as the Iraqis have continued to insist." (London Observer, 6-15-03) (Huddle in the White House: But isn't hydrogen used to make hydrogen BOMBS? Got it? Run with it....)

Al Qaeda and Iraq. What have come to be called "weapons of mass deception" as a basis for generating fear was joined at the hip from the beginning with the reasonably-sounding but totally invalid assertion that Saddam Hussein was a major source of recruiting for Al Qaeda and/or was providing it with WMD; explicitly or implicitly, as that justification grew, so was the image of the Two Towers.

(Where, lest we forget, WMD were <u>not</u> used; nor have they been by terrorists, ever.)

There were at least two problems with that assertion:

1) Osama bin Laden and his supporters in the Muslim world (particularly in Saudi Arabia) have long seen Hussein as an enemy, because of the secular nature of his regime. 2) Since 9/11 several Al Qaeda operatives have been captured. In addition to testimony from others,

> Two of the highest-ranking leaders of Al Qaeda in American custody have told the CIA in separate interrogations that the terrorist organization did not work jointly with the Iraqi government of Saddam Hussein.... Abu Zubaydh, a Qaeda planner and recruiter until his capture in March 2002, told his questioners <u>last year</u> that the idea of working with Hussein's government had been discussed among Qaeda leaders, but that Osama bin Laden had rejected such proposals.... Separately, Khalid Sheikh Mohammed, the Qaeda chief of operations until his capture on March 1 in Pakistan, has also told interrogators that the group did not work with Hussein.... /And it concludes by saying that/ "... no conclusive evidence of joint terrorist operations by Iraq and Al Qaeda has been found,..., nor have ties been discovered between Baghdad and Sept. 11, 2001...." (<u>NYT</u>, 6-8-03, "Captives Deny Qaeda Worked With Baghdad.") (My emphasis.)

So: Are we to take the terrorists' word as more truthful than that of the Bush Administration? There is good reason to do so (the implications of which are disgusting): They had nothing to gain by going against what their interrogators wanted to hear, and reasons to fear some hard times ahead—not excluding **torture**—for saying what they (separately) said.

On the other hand, the Bush team had much to gain from its deceptions—with even more to lose if found out—and could count on getting away with it, no matter what: polls show that at least half the people in the USA still believe in both the WMD and al Qaeda assertions.

There's a good lesson for you, children: As Goebbels used to say, big lies work better than little ones; just keep repeating them, over and over and over...: WMD, WMD, Al Qaeda, Al Qaeda, WMD, Al Qaeda.... All this could have been amusing had the leaders of the USA and the UK been caught cheating in a baseball game or a cricket match. But this was done to wreak <u>war</u>; only the latest and probably not the last of a series of lies, deception, and killing in a long procession that includes, not least, **Vietnam**.

For many years after that war, the "Vietnam Syndrome" filled the political air. Although few of our people have ever shown signs of mourning the millions of Indochinese deaths from that war, the tens of thousands of U.S. GIs who were killed (with a large multiple of that damaged for life), plus the associated national disgrace of <u>losing</u>, did act as a brake on similar brutal and destructive exercises; for a while.

Now that the USA has successfully spent hundreds of billions of dollars in order to perfect advanced weaponry assuring few deaths for our forces and many for our assigned enemies, the U.S. public seems willing now to permit, even to cheer, the resumption of that procession. And if those advanced weapons lead to uncounted thousands of deaths and injuries (called **collateral damage**), why, whose fault is that?

<u>So, then: Why **did** we invade Iraq</u>? It is useful to seek an answer to that question by asking another: Why, from 1948 on, did the USA become the major economic and military supporter of Israel in the **Israel/Palestine** conflict. "Useful" because then and now in the Middle East there were several mutually supporting and comparable reasons: (see EVEREST; BLIX; CLARKE for details)

1) Israel's mere location in the Middle East made it valuable for a USA newly-embarked in its Cold War and toward global socioeconomic hegemony;

2) Israel could be seen as a hub for access to oil; 3) although Jews are a tiny minority of the casually or strongly anti-Semitic U.S. population, they are key elements in three of the politically most important states (California, New York, Florida):

<u>Item</u>: In 1962, a secret nuclear reactor under construction (by the French) in Israel was discovered by a U.S. "overflight." After **JFK** was informed and did nothing—and despite all the no-more-**nukes**-except-for-us yammering—when asked why he wasn't trying to stop it he said, "You wouldn't ask if you were a politician facing another election." (ELON)

A moment's reflection shows that those three elements were present also for Iraq with, of course, variations:

1) The first Cold War is "over" but a second and hotter one,

called the "War Against **Terrorism**," has begun;

2) Access to the oil of the Middle East and, now, of Central Asia (see **Afghanistan**) is more important than ever;,

3) Because the Israel/Palestine conflict is always more intense and dangerous to stability and Israel could cease being an ally "with value" in the Middle East; and because non-democratic Saudi Arabia, our other major ally, is internally now problematic as well as the main source of Al Qaeda... well, my fellow Americans, it pays to make new friends: any which way.

More's the worse, to those "reasons why" a fourth must be added: the **Bush II** administration is without question representative of the tightest concentration of socioeconomic power and more confidently driven by rightwing ideology than any other in our entire history. Sitting at the hard center of the economic core are the inter-dependent industrial giants of **oil**, **milex**, and **cars**.

Ominous enough though that is in itself, what is called the "social" element of "socioeconomicpower" makes Bush II considerably more dangerous. The reference is to the "religious right," to its avid rejections of civil and human rights and their chumminess with the "military right"—a bizarre (and acknowledged) component of which is that the "born-again Christians" (Bush II among them), believing in and expecting a Second Coming of Christ, also believe He will not come except to "Israel"—by which they don't mean an Israeli State sharing the holy sites with a Palestinian State. Setting all else aside, and it's a lot to "set" (see **Bush II**), that is <u>heavy</u>.

The main geographic center of all that is the "reborning South"—a "South" increasingly more "Texan" than "Mississippian" in its ways and means. The spirit now leading that rebirth is **Bush II + Cheney**. Two ole boy southern wannabes from the North. Both are positively <u>dripping</u> with oil connections and (neither ever having heard a shot fired in anger) both are exuberantly militaristic war lovers: "bring 'em on!" incarnate.

Still, having cited these several reasons, oil may be seen as the most compelling. Of the top eight areas of known crude oil reserves, five are in the Middle East with the expected treasures of Central Asia nearby. (The other three are Canada, Venezuela, and Russia.) And, of course, the profit interests of the oil companies are tightly knit with our political/military aims in the Middle East.

<u>So: Quagmire Number Two?</u> Maybe so, maybe worse than a

quagmire—for many reasons, beginning with the rationale for the invasion.

However fraudulent the reasons given for previous wars, not even that for Vietnam could match the dizzying justifications for invading Iraq. As each of those become casualties of truth, much of the U.S. public and most of the world moved toward skepticism and disgust. Because, like Vietnam, this war is much-reported on the field of battle as well as at home, it also undermines troop morale and feeds fears in ways and to degrees that are new because of what is new about this war.

Understandably. For the GIs in Iraq, endless confusion as to why they are there and for how long mixes with ongoing daily horrors. For them, these are not matters of politics, but of life and death—and of betrayal. The betrayal of Iraq differs greatly from that felt in Korea and Vietnam.

It seems years now since the disgracefully costumed Bush strode across that carrier's deck to tell us our mission had been accomplished; tell it to the marines, and the other G.I.s in Iraq: surrounded 24/7 by people with whom they cannot communicate _at all_, whose strange clothing might conceal various lethal weapons; trying to work with and live beside people many of whom may well have feared and despised Hussein but now despise the U.S. occupation; facing people suffering greatly from U.S. errors of omission and commission as you, the well-fed, heavily-armed, and grotesquely attired GI walk among them, weapon at the ready—all that and worse for aims which _might_ include realization of a western definition of freedom and democracy, but which _surely_ include oil and regional power. It makes one shudder to even think of having to be one of those GIs—_or_ one of those newly-free Iraqis.

The status of the troops in Iraq is of great importance in terms of their morale. There are no draftees in Iraq, only volunteers of three types: career soldiers, those who enlisted for long enough to get an education and training for a civilian job, and called-up reservists. The reservists _never_ expected to be "in harm's way" _at all_; the others expected a quick and easy win, with a maximum 3-5 month hitch in Iraq.

In Vietnam it was a one-year ordeal for most; in Iraq all face being in Iraq for at least a year, then back home, then back to Iraq in a process that has no predictable end. (Although the British

Foreign Office in January, 2004 predicted five to seven years of "peaceful occupation." Next step: demoralization.

Who wouldn't be demoralized? Combat always produces emotional as well as physical damage, and governments always stretch to conceal rather than tell the truth about casualties; but this war is breaking new ground in every way.

1. Our military strength is incomparably superior to that of any in the world, in everything; the United States can prevail over any other power in a conventional and non-nuclear war. But this war, like that in Vietnam, is not the kind of war for which the United States is, or, given our history, ever could be prepared.

2. Few indeed of our armed forces expected to become casualties in Iraq; our easy victory was assumed from the start. Even fewer, it may be assumed, expected anything like the always changing mix of deadly forces and tactics against the U.S. now common: the 500 + U.S. dead in the first nine months in Iraq already exceeded our first three years in Vietnam.

3. This war was expected to be easier and shorter than its regional predecessor, the Gulf War: Our troops would invade, be greeted, mop-up, and leave—or, the thinking may well have gone, in the White House, stay, but on our own terms. Not quite.

4. Fear is intrinsic to all combat; but the fear in Iraq is very different from that of the European and Pacific wars, even including Vietnam: we have always known the who, usually the where, and often the when. Now our troops in Iraq (among others) never know what to expect, or from whom. Or when. That kind of fear, "from out of nowhere," can easily become unbearable as, day after day, the attackers recede back into their "nowhere."

5. In contrast with the broad and, after Pearl Harbor, the unquestioned support for World War II, the justification for the war in Iraq was doubted by a sizeable minority in the States and a substantial majority among our normal allies abroad before the invasion. After it, as usual, almost all "rallied 'round the flag." As doubts inexorably spread and deepen most perilously among the U.S. troops in or likely to be sent to Iraq, a growing number of politicians just could look

for ways to be courageous.

6.   Put all that and more together and the appropriate question is not why demoralization and suicides rise among U.S. troops, but how much more of the same—or worse—is to be expected? And what could plausibly reverse such processes?

They will not be reversed by ongoing **spin**, let alone by shameful efforts such as the Pentagon's provision of hundreds of identical letters from G.I.s (October, 2003) supporting the war—written by that same Pentagon.

What all this portends for the future cannot be known. "Quagmire" has ceased to be a four-letter word, and references to Vietnam are becoming always more numerous. But Vietnam was a very different war.

In that the current strategic thinking in the White House threatens to become what once was thought impossible, namely, to be more arrogantly puerile even than that of Vietnam, the outcomes of our latest criminal lunacy could well be worse in more ways than one. We were able to get out of Vietnam with "nothing lost save honour," tens of thousands dead, more than twice that wounded, and who knows how many with their lives turned into a chamber of horrors.

In Iraq we must confront what seems to be emerging as a fact: we can neither leave nor stay in Iraq without calamitous consequences at home and abroad, both stretching over a time period whose end one knows not.

The arrogant are almost always ignorant; those in the White House belong to that majority. We may assume they will not find the solution to the leave/stay conundrum; we may also assume that, left to themselves, they will seek to resolve one disaster by creating another and worse one—ad infinitum, until, as Tom Lehrer put in his 1960s song, "we'll all go together when we go."

One day in October, 1969, peaceful demonstrations all over the country resulted in an estimated 20 million of us standing somewhere in stated opposition to the war in Vietnam. It was called Vietnam Moratorium Day, the result of the combined organizing work of the two main antiwar organizations, "The Moratorium" and "The Mobe." A few days later, Vice President Spiro Agnew described the organizers as an "effete corps of impudent snobs." A year or two later, Nixon crazed by criticism, and although he was clearly on his way to an overwhelming re-election, hired thugs to find incriminating evidence against organizers, Democratic officials, anyone, anything to stop them.

Subsequently we learned (from ELLSBERG, who served at the highest level in the National Security Council) that Nixon was fully prepared to use nuclear weapons in Vietnam if defeat were the alternative. From Nixon's "right-hand" man HALDEMAN we also learned that the mass demonstrations against the war were the key factor in leading him to the stupidities of Watergate and the break-in of the office of Ellsberg's psychiatrist. The consequences of those acts were the forced resignation of Spiro Agnew and, in the face of certain impeachment, the resignation of Nixon.

As one of the teach-in-ers and a founder of "the Mobe," I know that nobody involved in those efforts ever held the hope or expectation that such might be the result of our activities, directly or indirectly. But it was.

It would be unrealistic to expect such results from similar efforts concerning Iraq; nor should our efforts depend upon such hopes. Neither should we allow ourselves to be overwhelmed by what seems to be an omnipotent White House. There are many reasons to believe the opposite:

1) The opposition to the war in Vietnam didn't gain momentum until we had been deeply involved for many years; the opposition for this war began before the war itself began. Given the ongoing evolution of conditions on the ground in Iraq, the morale of the troops there is likely to disintegrate at the same time as the opposition to us in Iraq and the opposition by us here at home are rising.

2) The Cold War atmosphere accompanying Vietnam put those at risk who took part in any resistance, in terms of jobs, friendship, even personal safety and freedom; Ashcroft's Patriot Act is a means to reproduce that atmosphere but the opposition to it has already been strong, and grows.

3) The antiwar demonstrations of the 1960s depended very much for their strength on draft resistance. There is no draft now, but the antiwar demonstrations have nevertheless been dominated by young people—a significantly encouraging sign of political awareness and concern going beyond that of the 1960s: Then, young people were either seeking to avoid

the army and/or were disillusioned; today, young people seem not to have many illusions about their society.

The potential to stop this war and, in the process, to begin to move our society toward what it could and should be, is great. Potential can become reality only through hard and persistent political effort. It is more necessary today than it was in the 1960s, but it is at least as possible.

So, there we are. While slowly being suffocated by the carbon dioxide in the air—most of it from "oil"—we are somewhat more rapidly murdering others for it. The Good Life, Inc.

Postscript: The foregoing was completed in the winter of 2004; in just a few months between then and this writing, as summer begins all hell has broken loose in Iraq, with appropriate reverberations at home:

1) A rising and spreading insurgency in which the rivalry/hatred between the Sunni and the Shia has been temporarily overcome by their mutual hatred of the occupiers.

2) The need for the USA to insist on this but to accept that (most prominently, but not only regarding "cease-fires" with insurgent forces that remain armed and active);

3) the almost (but not quite) comical revelations that those Iraqis we have chosen to lead have included a) former top officials of the Hussein regime, b) that our lovingly chosen leader Chalabi had to be rudely kicked out; and

4) the always increasing revelations about torture in Iraq, Afghanistan and Camp X-Ray.

What's next? It is likely that the **Kurds**, having found themselves betrayed by the USA for the third time in a dozen years, will be at the center of a civil war; but reliable predictions about chaos are impossible. It is very probable by now, however, that the Bushies wish to hell they had lied about and invaded some other—any other—protuberance of the axis of evil. It would never occur to them not to invade some little country; after all, if you're a Crusader you gotta crusade, no?

Israel/Palestine

The always deepening tragedy of these peoples goes back very far in time; in December of 2001, when it was moving into its most ominous stage ever and as I sought to understand and explain the developments of this century there, I wrote the article that begins below (for <www.zmag.org>. It will be followed by a brief comment on subsequent events.

From the Unthinkable to the Probable in Israel/Palestine

Since our birth in 1776 and Israel's "rebirth" in 1948, the two nations have had some important things in common: In both countries, most of their peoples—if never all—have seen their nation's birth as an historic act of heroism and have seen their nation as above reproach; no matter what. Without forgetting how very different the two nations have been and remain, It is useful to give at least a brief glance at some of their other similarities.

What strikes one first is that both came into being by ferociously displacing the peoples who were there prior to, during, and after their birth processes: the Palestinians in Israel, the numerous "**Indian**" tribes in North America.

In neither case have most of the people of either nation ever comprehended their deep wrongs against the original peoples, from the beginning to the present. Indeed, something like the opposite of comprehension defines the attitudes of most of the citizens of both countries.

In the USA such attitudes have been long and continuously represented in books and films, implanted in our minds from childhood on, where "the redskins" are caricatured and bestialized, their killers given heroic status. In Israel, the Palestinians who fight against the loss of their land, their rights, and their lives are similarly misrepresented when they are almost uniformly described as "terrorists."

In our earliest days, those who sought to oust the British from the colonies were called "patriots"; the Zionists who blew up Jerusalem's King David Hotel in 1947 are seen as heroes by Israelis, but it was described by the British as "a terrorist attack."—the first recorded usage of the term "terrorism" (other than during the French Revolution). Whatever else must be said about **terrorism**, like beauty, it is in the eye of the beholder.

There are many other similarities. But let me turn to some differences. The Jews who created the Zionist movement over a century ago also began gradually to emigrate to Palestine early in the 20th century. That process sped up and its numbers multiplied with the spread of fascism, and even more so after World War II. The first settlers had good reasons to leave the ghettoized lands of Europe; from the 1930s on, those who faced mass slaughter had even stronger reasons.

The emigrating Jews were able to see themselves as returning to the lands of their distant ancestors; the same could not, of course, be said for those who created the American Revolution. In both cases, however, the "newcomers" were stealing the lands and ruining the lives of those already there.

Moreover, today we can see an all-too-close comparison between the "Indian removal" of the entire 19th century and that of Palestinian removal after the 1967 occupation. That process has been seen as illegal in the UN by all members except the USA and Israel.

The "removed Indians" were robbed of what they saw as their sacred lands and the socioeconomic culture associated with them, all within the context of intermittent war. Among other consequences, it is estimated that in what became the USA, six to nine million "Indians" lost their lives from starvation, illness, or murder.

Those procedures were spread over three centuries; Israel has existed for but half a century. But consider what has already happened to the Palestinians in that brief period, what is happening to them now, what will happen to them tomorrow. Three generations have lost a goodly portion of their lands, their livelihoods, and the power to control their own destines as individuals or as a people; they have lost their freedom and their dignity.

After 1967, it was often noted that the daily life of most Palestinians and the blacks of South Africa were becoming nearly indistinguishable. But as South Africa moved from 1967 to the present, the native peoples were throwing over their oppressors, while the oppression of the Palestinians was deepening.

In retrospect, it is clear that for Israel to maintain its occupation of Palestinian lands, not only those lands but Israel itself would inexorably and unconsciously become militarized, both in attitudes and practice—as happened with the attitudes and practices of the USA as the **Cold War** evolved.

For the USA this meant a steady rightwing shift in our politics, an acceptance of the monstrous, costly, and wasteful **military-indus-**

trial complex which, along with its close pals **oil** and **cars**, provide the main impetus to our economic and social evolution. For Israel, it was just a matter of time until it would accept the murderous General Sharon as its Prime Minister, and live by the slogan "Cry Havoc! And let slip the dogs of war." Not quite what the Jews of the Zionist movement had in mind.

Whatever the heroism of the Jews who fought against the British in 1947, for the State of Israel to come into being, multi-faceted U.S. support was essential. Again, what has motivated the USA from that beginning to the present? And why was it so <u>easy</u> for us to ease Israel into becoming a nation in the Middle East?

It is widely-believed that the Jewish population of the USA was important; as noted in **Iraq**, it is; however, given that anti-Semitism was and remains strong here, that element is but part of the truth. What has been and remains most basic centers upon oil and global political-military strategies. In both respects, the Middle East is a hot spot. Europe's—especially Britain's—weakness right after World War II provided both opportunity and need for the USA to move into what was becoming a power vacuum.

Britain had long been <u>the</u> Mediterranean power; as regards Palestine, it was very much so after 1917. But after 1945, once mighty Britain was flat on its back in all respects, and desperately in need of a multibillion-dollar loan from the USA. It got its money in 1947—in exchange for getting out of Palestine and getting out of the Asian sub-continent, gracefully or not.

This was just when the soon-to-be Israelis began their "terrorist" uprising. They <u>might</u> have prevailed in this uprising without U.S. help, but the odds were 50-50 at best. Getting the British to step aside was easy compared with trying the same with the Palestinians. It was <u>their</u> home they were supposed to give up. Money wouldn't do it, and the mere rifles and grenades used by the Zionists against the UK would not suffice; both <u>heavy</u> weaponry and, at least as important, political support from the U.S., the UN, and Europe were needed.

As one year followed another, the USA provided all that was needed:

1) Vetoes in the UN in favor of Israel when, as was often. Israel was condemned for its behavior;

2)   More economic aid than for any other nation, from 1948 until today;

3)   Military materiel, again more than for any other nation. (Turkey has been second.)

In the past year or so, as the casualties of both Israelis and Palestinians have mounted (the latter a large multiple of the former), it has become clear that Sharon is determined to "settle" the conflict by any means necessary. The "second-intifada" that began in September, 2000 was, it is generally agreed, deliberately provoked by Sharon in his arms-accompanied "visit" to the Temple of the Mount. Such provocation has become his trademark, going back to 1982 and the slaughter in Lebanon.

Sharon's more recent and successful trick has been to deem Arafat (and everyone else of position) "irrelevant" and to gain de facto support from the USA in doing so (sometimes with a mild whine on the side). Serious negotiations have wavered between the difficult and the impossible.

In addition, Sharon <u>must</u> know that if or when Arafat is rendered entirely impotent (or assassinated) that the greatest likelihood is that he would be replaced by Hamas or some other group that denies Israel's right to exist. Just what Sharon wants: Step up violence, men.

Sharon calls to memory Kurtz, of Conrad's <u>Heart of Darkness</u>. Kurtz saw himself as dedicating his life to "civilizing" the Congolese; but with his last breath he wrote "Exterminate the brutes!" The big difference is that Sharon has never tried to "civilize" the Palestinians; only to control and isolate them.

The Israel/Palestine conflict cannot stop there. The closer to "victory" Israel comes in its intended permanent subjugation of the Palestinians, the greater the likelihood that Egypt, Saudi Arabia, Jordan and Syria, to say nothing of Iran, will find themselves pushed or encouraged by each other and/or their own populations to take a strong stand against the many deals their countries have with the USA— or face the internal consequences. Some of that is already bubbling up as an element in the conflict between Pakistan and India, with both different and overlapping roots.

As Israel's oppressive rule has hardened over time, a meaningful peaceful solution steadily fades into the distance. The refusal to

even communicate with Arafat, the continuing intrusion of new settlers into remaining Palestinian lands, the arrest of the most prominent moderate—and among the most promising—of Palestinian
leaders for no identifiable crime, and the hell-bent determination
literally to wall in and wall off the Palestinians combines madness
and cruelty with ultimate self-destruction.

The USA, in single-mindedly pursuing its own interests in taking sides instead of honestly seeking to find a mutually acceptable
solution has been partner to creating an extremely dangerous and
disastrous conflict without end or border. It has been done for oil
and strategy, first and foremost; then, as time has taken us to the
present, in response to the minority religious pressures coming from
pro-Israel Jews and (as noted earlier) the fundamentalist Christians
who believe the Second Coming of Christ requires an existing Israel.

Postscript. That was written almost three years ago. Since then,
the USA has moved in and out, continuing to sideline Arafat, now
and then issuing a rebuke to Sharon. The rebukes have been followed shortly by indifference to Sharon's indifference, continuing
economic and military support until—in 2003—"the road map."

That step by the USA and subsequent adjustments in the
region allowed at least some hopes to be raised that peace might
come, if slowly; the Israelis and the Palestinians had at least begun
to communicate with each other (sans Arafat); better than nothing.
By early 2004 (as this is written), the violence has once more begun
to accelerate, fingers pointing in both directions. Both sides have
engaged in the killing of innocents, each with its own justification.
Fear and hate dominate in both camps now, more than ever before.

That both sides compromised for a while was encouraging; but
neither has been nor will be able to commit itself to a compromise
with the sufficiency and the sustainability that might allow either or
both to be inclined—or able—to act in such a way as to allow the
other to trust it enough to call a permanent cease-fire. That has to
be imposed by outside parties.

It seems to be taken for granted that the USA is the only "outside" party fit to do the job. That is difficult to accept, given our lam-
entable record for the past half century, and the expansion of our
aggressive position as regards more than a little of the rest of the
Middle East in those same years. The most powerful force the USA
could use would be to threaten to cut severely its annual $4 billions

of aid to Israel. That is extremely unlikely.

Is there no hope? Let us hope there is. But it is unlikely to come from any conceivable project originating in Washington, D.C. The latest U.S. intrusion in Israel has been that of Congressman Tom DeLay, the House majority leader. As one of the born-again Christians awaiting the Second Coming of Christ, he makes Sharon look like a sissy. The White House has said not one word of caution to Congressman de Lay; nor has it likely to find either the courage or the inclination to do so.

Meanwhile, 1) with each passing day The Wall snakes its way through more and more territory, most especially in the Gaza Strip. The Palestinians have—quite rightly—seen it as assuring that, like the blacks and colored in South Africa, the wall is meant to be the Palestinians "apartheid." It is unforgivable and it will be provoke, not diminish, violence.

Put yourself in the position of a young Palestinian. Your parents, and their parents, have gone through half a century or more of mistreatment, economic and social privation and harm, and present tendencies threaten to make the past be outdone in horrors by the future. What would you feel, think, do?

As recently as five years ago, polls showed that two-thirds of Israelis were "doves," ready, willing, and able to find a way to a solution agreeable to both sides; and they had their counterparts among Palestinians. Now?

As Sharon continues to "up the ante" and provoke with the Wall and intransigence, the "second intifada" has become an—understandably—continuous process, the "doves—also understandably—are now increasingly frightened of their and their families' lives. Amos ELON, one of the most fair-minded of those who seek to analyze and understand that conflict, has written in the NYRB that "By now, even 'Israeli doves... are among the most ardent advocates of 'the nuclear option.'"

That they would be destroyed in using it as much as they would be destroying others is only one instance of how utterly irrational our world has become; another instance is that (see milex) that the USA has been and remains fully prepared to use its nuclear weapons (now being prepared in small types) if anything or anyone stands in our way. As indeed we were prepared to do so in Vietnam (ELLS-BERG; YOUNG)

A final lament: Writing before World War I, as Zionism was becoming a movement to be taken seriously, VEBLEN wrote a short essay ("On the Intellectual Pre-eminence of the Jews in Modern Europe"—reprinted in the 1945 collection <u>The Portable Veblen</u>). He explains that "pre-eminence" this way: The Jews were in <u>diaspora</u> from their Middle Eastern beginnings soon after the Christian era began. From the medieval period on, when they began to settle in the cities of eastern and western Europe they were ghettoized. In consequence, over the centuries up to and including the beginnings of Zionism, each successive generation of Jews had two lives: one in their ghetto living quarters, the other in their activities outside the ghetto, in always more rapidly changing cities.

In the ghetto the rabbi dominated education and power, and the millenial-old torah formed the entire and <u>unchanging</u> basis of his teaching. However, in the life outside the ghetto modern society was racing forward by ever greater leaps and bounds. The sharp daily contrasts, Veblen argued, could not help but to create <u>skeptics</u> of a substantial portion of each generation.

And, skepticism—questioning, wondering, inquiring, imagining, each feeding and fed by the others—is the sine qua non of the intellectual energies that produce science, art, literature, and music. Thus did the Jews in Europe, always a slender minority of the European population, provide a disproportionate percentage of its scientific and cultural growth.

Concluding his alaysis, Veblen goes on to wonder: And if and when the Jews <u>succeed</u> in having their own nation-state? Then, he argued, they will become just like all other nation-states: greedy for power and resources, nationalistic, expansionist, militaristic, warlike. What a pity he was right.

Kurdistan

Of the many lands over the world that are mere words to the people of the USA, Kurdistan stands high on the list. It is a land of tragedies going back to time immemorial. Perhaps the best-known and, quantitatively, the worst of them occurred in our own era, most recently in **Iraq** and environs, following the first Gulf War.

Since the first days following World War II, the USA has become an always-growing presence in the Middle East. The Kurds were involved in both of our wars against Iraq—an involvement, like the U.S. occupation of Iraq since 2003, that has by no means been resolved. Any settlement of the Iraqi war will have a vital effect upon the Kurds, for better or for worse. In that the USA is the self-appointed arbiter of any such settlement, it is important for us to have at least a summary perspective on the Kurds and their lands.

I shall depend mostly upon the essays of Mirella GALLETTI in what follows. She is Italian, and very probably the best-informed of all Western scholars on Kurdish history; as a frequent visitor she is also well-informed concerning current conditions. (see EVEREST)

Left to themselves historically, the Kurds would today be living in their original territory. In what we call the Middle East, no people was left alone; for the Kurds as the 20th century opened that meant control over their lands and their lives by the Ottoman Empire—itself part of the spoils of World War I. Thenceforward, the Kurds lost what remaining control they might have had over Kurdistan, and instead were forced to live under the harsh dominion of the Turks, the Persians (later Iran), Iraq, or Syria. We begin with the dreadful meaning of that division of the spoils of World War I for the Kurds:

> In the twentieth century the Armenian-Kurdish region can be considered a region of genocide. A million and a half Armenians perished in the first holocaust of the century (1915).... More than two hundred thousand Turkish Kurds were killed and a million a half /had been/ deported to Anatolia /by/ 1938. Since the 1980s, thousands of Kurds have been massacred and hundreds of thousands deported. (GALLETTI)

It was in the 1970s that the Iraqi Kurds began their fierce opposition to the monstrous repression and slaughter by Saddam Hussein:

> Since the seventies the /Hussein's Baath/ has been applying a strategy of scientific genocide in Iraqi Kurdistan. Half a million Kurds... were deported (1976-1986). In 1987-1988 at least ten thousand Kurds were killed...; /in 1988/ from 50 to 100,000 Kurds were killed, 182,000 are "missing," a million and a half deported, and four thousand villages destroyed. (1987-88)

That takes us to the Gulf War of 1990-91, and the role played by the USA in the Kurds' consequent catastrophe. In that war, the Kurds sided with the USA against Saddam as they would again in the 2003 war—and for the same reason: "The enemy of my enemy is my friend."

They were suckered badly in 1991. After cooperating with the USA, the Kurds were abandoned to the fully predictable revenge of Hussein. As Iraqi soldiers slaughtered Kurds and burned down their villages in Iraqi Kurdistan, 1.5 to 2 million Kurds fled to Turkey and Iran as the lesser of evils, and a hostile form of safety. Subsequently the UN established a Kurdish "safe haven" in Iraq, with programs for their safety. The USA provided a program of its own, if also more for "protecting" its own interests than those of the Kurds. Its center-piece was intermittent but frequent U.S. planes, often bombing, in the region north of the 36th parallel where the Kurds still, or had returned to, live. (GALLETTI)

In 1992, the Kurds were granted "federated" status by Iraq. That was their status when the 2003 war took hold. As soon as it became obvious that the second war was on its way, the Kurds made it clear that they would—once more—work with "the enemy of their enemy."

Despite all, they remain hopeful; however.... The USA took the Kurds up on their offer and, for a while, remained "friendly" because Turkey at the last minute, unexpectedly and despite all, voted against joining the "coalition." Subsequently, largely because the presently "independent" Kurdish state is both blessed and cursed by ample oil deposits (at Mosul and Kirkuk), both Turkey and the USA have been acting in ways suggesting that the Kurds will have to fight once more to hold on to even part of their historic lands.

Writing before the recent war began, GALLETTI concluded her analysis of Kurdish history with the <u>caveat</u> that "the Iraqi Kurds are right to be cautious." As each month passes, within and border-ing Iraq the open and concealed conflicts between Sunni, Shiite, Kurd and Turk mount and heat up. That will continue and, given the systematic inability—even disinclination—of the USA to com-prehend Middle Eastern realities and the avid desire of both Turks and the USA to control those oil reserves, Galletti's advice must be seen also as a warning, and not only to the Kurds.

<u>Postscript</u>: On June 8, 2004, the UN passed a resolution put together by the USA and the UK—much to the relief of the White House. But not to the Kurds. That they are now anticipating a <u>fourth</u> betrayal by us was indicated when, the next day, they walked out of the present Council and made it clear that they were likely to secede from the new Iraqi government. Why?

They have supported the present Iraq war, but did so because of their belief that if and when Iraq formed a postwar government it would maintain the degree of independence now enjoyed by the Kurds—forced upon Hussein through covert bombing and sanctions after the Gulf War. As the UN resolution now stands, the Sunni and Shia will be able to deny the Kurds the rights they see as essential to their freedom within a new Iraq. That is, unless—as is most unlikely—the USA forces the Sunni and Shia forces to back down (and it was they who just caused <u>us</u> to remove the Kurdish guarantee) a bloody and endless civil war is virtually inevitable between the well-armed and experienced Kurdish minority and the more numerous Shia and Sunni population. The U.S. response?

> "American officials deny that they betrayed the Kurds and reject the idea that American diplomats should try to mediate a solution to Iraqi federalism." (Kurds Find U.S. Alliance is Built on Shifting Sands," <u>NYT</u>, Op-ed, by Steven R. Weisman, 6-11-04)

Saudi Arabia (see oil)

militarism/military-industrial complex/milex

For the past century or so, existing technology and productive capacities in agriculture and industry <u>could have</u> been used to provide everything needed by all the world's people for at least their health and comfort. In that same century, instead, rising billions of people—about 80 percent of global population—have gone without adequate food, shelter, medical care, and education; lives have been needlessly shortened, cramped, and miserable, with countless millions dead of starvation.

That stark contrast between what has been and what could have been took hold as the modern era began, with an always greater and more devastating degree of divergence between realities and possibilities. Militarism and wars have been both consequence and cause of that continuing set of tragedies; they have been a major component of the economic and social irrationality of the social order which has allowed and caused such gaps between need and possibility to persist and deepen.

R.H. TAWNEY foresaw that evolution succinctly and ironically in his <u>Religion and the Rise of Capitalism</u>:

> Mankind, it seems, hates nothing so much as its own pros-
> perity. Menaced with an accession of riches which would light-
> en its toil, it makes haste to redouble its labors, and to pour away
> the perilous stuff, which might deprive of plausibility the com-
> plaint that it is poor. Applied to the arts of peace, the new
> resources commanded by Europe during the first half of the 16th
> century might have done something to exorcise the specters of
> pestilence and famine, and to raise the material fabric of civi-
> lization to undreamed of heights. Its rulers, secular and other-
> wise, thought otherwise. When pestilence and famine were
> ceasing to be necessities imposed by nature, they re-established
> them by political art. The sluice which they opened to drain
> away each new accession of superfluous wealth was war. (1926)

And so it went from the 16th up into the 20th century, when—
the possibilities for general wellbeing having reached hitherto
"undreamed of heights"—a new series of savage and ferocious wars
began, always more damaging, always more destructive.

In **environment** and **waste** it may be seen that honors for massive misuse and destruction of lives, resources, and equipment do not
go only to war; the "surrounding" socioeconomic system when it is
at peace—itself a somewhat murky notion—is also critically responsible for the always rising amounts of the wasted and destroyed
human and natural resources.

Put differently, industrial capitalism has been simultaneously
the most efficient <u>and</u> the most inefficient system in all history; and,
like wars and preparations for wars, as its productive system becomes
always more efficient it becomes also more destructive. That is so
even were we to ignore the considerable contribution **capitalism** and
its siblings **industrialism, nationalism,** and **imperialism** have always
made for war. The history of the USA, far from an improvement
over that of its European parents, has been splotched throughout by
its declared and undeclared wars. As was delineated in the <u>Foreword</u>,
and although the USA had never suffered any military aggression
from abroad until 1941, it sent forces in military interventions on
over 150 occasions, before then—and many more after World War
II. All were <u>un</u>declared wars, some very small, some very large.

In itself, that does not set us apart from many other nations;
but, unlike those other nations, their military efforts, more often
than not, involved mutual animosities with <u>neighboring</u> states. We
have never had that excuse except—perhaps, and a very weak per-

haps—in the Mexican wars. In short, militarism is in our bones.

We begin with an examination of the language and rationale(s) of military expenditures (hereafter **milex**).

1) What here are called <u>military</u> expenditures are called <u>defense</u> expenditures by the U.S. government. Along with the **Cold War,** that terminology and other ways of "spinning" the language into pleasing shapes took hold in 1947, as did renaming the Department of <u>War</u> (as it was called from 1789 on) to the Department of <u>Defense</u>. It was in 1948 that Orwell wrote <u>1984</u>, whose themes were "doublespeak and doublethink." He got that right.

At the center of the milex rationale was a cultivated <u>fear</u>. The Cold War now presumably gone, fear is now again cultivated and exploited using 9/11 and **terrorism** for a renewed expansion of milex at home and their use abroad, most recently in **Afghanistan** and **Iraq**. The road for all of that was first paved in the Cold War by the Soviet threat. (see **USSR**) Among the many dimensions of that "threat" was the much-propagated "missile gap" exploited by **JFK** in 1960 in his election campaign.

That continued to be used as the justification for skyrocketing milex up through the **Reagan** years (as terrorism now does—ridiculously—for the creation of "small" **nukes**). However, ELLSBERG shows that the highly classified National Intelligence Estimates (of the U.S. government) revealed that though there <u>was</u> a very large gap—10 to 2—it was in favor of the USA, as all weaponry had been from World War II on. (see **Cold War**).

The accompanying growth of that and other myths led to the cancerous growth of the Department of "Defense." Chalmers JOHNSON, once with **CIA**, tells us that

> The actual Defense Department is an alternative government, running not just the Army, Navy, Air Force and Marine Corps, but numerous intelligence agencies, 725 admitted military bases in other people's countries (the actual number is considerably higher), a hoard of weapons of mass destruction that could wipe out life on this planet many times over, with plans to build battle-stations in outer space from which it can dominate the globe. ("Who's In Charge," <u>London Review of Books</u>, 2-6-03)

Now to the nuts and bolts of milex. The harmful socioeconomic consequences of our huge milex received considerable critical scrutiny as they took hold after 1947 (see CYPHER /1987,1991/; MELMAN). What such critiques demonstrate is 1) the prodigious waste of both human and nonhuman resources by milex (e.g., the Pentagon using as much oil as all but seven nations); 2) their serious distortion of educational and occupational structures and negative effects on economic productivity, and (among other matters) 3) their low-yield contribution of jobs and incomes for ordinary people when compared with the same levels of non-military government spending. To comprehend the socioeconomic importance of milex, two measures are central: 1) the percentage of milex to GDP, and 2) their percentage of total federal government expenditures.

First, the dollar amounts of both sets of figures are systematically understated because of what is not but should be included as military, and because of the ways in which the overall budget is structured, now examined in turn.

The average percentage of milex to GDP is regularly stated in single digits—presently, about 4 percent; the reality is more disturbing. A realistic accounting of the percentage of milex to total federal expenditures that includes what CYPHER calls "add ons" takes us well into double-digit land. (see below)

Consider first the interest on the national debt. John L. BOES has undertaken the most plausible and statistically thorough of milex. If, as he reasonably suggests, we assume that "the share of the U.S. debt resulting from security expenditures is equivalent to the share of on-budget expenditures to national security," we find that "Since 1948 national security and national security-related interest on the debt has absorbed some 57 percent of state resources." Further details of such analyses will be discussed shortly; but first, how explain what must be seen as continuing, even worsening, social irrationality in the face of always high and now rising milex?

The explanation is not to be found in any tangible military threats from abroad, whether in the years following World War II or now, but in the economic and sociopolitical developments that rationalized milex; they will occupy the discussion that follows.

At the center of those developments were the interactions of military Keynesianism, the **Cold War** and **McCarthyism** which—their paths greased by **consumerism** and the **media**—have qualitatively altered the consciousness and the social standards of the people of the USA: We the People of the USA have "learned" to acquiesce, to look the other way, to be numbed to the violation of our historic ideals; or, when we do note ugly realities, to shrug them off, with "If we're doing it, it must be OK," or, "So What?"

In support of that social indifference, as Paul BARAN (1969) put it, "We have learned to want what we don't need, and not to want what we do." Long ago Samuel Johnson observed that "patriotism is the last refuge of the scoundrel." The squalid uses of patriotism, like so much else under criticism in these pages, is neither new nor by any means confined to the USA. However.

The whys and the wherefores of our "Pentagon Capitalism" (MELMAN, 1970) and the brutalization of our society have a uniquely vivid meaning for us, here and now: it becomes inexorably more vivid as "the war on terrorism" has begun to spread into always more areas of our lives, as though a disease carried by the air.

Previous generations in the USA and elsewhere have found themselves confronted by horrendous developments; what faces us today has ever more terrifying and mutually worsening dimensions—not just military, but environmental, cultural, political. They must be understood and fought against effectively and soon, if life itself—let alone a decent life—on this planet is to be preserved. That is new, unique to this time and place; and the direct and the indirect effects of milex are central to that crisis.

Now to the whys and wherefores of that many-headed monster, born as World War II was ending.

The term "military-industrial complex" was first uttered as a warning by, of all people, General/ President Eisenhower. It is an intricate "complex" in its origins, structures, functioning, and effects. The following brief analysis seeks to reduce that complexity into several parts: 1) The iron triangle of milex; 2) Military Keynesianism ; 3) The socioeconomic costs of milex: Who benefits and who pays in the USA? 4) Who benefits and who is harmed abroad?

1. The iron triangle of milex.

The "triangle" metaphor was developed by James CYPHER (1987, 1998, 2002), generally seen as the most astute economist critical of milex. In much of what follows, he is either being quoted directly or paraphrased. (Some readers will be reminded—relevantly—of C. Wright MILLS's 1956 book The Power Elite, consisting of the "corporate rich, the political directorate, and the warlords.")

As noted above, the Cold War and McCarthyism were critical for the emergence and functioning of milex. They did not fall from heavens or rise from hell; they were created by the "three sides" of "the iron triangle." (CYPHER, 2002)

Two of the triangle's sides are governmental: civilian and military; at its "base," as Cypher points out, are the 85,000 + private firms that profit from the military contracting system; that number of firms in turn gives them considerable direct and indirect political influence—much added to by their sway over millions of "defense" workers—to push for ever-higher military budgets. We start with that economic base.

a) In addition to being a meaningful political bloc in and of themselves in the election booths, the weight of those companies is felt at least as effectively in the offices of our elected representatives and the White House, made so through the unremitting pressure of thousands of **lobbyists** and related **campaign finance**.

Given that set of enticements (treated below or in the just noted entries), we may then look at why businesses and workers have become so addicted to milex. The place to begin is the 1930s depression; that worst economic crisis in history for all nations was ended only by World War II.

The USA was the last to enter that war, but we had been its economic beneficiary for several years before 1941. From a nation which in 1933 had 25 percent unemployed and in 1940 still had 10 percent unemployment, it was almost entirely the war that brought us to our lowest unemployment rate ever in 1943 (one percent+).

If the 1930s were the worst economic years in our history, the 1950s and 1960s became the best. They were decades of hot war and cold war—and of high milex. Few failed to see that connection or the relationships between milex and cold war politics at home and abroad. (Of which, more below, re: "military Keynesianism.")

But 85 thousand firms? Yes, but the lion's share of military contracts then (and even more now) is delivered to a tiny and always shrinking fraction: During World War II, only 100 giant companies received two-thirds of the dollar value of milex contracts; in the past few years the top 25 companies get more than 50 percent, the top 10 get 40 percent; as **M&As** continue, they will get more:

> Since 1993, encouraged by the Pentagon..., consolida-
> tions have accelerated in speed and size. In early 1995,
> Lockheed and Martin Marietta merged to become
> "LockMartin"..., Boeing picked up defense pieces from
> Rockwell, Litton, and others and then in 1997... by swallowing
> its only U.S. aircraft rival, McDonnell Douglas, to become
> "McBoeing." Hughes Electronic, owned by General Motors,
> bought General Dynamics' missile division, the Magnavox
> defense division, and others, while Raytheon acquired Texas
> Instruments' defense division and assorted others. Then
> Raytheon bought Hughes from GM for $9.5 billion.(CYPHER,
> 2002)

Makes your head spin as 'round and 'round it goes, as it did others': It was more than coincidental that in those same years, U.S.
politics underwent a rightward shift. (see GREIDER, 1998; ALT-
MAN,"Ensuring Competition..." NYT, 9-15-02)

The two governmental sides are a) the civilian governmental
agencies that shape U.S. military policy: the White House, the
National Security Council, the Senate and House Armed Service
Committees, the CIA and the NSA; b) the military institutions,
including the Joint Chiefs of Staff, the top brass of the Air Force,
Army, Marines, and Navy, the powerful "proconsul" regional com-
mands ("CINCs"), and, in an important supporting role, veterans'
organizations.

It doesn't take much imagination to see how those three "sides"
taken together constitute a mighty pressure group; adding the pressures and inducements of **lobbyists** reveals "the iron triangle," the
most focused and effective pressure on our government.

In the past 50 years, it has been rare for there to be congressional opposition to the "triangle's" wishes—except for infighting
over particular and competing milex projects: a new weapon vs. an
older one; one new weapon vs. another similar new weapon; a "Star
Wars set of weapons vs. an older set of weaponry, etc. When that
happens, it is often one state against another: California vs. Texas,
Mississippi vs. Massachusetts, etc. But then the debate is not over
the size of milex, but who gets how big a slice of that very big pie.

2. Military Keynesianism

John Maynard Keynes (1883-1946) was the leading economist
in the English-speaking world in the 1920s and its chief advocate of

"**monetarism**"—a doctrine placed into scornful disuse by Keynes himself in his 1936 General Theory....

Only a few years earlier he had written a three-volume Treatise on Money, which the 1936 work contradicted. It was the depression of the 1930s—begun in his native Britain already in the 1920s—that caused his 180 degree turnaround.

Keynes argued that the depression was there to stay no matter what was done in the way of monetary policy; i.e., the manipulation of interest rates and the supply of money. The problem, Keynes argued (see **economics**), was not "money" but the inability for private demand by consumers and businesses to purchase a healthy economy's production at reasonable prices; thus it was essential for the government to provide the needed supplementary demand and to finance it by deficit spending. Spending on what?

His answer was "social consumption" and "social investment." The former would take various forms—governmentally subsidized housing, education, culture (which in the USA was done through WPA projects for music, literature, art, and the like /see **jobs**/); the latter, "social investment" included what we now call "infrastructure": bridges, highways, dams, etc. (accomplished in the USA through the PWA).

The items in both categories had in common that they were publicly financed and, as well, humanly and socioeconomically useful. Keynes, although not foreseeing either the qualitative or quantitative dimensions of post-World War II milex (he died in 1946), was nevertheless scornful of its historical predecessors: Ancient Egypt and its pyramids or, as he put it, "building battleships, sinking them" and then building some more, equivalent to "hiring some thousands to dig holes and others to fill them"—all job-creating, all useless and wasteful.

Which brings us to contemporary milex, with the additional comment that although Keynes was critical of **capitalism**, seeing it as a system "merely of possessors and pursuers," like PHILLIPS, he also thought it the least bad of all possible systems. Even so, from the 1970s on, and despite that his aim to save capitalism from itself was intrinsically conservative, his arguments and policy proposals came to be called "left-wing Keynesianism."

After World War II Keynesianism in its intended form was more or less adopted throughout the industrial capitalist societies;

"more" in Western Europe, "less" in the USA. What kept <u>our</u> economy buoyant after the war was a mixture of what Keynes intended <u>plus</u> much more of what he scorned: military Keynesianism." (Joan ROBINSON, who helped him write the <u>General Theory</u>, called it "Bastard Keynesianism." (TURGEON)

Unquestionably milex and related expenditures and the Cold War provided a firm base for U.S. economic buoyancy from 1946 to 2000; as it is also clear that the recessions of those decades, including that which began in 2001, were much shortened by ongoing large milex. Recessions cannot be avoided under capitalism but their collapse into depression can be barred by the steel gates of milex "+" (with the "+" to be discussed soon)—whether or not accompanied by "hot war" as in Korea, Vietnam, or the Middle East.

How so? Two matters are of key importance: 1) the <u>actual</u> as contrasted with the <u>official</u> statements of the annual amounts of milex; 2) the indirect economic effects of any given milex.

1) For the fiscal year 2003 (which began in October, 2002),

> the basic Pentagon budget (including "Homeland Security:) will reach $433.7 billion—coming close to the post-World War II high of $449 billion (adjusted for inflation) spent in 1968 at the height of the Vietnam War.... But this calculation ignores important "add-ons," such as foreign military sales, military space programs, veterans' benefits, military retirement, foreign military aid, and interest on the national debt attributable to past deficits related to military spending. (CYPHER, 7/8/, 2002)

Here a closer look at some of those "add-ons":

a) Interest on the national debt: At least half of our yearly interest payments on the national debt are milex-connected (the total runs at $200 billion + every year).

b) The share of the Department of Energy's expenditures on milex, not least those on nuclear development, where it is estimated at least $4 billion annually for nukes are "squirreled away" in its budget. (CYPHER, 1991)

c) The "Social Security matter": The federal budget for 2002 lists $460 billion as "Social Security expenditures." (ERP, 2002) However, until 1966, Social Security payroll deductions and benefits were—as they should be—"off budget." In that year, as the Vietnam war expanded, LBJ, in addition to understating milex by

$10 billion (= roughly 10 times that today) from the Budget Office, he decreed that Social Security payroll deductions and benefits be classified as taxes and expenditures and thus be "on budget." Why?

Because adding a large amount of non-milex to federal expenditures automatically reduces the percentage of milex to the total: good political sense, especially with an unpopular war going on. Note that the total of Social Security, as noted above, is greater than that of official milex.

Social Security benefits are not and should not be considered as "expenditures" because over time they are fully self-financed by the beneficiaries. Indeed, as Social Security payroll deductions have always far outrun benefits, the Treasury has borrowed hundreds of billions from the surplus every year, thus reducing its need to issue bonds, thus camouflaging the national debt.

However, if and when the Social Security surplus (the "lock-box") is emptied, it will be necessary for bonds to be issued to pay benefits; in turn, that will increase general income taxation. Thus, to the public's present payroll deductions one will have to add the taxes to be paid for, because of this skullduggery—not by the rich, but by the bottom 80 percent of us. (see **social security, taxes/tax expenditures**)

d) Milex are also hidden away in the expenditures on foreign aid, the CIA, space research, and "schools" (one of which, "the School of the Americas" has turned out at least 60,000 graduates /NYT, 10-1-96/; we can only guess at the total—except we know the CIA budget is well over $30 billion annually, and that it also receives "$5.6 billion for keeping secret documents secret." At that circus we are the clowns.

Conservatively adding all that up, we can easily agree with CYPHER when he says the add-ons "would increase the real level of military spending by more than two-thirds in a given year." (ibid.) That is, the real figure for fiscal 2003 would be something between $700 and $900 billion. Nor has Cypher included certain plausible items such as covert military activities on the part of the **CIA** and other governmental units.

Further, consider interest on the debt: it is of course paid to those who hold the debt (in the form of U.S. bonds, etc.). They are mostly financial institutions (that is, their owners) and others in the top 10 percent income receivers of the population. Apart from all else, then, the mere accumulation of debt from milex makes for always-greater **inequality** in a system of existing great inequality.

Nothing has yet been said of the terrible socio-economic **waste** of milex (pursued in detail under **waste**). Even if we were to grant that we need to be as "prepared" as we have been told—shown as most doubtful under **Cold War**—that still would not justify the exorbitant profits and wastefulness of milex. For example:

> In hearings before the House Committee on Armed Services in 1984—and in addition to showing that $750 was paid per toilet seat—the prices of ordinary tools at the retail level were compared with defense contractors' prices for 21 items. At your neighborhood hardware store, screwdrivers, wrenches and the like all sold for less than $13, and many under $5. The defense contractors sold none for less than $225 (a screwdriver, retailing for under $3), and their highest price was $1,150 -(a wrench, retail price $4.88). The total retail price for the 21 items was $92.44; but from the contractors, $10,168.00. (ADAMS/BROCK)

Screwdrivers, toilet seats, wrenches—peanuts. For the BIG profits, take a look at the giant companies and their giant contracts—for planes, submarines and missiles. They are the most expensive and most wasteful hard core of milex.

Of the tens of thousands of separate firms now contracting with the Pentagon, as noted above only a few companies take the lion's share of all contracts and farm them out to the multitude of other companies; altogether they hire about 3 million workers, and there are about a million civilian workers on the Pentagon payroll, plus a million paid reservists. What are we getting for our $400++ billions of direct and at least twice that indirect taxes? A lot of waste, more protection than we need, lots of jobs that could be used for better purposes, lots of profits which, by any reasonable definition are undeserved. (ZEPEZAUER/NAIMAN)

<u>Item</u>: Profit rates for milex companies are two to three times those for <u>all</u> other companies. And why not, given "cost-plus contracts" and virtually assured payments for cost overruns?

<u>Item</u>: The fabled B-2, or "Stealth" bomber." Set aside that it has never been used in combat. (The F-117A "Stealth" <u>fighter</u> was used, and flopped, in Panama and in the first Gulf War.) The first 1980s contract for ten B-2s set the price at $400 million <u>each</u>, or $4 <u>bil-</u>

lion; by 1990 that had risen to $870 million each; thence, in 1994 to $2.2 billion, each: $22 billion for TEN planes, and more than five times the original price.

Sounds awful? Try this: Standard Pentagon contracts allow— and pay for—correction of defects. The first B-2 had 110,000 defects (no misprint there: one hundred and ten thousand defects); the second had 80,000. Given that it's cost plus with defects plus-ed, and assuming (as **economics** does) that bizmen are "rational calculators," that would seem to be an incentive to the companies to make defects, no? Not to worry; in 1996 Congress appropriated $44 billion, enough for 20 B-2s. (NYT, 7-14-96)

And it doesn't stop with planes. In an editorial entitled "Jackpot," the NYT reported that "the Senate Armed Services Committee tossed $1.3 billion into its budget bill to order an LHD-7 amphibious assault ship the Navy did not want..." but that Senator Trent Lott (Rep. Miss.) did; happens it was to be constructed in his state. (7-19-95) One of those coincidences.

Lest we forget, one of **Reagan**'s favorites was "Star Wars." It was shelved after his departure from the White House, only to be revived by Newt Gingrich and Bob Dole (House and Senate leaders, respectively) in 1996. The Congressional Research Service estimated it would cost $60-70 billion. Gingrich, in support of his "Defend America Act of 1996," argued that "One day, mathematically, something bad can happen and you ought to have a minimum screen on a continent wide basis, and its doable"—as "doable," the American Physical Society pointed out "as deflecting a bullet in mid-flight by firing one of your own." (TN, 6-24, 6-25,7-8, 1996). And, of course, as with so much of the Reagan follies, the **Bush II** has brought Star Wars back.

2) In addition to the foregoing direct costs and effects of milex are many that are indirect. It is generally agreed that for every governmental dollar spent on milex, GDP will increase by three dollars. Why? Because those milex dollars go to workers and owners; they in turn spend most of what they receive; and those expenditures in turn generate more incomes, and more expenditures, and.... It is what is called "the multiplier effect." And it works the same way for all additional governmental expenditures.

In the years 1990-2002, official milex came to over $4 trillion. If you take that and add two-thirds of uncounted milex times the multiplier effect which triples it, it helps considerably to explain the "fabulous 90s"—quite apart from taking into account just how important milex have been for the main constituents of the "new economy": subsidized research, guaranteed markets, not least. Lots of economic wallop there, and just as much political wallop, if one considers the "multiplier effect" of economics on politics. (ERP, 2002)

3) The socioeconomic costs of milex: Who benefits and who pays in the USA?

The answers are both very simple and very complex. Those who benefit economically are the owners and executives of the milex companies and, as well, their workers. However:

Although in principle there is no inflexible reason why the "health" of the milex companies and their workers must have adverse socioeconomic effects, in reality there have been and remain serious negative consequences: they can be, have been, and are currently used to forestall or cutback needed social spending: "Can't afford it." (see **deficits and surpluses; Greenspan/monetarism**)

From the late 1970s on, and increasingly from the 1980s until today, high milex, almost always supported by business and labor, has regularly been used as an excuse to "crowd out social programs supported by public-sector funds, such as healthcare, public transportation, education, and environmental protection." (CYPHER, 7/8- 02; and MELMAN, 1965, 1970) That became an odious, ideological and dishonest, excuse in the **Reagan** years, as it is still. (STOCKMAN; ZEPEZAUER/NAIMAN)

Continuing high milex depend upon the creation and persistence of real and imagined threats of and/or military engagements from abroad, and accompanying attitudes of fear and hate and nationalism. The **Cold War** served that purpose from 1947 on, aided and abetted by the ways in which political dissent was punished and/or stifled by attendant **McCarthyism.**

Behind that generalization exists a tangled and dirty mess of developments which, for the past half-century, have qualitatively altered the average political outlook of our people.

Difficult though it may be to believe now, the mind of the U.S. public before World War II was in general non- or anti-militaristic, even pacifistic, mostly in consequence of World War I. In the entire period between 1918 and Pearl Harbor, World War I was seen as having been not only unprecedentedly destructive, but as senselessly so, as a European catastrophe at least partially brought about by fools and munitions makers: "the merchants of death," as they were popularly known. Good thinking.

Item: Throughout the entire 1920s—incredibly for us today—federal expenditures on the Post Office exceeded those of milex; something the militarists and "the iron triangle" neither forgot nor forgave.

The Cold War and McCarthyism changed all that, even taking into account the flare-up of antiwar sentiment during the 1960s. But the antiwar movement was a consequence 1) of a very unpopular draft, and 2) what became the undeniable fact that the USA could not win the Vietnam war except with **nukes**. That movement and that realization, combined with the fatal **arrogance** of **Nixon**, brought the war—but not milex—to an end. Both during and after Vietnam, among the war's principal supporters—as well as its principal casualties—were workers.

The consequences went well beyond milex alone and they continue to do so. The reference is to what happened to the consciousness and the culture of the USA. In several overlapping and interacting realms—entertainment, education, politics, and unions—the Cold War and McCarthyism acted to stifle criticism, dissent, even creativity, liveliness—"difference."

All this was done in the name of holding back a Soviet—"communist"—threat. But the human and economic destruction to the **USSR** was far beyond that of any other country—Germany, Japan, Italy, the UK, anywhere. It was estimated that 60,000,000 soldiers and civilians were killed in the European war; at least 28,000,000 of those were in the USSR. (FRUMKIN) On top of which, the destruction of its entire rail network and its productive facilities was almost complete.

There was a threat, however. It was a political threat of a general movement to the Left in most of **Europe**—a movement which (as argued under USSR) would have existed had there never been a Soviet Union. Why? Because the political leaders and the economic system of most European nations—from Greece to Italy to Spain to France to Britain to Holland to Norway—had undergone a disastrous and two-decades long depression under right-leaning governments, all too many of which leaned very close to, or became, fascist. Nor would many forget that the resistance to that rightward shift and to fascism itself was made up predominantly of those who were left of center. As will be seen in our discussion of **Italy** and **Greece** (see **Europe...**), if <u>any</u> interference in the internal affairs of European countries was to be feared, it would be that of the USA.

At home, from 1947 on, whether for workers (with the **Taft-Hartley Act)**, or actors, or writers, or professors, or politicians..., anyone, those who dared to function as they had <u>before</u> the Cold War often paid the price; and others who might have thought of resisting such conformity learned instead to... **conform**. The price paid in all those realms was high each step along the way and its effects continue in terms of persisting difficulties in the organization and effective strength of unions, politics, **education** and **entertainment**.

In addition to our having an always more militaristic and probig business government and flaccid educational system, perhaps it is all epitomized by an entertainment diet in film and **TV** which finds us "amusing ourselves to death." (POSTMAN)

Milex was by no means the sole cause all this but did more than its share, as was essential: the milex we support <u>requires</u> a population either supportive or indifferent—and gets it. The USA spends more on milex than most of the rest of the world combined—and half of what the rest of the world spends on milex it buys from the USA. (CYPHER, 2002) It is our position, our claim, that we must do this to protect ourselves—from what is now seen as an "axis of "evil." Whatever works.

4) Who benefits and who is harmed abroad?

Substantial answers to those questions are put forth in the separate country discussions under **Africa, Asia, Latin America** and **Europe**. But here we may point to the most general consequences of milex and related policies. As might be expected, the benefits from U.S. milex and its cold war accompaniments went mostly to those at the higher levels of income, wealth and power within those countries affected by our policies (which is to say, much of the world), and that most of the harm done—both qualitatively and quantitatively substantial—fell upon those at the bottom and middle levels of income, wealth and power. A major explanation of those effects is that in the name of freedom and democracy and economic well-being U.S. foreign policy has effectively <u>distorted</u> the economic development of the weaker nations and has led to <u>reduced</u> rather than increased democracy in them.

The Cold War militarized global politics; in doing so, it served to maintain long-standing conservative/ dictatorial governments, and/or to aid in the installation of **fascist** or quasi-fascist governments in all quarters of the globe.

That said, it becomes essential to see "benefits" as a euphemism, and its normal meaning twisted to cloak what should often qualify as criminal activity. A reading of what the USA has done to countries discussed under **Asia** and the other regions can sensibly come to the conclusion that the **Cold War** and its milex over the past half century was a calamity for dozens of other societies and, in the future, for the entire world.

An immediate rejoinder comes to mind: wasn't all that essential if the tyrannies of the USSR, and China, and Cuba, and Vietnam and Chile... were to be displaced?

To answer that question affirmatively requires the acceptance of the U.S. rationale for the Cold War. At least two points here, with more in the discussion under **Cold War** and the regional entries.

1. From the beginning of the Cold War until its presumed end, we were always told of how we had to "keep up" with the USSR's vast milex; in JFK's time (as noted earlier) this took the form of a frightening "missile gap" (which was soon found to be non-existent). While all that was going on, well-based critiques also emerged; best known of them was that of a Prof. Franklyn Holzman, an expert on the USSR. When he died in 2002, his <u>NYT</u> obituary noted that he had become best-known for his strong accusations (put forth long ago, in the 1970s and 1980s) that the USA—most notably, in the **Reagan** years—"drastically overstated Soviet military spending in an effort to sway budget decisions at home."

2. More generally, an acceptance of the cold war position of the USA requires a reading of history that ignores the ways in which the careers of all the targeted societies were altered and distorted by the hostile policies of the USA (and other western powers) from their revolutionary beginnings; never given a chance.

Keynes has been discussed above; there it was pointed out that he was a worried supporter of capitalism.

Here it is worth repeating his thoughts after an official visit to the **USSR** in 1925:

> So, now the deeds are done and there is no going back, I should like to give Russia her chance; to help and not hinder. For how much rather, even after allowing for everything, if I were a Russian, would I contribute my quota of activity to Soviet Russia than to Tsarist Russia! I could not subscribe to the new official faith any more than to the old. I should detest the actions of the new tyrants not less than those of the old. But I should feel that my eyes were turned towards, and no longer away from, the possibilities of things; that out of the cruelty and stupidity of Old Russia nothing ever could emerge, but beneath the cruelty and stupidity of New Russia some speck of the ideal may lie hid. (KEYNES, 1931)

Well, we (and Britain, France and others) did nothing to help and quite a lot to hinder. We and they sent military aid to the White Army, and thousands of soldiers to try to overthrow the revolution—and we repeated all that, with variations, in Allende's **Chile** (see **Kissinger**), Mao's **China**, Castro's **Cuba**...; and denounced each and all of them for protecting themselves from us.

All of that is discussed in the respective entries of the countries just noted, as it is for most of the others in the "regional" groups (**Latin America....**).

Meanwhile, the **Cold War** has ended and Hot Wars threaten to become common. Consequently, to the joy of milex **lobbyists** and their paymasters, Congress has just enacted "the costliest defense budget since the cold war—$400 million and counting...." (NYT, Editorial, "The Defense Budget Spills Forth," 5-20-03). Military spending has been rising since 1998, and the current official milex budget of $447 billion does not include the $87 billion minimum expected cost of the Iraqi occupation. ("Military Revival After the Vietnam Trauma...," NYT, 8-15-03)

For both the inquiring and the skeptical reader of these words, I add that in order to replace the "common sense" view that has supported U.S. policies with "good sense," it is essential to undertake much study. Here, then, is a listing of some works (also listed in the Bibliography) useful for opening the doors to the questioning our policies deserve.

It will be noted that some of those listed concern pre-World

War II developments—e.g., as regards the USSR after 1917, Germany under Hitler, Spain under Franco, etc.; that is because they are essential for understanding what happened <u>after</u> World War II.

Brady, Robert A. The Spirit and Structure of German Fascism.
Breitman, Richard. What the Nazis Planned, What the British and the Americans Knew.
Cumings, Bruce. The Origins of the Korean War.
Dobb, Maurice. Soviet Economic Development Since 1917.
Eisenberg, Carolyn. Drawing the Line: The American Decision to Divide Germany, 1944-1949.
Gurley, John. Challengers to Capitalism: Marx, Lenin, Stalin, and Mao.
Kennan, George F. "Letters from Germany," "The US and the World: An Interview," New York Review of Books, 12-3-98 and 8-8-99.
Kofsky, Frank. Harry S. Truman and the War Scare of 1948.
LaFeber, Walter. America, Russia and the Cold War.
Leffler, Mervyn P. A Preponderance of Power: National Security, the Truman Administration, and the Cold War.
Oglesby, Carl and Shaull, Richard. Containment and Change.
Shawcross, William. Sideshow: Kissinger, Nixon, and the Destruction of Cambodia.
Wittner, Lawrence. Cold War America: From Hiroshima to Watergate.
Young, Marilyn Blatt. The Vietnam Wars: 1945-1990.

monetarism/the Fed/Greenspan

Monetarism is that set of economic theories and policies that sees only one justifiable intervention with the otherwise "free" workings of the economy; namely, to take steps to increase or decrease the supply of money and/or to lower or raise the rate of interest on borrowed funds.

That is the stance which has presumably guided thought and policy in the USA (among other places) since the 1970s—"presumably" because in fact those who preach that doctrine, whether in the business or the governmental world (or, as is common, passing back and forth between them) have seen innumerable reasons to intervene in the economy—through export subsidies, spending programs (not least on **milex**), manipulation of personal and business **taxes**, protective tariffs (at home, while condemning them elsewhere)...; the full list would consume many more lines of print.

Monetarism also dominated thought and policy (in principle) in the 1920s. Probably its most influential theorist was John Maynard Keynes, who topped off his work in 1930 with his three-volume Treatise on Money.

And then, in 1936, turned those same ideas on their head (as noted under **milex**) with his General Theory of Employment, Interest and Money. (see **economics**) What caused him to change his mind so completely was the depression of the 1930s—which, however, had begun in the 1920s in his native Britain, where it averaged 10 percent unemployment throughout the 1920s.

In the face of that enduring and stubborn unemployment (and an associated weak national and global economy) Keynes saw the light: capitalism, far from being how economists see it, a self-curing system, is not. Indeed, if left to itself, either in general ("macroeconomically") or in particular ("microeconomically") it was likely to cut its own throat. Macroeconomically, to be more precise, intermittent minor recessions can and will reverse themselves, with only minor assistance—that is, the assistance of a stimulating (low interest rate, expanding money supply) set of policies. And the stimulus would come (in his country) from the Bank of England; through the Fed in the USA. The Fed was then and still is privately owned (its shareholders being the member banks), although its directors (presently Greenspan, and the 7 governors) are appointed by the White House—with the substantial "assistance" of the financial world. But the 1930's collapse was not "minor."

Keynesianism came into use and dominance in the USA through the New Deal (and, in Europe, social democratic governments). Although monetary policy continued to be used throughout those years (late 1930s through the 1960s) what was crucial were **fiscal policies**; that is, deliberate governmental intervention through tax and spending policies.

The spending, called "social consumption and social investment" by Keynes, emphasized deficit financed expenditures in the realms of education, health care, culture and for governmentally financed infrastructure (bridges, dams and the like).

As detailed under **milex**, social spending in the USA after World War II came increasingly to be much outdone by **military expenditures**; so much so, that as the 1960s ended, Keynesianism in the USA had come to be described as "military Keynesianism." However, insofar as that was happening within the political framework of the **Cold War** and **McCarthyism** and the economic framework of an always increasing political role for **big business**, it was easy for a general conservatism to dominate not only economic policy but, as well, economic thought.

Thus it was, by the 1970s, and accelerating into the 1980s and up to the present, that whatever reformist influence Keynesianism might have had fell into not just disuse but disrespect.

In the USA the thinker who took Keynes's place was **Milton Friedman**, (see **deregulation** and other matter under his entry) and what is called "the Chicago School." where he both studied and taught.

When **Nixon** was in the White House (1969-73), economic policy was what now would be seen as "liberal" (or New Deal-ish); which is to say that he was merely continuing in the footsteps of his (mostly Democratic) predecessors. But as Carter became President (in 1976), the tendency of economic policy began slowly to shift toward what it has now become with regard to social spending and taxes. All this was to accelerate and become transformed in the 1980s.

The 1980s were, of course, the years of **Reagan** and **"Reaganomics."** And in those years (and those of the **Bush I** administration), what was discussed in the opening paragraphs of this entry—i.e. the presumable confining of intervention to the money market—moved from farce to scandal: literally scandalous as regards what was universally termed the **S&L scandal**.

The latter is discussed in detail in its own place; suffice it to say here that the savings and loans banks had their specific function upended and destroyed when, under pressure from influential financial figures, those small banks were entirely **deregulated** and their nature transformed to be whatever their mostly new owners sought to make them (**Glass-Steagall**). Many of those new owners were quite simply gamblers, some of them were gangsters. (PIZZO, et al.)

The "freedom" thus achieved was not entirely unlike giving the key to the safe to bank robbers; even better, after the bank has been robbed, to use taxpayers' funds to restore the banks to solvency, as almost all the robbers went off to their resorts and palaces.

As all this—and much more—was being done, the "monetarists" looked the other way, continuing to murmur their mantra of non-intervention and freedom; some even found ways to explain away what had been done in the name of "free enterprise." It was in those years the seeds were planted that nourished the growth of Enron and many other socioeconomic misdeeds which are usually treated as civil transgressions rather than the major crimes they are. (see **CEOs**)

All this transpires no matter which party is in control of Congress or in the White House. It was more than a nonchalant use of four-letter words when, in his first year as President, Clinton muttered (in the presence of the press) something about how he (saw himself) as constrained first and foremost by that "——ing bond market." That "market," along with the bankers who dominate it, also chooses who shall run the Fed, and what degree of opposition or support it will receive for a given change in policy.

And now **financialization** of the economy is in full swing and it and monetarism rule the roost all the more at home and, through the **IMF. et al,**, abroad.

But perhaps they are right? Let us look only at two economies in two periods to see what has been accomplished in hard times when monetarism has had its way: the USA, 1929-1933, and Japan, 1991-2002.

1. The USA. It is popularly believed that the Wall St. crash of October, '29 opened the gates to depression. Doubtless that crash did make a bad situation worse, but the economy had been in trouble already in 1928.

Trouble =? What it usually means in an advanced industrial capitalist economy is that productive capacities are greater than money demand. Lowering interest rates is meant to stimulate purchases by businesses (for expansion) and by consumers. But when there is excess capacity, only fools would tread the path toward increasing it; or, as Keynes put it, you can lead a horse to water, but if its belly is full, it won't drink. In the face of that condition in 1928, Harvard prof Irving Fisher, the leading economist of his time, famously proclaimed that the U.S. economy was on a "high and rising plateau" and that "the business cycle was dead." No more ups and downs. He was right about the "ups" part. Nobody's perfect.

The economy continued to hiccough its way down (not in a straight line; that isn't how the economy or the stock market go either down or up): bears turned to bulls again in 1930, and then, kerplunk! Then again, as 1930 went on, up went the market, and then kerplunk! And again in 1932, finally hitting bottom in March 1933, as FDR entered the White House.

He continued the conservative ways he had as governor of New York until the elections of 1934 brought a whole bunch of "liberals" into the Congress—a result of the political and labor tumult and unrest shaking the country. His main advisors, Harry Hopkins and Eleanor Roosevelt persuaded him to become the **FDR** we remember.

But his "New Deal," wild though it seemed to the conservatives of the time and helpful though it was, was timid by comparison with what was needed in an economy with 25 percent unemployment. Thus, still by December 7, 1941 there were 10 percent without jobs.

2. Japan. It is the second largest economy in the world. In the 1970s and 1980s, it was widely seen as not only the technologically most advanced country but as economically invincible. And why not, with all of us Yankees (among others) driving Japanese cars and using Japanese electronic stuff? And then, as the 1990s began, it went into recession. And did nothing. And stayed in recession. And did nothing. And so on. Nothing? Not quite, they did a lot of diddling down with the rate of interest (aided and abetted by considerable U.S. advice to do just that, but only just that.) Ten years later, 2001, it was still in recession (interrupted slightly now and then by a little uptick, which then dropped again).

By then the rate of interest on borrowed funds became minus one-tenth of a percent. That is, in principle, if you borrowed some money, your creditor owed you. They are still in recession; having a cocktail party to celebrate when the economy expands by one percent (anything below 3.5 percent is bad news).

A few years ago, the Japanese would begin to worry when their Nikkei stock index (something like a composite of our Dow, Nasdaq, and S&P) started sinking below 14,000. In late summer 2003, when it rose just above 10,000 it was called a sign that—how does that go? —oh yeah, "prosperity was just around corner."

It's not that the Japanese haven't done anything but lower

interest rates; it is that they haven't done anything else they should have done: deficit financed social consumption and social invest-ment in ways that would demonstrably stimulate the economy while also being humanly and socially useful.

Greenspan. It's a good bet that a few years from now he will be seen as having been the beneficiary of the biggest con job in mod-ern economic history: the magic man, who was able to conjure up good times when all around him were dumbstruck. The truth is that Greenspan's reign embodies the truths of monetarism: If and when the economy is in no need of serious remedies, monetarism works just fine; when things get serious, it makes thing worse by seeming to provide a cure when it isn't—something like an ill-trained med-ical doctor looking really great when he takes care of a healthy per-son; but when that person develops a serious malady, it's harmful not helpful to even have him around.

One of the popular characterizations of Greenspan in his hey-day had to do with his ways of presenting his ideas before congres-sional committees (he seldom if ever speaks publicly anywhere else), always reading long and complicated sentences with qualifying phrases that require much interpretation, etc. The Wizard of Oz in economics clothing.

However, as the soggy economies of 2001-2002 mushed along he did what those in the high seats always do: he was either non-committal or wrong. If you are an influential public figure, you daren't say anything seriously negative about the economy, for fear 1) of making a bad situation worse, and/or 2) being made less influ-ential because you were negative. It's OK to use cute phrases like "irrational exuberance," when they're not connected to any policy that squeezes the irrational ones. Or, as Paul Krugman in "Passing the Buck" puts it: (NYT, 9-2-02, Op-ed)

> You see, Mr. Greenspan is the only economic policy maker we have. Fiscal policy is effectively off the table because of long-run deficits worsened by Mr. Greenspan's own bad advice. Funny how he wasn't sure that Nasdaq 5,000 was a bubble, but believed that 10-year surplus projections were reliable enough to justify a huge tax cut... urged on by the Bush administration's relentless opportunism; every proposal for short-run economic stimulus turns into an attempt to lock in permanent tax cuts for corporations and the wealthy. So, if the recovery continues to lose momentum, it's up to the Fed to take matters in hand.

.... a worry I've had for the past few months /is/ that Fed officials will respond to continuing economic weakness not with action but with excuses...; a process we've seen all too clearly in Japan...; rather than risk trying to solve Japan's problems and failing, the bank has repeatedly redefined it mission so that it doesn't even have to try. I never thought the Fed would go down the same path. But after listening to Mr. Greenspan explain why he couldn'ta and shouldn'ta, I'm starting to wonder.

It would be better to start worrying. Here's what Alan was up to in February, 2004: "To Trim Deficit, Greenspan Urges Social Security and Medicare Cuts." (NYT, 2-28-04) He went on to say that "the real fiscal calamity is not this year's deficit /$500 + billion/ but the soaring entitlement costs that will come when the baby boom generation begins to reach retirement age."

That is so wrong—see **Social Security**—that one is led to ask which of these three statements is correct: 1) Greenspan is ignorant. 2) He is a liar. 3. 1 + 2. Woe is us: In the realm of policy-making, he and **Friedman** rule the roost, i capi dei capi, in Mafia talk.

Monroe Doctrine (see Latin America.....)

multinational corporations (MNCs) (see big business)

NAFTA (see free trade, globalization)

napalm (see collateral damage)

nationalism/patriotism

There are certain "big words" with so much of both the useful and the harmful, positive and negative attached to their existence that it is difficult to have a lucid discussion about them. **Technology** is one of those words, nationalism one of the others, in part because it is so tightly linked to patriotism and almost as much with democracy—two other big words. (HOBSBAWM, 1990; VEBLEN, 1917/1945)

The qualification "almost" regarding nation-states and democracies arises because there have been so many very <u>un</u>democratic nation states and, as well, democratic societies that did <u>not</u> exist within what we mean by a nation. Here we note only three:

1. In his translation of <u>The Laxdaela Saga</u>, VEBLEN showed that after the 10th century Iceland moved toward becoming at least as democratic as any society since then. By the 13th century Iceland had become a republic—without, however, a central state, an executive, or police. Alas, Veblen pointed out,

> their republic of insubordinate citizens presently fell into default... after some experience at the hands of able and ambitious statesmen in contact with an alien government drawn on the coercive plan. The clay vessel failed to make good among the iron pots, and so proved its unfitness to survive in the world of Christian nations... (VEBLEN, <u>The Nature of Peace</u>, 1917/1945)

Veblen's writings were always ironic, and the more so as his deepest feelings were involved. He was a passionate democrat and at least as passionately opposed to war and the nation-state. He saw them as facilitating and multiplying war and its damages; his <u>The Nature of Peace</u> is really about the roots of war, and when he refers to "insubordinate citizens," it is admiringly.

2. On the other side of the planet, a long-standing set of democracies was also destroyed by "iron pots" many centuries later. Before the French invaded and occupied what came to be called Vietnam, the peoples there had an Emperor, but he was more of a figurehead even than today's British Queen; a functioning democracy was common in the villages, especially in the North. (KAHIN, 1968)

3. The histories of the USA that discuss "**Indians**" see them not only as "savages" but their "chiefs" as ruling tyrannically. However, in a long and informative article concerning the tribes native to the Missouri Valley, Tim Egan noted this:

> What the natives who descended from those tribes want people to know is that they already had an advanced society when Lewis and Clark arrived. It was a sophisticated agricultural society, with clans and large earth lodges run by women. ("Two Centuries Later, A Moment for Indians to Retell Past," <u>NYT</u>, 6-15-03)

The foregoing refer to small groups; the societies that first became major nation-states and, ultimately, political democracies, were part of the European evolution toward industrial capitalism. The driving force of those movements was not democracy, however; it was **power**—power for the rising business class to have the first and final say over how the nation's human, natural, and military resources were to be used.

What democracy was achieved came much later, and always after much struggle: Whether in Britain, France, Germany, Belgium—wherever (including the USA)—the right to vote was restricted by property and, until the 20th century, by gender (and in the U.S. South, by color, until the 1960s).

Nationalism in the colonized and imperialized societies usually had democracy as both its origin and its goal, as they sought to throw off the foreign rule that had crippled or destroyed their societies. In the richer countries, however, nationalism's driving force was usually some combination of militarism and expansionism with, just as usually, considerable popular support.

As a term, "nationalism" is sufficiently confusing unto itself; but it has not been left to itself, it has come to be used interchangeably with "patriotism." Once there was a fine saying, "My country, right or wrong, but my country!" "Fine," because it could be followed by constructive criticism, to right the wrong(s). Nowadays it is more likely to come out as "My country right or wrong; and those who say it is wrong are unpatriotic—and they'd better watch out." That is, those who are patriotic must also be nationalistic.

In the USA such attitudes did not begin with the Iraqi war; its seeds were planted as we broke loose from Britain and blossomed as the USA began its overseas expansion in the 1890s. Then (to mix the metaphor), when we entered World War I they "tied the knot": nowadays we live with the lethal offspring of that marriage.

Nationalism paved the way for the nation-state but was itself a product of the felt need by newly-emerging centers of economic power to have recourse to political and military power. Underneath and enabling all of these drives were technological developments—in production and transport and in communications.

Put together, the latter were in turn stimulated by their existence and growth in other and competing national economies and by the upsurge of **imperialism**. Those varying sources and degrees of fervor were all given added strength by the ways and means of the ever-modernizing **media**.

All this was becoming evident in all the participant powers just before and during the first world war (1914-1918). The following comments by Veblen, written in 1916 and 1917, could have been written yesterday.

> Among English-speaking peoples much is to be gained by showing that the path of patriotic glory is at the same time the way of equal-handed justice under the rule of free institutions; at the same time, in a fully commercialized community /such as ours/, material benefits by way of trade will go far to sketch in a background of <u>decency</u> for any enterprise that looks to the enhancement of the national prestige. But any promise of gain... will not of itself carry full conviction to the commonplace modern citizen; or even to such modern citizens as are best endowed with a national spirit...; no contemplated enterprise... will fully commend itself to the popular sense of merit and expediency until it is given a <u>moral</u> turn, so as to bring it to square with the dictates of right and honest dealing.... To give the fullest practical effect to the patriotic fervor that animates any modern nation..., it is necessary to show that the demands of equity are involved in the case; the common man must be persuaded that right is on his side....; and on the whole it is not difficult to arrange.... It is not that the... patriotic policy entered upon with the support of popular sentiment need <u>be</u> right and equitable..., but only that it should be capable of being made to <u>seem</u> so.... The higher the pitch of patriotic fervor, the more tenuous and more threadbare may be the requisite moral sanction. By cumulative excitation some very remarkable results have latterly been attained along this line.
>
> A corollary...: Any politician who succeeds in embroiling his country in a war, however nefarious, becomes a popular hero and is reputed a wise and righteous statesman; at least for the time being. Illustrative instances need not, and indeed can not gracefully be named; most popular heroes and reputed statesmen belong in this class. (VEBLEN, <u>Nature of Peace</u>, 1917/1945) (emphases added)

NATO (see Cold War)

needs

As noted under **economics**, the word "need" is not to be found in economic theory. To be sure, once in a while it may be heard in an economist's conversation: "I need a drink," or, "I need a promotion..., a larger office"; don't waste your time looking for it in an econ textbook.

That should come as no surprise; mainstream economics is a tool for maintaining and strengthening the status quo; the status quo is a business society; <u>its</u> need is to be ever more profitable. If, in passing, some human, social, or environmental needs are met, OK; but that's not the name of the game.

On the other hand, economics has spent much time with analyses of <u>wants</u>; and business has done what it can to create, multiply, and stimulate them. The distinction between needs and wants is simple, but no less important for being so: our needs prompt the desire (or want) for their satisfaction. In our modern era, however, our wants have been created through **advertising**, and decreasingly prompted by our needs. Indeed, in our attempts to satisfy created wants we are often led to act directly or indirectly to thwart public policies required to satisfy our needs, such as public transportation and **health care**.

Our needs arise out of our nature as human beings; primary among them are what have come to be called "basic needs": for nutrition, shelter, health, education and, especially in our time, the opportunity to appreciate and develop our possibilities. Education and opportunity are different from the other three; we can survive physically without education and opportunity; but it is in the very nature of our species, for better and for worse, that over time we not only can but must change the conditions under which we live; and that requires education and opportunity for all. (See SEN; STREETEN; STRETTON; <u>Afterword</u>)

As noted elsewhere, what distinguishes us from all other species is our ability to <u>imagine</u>, and our inability <u>not</u> to do so. This has led to all of our creations, constructive and destructive, beautiful and horrifying; it is also the source of our hopes and our fears, along with much else.

It has become a commonplace that the technological progress of the past two centuries or so in the USA (and elsewhere), although it has done much to improve our living conditions has in the same processes made daily life a constant struggle to "get through the day," has not only provided us with innumerable "things"—many of which increase rather than satisfy our needs—but has caused the levels of tension and anxiety in our lives to rise as we wait in lines, are stuck in traffic jams, work our way throughout crowded malls, ponder our credit card debt, our children's behavior, and so on.

But behind any such listing is something more fundamental and disturbing. In the process of seeking to meet our created wants, we have lost our bearings as to what our basic needs are and how they easily they might be met. More generally, our species, which from its beginnings has been driven by both constructive and destructive "instincts," (see VEBLEN, 1914) has allowed the latter to crowd out the former.

We plunge into ever-more destructive wars accompanied by **environmental** recklessness while, as individuals, we find it ever more difficult to construct a calm and pleasing life for ourselves—as distinct from having a shiny car, lots of appliances, and a houseful of throw-away objects purchased through debt. On top of which, instead of assisting us all these "things" have come to dominate us. We are descended from chimpanzees and, perhaps, some of their cousins. When we observe them in the **zoos**, we laugh and feel superior. The last laugh would be theirs, were it not that we will take them down with us.

Nixon, Richard M.

Hatred is harmful to the hater, as well as to the hated, and we should do our best to rise above it. For me, after having to put up with Nixon and J. Edgar **Hoover** and Joe **McCarthy** and their ilk year after year—and now **Bush II!**—that is easier said than done. Nixon himself hated so many and so much that we inhaled it from him, as with second-hand smoke; he was an infectious disease.

Here, for example, are two excerpts from the long-suppressed White House tapes, the first with his Chief of Staff (**Haldeman**), the second with his Secretary of the Treasury (**Connally**).

Item: After Arthur Watson, Nixon's Ambassador to France, was publicized as having groped an airline stewardess, his response to Haldeman was "It's better to chase girls than boys. Now that's my position and let's stop this crap. Understand!"

Item: In discussing what Nixon termed a "terrible Jewish clique," Connally agreeing, he added "it erodes our confidence, our strength. They're untrustworthy." After a few more such comments from both of them, they agreed that Nixon should try to reduce the Jewish influence in his second term. (WP, 3/2/02)

He was one of the most powerful politicians ever in our history, but sloshing around in him like a poison was his need for always more power—no matter how gained, no matter what the purpose. That need splotched him like measles, kept him in a continuous high fever, unbalanced him; finally did him in.

But what a wall that Humpty Dumpty climbed before he fell! In 1946, Nixon was a virtual unknown from the Styx of Southern California; only six years later, Eisenhower was forced to accept him as his running mate. How did he do it? How rise from being "whatshisname?" to Veep and ultimately to the Oval Office? Twice, yet. The short answer is that his climb was almost entirely a product of his relentless use of character assassination. (WILLS, 1969) It began with his virulent congressional campaign against the moderate New Deal congressman Jerry Voorhis, in 1946.

Precocious cold warrior that he was, Nixon portrayed Voorhis as a leftist. Then, along with honing his skills and enlarging his publicity with the **House Un-American Activities Committee,** he used the same weapons in 1948 against another decent liberal, Helen Gahagan Douglas ("a pink right down to her underwear," said he). That got him into the Senate. And then, in order to satisfy the GOP right, Eisenhower made him his running mate in 1952.

Most think Nixon rose to power by hanging onto to the coattails of Joe **McCarthy;** the truth is quite the opposite. An entirely lackluster senator, McCarthy was a stupid lout, but he was not unobservant. He used Nixon as a role model; and it was by using Nixon's tried and true techniques that in 1950 Joe rose to public prominence when he held up that piece of paper on which, he said (lying as usual) were "the names of over 205 members of the Communist Party now serving in the State Department...,"

That the list was never seen by anyone; that never one name

from that list was ever provided, should have disadvantaged Joe; but when it comes to "anti-communism" anything and everything worked (as now with **terrorism**). McCarthy (or his advisers) took their lessons from the **Red Scare** of the 1920s, but it was Nixon who honed that into his personal weapon.

The term paranoid seems to fit Nixon all too closely: remember, we're talking about a President of the USA. He almost always seemed as though he were getting even, working out a grudge. He was said to be unprincipled: wrong. He had at least <u>one</u> principle, and it served for all occasions: "What's in it for me?" There are, of course, many in the business, political, educational and medical worlds (among others) who live by that standard, but Nixon ran away with the prizes.

However, and interestingly, although his <u>a</u>morality led him to propose or accept innumerable disgusting and destructive policies, it also let him go along with certain <u>desirable</u> socioeconomic legislation that no subsequent president has been able or inclined to see passed—among them, clean air and water legislation. "Wotthehell," one can imagine him saying to himself. Nixon's tendency to personalize domestic and foreign policy did him in when it became his turn to deal with the war in Indochina. It was in trying to protect himself and to "get" his enemies that tied him in knots and threw him down. His role in the war will be noted when **Vietnam, Laos**, and **Cambodia** are discussed (all under **Asia...**) and under **Haldeman**; here just a few more comments in that respect on Nixon himself.

In his winning presidential campaign in 1968, Nixon promised to get us out of Vietnam—by "Vietnamization." What he had in mind was not ending but winning the war without <u>U.S.</u> casualties. Let the ground war be fought by the Vietnamese while we **carpet-bomb** from 32,000 feet up; if that failed to turn the trick, well, we'll just have to nuke 'em. (ELLSBERG)

Politically, his strategy was a good one; by a steady withdrawal of U.S. troops and declining U.S. casualties he was able to end the draft and, at the same time, to take much of the steam out of the antiwar movement. Fortunately, we'll never know about those **nukes**, because Watergate got him kicked out of the White House with the war still on.

His response to the Watergate accusations were highpoints (or lowpoints): His ongoing reply to each new piece of evidence was to employ what he termed "the modified limited hang-out": admit to previously proven acts—"mistakes were made"—but not the latest ones. Sound familiar? (Or maybe they <u>have</u> found those weapons of mass destruction in Iraq?)

I cannot leave Nixon without the simultaneously absurd and poignant note furnished us by the late H. R. **Haldeman** in his memoirs. He was Nixon's confidant and right-hand man for domestic political strategy. **Kissinger** served that purpose for foreign affairs. Among the many juicy tales recounted by Haldeman—who frequently and dispassionately notes the distrust, dislike, and jealousy between those two power-hungry servants of the USA—is this one concerning an incident at a time of high intensity over Vietnam: Tricky Dick and Henry the K.—one resembling an uptight mortician, the other the good Dr. Strangelove—were found by Haldeman kneeling on a carpet in the Oval Office, fixed in prayer. We shall never know to whom or for what they were praying, but we can be sure of one thing: it had nothing to do with the well-being of the people of the United States of America (or anywhere).

Despite all, a few years after Watergate, that charmless man with the charmed life had the <u>chutzpah</u> to begin to resume staged appearances in public, with always more fanfare. And it worked. So it was that Richard Milhous Nixon emerged from obscurity a second time, this time to be seen as a respected elder statesman. Gulp.

Back in the early 1970s, my aged Russian Jewish immigrant Uncle Louie summed up Nixon well and succinctly: "Vot a <u>schlemiel</u>!"

nuclear weapons (nukes)

It has been said that the <u>interaction</u> of just three technological developments of the past century are sufficient to bring an end to (at least) human life on this planet: **TV**, **cars**, and **nukes**. TV has been central to the **commodification** of almost everything in sync with **consumerism** (in which **cars** are the main obsession) and the always deeper **corruption** of politicsm the **media**, and almost everything else. So where do nukes come in?

Once the damned techniques were mastered, whether for war or peace, it had become essential to rid ourselves of them: entirely. They are too dangerous, not only in war but also, as is clear (but not easily visible through the media camouflage), when used for energy production. (see **environment** and **waste**)

The history of our species suggests it would be difficult enough to contain that technology in a world <u>without</u> consumerism and TV; with them, it may well be impossible. The need is great to learn the facts concerning nukes and to pay attention to the ongoing developments—here, there, and elsewhere.

To meet that need, that is, to have a sufficient percentage of the population bring their powers to bear to prohibit <u>any</u> use of nuclear technology, would be difficult under any circumstances, given the several powerful vested interests involved in business, politics, the military. In today's world of mystification, deception, and bewitchment, institutionalized confusion and boredom constitute imposing obstacles to good sense on this (or any other) matter.

That the foregoing has the sound of hysteria to it is its partial confirmation; we have not learned "to love the bomb," but we surely have "learned" not to worry about it (and its offspring) as much as realism demands.

So what's all the fuss about? We look first at nukes as weaponry.

<u>Hiroshima to today</u>. As was pointed out in **Hiroshima...**, there was no need to use the bomb there, let alone again at Nagasaki—except to see if they really worked and, more importantly, to warn the **USSR**. (ALPEROVITZ) If such weapons were used for such disgraceful purposes at a time when our political leadership, bad as it may have been, was first-rate compared to now, how can it be believed they won't be used by us—and/or others—for equally or even more monstrous purposes? (BIRD/LIPSCHULTZ)

Immediately after Hiroshima the Federation of Atomic Scientists and some politicians sought to prevent nuclear proliferation and to assure it by promising that we would get rid of our own nukes. The knowledge would remain; the weapons would not.

Good try, but they didn't have a chance. Soon after the war proliferation began and has never stopped; now there are nukes in countries large and small, rich and poor, some in countries seen as friends, some in those seen as foes. Along the way, we and the **USSR** have more than once stumbled to the edge of using them against each other. (ELLSBERG; JUNGK)

Ah! The nuke-lovers will say, but didn't MAD (mutually-assured destruction) work? Didn't the **Cold War** end without them being used? Yes and no.

First, the yes. It applies to the use of atomic/hydrogen bombs. We didn't use them, but we came perilously close to doing so in the Cuban missile crisis, under "good" president **JFK**; and we know that **Nixon** was prepared to use them against Vietnam, except that he didn't last long enough. (ELLSBERG)

More recently, there have been more than a few suggestions that we just might have to consider using them against North Korea, if.... (See **Cold War** and **Vietnam** and **Cuba** for discussion of how unjustified all those conflicts were—and might not have gone as far into horror as they did had we <u>not</u> had nukes and the **arrogance** that accompanies them.)

Then there is the "no" side. It has to do not with the Bomb but with our use of "depleted uranium"—which, it turns out, is <u>not</u> depleted. In recent years there have been complaints from the **Okinawans** (among others) about sicknesses arising from our use of depleted uranium in practice bombings; (JOHNSON, C.) The problem there, grave though it has been for too large a number, pales in comparison with the **collateral damage** of the first Gulf War. The details are sordid, both in terms of the hundreds of thousands of injured <u>and</u> the U.S. response.

In a recent book, the British journalist John PILGER shows that over 300 tons of weaponry using depleted uranium were used, fired by tanks or aircraft. He quotes Professor D. Rokke, the U.S. Army physicist responsible for "cleaning up" Kuwait at war's end:

> I am like many people in southern Iraq, I have 5,000 times the recommended level of radiation in my body. The contamination /of air and water/ was right throughout Iraq and Kuwait.... What we're seeing now, respiratory problems, kidney problems, cancers, are the direct result of the use of this highly toxic material. (PILGER)

And he goes on to cite the "denial of medical care to American and British and other allied soldiers and the tens of thousands of Iraqis contaminated," adding that "the Iraqis didn't use depleted uranium; it was not their weapon; they simply don't know how to get rid of it from their environment." Does anyone?

Meanwhile, to cut this short, we, the USA, are now taking a step toward even great danger, even greater likelihood that there will be an unstoppable nuclear war in the foreseeable future: with <u>little</u> nukes.

First, we note where nuclear weapons exist or are on their way to becoming:

> Confirmed: USA, Russia, China, France, Britain, Israel, India, Pakistan (about 32,000 known warheads in toto, 20,000 of them ours). Unconfirmed: North Korea,; Countries reported to be trying to make them: Iran, Libya, Iraq. (12 countries have disbanded nuke programs.) ("Bush's nuclear arms plan," <u>SFC</u>, 5-11-03).

Second, let the headlines in early 2003 suffice to make the point: "Senate Panel Votes to Lift Ban on Small Nuclear Arms." (<u>NYT</u>, 5-10-03) "The Thinkable: The Second Nuclear Age is About Insecure Nations..., unaligned with and resentful of Western Power." (<u>NYT</u> Magazine, 5-4-03) "Noted nuclear scientists reject nuclear quest: U.S. research would give legitimacy to others to develop low-yield bombs..." (<u>SFC</u>, 5-20-03)

If that is not enough to make your skin crawl, consider what gives with the peaceful uses of nuclear technology.

Most who read this were children when the peaceful uses of nukes showed <u>their</u> catastrophic side: Three-Mile Island (1979, Pa., USA) and Chernobyl (1986, Ukraine, USSR).

The people living in or near both regions have not been able to forget those disasters; their consequences live on, whether because of family members lost or badly-harmed, or ongoing severities. In Chernobyl, "when the facility's roof blew off—releasing 30 to 40 <u>times</u> as much radioactivity as Hiroshima and Nagasaki <u>combined</u>, many were killed instantly and 135,000 had to be evacuated: permanently. As recently as 2000, the Ukraine government was spending 5 percent of its GDP to mitigate the disaster's consequences." ("REACTOR: Steel shell to encase ruins of Chernobyl," <u>NYT</u>, 11-30-02) (emphasis added)

So, that was in the Ukraine; couldn't happen here. But it did, at Three-Mile Island in Pennsylvania; and there have been premonitions of new Three-Mile Islands in the air: Two incidents, in 2002 and 2003, gained attention, this time in Ohio and Texas; in doing so they have revealed a more general set of dangers.

In a <u>NYT</u> Op-ed piece by Daniel F. Ford (once director of the Union of Concerned Scientists), "The Hole in the Reactor: A

Safety Lapse in Ohio is All Too Unsurprising," we read that the First Energy Corporation's 25-year old Davis-Besse nuclear plant (near Toledo) is planning to weld "a steel Band-Aid to the top of the plant's cracked nuclear reactor, now so corroded that 70 pounds of steel have been eaten away." Did you say <u>cracked</u> <u>nuclear</u> <u>reactor</u>? That's what he said; that and this, and not just about Ohio:

> Today we have dozens of aging (and corroding and leaking) nuclear plants, licensed in the 1970s, operating close to our major cities. The reactor with a hole in its head at Davis-Besse is proof that the reforms and safety upgrades promised.... after Three Mile Island and Chernobyl have not, to put it delicately, had full success. The Nuclear Regulatory Commission has let Davis-Besse operate /for years/ with documented bad maintenance.

Well, that was written in April, 2002. In May, 2003, we read that in Wadsworth, Texas an "Extraordinary Reactor Leak Gets the Industry's Attention." (<u>NYT</u>, 5-1-2003) The subtitle tells us a bit more: "It's at the Vessel's Bottom, a Troubling Sign." What's troubling about it is that "until that discovery, the Nuclear Regulatory Commission believed that it understood the mechanism for leaks in reactor vessels." In other words, it is likely to turn out as being not "extraordinary" but merely the first of a series.

The presumed cause—"stress correction cracking"—came as news to the Commission. If the presumption is correct, "That would be bad news for the nation's 102 other commercial power reactors...." It could also be seen as "bad news" for the millions of people within radiation distance from those 102 reactors. But surely the Nuclear Regulatory Commission, its members appointed by the **cor**-**ruption**-free Bush Administration, wouldn't have reduced its regulations unless they were <u>absolutely</u> sure that everything is OK? Of course not!

On top of which, there is the problem of nuclear **waste**—which is discussed under that heading.

Meanwhile, stop worrying. Party!

oil

It is close to impossible to comprehend what our world would have been like <u>without</u> its innumerable uses for oil in the past century or more: for **cars** and other modes of transportation, for all of industrial and much of agricultural production, for our heat, our cooking, for..., you name it. Here, however, it will be contended that—all things considered—the past few generations (and, even more so, upcoming generations) would have had a better life without it. What's so bad about oil?

Here are the main elements of those "all things" that need considering": 1. War. 2. The economy. 3. Politics and power. 4. The environment. (Here we comment only in passing about natural gas, oil's near relative in all such matters).

At the outset, let it be understood that the critical positions now to be taken are not meant to suggest that without oil there would not be nor ever have been problems in any of those realms; only that with oil the separate sets of problems and their interactions have long made increasing contributions to hellish troubles, the accumulation and worsening of which now threaten unprecedented disaster(s).

1. Oil and war.

All of history and probably most of prehistory have been afflicted by military conflicts; but the differences between the enormities of conflict in the pre-oil epochs and the past century or so are great indeed, whether viewed quantitatively or qualitatively. Moreover, it is telling that as we approach the present, oil tends has become the major contributing cause of military conflict—obviously in the several conflicts in the **Middle East** since World War II; less obviously for decades going back to the beginning of the 20th century. (see EVEREST)

That such should be so arises mostly from two facts: 1. All but a very few countries depend increasingly upon supplies of oil to keep their economies running, while 2) a handful of giant oil companies' profits depend upon their continuing access to proven and probable oil reserves. Our emphasis will be on U.S. companies and U.S. foreign policy.

First, a bit of what now seems ancient but remains relevant history. Those who came to social consciousness after World War II might be surprised to learn that oil first became significant economically in the USA, that we possessed huge oil reserves, and that it wasn't until after World War II that oil would have any connection with war for the USA.

Oil was discovered and used for "primitive" purposes by the tribes indigenous to what became Pennsylvania; it first became a commercial product after the Civil War, mostly as kerosene for illumination and as a lubricant. Even so, as its uses spread both in function and geography ("oil for the lamps of China"), it became the foundation of Rockefeller's wealth.

Already in 1873 John D. had pulled off the large group of **mergers & acquisitions** that became the Standard Oil Company: The key elements were his purchase of many oil refineries while, at the same time, making secret deals with the railroads to carry his oil at cheaper rates than his remaining competitors. By the end of the century, he controlled over 90 percent of all oil production—a precocious step toward the giantism that would come to mark U.S. business before World War I and that made him the first U.S. billionaire as the 20th century opened. In doing so, Rockefeller (as did Carnegie, in steel) manifested his religious zeal when he proclaimed that his new monopoly was "a matter of conscience..., it was right between me and my God." (PHILLIPS, 2002) He and **Bush II** (from an oil family himself) and **Ashcroft** would make a helluva team.

The impact of the "Muckrakers" and their critiques of the "robber barons" (JOSEPHSON) combined with the fervor initiated by Teddy Roosevelt led in 1911 to the first major case against monopoly in our history. The indictments for violating the 1890 Sherman Antitrust Act led to the breakup of Standard Oil into 34 separate companies which, since then, have become intimately associated again: notably, Socony (NY) begat Mobil, which joined Standard of N.J., which begat EXXON, and they then begat EXXON MOBIL, whilst Texas Oil begat Texaco and Standard of California begat Chevron and they begat CHEVRONTEXACO. Saves gas for family reunions.

As domestic and industrial electrification and **cars** (among other uses) caused the demand for oil to skyrocket, reserves were sought for and found throughout the USA—beyond Pennsylvania to Texas and Oklahoma, California, and the Northwest. The riches to be made from oil brought out the worst in the business world as regards **corruption**, violence, and dishonesty, all fanned by **greed**.

As might be expected, all this was displayed flagrantly not only in Texas, but in the glamorous new developments that became—the saints preserve us!—Southern California, with its sunshine and beaches and, not least, its rich oil deposits. Both your funnybones and your sense of horror can be aroused by a reading of Oil! by Upton SINCLAIR (1926), or by the film "Chinatown," both of them concerned with the high-rolling corruption provoked by oil and water in the social context of the L.A. region in the 1920s.

Alas! What led to all that also determined that all the U.S. oil regions would abuse their enormous oil resources in such a technologically insane manner as to make us become prematurely dependent upon foreign oil as World War II approached.

As noted elsewhere (**Middle East**), "prematurely" because the USA had the distinction of pumping its oil out competitively; great for some moneymakers, sheer stupidity by engineering standards. The land under which oil was expected to be found was marketed in relatively small parcels, on each of which competitive drilling then took place. If you didn't pump out as much as you could, fast, the other guys would empty the pool.

Elsewhere—in the Middle East, for example—the drilling was and is done on a "unit" basis, where the unit is the entire oil field. Doing so not only eliminates competitive drilling, but also allows the field's natural gas to assist in "pushing oil up." (BLAIR)

The USA is the hungriest of all nations for oil. At the end of the war we were indisputably also all-powerful. As such, we set about 1) to organize and dominate the global marketing of oil, and 2) to gain control over reserves wherever they might be—which meant, first the Middle East, then Latin America, then Africa. (see SAMPSON, TANZER, RIDGEWAY, ENGLER)

Britain had been the major oil power in the Middle East in preceding decades (see **Middle East....Iran, Iraq**); but Britain, as with the rest of Europe, was distraught and unable to maintain itself, let alone its empire, as World War II ended. Adding push to shove, the **Cold War** began.

The first U.S. steps were to support those seeking to create the state of Israel. That meant, first and foremost, getting the British out; that done, the next task was to keep the Israelis in, that is, to assist them in the **Israeli/Palestinian** conflict. In the same years, the USA began its efforts to "fill the vacuum" left in Iran, Iraq, and Saudi Arabia by the departing British. In some degree we succeeded; in some degree we failed: see **Iran** and **Iraq**.

Apart from Israel, our greatest "success" was in Saudi Arabia, both as a source of oil and as a military base. By now, however, Saudi Arabia has become a leading instance of the "Blowback" analyzed by Christopher SIMPSON—only the initial manifestations of which are the activities of the Saudi Osama bin Laden and Al Qaeda. The capture of bin Laden will end his career, but not that of Al Qaeda. So it goes.

The future is unpredictable in these respects, but it would be foolhardy to ignore some dangerous probabilities edging over the horizon. Among them are a continuation and enlargement of the anarchy in Afghanistan and the return of the Taliban. That "nation" is critical to us because it is a key part of the sector of what is hoped to become the main oil pipeline to the beckoning reserves of Central Asia—an effort in which Unocal has been involved for ten years or more.

Then there is Indonesia, a seemingly permanent area of social and military eruptions, teeming with mineral resources; and Latin America, most of all Venezuela, with its left-leaning government and its rich oil resources; and Nigeria, another Indonesia, with even greater instability and anti-Americanism centering upon CHEVRON. Nor can it be forgotten that although the **Cold War** is "over," our conflicts with Russia are not; the Russians are among the high oil reserve countries in the world, have close relations with Iran, and have their own plans for Central Asia (as does China). Understandably, they are among the most restive of the Europeans as regards our bristling new **preemptive** foreign policy.

There are other regions and other reasons that could bring us to war; those concerning oil are sufficient to provide deep concern. But that is only one of the vital reasons for us to seek to reduce our dependence upon oil, rather than to seek control over global reserves.

2. Oil and the economy.

As with war, there are enough reasons to worry about the economy's health and dangers without having to bring oil into the equation. Because the supply and the price of oil affect so much of our consumption and our production and, as well our foreign trade and financial and service sectors—is there anything left?—when oil is in trouble it is likely the economy will be close behind.

What troubles? Although both oil and natural gas prices are presumably regulated—oil by the major oil producing companies through cartel arrangements such as OPEC and by the several major western companies (SAMPSON), and natural gas by (always weakening) federal and state regulations (see **deregulation**)—one might think that neither of the controlling private and public institutions would be foolish enough to let their search for profits (or fear of losses) lead them to price manipulations that might cause the entire world economy to move into crisis.

In thinking that, one would be wrong—as illustrated most easily by 1) the "oil crisis" of the 1970s, seen as being caused by OPEC, 2) the more recent natural gas "Enron-connected" crises as the 1990s ended, and 3) the horrendous "blackout" of 2003. Their causations were both different and similar: different because OPEC raised the prices of oil (to counter the preceding and ongoing inflation affecting their imports), Enron (et al.) restricted natural gas production in order to make greater profits from **speculation**, and the blackout was caused by the sheer absence of preventive regulation; similar because in all cases it was concentrated private power working in collusion with corrupted governments to maintain or enhance profits; let come what may.

The OPEC price increases, initiated in 1973 and worsened five years later, moved inflation from mild to severe, as unemployment also rose in most of the major economies. (It was called "stagflation"; see SHERMAN). One would hope that responsible governments, seeing the dangers associated with economically dangerous uses of private power would act to constrain that power; once again, one would be wrong—this time because the line between the concentration of business power and the concentration of political power is difficult to find—except in the imaginations of mainstream **economics**. Which takes us to:

3. Politics and power.

There are many similarities between the USA of the 1920s and today; among are those having to do with oil and politics. The 1920s were rocked more than once by corruption scandals; the most publicized among them was "Teapot Dome."

You've guessed it, the government property called Teapot (in

Wyoming) was filled with oil. The oil reserves were "reserved" for the U.S. Navy under the control of what was then accurately called the War Department (now, of course, "Defense"). Our president then was Warren Harding, a hard drinker and womanizer whose Secretary of the Interior was a one-time oil developer named Albert Fall. (And you thought the White House only became oily a couple of years ago?) Harding, who gave the impression of having been <u>born</u> corrupt, transferred the Naval reserves to the Interior Department, and Fall leased them out to private developers (as he did also with some governmental reserves in California): greater efficiency; less governmental waste, y'know. (BLAIR, ENGLER)

As a Wyoming person, V.P. **Cheney** didn't have to be a historian to know about <u>that</u>; who said that history doesn't repeat itself (if with variations)? So we not only have an oil guy for V.P., but an oil guy for P. as well. No sweat; their holdings are all in blind trusts or something, no?

So Halliburton (Cheney's "ex"-company) got that big contract for post-war Iraq because it <u>deserved</u> it, and Bechtel (run by **Reagan's** Secretary of State George Schultz) got its big slice of the pie because <u>it</u> deserved it, and WorldCom got its juicy Iraq contract without competitive bidding perhaps because having just been fined $500 million for defrauding its shareholders of $11 <u>billion</u> it really needed the money. Aw, shucks, what are friends for? (IVINS, "The War? Just Business." <u>SFC</u>, 6-20-03)

All that looks a lot like **corruption**, and is; sure it is, but as Coolidge said, "the business of government is business." Change that to **big business** (especially the oil bidness). It's "normalcy" (a word Coolidge made part of our vocabulary): When people who have <u>been</u> in **big business** become part of big government swinging big deals in D.C. instead of Houston—why, that just means a slight voice change as you drink wine instead of beer.

So what was good for Halliburton before is now good for—I've got it!—the people of the United States of America! Let's drink to that. Would that oilers were the only giant companies who sit at the table of government largesse.

4. Oil and the environment.

This relationship is treated at some length in **environment, cars,** and **waste.** Suffice it to say here that both the search for oil and its multiple uses are destructive, first to the natural environment (most recently, in Alaska—much of it already accomplished through pipelines—with more to come), and have done and do irreversible sociopolitical harm done to the peoples of the countries where the oil is found.

Plus: It is both tragic and remarkable that the truly obvious existing damages—most especially in our polluted air—are widely-known and yet, at the same time, the craving for more and bigger **cars** rises rather than falls, the support for safe and efficient and cheap(er) public transportation falls, rather than rises—and so on: The consciousness industry has done its work.

But those who sit in the catbird seats of power never let down their guard. Just as the EPA was preparing to publish its report on environmental conditions in the summer of 2003, some EPA staff member furnished reporters with the kind of disturbing information that has come to characterize our invasion of Iraq. Two headlines tell the tale:

"White House rewrites EPA report: Risks of climate change edited out." (<u>SFC</u>, 6-20-03)

"Censorship on Global Warming." (<u>NYT</u>, Editorial, 6-20-03)

No response from **Bush II**; he was out raising money for the 2004 campaign. Plenty of it; some of it, probably, from the gas mask industry: He is <u>good</u> for them.

The foregoing discussion took off from the outrageous suggestion that we'd have been better off had we confined our uses of oil to its 19th century uses.

Does that make me a "Luddite?"—that is, a "machine-breaker"? (The reference is to those workers who, as the industrial revolution was emerging gained that reputation—unjustly. /see HOBSBAWM, 1964/)

The serious as distinct from the dramatic element of that position is that our lives would have been and in the future would be, safer and saner <u>and</u>, finally, more comfortable had our uses of oil been guided by intelligence rather than business greed and consumeristic idiocies.

That is saying something else: Only in a society wherein vital decisions are made in terms of human and social needs and possibilities can the positive rather than the negative meanings of **technology** be trusted. (see <u>Afterword</u>)

Okies (see Dust Bowl)

oligopoly (see big business)

Operation Just Cause
(see Latin America... Panama)

Palestine (see Middle East: Israel/Palestine)

pharmaceuticals

Prescription drugs are obtained as though they are among the "consumer" products that the "free market" should "ration." However, and as with health care, education, and housing, medications should be made available according to need not purchasing power, as "for-profit commodities" in keeping with "tastes." Some who read this will remember that during World War II there was price control and rationing. They were meant to see that purchasing power not determine who should have how much of needed goods. And it worked. There was a war on then, of course; but, as the philosopher William James once put it, surely there is—or should be—a moral equivalent for war? Is not the pained life of a child with Down's Syndrome deserving of consideration beyond its parents' incomes? Do we not give free health care to war veterans? (Although that too is now being cut.) Does a fibrillating heart threaten a rich man more than a poor one? Etc.

What is it about pharmaceutical companies that makes their products so different from those rationed in wartime? And what we are to make of the claims of these companies, with the tightest and most wealth-yielding patent protections of all, to be part of a "free market"? That's a good place to start.

Patents. When patents began in 17th century England their full name was "patent of monopoly." The justification for continuing patent monopolies is that they provide an incentive for costly research which, it is presumed, otherwise would not occur. That is a respectable reason, but one that ignores many matters:

Item: In both past and present there have been long-standing other research efforts—governmentally-financed private and university research labs, as well as charities and private foundations—which have provided important drugs (penicillin, polio vaccine, AZT, taxol, among many others). (BAKER, D&S, 5/6-2001)

Item: A conservative estimate of the cost of patent protection is that prescribed drugs would sell for just 25 percent of their prices without that protection; a $79 billion savings to patients in the year 2000. But didn't they need that money to do their research? No. The drug industry's net costs of research in that year came to $19 billion. No bargain for us there. So where did the other $60 billion go? Here's where:

Marketing. NYT, 11-17-2000: "Overall spending on pharmaceutical promotion in the United States increased more than 10 percent last year, to $13.9 billion from $12.4 billion in 1998." That was not for advertising, but for visiting doctors: From 1990 to 2000, "there was a 57 percent increase in the number of pharmaceutical salespeople visiting physicians, from 56,000 to 88,000," (K. GREIDER)

Three years later,

> the Bush Administration told drug companies that many of the techniques they use to sell their drugs run a high risk of violating federal fraud and abuse laws...; that they must not offer any financial incentives to doctors, hospitals, insurers or pharmacists to encourage or reward the prescribing of particular drugs. ("U.S. Warns Drug Makers...." NYT, 4-28-03)

The article goes on to list many of the other questionable practices of the drug companies, such as "extraordinary incentives to sales reps to induce sales through lavish entertainment, etc." As it happens, a tennis mate of mine is the chief pharmacist for a large hospital in our area. He is also a skier; he loves to visit Paris and..., you know. Well, every year, at least once, we have to interrupt our tennis engagements because he is off to the Alps to ski (and sit in on meetings), or Paris (and sit in on meetings) or somewhere, all expenses paid (to sit in on meetings). Does it influence his behavior as a pharmacist? Of course not!

In that **corruption** is king, that's not the end of the story (nor will this be): One of the largest of the drug companies was forced to admit publicly that "it could soon be indicted in a host of federal charges, including /the/ destruction of documents related to a government investigation into its marketing practices for prescription drugs." (NYT, 5-31-03)

> Prosecutors are examining whether Schering-Plough illegally gave financial grants and other items of value to doctors and other customers, whether it marketed drugs for unapproved uses, and whether it submitted false pricing information to the government so that Medicaid paid too much for its products.... /This and/ other cases have been spurred by rapidly rising increases in the costs of prescription drugs and the burden those costs place on governments, employers and patients.

Will the drug companies stop being naughty now that the government has waggled its finger at some of them? Of course! But that's not all.

Advertising. Until 1997, the category of direct-to-consumer ads for prescription drugs did not exist. Then, the Food and Drug Administration—"encouraged" by lobbyists—loosened the relevant restrictions; "...now it is a $2.5 billion a year business—exceeding the amounts spent advertising over-the-counter drugs (vitamins, analgesics, etc.; another $2 billion +) and, as well, yearly outlays marketing insurance, real estate, apparel and alcoholic beverages." (NYT 7-12-02)

Plus: "most of the prescription drugs promoted directly in magazines, TV, and elsewhere are the newest, most expensive products, offering their makers the highest profits."

Plus: Advertising expenses are fully deductible business expenses.

Plus: In response to a research survey on the matter, 25 percent of respondents said they had been prompted by ads to call or visit a doctor to discuss the advertised product—often placing the patients and doctors in "an adversarial relationship," with even the doctors being "as misled as the patients." (ibid.) The drug companies respond to such criticisms on the grounds that advertising falls under the categories of freedom of speech. Sure it does; wasn't it Thomas Jefferson who said "Without advertising—especially of pharmaceuticals—we might just as well be occupied by the British!" Right.

But the advertising and marketing efforts of these companies may much exceed what has been stated above. According to a report in the LAT (7-12-02), "pharmaceutical companies often spend twice as much on overhead, marketing, advertising and promotion than on research and the development of new drugs"; namely, "$45.4 billion for the 50 most-prescribed drugs for seniors, compared to $19.1 billion in research and development." (HC, 7-18-02)

Fear not, self-reform by the business world is just around corner: "CNN to Reveal When Guests Promote Drugs for Companies": (NYT, 8-23-02)

> In the last year or so /only then?/, dozens of movie, television and music stars, as well as sports celebrities, who are paid by drug and medical device companies, have appeared on talk shows and morning news programs to discuss ailments they or people close to them have. They often mention the drugs or other medical products by brand name without disclosing their ties to the company. /See **advertising** for Lauren Bacall's venture into those murky waters.)

Protecting patent monopolies. Among the most important ways of doing this are:

1) "A company whose main patent on a drug is about to expire can win a reprieve by suing a potential generic competitor for infringing peripheral patents on packaging, dosing schedules or other secondary issues. Under a loophole in federal law that automatically triggers a 30-<u>month</u> delay in the entry of the generic..; or, a company about to lose patent protection on a brand-name drug can simply pay a potential generic competitor millions of dollars <u>not</u> to produce the cheaper version of the drug." (NYT, 6-10-02) These "30-month delays" have allowed drug companies to "delay generic competition repeatedly," reports the NYT (7-12-02) Makes you wonder how those little "loopholes" got there, don't it.

2) "Pharmaceutical companies regularly stand near the top in contributing to political campaigns." (BAKER, op.cit.)

3) Phony "new" drugs: "Two-thirds of the drugs approved from 1989 to 2000 were modified versions of existing drugs or even identical to those already on the market," according to a study of the National Institute for Health Care Management Foundation;.., "The modified medicines were often more expensive than the older medicines, even if the F.D.A. had found they did not offer significant advantages." (NYT, 5-29-02)

4) <u>Profits</u>. The industry consistently ranks at the top in return on investment..., more than $20 <u>billion</u> in profits in 1999, a rate

about 4 times that of the <u>Fortune 500</u> companies. (BAKER, op.cit.)

5) **CEO**s pay: "The highest-paid executives of the nine top pharmaceutical companies received an average of nearly $19 <u>million</u> each, without counting unexercised stock options, which were valued at nearly $900 million for the nine executives. (<u>MM</u>, 9/2001)

Spending on medications in the USA rose by 19 percent in 2000, and an additional 17 percent in 2001. There is no reason to expect that precipitous rise to slow in the future. For some years now, efforts have been made to provide relief for at least the old and the poor for medications; every year the attempts in Congress are foiled, either voted down or, as now, tabled and allowed to die.

With the elections of 2004 looming up, Congress and the White House, Demos and GOPs, went to work to produce something—anything—to convince the public (especially its older voters) that they "felt their pain" at the high cost of prescription drugs. What they came up with and passed in early 2004—the Medicare Act—is most likely to do this: 1. Raise the cost of prescription drugs for most, including those on Medicare; 2) leave the poor now aided by Medicaid worse off; 3) amount to a major step in the privatization of Medicare. Just what is wrong was lucidly summarized in the Op-ed essay of Jacob S. Hacker (<u>NYT</u>, 7-2-03):

> Neither the House nor Senate legislation... provides what the majority of Americans want: a drug benefit <u>within</u> Medicare itself. Instead, beneficiaries would be forced to turn first to private /profit-making/ insurers, which would be able to set their own premiums for drug coverage.... Both bills feature an upfront deductible of $250 or more, require significant co-payments above that amount and force beneficiaries to pay a huge amount out of pocket before catastrophic protection kicks in. As a result, an elderly woman with $6,000 in total drug costs would end up paying more than $4,000 of her own money under the Senate bill, and even more under the House legislation.... The real solution is no secret: make the drug benefit a part of Medicare and, yes, spend more money on it.

Only rarely does anyone in Congress, and never in the White House, mention or acknowledge that in none of countries of the European Union (among others) is there Medicare or Medicaid. Shocking? Not quite. They don't need it, they all have one version or another of the universal health care—which takes care of all medical problems and prescription drugs.

As noted in **health care**, someone like myself, with both Medicare and my California state health care program to protect me, and even without any illness or drug needs whatsoever, $5,000 is deducted from my pension payments; then, if drugs are needed, Medicare pays for nothing, and my California plan has significant co-payments and deductibles.

Meanwhile, a bit of encouraging news. Maine and Oregon are taking matters into their own hands for their citizens while some in Congress (from both parties) are seeking to legalize "reimportation" of (U.S.-made) drugs at, of course, much lower prices: in 2002, "average drug prices in the USA were 67 percent higher than those in Canada and about twice those in Italy and France...." ("Measure to Ease Imports of Drugs is Gaining in House," NYT, 7-22-03). The sub-head on that story, however, was "Drug Manufacturers Scramble to Lobby Against Bill That May Cost Them Millions." That was preceded a month earlier by "Drug Companies Increase Spending on Efforts to Lobby Congress and Governments," NYT, 6-1-03) And it's all tax-deductible.

Then there is this: "The New England Journal of Medicine /most respected of all such journals/ is relaxing its strict conflict-of-interest rules for authors of certain articles because it cannot find enough experts without financial ties to drug companies." (NYT, 6-13-02)

All the foregoing might sound a bit ominous for those worry-warts who are having trouble getting what they need to keep (or get) healthy. Stop worrying! One of the drug companies—Pfizer—is so good and strong that some high governmental officials from the Pentagon, asked for and got a meeting with the top guys at Pfizer to ask for its advice on how to run a really big outfit. And Pfizer is really big: Fortune (in its essay King of the Pill," 4-14-03) reported that Pfizer's purchase of another big drug company, Pharmacia—for $60 billion)—will make it one of the Top Ten giant companies in the USA, right up there with **GM, GE,** and **EXXON MOBIL.** Sure enough, it's now in the Top Ten.

Don't worry. They'd never use all that economic and political power in any ways other than to help us all toward better (and cheaper!) health. Relax! Take a pill! Use your credit card! Light up!

Philip Morris (In January 2003 they spun their name to Altria Group: Good thinking. **See tobacco**)

political correctness

That phrase began to be heard regularly in the 1980s. Contrary to popular belief, those who began to use it were not supporters of affirmative action, or of social and political equality, or of equal economic opportunity for all, or of anything of the sort.

Just who was first to use the term, I can't remember; I do know that it gained currency among the <u>opponents</u> of the laws and policies that aided or protected the victims of racism, sexism, poverty, and the like. It was used quite obviously to allow them to make disgusting remarks, as in the past.

<u>Item</u>: "I know it's not politically correct to say this, but if those babes want to be treated like men, why in hell don't they act like men?"

<u>Item</u>: "I know I'm going to be called politically incorrect for saying this, but hasn't it ever occurred to these weepy-eyed liberals that if blacks want to live better it would help a lot if they went out and got a job?"

<u>Item</u>: "The next time you see some queer out there complaining because he's being discriminated against, whether it's politically incorrect or not tell him what he needs is a good swift kick in the ass."

But by the 1990s, if not earlier, it was not only the rednecks and their ilk who were saying "political correctness"; they had been joined by conservatives and politicians, by TV programs, you name it, all using the term as some sort of sly joke, all in some way or another denigrating those who have fought for universal human rights. And a dirty confusion was king.

Those who are mocked by the term are those who have been working for political <u>decency</u>; it is a measure of just how indecent our society is that those who support the status quo (or something worse) have won the battle once more that makes something good sound rotten.

poverty

Some questions: 1. How <u>many</u> people live in poverty in the USA? In the other well-off countries? In the badly-off countries? <u>Why</u>? 2. What are poverty's <u>consequences</u>—to the poor and to their society? 3. Could poverty be <u>reduced</u>, even <u>eliminated</u>, in the USA? Elsewhere? <u>How</u>?

It will be necessary to begin with definitions. Don't say ugh; it will be seen that the way in which the U.S. government <u>defines</u> poverty—even as contrasted with other rich countries—has from the beginning allowed poverty's nature, causes, and consequences to be given short shrift.

1. <u>Some definitions</u>. Poverty is both a <u>relative</u> and an <u>absolute</u> condition; in practice they overlap and interact. a) <u>relative</u> poverty exists within a particular society when, those in (say) the bottom third of the society's income distribution are likely to "feel" poor, even <u>if</u> they are living better than their grandparents and parents, because their purchasing power is inadequate to meet the ongoing living <u>standards</u> of their nation; b) even the middle-income people in a poor <u>society</u> (e.g., India) are likely to feel "poor" if and when they compare their lives with their counterparts in a rich society. (Claire BROWN)

b) <u>Absolute</u> poverty exists when people's health and life-spans are reduced by their inaccessibility to adequate nutrition, shelter, and health care—usually because they are also unable to have access to the education and job-training that might lift them and their children up <u>out</u> of poverty.

However: Interestingly and confusingly (and not necessarily in contradiction), some research at Harvard found that "mortality rates were more closely linked to <u>relative</u> than to <u>absolute</u> income, with rising inequality meaning higher mortality." (PHILLIPS, 2002). Vincente NAVARRO, professor in the Johns Hopkins University School of Public Health, has shown that "countries with strong unions and labor movements that have developed strong redistributive policies and inequality reducing measures have better health indicators than the United States," and concludes that "the most effective public intervention in reducing mortality in the United States would be to reduce social inequality." (<u>MR</u>, 6/04, "Inequality is Unhealthy.")

<u>How many are poor</u>? Now we examine both (a) and (b) as they

exist in the USA. Most urgently in need of examination is how the U.S. government <u>defines</u> absolute poverty.

As discussed under **inequality**, despite the grinding and widespread poverty of the 1920s and 1930s in the USA, we did not even <u>have</u> a definition of poverty until the 1960s. Before then, there had of course been poor and even some programs—breadlines and soup kitchens, some shelters and skimpy welfare agencies—to assist the poor on the local and state levels. But that was all.

The 1960s turned out to be the longest and strongest period of sustained economic expansion in our history; it was also the decade of **Vietnam** when, in 1963, **JFK** was assassinated, and his V.P. **Lyndon Baines Johnson** took over.

LBJ was a master of political dealing, for better and for worse. As his administration began in 1964, he sought to make it for better (if only to keep the war in the background). He hoped to put the USA on the path toward becoming "The Great Society."

As he was doing so, a startling book had become popular: <u>The Other America</u> (1962), by Michael Harrington. The "America" the USA had been congratulating itself on was GALBRAITH's <u>The Affluent Society</u> (1958); but Harrington argued that there were many millions of families and individuals who were <u>poor</u> and struggling in this, the richest society in history. For **LBJ**, what with the assassination and the beginnings of protests against Vietnam and the draft, <u>The Other America</u>, as the saying goes, came on as a loud belch in church.

He decided to declare his "war on poverty." But what did we mean by "poor" and how many were there? LBJ needed a definition to get the program going. He ordered his Council of Economic Advisers to give him one. After a long scramble, they did; and what a definition! It is <u>still</u> the definition; so it needs quoting at length:

> It was based upon a study by the Social Security Administration of the income needed to support a nonfarm family of four. The SSA had established two standards for such a family, both based on estimates of dietary costs prepared by the Department of Agriculture: 1. A "low-cost" budget, permitting the minimum diet consistent with the food preferences of the lowest third of the population and adequate to avoid basic nutritional deficiencies.... The resulting budget stood at $3,995. This called for a higher budget than welfare agencies were allowing for families receiving public assistance. <u>To meet the administra-</u>

tive need of these bodies, the SSA prepared.... 2) an "economy
budget" based on a deficiency diet designed for temporary or
emergency use... setting the total budget at $3,165. On the basis
of this figure, the Council adopted $3,000 as its family poverty
line..., and $1,500 for a single individual. It thus found... some
35,000,000 people, a fifth of the nation, to /have been/ in poverty in 1962. (WILCOX) (my emphases)

It is bad enough that both the $3,995 and the $3,165 were
"rounded down." More important were two other matters, ranging
from the absurd to the incorrect: 1) "the emergency use diet" was
itself put together by the Office of Civil Defense for a post-nuclear
attack period. 2) The cost of the diet established ($1,000/year)
assumed that food constituted one-third of a family's expenses; so
multiply by three, and there you've got it. Neat.

That formula, quantitatively altered in keeping with inflation
over time, remains the basis for today's definition of poverty—even
though the "post-nuclear attack" diet was ludicrous to begin with
and even more so over time; even more important is that the structure of household expenses has altered drastically since 1962; it is
widely-agreed that most low-income families pay out at least half of
their income for rent. (EHRENREICH)

Nor is that all that's wrong. Jared Bernstein (senior economist
with the Economic Policy Institute) points out several other major
problems (and setting aside the nuke budget and that the food costs
were those of 1955):

> 1. It neglects rising costs of housing, health care and trans-
> portation for poor families; 2) it "ignores important costs to low-
> income families.../such as those for/ many more women with
> young children working /and needing/ child care....and that
> alone lifts the poverty rate to include 9 million more Americans
> whose incomes are inadequate for their basic needs." ("Who's
> Poor? Don't Ask the Census Bureau," NYT, 9-26-03)

But what about other countries; maybe they are even more
dumbheaded than we are? Not quite. The official measure of poverty in Western Europe, for example, is that a family is poor if its
income is less than half of the median income. (OSBERG) That is,
if half the population receive above $50,000 annual income, and
half below then those with less than $25,000 are in poverty. When
we look at the actual data shortly, it will be seen that such a meas-

ure virtually doubles the U.S. poverty rate—as adopting the European measure for **unemployment** also doubles that rate for us (and for Japan, which copies us).

Elsewhere? In other rich countries, there is also too much poverty, but even though we are the richest of all, we also get the booby prizes 1) for the overall percentage of our people in poverty, 2) the percentage of children, and 3) how long their poverty endures: Of 19 European countries (plus Canada and Australia),

> the United States, with 16.9% of its total population living in poverty, has the highest level of overall poverty...; poverty is also more enduring in the U.S.; /and/ the United States is also unique in that it has the highest rate of child poverty (22.3%). (MISHEL, et al., 2003)

That quotation is from The State of Working America: 2002/2003. It is, as PHILLIPS is quoted as saying on the cover, "The ultimate authority on what the American economy means to ordinary Americans." For those who wish to know about and understand all the dimensions of the distribution of income in the USA (along with comparative information on other countries), this biennial work is indispensable. (Also very helpful are the excellent and readable compendia of data put together by HEINTZ & FOLBRE for the U.S. economy and by ANDERSON & CAVANAGH for the global economy.)

There are 193 countries in the world now; most of the people in most of those countries are really poor; a horribly high percentage of them absolutely poor: 15-20 million children die every year from malnutrition; they live with a billion or so adults who are on the edge of starvation. (UNICEF)

The cheerleaders for **globalization** like to say that "a rising tide lifts all boats." Most people in the world do not have a boat; many who had something like a boat had it swept away by the tides benefiting the **MNC/TNC**s. The latters' great pushes into the "developing countries" were facilitated by U.S. programs from the 1960s on, with this effect: "The gap in per capita income between the industrial developing worlds tripled from 1960 to 1993...; by 1999, the wealth of the world's 475 billionaires was greater than the combined incomes of the poorest half of humanity (3 billion people). (ANDERSON & CAVANAGH)

But surely as that gap widened it was also probable that the bottom level was nonetheless rising? Surely, although the poor may have been <u>relatively</u> less poor, they were <u>absolutely</u> better off? Sounds good; tell it to the Mexicans at work in the <u>maquiladoras</u> who make around $2 a <u>day</u>; or those in Indonesia, or in Thailand, or in Nigeria or in Argentina or, for that matter, in Detroit, even in Silicon Valley, with its hordes of minimum wage workers in the highest techs of all.

In short, there are poor people all over the world, more now than ever, and not just because there are more people.

<u>Why</u>? Put your "man from Mars" hat on; that is, try to shed our socialized presumptions and reasoning and cope with the following. Fact: agricultural and industrial productivity have increased at logarithmic rates in the past two centuries or so—rates much higher than population growth. <u>Pace</u> Malthus. How is it then that there are so many more people living <u>very</u> badly, in both absolute and relative terms? Why so much poverty in the midst of so much prodigious <u>plenty</u>?

Some of the answer is found in entries such as **capitalism, exploitation, waste, imperialism, globalization, power**, et al. They should be consulted on this matter; but there is something else, something related to the "entries" just noted, but which needs specific statement here: In the modern world, the ideology we live by has "taught us" to think about the social process, if at all, in ways that confuse and obfuscate rather than enlighten. VEBLEN called it "a trained incapacity." (1919.)

It is hard to pin down, as would be the case with any ideology, but it centers upon what we have come to mean by "individualism." Individualism is a lovely word; one couldn't live decently without it; at least yours truly couldn't. In practice, however, it has evolved from a word pointing to the high value placed on the individual— as regards freedom, choice, opportunity and the like—to something different, but with the same name: the high value placed upon what we <u>have</u> and can <u>get</u> and, relatedly, our <u>status</u>. Instead of individualism finding its definition in the qualities of society, it does so in the goals and accomplishments of <u>a</u> person.

That being so, "individualism" becomes a spun word for selfishness—a trait absolutely essential to the functioning of **capitalism**. If you study hard enough, work hard enough, have the "right stuff," and so on, you'll "make it." If you <u>don't</u> "make it," logic informs us, it's because you don't have the right stuff: Q.E.D.

From such reasoning, it is but a short step to "blaming the victim." (RYAN) Color, gender, religion, whether of rich or poor parents? Irrelevant. We have a well- socialized tendency to view the very rich as having "earned" and "deserved" their wealth and to blame the poor for being that way. And after all, haven't some very rich people in fact risen from poverty? Indeed there are some of those; even more striking is the continuation over many generations of maintained, usually increasing wealth <u>un</u>accompanied by unusual ability or even exertion—of which **Bush II** is a prize example. (see PHILLIPS /2002/ for details)

Stephen Jay GOULD (as quoted in **education**) put it well when, in commenting upon Einstein's brain, he said he was "somehow less interested in the weight and convolutions of Einstein's brain than in the near certainty that people of equal talent have lived and died in cotton fields and sweatshops"—from which the rich benefited.

It isn't that one <u>cannot</u> rise from the slums and the ghettoes; it is that it takes what must be seen at a superhuman effort and <u>unusual</u> talent to do so—in comparison with, say, the aforementioned **Bush II**, who becomes a millionaire and a governor and a nation's president without breaking a sweat; who, it will be asserted here, had he been born into a poor family would probably have ended up in a "poorhouse."

<u>Poverty's consequences</u>. Those of us in the better-off top income layers of the USA (say the top one-third) are more likely than not to have gained our understanding of what it means to be poor in this country from the stereotypes provided by the media; mostly, though not entirely, the picture we are given combines laziness with violence with crime with dissolute behavior in one mix or another; pretty much what we think of when we hear the word **homeless**. That <u>some</u> of that is accurate is likely; that it is an adequate explanation is not. (RYAN)

To begin with, take laziness. Almost all of those who are poor have jobs; by official definition, their income is something under about $17,500 a year. Almost all of <u>those</u> work much harder than you or I, and under both social and physical conditions that are likely to be more tiring, both physically and emotionally. As someone who began to work when I was about eleven, and did all kinds of "shit work" for seven or eight years, I know about that kind of work; then, as someone who after the war, made all of my income in the university, I know a lot about that also.

Had I my life to live over again, I would happily do the university work for the wages I got as a kid; and I wouldn't do that other work except for two or three times as much as I have received as a prof. As noted under **jobs**, Plato put it well some millennia ago when he argued that those with good jobs should receive the lowest incomes (so long as they can be comfortable), and those with lousy jobs should be compensated with high.

The reality is the opposite, of course. (see TERKEL, Working....) It's worth thinking about; but such thoughts are not encouraged.

The low wages and the hard work are bad enough; being pushed around, treated like dirt, without security, without comfort, without... almost everything, is hard enough; trying to support and enhance a family life is even harder. It is hell, for worker and family; not least for the children. All that is made worse by poor childrens' treatment in (usually a lousy) school, with predictable effects on morale and, among other matters, health. For example,

> Research in the 1990s demonstrated how the paint and pipes of slum housing—major sources of lead—damage the developing brains of children...; a 1990 study published in the New England Journal of Medicine showed that youngsters with elevated lead levels have lower I.Q.'s and attention deficits.... (David K. Shipler, "Total Poverty Awareness," NYT, 2-24-04)

If one lived in a decent society, one where those who are poor are treated as essentially unlucky human beings, it would be bad enough; however, to be poor in the USA is to have insult heaped upon injury; to be treated despicably even, perhaps especially by people who themselves are not far from poverty, to have remaining elements of dignity shredded; it is to see yourself portrayed in the **media**, by politicians, even by teachers, as semi-human, as dregs.

None of the foregoing, unfortunately, is an over-statement, whether at work, in treatment by strangers or acquaintances, not just in the USA, but everywhere. (For the USA see, for example, GANS and PIVEN & CLOWARD, and the remarkable study of FINNEGAN, for the lives of poor and almost poor; for the poor countries, see GEORGE /1976/ and de CASTRO and SEN.)

The consequences for individuals and their families and the ways in which they are treated by the society cannot help but have serious deleterious effects for the society as a whole. Those effects are measured in terms of how **crime** is defined and criminals treated; by the **corruption** not only of government and business but of the people as a whole in terms of the attenuation of anything that could be called morality; by the disintegration of anything that might be seen as a social, as distinct from a self- and greed-centered, polity; by the growth of fear, and hate, and envy, and violence.

Is there no way out? There are ways out, both at home and abroad, but we have not chosen them. Better ways of treating poverty require first and foremost different ways of viewing the poor. Our way has almost always been to resent, scorn, even to hate the poor, whether as regards **homelessness, hunger, health care, education**, or welfare, all of them almost always linked to inadequate (or no) income. (RYAN)

The welfare system of the USA, although it does not cover all of the above, embodies the attitudes and behavior of the agencies that do. In confronting those agencies, those in need are virtually always met with attitudes of suspicion, hostility, contempt, disdain, and/or fear. (GANS, PIVEN/CLOWARD)

Of course some of those in need are often shiftless, and/or dirty, and/or lazy, and/or addicts, and/or something else unattractive. Seldom, if ever, are they given the benefit of the doubt, where the "doubt" would refer to their being victims of parental abuse, of untreated disabilities, of terrible housing and educational conditions, of war-induced physical and/or psychological injuries, and/or, despite having worked full-time have received wages that do not permit anything approximating a living wage.

President Clinton and the Congress of his time, prodded for years by **Reagan** and his followers, prided themselves on having resolved this set of problems with their "workfare instead of welfare" programs (and earned income tax rebates). To be sure, the traditional welfare program was always inadequate and, usually, rife with insulting treatment; but the "welfare reforms" of the 1990s made a bad situation worse.

States that pushed people off welfare could do so conscientiously only if 1) there were jobs to go to, 2) all who needed assistance could work, and 3) when mothers and children were involved, provisions for child care would be assured. <u>Some</u> of those subsequently deprived of welfare could meet all three conditions; <u>most</u> could not; some could not meet any of them—and <u>none</u> could have if the standard of sufficiency had been a "living wage."

Of that principle, more in a minute; suffice it to say here that even in the "new economy" of the 1990s, of the six million or so who left or were pushed off welfare after 1996, most did not have enough to eat. That says nothing of their housing, of what <u>kind</u> of work they got, with what kind of hope attached, what benefits, what <u>dignity</u>. (EHRENREICH) What is "a living wage"?

> The Economic Policy Institute, an independent research group, estimates that for a family of one adult and 2 children that would mean full-time work at $14/hour (= $30,000/year); it would cover health insurance, a telephone, child care at a licensed center, groceries, and the like; but <u>no</u> restaurant meals, video rentals, internet access, wine, liquor, cigarettes, lottery tickets, or even much meat. A substantial majority of U.S. workers, <u>60 percent</u>, earn less than $14/hour— many with two wage earners, a spouse or a grown child, some with food stamps. (EHRENREICH; my emphasis)

When we consider what kinds of jobs those 60 percent have, a poll of their employers would doubtless tell us that they could not function were they required to pay that living wage; and they would be right. So some things have to change, or see ourselves, rich as we are, as an indecent society: the present <u>minimum</u> wage of $5.15/hour at full-time work leaves one below the poverty level of $17,500, itself but half of a living wage.

The minimum wage must be raised to at least $10/hour; universal **health care** must be provided by the federal government, as must affordable and decent housing; those who are old and/or disabled must be supported adequately for all their needs, for which **Social Security** payments are substantially inadequate; educational opportunities must be qualitatively and quantitatively changed for the better so as to stop the passing of poverty from one generation to the next; child care must be subsidized by the government. All that, at least, if we are to put an end to the disgraceful situation of the past and present:

> The working poor... are in fact the major philanthropists of our society. They neglect their own children so that the chil-

dren of others will be cared for; they live in substandard housing so that other homes will be shiny and perfect; they endure privation so that inflation will be low and stock prices high.... (EHRENREICH)

In a world that tends always more toward self-destruction, any changes for the better are difficult; not least is that so for the reduction, let alone then the elimination, of poverty in the USA, given its close affiliation with **racism** and **greed**. It is at least as difficult in the poorer countries, both because any changes for their betterment depend upon outside cooperation (or the difficult breaking of ties), and because there are so many who are so very poor.

In the Afterword more will be said in these respects; here a few summary statements. It should be clear that poverty hurts everyone, not just the poor; to reduce it or get rid of it would also benefit everyone (except those who get their jollies from fear and hate). There are many bases for those generalizations;

1. Poverty is enormously wasteful of human and nonhuman resources, both for those who are poor and for the society. Unless you believe that the poor are that way because they are incorrigibly dumb, weak, lazy, or something of the sort—and if you do, you are ignorant—then that they are doing work that requires no talent reflects considerably more on the educational (and related social) system than upon them; there is a lot of potential talent going to waste.

But if it would take more and better schools and not unimportantly, more and better housing to change that, and that would cost many billions—and where would the money come from? Here is part of an answer: Better schools and housing require teachers and construction (among other matters); in turn they produce higher incomes for those who train the teachers and put up the buildings (workers and businesses). In that this would mean a significant increase of related jobs (among other matters) it would also mean more job opportunities (and training jobs), and higher incomes for all—a large percentage going to those who previously had low-paying and stupid jobs—and were poor: round and round it goes. In his General Theory of Employment..., KEYNES called the process "the multiplier effect." (see **deficits and surpluses**, and **economics**)

But where would the money come from to do that "reconstruction"? As suggested above, over time it would come from the higher national income; initially it would come from borrowing (we do it to make missiles, no?) and/or from making our tax system more progressive (rather than, as we have been doing, making it very much less progressive). And from reducing **military expenditures** instead of increasing them (as now).

If all that sounds like a fairy tale, thank today's economists (most of them), and politicians (almost all of them), and the **media** that carry the message for fuzzing up your head.

And you may be encouraged to know that as of 1999, at least 16 major cities had adopted living wage policies for their employees, with more on the way. Also good for one's morale is that, beginning with Maine, one state after another now seems bent on having its own **health care** system, moving in the direction of Canada's single-payer plan.

See? Where's there's life there's hope.

power

First, what is it? It is the ability to act effectively, to cause things to go one's way and to remain so; or, equally important, to keep others from having their way—for example, to be able to block a single-payer **health care** system. The Latin root for the noun power and the verb to be able is the same.

Where does power come from? Most simply, social power is held by those who control what is, has been, and is coming to be valued in their society; it may be something tangible (productive assets or weapons) or intangible (the ability to formulate or represent cherished beliefs or aspirations).

Control over the means of material survival places its possessors at the center of power in all societies. The forms and functions associated with such control have of course differed substantially over time: the priesthood in Ancient Egypt, the Church and warriors in medieval Europe, private control over productive wealth in the modern world. Indeed, that source of power is the very definition of **capitalism**; it also explains the extraordinary dynamism of capitalist development—for better and for worse.

The survival and strengthening over time of capitalist social power has depended upon more than its mere ownership and control of the means of life; its economic power needs to be seen as the apex of a <u>pyramid</u> of power. The metaphor of "pyramid" is itself an over-simplification, but it is a useful way to begin.

Perhaps the most insightful (and readable) modern analysis and discussion of the structure of power in the USA was that of C. Wright MILLS, in his <u>The Power Elite</u>, written in 1956, as our present structures were moving toward maturity. It was composed of three sectors: the economy, politics, and the military.

Within that triad there are, of course, many other structures; in the economy, for example, are industry, trade, finance, agriculture, and the media; each with its own functional structures and power, each with its own "pyramids."

Vital to the existence and behavior of power structures are their <u>interactions</u>; in a capitalist society, the main consequences of those interactions are established at the pyramid's economic apex: the power of **big business**.

A clear example of all that is found in the relationships between big business and the military. As is discussed at length under **military-industrial complex**, the largest producers of **cars**, aircraft, steel, chemicals, electrical products, ships, and munitions are <u>also</u> the largest producers of military products. Their **lobbyists** have assured that military contracts will go to them <u>and</u> that there will be an abundant supply of such contracts over time: they, taken together with an always cooperative **media** (also sitting at the table of power), persuade Congress and the public to accept—even to applaud—a set of aggressive foreign policies and conservative domestic policies that thus come to seem as just what the doctor ordered; Dr. Capitalism, that is. Power does not reside only at the top, of course; it exists on all levels, in all nooks and crannies of the society—at the state, county, and local levels, in the classroom, in the office, in every social setting—between **boys and girls, men and women**, and the various strata of **racism**.

Saying so, and whatever the complexities and however constructive or destructive all those power relationships may be, what ultimately sets the rules and determines the rewards and punishments within which almost all of that takes place is "the power elite"—which, in its turn is ruled over by **big business**: "The ruling ideas of any era are the ideas of its ruling class." (MARX/ENGELS, 1845-46)

What has been true for all modern societies has been especially so for the USA, the most capitalist of all capitalist nations. So it is that from its beginnings the USA has been the least constrained by the long-established traditions common to <u>all</u> others.

The great differences between us and all other industrial capitalist societies as regard the socioeconomy—most obviously, health, education, the old, the poor, the environment—are to be explained by three other major differences: 1) others' capitalism grew out of long periods of <u>non</u>-capitalist history, whereas we <u>began</u> that way; 2) in the USA there has been an absence of anything approaching the conscious class divisions (and associated politics) elsewhere; in the USA we have had trade <u>union</u> movements (called, appropriately, "business unions") whose focus has been predominantly on the company, while elsewhere there have been strong <u>labor</u> movements (which have sought and gained <u>social</u> power)—power that brought not only higher wages and better working conditions for unionized workers (as here), but significantly transformed the socioeconomy; 3) the social role of organized religion, especially in Western Europe, has had a mitigating effect on the "rugged individualism" unique to USA.

On top of which, along came **consumerism**. It began first in the USA in the 1920s. It could not spread to our entire population until after World War II, enabled to do so then by the combination of sustained economic growth, the introduction of consumer **debt** on a large and always growing scale, and the transformation of the **media** into a combination of sorcerer and hypnotist.

The always-stronger preoccupation of our citizenry with buying and borrowing had as its predictable and obverse side a lessening of an always-low level of social concern. The narcissism accompanying consumerism and debt inexorably diminished whatever sense of social solidarity ever existed in the USA, while assuring success for a conservative political/media orchestrated campaign against the **taxes** said to be benefiting the black and the poor at the expense of the "middle class."

Taken together, all those developments had the effect of enfeebling a never powerful liberal/left consensus and—since "power cannot stand a vacuum"—not only strengthened already strong conservatives, but allowed a genuine right wing ideology to become always more influential: in cities, states, in Congress, in the White House, and in the Supreme Court.

If, as Lord Acton sagely remarked, "power corrupts, and absolute power corrupts absolutely," then We the People of the

United States of America are in <u>deep</u> trouble. And, given our power over the entire globe, who is not?

preemption

In his second year as president, **Bush II** announced preemption as a new component of U.S. foreign policy. It is a reprehensible policy, but it is not—alas!—new: the USA has been attacking others "preemptively" throughout our entire career as a nation; indeed, we began to do so well before we <u>were</u> a nation.

We began that way against the originally friendly "**Indians**," aggression piled on aggression, as we took what we wanted in North America. Then there were the preemptive conflicts against the Spanish in Florida, the French in Canada and Louisiana, the Mexicans in Texas, the Southwest, and California, the British in the Pacific Northwest ("Fifty-four Forty or Fight!"), the Eskimos and Russians in Alaska..., until we had what we wanted: in North America, that is.

Our overseas preemptions began with Hawaii and other islands of the Pacific, continued with the intervention in the Cuban-Spanish War that gave us control over Cuba, on to the Philippines, and Puerto Rico, and....

The "undeclared wars" discussed in the <u>Foreword</u>—of which there were more than 150—included many that today would fit into the highly elastic category of what Bush II's groomers have had him call "the axis of evil": Today, **Iraq**, **Iran**, North **Korea**; "tomorrow," as some guy in Europe once put it, "the world"?

prematurely anti-fascist

No big deal this particular phrase today, because it has gone out of use—only to have its function served by other terms which, for the general public, brand any and all dissent as fearful. But in that this one was used in a most revealing way "close to home," I tell this story.

As noted in the discussions of **fascism**, the most thorough study of its German variant (at least in English) was that of Professor Robert A. Brady, <u>The Spirit and Structure of German Fascism</u>. Brady was a noted scholar of 1920s Germany, had lived there for many years, and was there as the Nazis took power. His book came out in 1937; it served then and it serves still as a warning of the ways and means by which fascism comes to **power**, and how it uses it.

It is often forgotten now, but U.S. participation in World War II was more often than not described as "a war against fascism." Fascism had begun in Italy and by the 1930s had spread to Japan, Germany, Spain, and Portugal and was beginning to take hold in, among other nations, France. A good time for Brady's book to be studied.

It was given a look by the **House Un-American Activities Committee**. They didn't like it, and called Brady before them. The upshot was that Brady was publicly branded by them as "prematurely anti-fascist." At that same time, the USA (see **fascism**) was acting in ways either indifferent to or friendly with what would be its enemies in World War II. That is, we were "belatedly anti-fascist." And then, after the war, notably but not only in **Korea** and **Chile**, we became indifferent to, supportive of, even positively cuddly with fascism. Takes all kinds.

prison-industrial complex

Just as the land of the free and home of the brave is #1 in **military expenditures** so it is in expenditures for prison construction and personnel. Perhaps that may be explained by the fact that we are such a large country? No, China and India both have larger populations, and only China exceeds us in raw (absolute) numbers. Measured relatively (as percent of population) no nation even comes close in the number incarcerated.

> In 2003 there were 2.3 million federal, local and state prisoners in the USA; almost 600 per 100,000. Compare that with the Russian Federation: 335; the UK: 93; France and Germany: 80; the Netherlands: 40, Philippines: 22, France: 81; Japan: 10. (HERIVEL/WRIGHT)

Those numbers are bad enough in themselves; add to that the notorious contrast between rapidly rising expenditures on prisons and rapidly rising tuition fees for higher education. In 1999, for example, California (prison ratio: 700/100,000) spent $5.6 <u>billion</u> on incarceration and only $4.3 billion for higher **education**. The beginnings of that surge were in the 1980s; between then and 2000, tuition costs had jumped under $800 to over $5,000 in the University of California system, from $231 to $2,976 for the state colleges and from zero to $18 a unit in the community college system; meanwhile California's K-12 fell from top in the country to being equal with Mississippi (see **education**). (SFC, 8-22-03, "Rising Tuition....") That now worsens all over the nation as the **Bush II** tax cuts + increased **milex** have been accompanied by reduced federal grants to the states. Result? Schools are cutting down on school days, handing out pink slips to teachers, making classes larger. No problem for prisons, though; they are continuing to be built.

There are many "popular" reasons for vast prison budgets. Many communities see more prisons as more jobs, and broader public support is provided through media and politicians' crime frenzies. Most important, however, have been racist arrests and convictions, and the successful **lobbies** of both the prison construction industry and of guards. We examine them in turn.

The main elements of **racism** are discussed under that heading; here we note only the role it plays regarding imprisonment; that relating to drugs is perhaps the most obvious.

First, note the disproportion between population and imprisonment percentages: In California, for example, blacks are but 6.8 percent of its population, but 31.6 of its prisoners; for Latinos the figures are 25.1 to 33.9; for Whites 55.6 to 29.6. In the separate discussion of the **death penalty**, it was shown that this pattern is even more flagrant.

Of the top five charges leading to imprisonment, three concern controlled substances—possession, possession for sale, and sale—all non-violent offenses. The two drugs most involved in such offenses are crack cocaine and powder cocaine; arrests for crack possession far outweigh those for powder cocaine. As law professor Marc Miller (and once co-editor of the Federal Sentencing Reporter) put it, "... low-level (retail) crack dealers /are/ far more severely punished than their high-level (wholesale) suppliers of powder cocaine that serve as the product for conversion into crack." Relevantly, crack users are predominantly poor and black, while the more expensive powder cocaine is accessible generally only to the non-poor. (TN, 12-4-95)

Then there is the three-strike law. California was the second state to adopt it (Washington was first); it is usually accompanied by the two-strike provision. The former means that on a third felony conviction, the minimum term of imprisonment shall be 25 years; the two-strike means that the sentence for a second felony conviction must be the double of the first.

A recent study shows that the major consequences of that law in California (enacted in 1994) are 1) there are 6,721 "three-strike" and 43,800 "second-strike" prisoners; 2) one can become a "three-striker" for a crime as mild as stealing a pair of sneakers, or possessing 5 grams of crack (an amount so small it would fit on your thumbnail); 3) prisons are already becoming stuffed with elderly inmates; 4) the overwhelming number of sentences are for nonviolent offenses (mostly drug possession), and 5) the need for new prisons accelerates. (<u>NYT</u>, 8-23-01). An editorial that same day pointed out that

> New York's drug-driven expansion, while providing jobs to largely white upstate communities has devastated black and Hispanic neighborhoods in the cities. Though most drug users are white, 94 percent of the people jailed for drug offenses are black or Hispanic. (<u>NYT</u>, 8-23-01) (and see DOMANICK)

New York's contemporary situation of overcrowded prisons, largely for drug convictions, stems from the "Rockefeller drug laws" of the early 1970s. They were intended to deter drug use by providing very harsh sentences for users and dealers. In the <u>NYT</u> (5-10-02), ex-State Senator John R. Dunne, who sat on the Senate Committee that wrote and passed those laws—and which he sponsored—stated that "after three decades it is clear to me and others that this approach has not worked. Instead, these laws have been responsible for a steep and steady rise in the number and proportion of prisoners convicted for low-level, non-violent drug offenses."

It has long been argued by those from groups as diverse as psychiatrists, medical doctors, police, and many drug addicts a) that drug addiction leads to criminality, b) that, other things being equal, imprisonment <u>increases</u> criminality, and c) that drug treatment without imprisonment <u>reduces</u> both drug addiction <u>and</u> criminality. Details, details....

Now an authoritative report from the Yale School of Public Health: Studying 3,500 inner-city drug users receiving treatment in the Philadelphia area, the authors found that "treating drug abusers reduced the crime they committed by 51 percent...; and that a year in prison costs $23,000 per inmate, compared with $3,000 annual costs for methadone treatment of heroin addiction." (<u>BW</u>, 8-5-2) Bushwa, say the prison construction industry and the prison guards, the highly effective **lobbyists** for more and fancier prisons, east, west, north and south.

In the 1990s in California, 20 new prisons were built, as compared with two university campuses. As with military expenditures, their advance accelerates not only for sheer political reasons, however misguided, but also because of the feverish advance of technology: as the 1990s began, the cheapest kind of minimum security cell cost $100,000, $50,000 "up front" and the rest in interest.(D&S,9-91) Add in the costs of food, clothing, guards, post offices, libraries and medical costs.

Item: In California, the average annual pay for a prison guard is now $64,000; higher than that of an experienced school teacher or a new university prof.

Item: Between 1982 and 2001, as police arrests rose by only 13 percent, the expenditures on criminal justice rose 154 percent and those for federal and state inmates by 228 percent. ("With Longer Sentences, Cost of Fighting Crime is Higher," NYT, 5-3-04)

And all of this competes with and wins against all other badly-needed social expenditures.

But even if building prisons to deter crime is costly in itself and at a loss to other social needs, it's worth it, no? No. In a 2002 study prepared for the Bureau of Justice Statistics, it was found that in the first decade after the prison-building boom that began in 1983, convicts released from prison were more likely than ever to commit new crimes. Why?

> The main thing this report shows is that our experiment with building lots more prisons as a deterrent to crime has not worked...; state governments, to save money and to be seen as tough on crime, cut back on rehabilitation programs, like drug treatment, vocational education and classes to prepare prisoners for life at home....and, unable to find jobs, and from living in public housing projects, they return to crime." (NYT, 6-3-02)

It has been said that "facts are stubborn things"; uh-uh, not for those who are behind the recent "prisons for profit" campaigns; in addition to more and more new prisons being built are more and more being **privatized**.

The nation's largest operator of prisons for profit is the Corrections Corporation of America (CCA). It began in the fabled **Reagan** years and now has more than 60 prisons, jails and detention centers. It's been doing its job, if its job is to make profits. If—don't laugh—its job is to run prisons better than governments? A new report (from "Grassroots Leadership") shows that

> CCA's and other for-profit prisons 1) fail to provide adequate medical care to prisoners, 2) fail to control violence, 3) provoke prisoner protests and uprisings because of their substandard conditions, and 4) that many of their employees are involved in criminal activity. ("Jail 'em!") (<http:www.alter-net.org>m 12-15-03)

Privatization is not new to the past two or three decades, but it has now become an epidemic, not just for prisons, but for **health care** and **education** and the **military**. See **Friedman**, and read what's next:

privatization

The meaning and purposes of privatization are not obscure: it means transforming an institution whose purpose is to provide a vital public service under governmental supervision and control into a private enterprise whose purpose is to make profits <u>and</u> which is presumably going to do so better and at lower costs.

As is true for its brother-in-arms **deregulation**, it is difficult to find any sector of the society in which such privatization has not already occurred in some degree—whether in **education, health care**, the military (see **milex, Iraq**), in **prisons** (for construction, ownership, and control), safety (whether for boarding or controlling aircraft), **welfare**, the **environment**—for any service or any product.

The marked swerve to the right in the USA over the past quarter century has meant that whatever can be made to produce a profit: Go for it! If and when the news arrives that the "experiment" costs more and functions worse than its public predecessor, why, shoot the messenger!

In a democracy that has become as plutocratic and as corrupted as ours by big money, if it is to maintain even the semblance of democracy it must find a rationale for foul policies. For privatization, the rationale is that the grungy, creaking giant bureaucracy of government is inherently inefficient; put the same thing in the hands of the free market and—<u>voila'</u>—it will become <u>efficient</u>. Thus it becomes necessary to take a closer look at that word "efficiency."

It means that more will be gotten for a given use of human and other resources; or that the same amount of service or product can be gotten while using fewer of those resources: inefficiency replaced by efficiency means that everyone is better off.

But efficiency is not the aim of business; **profits** are. So, how does it work, privatization? Have privatized entities in fact 1) cost less per unit of service and/or 2) done the job better? And another question: 3) if and when they make profits and—as often happens—the answers to (1) and/or (2) are <u>negative</u>, then what? Do we "<u>un</u>privatize them?" 4) Do you believe in the tooth fairy?

Here we look only at some of the realms: the military, health care, education, prisons (for fuller treatment of which, see the relevant essays).

How it works is like this: 1. No sane business is going to be a party to privatization unless it expects a profit. How does it make a profit from, say owning and running a <u>prison</u>? Well, the prison's <u>construction</u> is subsidized by the government or built on a "cost-plus" basis; that is, BIG profits are <u>guaranteed</u> (as with **milex**), and then the state or local or federal government awards the Prison Company a block sum or per capita amount for managing prison life. If that is <u>not</u> done on a cost-plus basis, the Prison Company will then pursue normal business practices: it will cut costs and/or seek (through **lobbying**) to raise the rate per prisoner it charges the government. After all, it's a business now, and business is—how does that go?—business.

Meanwhile (see **prison-industrial....**) to reduce its costs The Company will reduce its "services" to the prisoners (in re: food, sanitation, clothing, medical care, recreation, space); why not? They're all <u>cons</u>, aren't they? (see Judy Falk, "Fiscal Lockdown," <u>D&S</u> 7/8 and 11/12, 2003)

Fill in the blanks. And then apply that to elementary and high school **education** (charter schools, or GM-written textbooks, billboards in the schoolyard, **TV** in the classrooms with 40 percent **advertising**), to **health care** (where hospital nurses are being replaced by "orderlies" and, to shorten a long list, in the **military**. (see P.W. SINGER) In that the Iraq "mission" does not yet seem to be "accomplished," here a quick look at a especially scandalous instance.

At the very top of the list of business beneficiaries from the Iraq war is the oil industry giant Halliburton. As is discussed further under **Cheney**, he was once its **CEO** (and still receives $180,000 a year from them). One of that company's main divisions is KBR. In a lengthy

NYT article describing KBR's juicy contracts for **Iraq**, one that is relevant here is the 10-year contract that privatizes military operations:

> KBR... holds a contract that is in many ways more important, and potentially bigger, than the one /it received/ to repair the oil fields: the Logistics Civil Augmentation Program, or Logcap, which essentially turns KBR into a kind of for-profit Ministry of Public Works for the Army... KBR is on call to the Army for 10 years to do a lot of the things most people think soldiers do for themselves—from fixing trucks to warehousing ammunition, from delivering mail to cleaning up hazardous waste. KP /kitchen work/ is now history; KBR civilians now peel potatoes...., do the laundry..., fix the pipes and clean the sewers, generate the power and repair the wiring....
>
> Writing the oil-field contingency plan was only one of a thousand things KBR did for the Army last year under Logcap. (KBR has a similarly broad contract with the Navy, under which it built, among other things, the cages for suspected terrorists at Guantánamo Bay. The technical term for Logcap is "cost-reimbursement, indefinite-delivery/ indefinite quantity," or "cost-plus," meaning KBR spends whatever it believes necessary to get a job done, then adds from 1 to 9 percent as profit. /Wanna guess whether it's closer to 1 or 9?/ ("Nation Builders for Hire," by Dan Baum, NYT Magazine, 6-22-03; emphasis added)

A reminder: The provision of certain services by state and federal agencies arose because they were <u>needed</u> but not available through the for-profit free market; the aim was to provide the service, not either to save or to make money.

To be sure, big government can be and often is <u>in</u>efficient; as is **big business**; I know, In the late 1930s I worked both for a governmental office (as a court reporter!) and for a giant corporation (in the San Francisco offices of U.S. Steel, then the largest steel company in the world). They were both and equally inefficient.

In both cases, it was clear to me, part of the inefficiency was due to the institutional lethargy that goes with great size (and most of the beneficiaries of today's privatizing contracts <u>are</u> giants), part to low morale, part of it to managerial dopiness. The point is, <u>both</u> were inefficient.

In private companies it is possible to have "efficiency" without harsh exploitation—when they are very small <u>and</u> when the jobs carry some responsibility <u>and</u> allow some initiative <u>and</u> are properly-paid; in public institutions, all can go well if and only if the public mission is being carried out with integrity <u>and</u> those doing it are allowed some responsibility and dignity. Sometimes that happens.

Then there is the possibility of thinking through and working for different ways of organizing our lives, of working toward a society whose guiding principle would be its insistence on genuine democracy: economic, political, and social.

Neither the thinking through nor the working for such a society would be easy or quick; whatever its name, if it were to be fully democratic it surely would not resemble **capitalism**. See the <u>Afterword</u> for further discussion.

profits

Mainstream **economics** today purports to explain the whys and wherefores of profits, but does not; but the founders of economics—Adam Smith (1723-1790) and David Ricardo (1772-1823)—at least got a leg up on it. Significantly, what since the 1860s has been called "economics" Smith and Ricardo (and John Stuart Mill) called "political economy." A consideration of the contrasts between their time and ours reveals why.

Examine any contemporary econ text and you will be informed that the recipients of all four kinds of incomes—interest, profits, rent, and wages—receive what they get for their contribution to production. Thus it is, for example, that profits are now normally discussed as **earnings**. Believe it or not, economists really take that seriously. No kidding.

On the other hand, the earlier political economists saw the distribution of incomes as consequent upon **power** relationships: thus "political" economy. The economic theory at the center of Smith's/Ricardo's analyses was called "the labor theory of value"—the very theory whose logic Marx "deconstructed," revealing it to be a theory of **exploitation**—a major reason that political economy was transformed into what was first termed "neoclassical economics" and then, "economics." (ROGIN)

As neoclassical economics evolved, what had been a plausible explanation of the source of profits was transformed into an ideological defense of **capitalism**; in that same process most (not all) economists became cheerleaders for capitalism. Such generalizations demand at least some explication.

The classical political economists (up through John Stuart Mill /1806-1873/) took it for granted that workers received <u>subsistence</u> wages—just enough to keep them and their families able to work and survive: What they received had <u>nothing</u> to do with how much or how little they had contributed to production. What <u>did</u> it have to do with?

As discussed at length under **capitalism**, the working class was made up of those who, once "the proud yeomanry" of Britain, had been pushed off the land by "the enclosure movement." That movement, in "rationalizing" British agriculture also created a powerful "landed gentry." They, with the Lords, were the hard core of British power until the mid-19th century); most of the rest were the <u>disem</u>powered who had lived on and worked the land. (MANTOUX, HAMMOND/1924/)

By the early 19th century, as coal mines and ships and factories were in need of rising numbers of workers, the employers were usefully faced with an abundance of desperate men, women, and children, all <u>utterly</u> powerless to make even the slightest demand, whether for more wages, fewer hours, or better working conditions. Taken together, their deprivations and overwork caused the average worker's life span to <u>decrease</u> by 20 percent in the first three decades of the "industrial revolution." (HOBSBAWM, 1968)

The word for what was occurring was **exploitation** which, like **needs,** is not to be found in the lexicon of economics. Exploitation of the powerless was the basis for profits then; it still is, though now it is joined by the what we may call exploitation through **taxes** and, less obviously, through the cultivated irrationality of **consumerism**.

Marx's emphasis was of course on worker exploitation; Smith and Ricardo were in agreement, and saw exploitation as a necessary if unpleasant ingredient of the emerging industrialization process they both prized. Smith explicitly hoped worker exploitation would be substantially ameliorated over time, though never ended. (GINZBERG, 1964)

OK, you may say, but in a private enterprise system do not those own and manage deserve something for their efforts? Within such a system of private ownership and control, of course; but what they would receive in a competitive economy (the one found in all textbooks) would be equivalent to the interest paid on borrowed funds and a return for their managerial contribution, not as legalized payment for their power over the powerless. Note: the competitive economy advocated by the political economists (Smith et seq.) meant there would be no firm (or a few firms) big enough to be able to control any aspect of the market: prices, wages, quality..., anything. (See **big business** for the modern economy's realities.)

What led to today's humongous companies was prompted by the needs and opportunities accompanying modern industrialization. Today's corporate form was "invented" simultaneously in Britain and the USA in the 1850s. Thenceforward, as large-scale production became dominant, so did the modern corporation.

Great size required investment capital in amounts going beyond the profits and savings of small owners; so corporations sold shares. To shorten a long story, the always-larger companies used their growing market power to make greater profits by (among other means) eliminating competition.

By the 20th century the ensuring profits were going to shareholders who do nothing but own—and to executives. More recently the proportion going to **CEO**s has risen substantially—a significant amount of which is a return not for "risk-taking" but for criminality.

But the reasoned basis for profits in the past remains its basis in the present. What began as rugged—read: ruthless—behavior on the part of early capitalists, after an interval in the 1950s-1960s, has returned to become normal: working hours increasing, social benefits decreasing. (see **big business**)

What about incomes other than wages and profits; that is, interest and rents? Interest is received as a return on borrowed money. The lender has done nothing but to postpone consumption; if that. Today almost all interest goes to those in the top 10 percent of incomes, and they are foregoing nothing; their problem is to find something more to buy when they are already suffocating with $5,000 watches and $150,000 (+) **cars**, and $4 million dollar homes, and global cruises, and.... wanting MORE.

Rent is more interesting. Ricardo described rent as, simply, "unearned income." He had a good point. He used the term "rents" to describe an important portion of what the landed gentry were receiving as prices for their crops. Why? Because those prices were made artificially high by tariffs on imported grains (the tariffs themselves decided upon by a Parliament dominated by landowners): If no foodstuffs (grain, etc.) could come into Britain below a certain price, then that price (irrespective of domestic costs) became <u>the</u> price. Thus an "arranged profit," or "rent": unearned.

It is relevant that Ricardo was a successful financier; he knew whereof he spoke. He, like his forerunner Smith, was an ardent supporter of British industrialization; he saw that keeping food prices artificially high necessarily raised the cost of "subsistence" and therefore money wages; in turn that lowered profits and hindered industrialization.

The subtitle of Marx's <u>Capital</u> (1867) is "A Critique of Political Economy." He simply took Ricardo's "labor theory of value" and, seemingly without changing much took it to its logical—and radical—conclusion. Consciously or not, the economists after the 1860s steadily abandoned "political economy" and the "labor theory of value," moved toward ever-higher levels of abstraction, changed the focus from production to consumption, and lived happily ever after.

If you have studied economics, you will know that little is ever said about the <u>source</u> of profits, but economic theory places much emphasis on profit-<u>maximization</u>. There is good reason to do so—but <u>not</u> to do so <u>as</u> they do; a meaningful discussion needs many ifs ands and buts. Here a handful.

The assumed maximization of profits by businesses is linked to the key assumption of <u>rationality</u>. A caution: As with other concepts in economics, this one doesn't mean what most of us would expect. It <u>doesn't</u> mean, for example, being "reasonable," or "thinking things through." No, it means "calculation," no more and no less. But even that has a catch: a rational business seeks to maximize its profits; it does so by "calculating," which, in turn, means by being "rational" which, in turn means "calculating" so as to maximize profits. Does that sound like circular reasoning to you? Good for you; that's what it is.

<u>Of course</u> most people who run a business, especially if it is a small business, <u>must</u> "calculate" and think in terms of profit maximization (or, its other side, loss minimization). Or else. But many other things also need doing for a firm, things that require thinking through a changing and unpredictable future: Expand or not expand? Try this new product, or not? Borrow to expand, or seek an additional partner, or go public and sell shares? And that's not all, of course.

Quite apart from the fact that, formally, economic theory assumes away time and change (along with almost all the rest of reality), one can "calculate" 'til the cows come home, and never be "rational" as normal human beings (as distinct from economists) think of it. And, in any case, "normal" human beings also "normally" are affected by thoughts and moods and hopes and fears and so on that affect their "calculations." Even of they run a business.

But that's only part of the problem and, today, not the largest part. Today, as recent and ongoing scandals have shown (see **CEOs, big business, financialization**) the giant companies that count most in terms of power have come to behave as though their business were a gambling casino, and not a very honest one at that.

The **mergers and acquisition** frenzies of the past 25 + years have not been rational, nor have they been about profit-maximization; mostly they have been about power, and greed and driven by **speculation**—itself exploding with irrationalities.

When Cartwright steamed up the power looms in his textile factory in the first factory (1815), he may have been prompted solely by "rational" considerations (although I doubt it). But the world has changed enormously since; not least the world of business. You'd never know it by reading economic theory.

Today's economists' analyses of business behavior combine ideology with games-playing with sheer irresponsibility. Presumably many mainstream economists read the financial news in the NYT, the WSJ, BW, etc. If they do, it doesn't show up in their public statements or in their professional articles. It's as though the economy consisted of thousands of Arkwrights, run by dedicated (and honest) people who, like their workers, receive an income proportionate to their contribution to production (their "marginal" contribution).

Something like that might apply to many of the really small businesses that exist in the millions in the USA: bookshops, the corner grocery, the dry cleaner, the bar around the corner, the shoemaker...; usually very hard-working souls (often families). Very often their little business, whatever else it might be, makes sense to them because the alternative is to close their shops and work for someone else (perhaps even at a more assured income and fewer worries). However.

Although what they are doing might be seen as sensible and life-preserving (and very useful for their customers), it is not "rational" as economists use the term; as economists "measure" things, that little shop around the corner is just plain "irrational."

This is not to say that **big business**, "non- or irrational" as it may be, has not piled up profits in recent years; indeed, they have piled up more than ever in history, and by a long shot: Using data from the Economic Report of the President (2001), PHILLIPS (2002) notes "a striking increase in profits for all U.S. corporations between 1980 and 2000, with the big surge coming in the nineties":

> Profits in 1980 were $209 billion, rising to $389 by 1990, and to $930 (est.) in 2000. The top one percent of shareholders owned 62 percent of business assets, 50 percent of stocks, and 62 percent of bonds (the top 10 percent owned all but 9-24 percent of all the foregoing).

However, in those same years, a great and ominous shift was taking place in the structure of power in the economy. One need not be enamored of corporate profits to believe that within the framework of a capitalist economy profits going to those involved in production are more likely to be useful for the economy than incomes derived from sheer ownership of or speculation in, financial assets. But note the tendency since 1949:

> Corporate profits were more than ten times as high as net interest in 1949, more than five times in 1959, and more than two-and-a-half times in 1969, but only a quarter more in 1979; since then corporate profits have been less than interest. (ERP, 2000)

The accumulation of **debt** (consumer, business, governmental, and foreign) accounts for much of that; but there is more. Again, PHILLIPS: (his emphases)

> In the early 1970s... the financial sector was subordinate to Congress and the White House, and the total of financial trades conducted by American firms or on American exchanges over an entire year was a dollar amount less than the gross national product /GDP/. By the 1990s, however, through a twenty-four-hour-a-day cascade of electronic hedging and speculation, the financial sector had swollen to an annual volume of trading thirty or forty times greater than the dollar turnover of the "real economy." Each month, several dozen huge domestic financial firms and exchanges...electronically trade a sum in currencies, futures, derivative instruments, stocks, and bond that exceeds the entire annual GDP of the United States! Lots of profits there; precious little "rationality"; and precious few of those of them were "earned."

propaganda

The term is not new to our time; it was used first in the 17th century. According to Fowler's <u>Modern English Usage</u>, it is in fact a curtailed phrase: <u>Congregatio de Propaganda Fide = Board for Propagating the Faith</u>. The wheel is not new to our time, either; but just as its function has changed from easing the path of a wagon to its manifold uses for all vehicles, computers, missiles, gambling casinos, and..., so has that of propaganda.

In "propagating" its faith, the Roman Catholic Church was—as the saying goes—"speaking to the converted"; propaganda in our time is "speaking to the vulnerable"; an essential means for gaining and holding economic, political, and social **power**, and for making **profits**.

Whether for commercial, political, or national aims, modern propaganda, channeled principally through the **media**, most especially by **TV**, has the <u>aim</u> of causing us to do something for the specific benefit of the "sponsor": business, politician, party, nation. Its ways and means leave no essential difference between a beer ad, a candidate's TV performance, presidential speeches, or many essays and books—to say nothing of films: A fine representation of those overlaps is found on the cover of a book by the journalist Joe McGinnis, who accompanied Nixon on the 1968 campaign trail, <u>The Selling of the President</u>: It shows Nixon's head emerging from a package of cigarettes.

To be sure, the Church was doing something like the same thing; in serving itself it was acting to control the social process, for better and for worse. But "something like" when the reference is to capitalism and the capitalist state is as different as a box of crayons is from a case of dynamite: the combination of economic and political power held by the few today pervades every corner of current existence in every moment, everywhere: always for less better, for more worse.

Whatever else is true of advertising and "public relations," what stands out is that their successes depend upon their ability to play upon our emotions, not our reason; to replace reflection with triggered responses to images and sounds; to exploit our weaknesses, heighten our fears, anxieties, our greed and our insecurities; for business or political ends, it speaks to the child or the adolescent in us, to the bigot, to the snob, to our frustrations and inner rages:

Propaganda brings out the worst in us, and paves the way for social and self-destruction.

BARAN (1969) captured an important element of it when, in his "Theses on Advertising" he saw it as "teaching us to want what we don't need, and not to want what we do." True, the Church has done its harm (as witness the Crusades); but it has also had the effect of bringing out the good in some. Not so with today's propaganda.

We live in an era in which social and self-destruction have become rife; for that to happen, it has been up to those in power to assist in bringing it about through half-truths, lies, and deception. In doing so, they persuade us 1) to overlook the dangers associated with how we live—not least as regards the **environment**, 2) to support military invasions (e.g., of **Vietnam** and **Iraq**) in the name of freedom and peace which had nothing to do with either, and, neither last nor least, 3) to acquiesce in an always deeper system of **corruption** and **lobbyism** that allows those in power to maintain and strengthen that power.

The USA and—because of our great power and the ways in which we use it—the entire modern world face an ever-deepening crisis. It is not the first time, of course; it is very likely to be the worst.

The two previous modern crises exploded into the two world wars; both were accompanied by intense propaganda campaigns in all the contending nations. It is still difficult to find any reasonable justification for World War I. Although on the side of the Allies it was portrayed as a struggle between decency and savagery ("German soldiers cutting off the breasts of Belgian nuns....") the Versailles Treaty's provisions revealed that the fighting was about power and resources, and imperialist pie not large enough to satisfy all appetites.

In its origins World War II was different: it <u>was</u> essential to stop the spread of fascist imperialism in both Europe and Asia; thus the propaganda for the war had a real base—although, as discussed under **fascism**, the opposition to it by the USA (until Pearl Harbor) was, to put it politely—underwhelming. And when the **Cold War** took hold, it was accompanied by a clandestine support and utilization of "ex-" fascists in Germany, Italy, and Japan—and the importation of known to be Nazi scientists to the USA to assist in weapons development. (WITTNER, ALPEROVITZ) To say nothing of the propaganda campaign accompanying what was not, after all, a "cold" war—unless one ignores the 100,000 or so U.S. deaths in Korea and Vietnam, and the several <u>millions</u> of dead Koreans,

Chinese, and Indochinese.

The promises that led us into those wars—I: "The war to end all wars," and II: "The war against fascism"—were, to say the least, not kept. In both cases, it seemed for a time that we had learned something, as symbolized by the creation of the League of Nations and the United Nations; in both cases the USA (and other major powers) spent more time and energy in creating than resolving problems; most recently, in **Iraq.**

As World War I broke out, VEBLEN (1914) saw it as a triumph of "imbecile institutions"—by which he meant "the system of business enterprise," its nationalistic and imperialistic state and close partner, militarism.

Those institutions became ever more imbecilic between the two world wars; after which, the **Cold War** and, soon after, **globalization** signified that we had learned nothing—or, more accurately, that we had been <u>taught</u> to unlearn what makes sense and to acquiesce in or even become enthusiastic about the strengthening of the very institutions that had produced the deadly crises of the past—if, now, in different garb.

When World War II ended, Wolfgang BORCHERT, a German soldier who had been imprisoned twice in Nazi prisons during the war, and who had contracted a fatal case of malaria at Stalingrad, returned to Germany. In the two years before his death (at the age of 26), he wrote dozens of short stories and a play. The theme is the same in all of them: the stupidity, horror, and terror of the modern world. His last story, published posthumously, speaks his main message, one we should heed, as soon and as well as we can. It was called "There's Only One Thing"; it specifies about 15 different situations, in which the "one thing" is to say NO! to all forms of propaganda and repression and their accompaniment, the processes that lead to war.

Here a few of them:

If tomorrow they tell you to make not more water-pipes and saucepans but to make steel helmets and machine-guns, then there's only one thing to do: Say NO!

You. Research worker in the laboratory. IF tomorrow they tell you are to invent a new death for the old life, then there's only one thing to do. Say NO!

You. Priest in the pulpit. If tomorrow they tell you are to bless murder and declare war holy, then there's only one thing to do: Say NO!

You. Pilot on the aerodrome. If tomorrow they tell you to carry bombs and phosphorus over the cities, then there's only one thing to do: Say NO!

You. Mother in Normandy..., in the Ukraine..., in Frisco and London, you on the Hwanghoo and on the Mississippi, you, mother in Naples and Hamburg and Cairo and Oslo—mothers in all parts of the earth, mothers of the world, if tomorrow they tell you are to bear children, nursing sisters for military hospitals and new soldiers for new battles, then there's only one thing to do: Say NO!

For if you do not say NO, if YOU do not say no, mothers, then:...the big ships will fall groaningly silent..., the trams will lie like senseless shineless glass-eyed cages... in lost crater-torn streets...; a slime-gray thick pulpy leaden stillness will roll up, devouring, growing, will swell.... and spread; the sunny juice vine will rot on its decaying slopes, rice will dry in the earth.../and he goes on to conclude:/ all this will happen tomorrow, tomorrow, tomorrow perhaps, perhaps even tonight, perhaps tonight, if —— if —— you do not say NO.

Saying NO! is necessary, but it is not sufficient to hold back and reverse the evolving anti-democratic, plutocratic, aggressive juggernaut, the "Amerika!" we are coming to be. We must do more than say NO!; much more. Some of what that might be is discussed in the Afterword.

public relations (see advertising)

public utilities (see deregulation)

Quayl, Dan

Some who read this are too young to remember him; you're lucky. He was the V.P. of **Bush I**. His only claim to fame was when he was caught spelling "potato" with an "e" on the end. I have set things right here. Now he's even.

Like **Bush II**, Quayle was born in the lap of luxury. His daddy was not in **oil**, but in the **media**. Dan the Q. made a try to get the

GOP nomination for president and failed: Oy. He did himself in, and we all exhaled. Little did we know, how could we possibly have imagined, that an even worse fate awaited?

History Lesson Number One: There are always depths below depths.

racism

Introduction. What we call "racism" probably began as our species came into existence, as human beings viewed each other with attitudes of envy, fear, and hatred. In the primitive world of enduring scarcities and the mere beginnings of technology, such attitudes and associated behavior patterns were considerably less irrational than today's.

Despite that, however, it is clear that those early peoples must have cooperated more than they fought with each other, or else our species wouldn't have survived; consciously or not, they must have recognized that the differences among and between them were minor when set against their similar needs and possibilities. Would that we could do the same; now as then, we are all members of the same species, of the same "race."

Quotation marks are placed around "race" to emphasize what should be the starting-point for discussing racism:

> There is no biological basis for distinguishing human groups along the lines of "race," and the sociohistorical categories employed to differentiate among these groups reveal themselves upon serious examination to be imprecise if not completely arbitrary. (WINANT; OMI/WINANT)

The bases for racism are "sociohistorical" rather than "biological." Most of us think of skin color when thinking of "racial" matters; in practice, however, color is only one of many its bases. Think only of the "racial theories" of the German Nazis, which focused more heavily upon Jews than any others—despite that 1) most—not by any means all—Jews are "white," and 2) when Jews are victimized, it is usually under the banner of "anti-Semitism," although not all Jews are Semites and not all Semites are Jews. Note this definition in Webster's New International Dictionary (1911):

> Semite: A member of a Caucasian race /sic!/ now chiefly represented by the Jews and Arabs /!/, but in ancient times

including also the Babylonians, Assyrians, Aramaens, Phoenicians and others....

But what about "black and white and brown and yellow <u>genes</u>"? Or, for some whose religious and national prejudices edge over into racism, what about Jewish, Catholic, Protestant, Muslim, and Buddhist...., German, French, Italian, Turkish, Greek.... genes? Moving from color to religion to nationality and the intense feelings involved in all of those and other hate- and fear-raising differences would bring strong affirmative answers from those who hate and fear in "racist" terms: It's <u>genes</u>. But the differences among peoples <u>within</u> a given category—color, religion, etc.—are at least as great as those <u>between</u> those different categories—whether the measuring criteria are those of intelligence and strength or, to shorten the list, bravery and honesty and health. (BALIBAR & WALLERSTEIN)

There are of course oft-cited data regarding crime, and education, health and..., that seem to (or are meant to) confirm racist views. But, and merely as an instance of what will be discussed more fully below regarding various economic and social indices, consider the most "physical" of these: <u>health</u>.

In the <u>NYT</u> feature article "As Black Men Move Into Middle Age, Dangers Rise," (9-23-02) the data provided

> showed conclusively that the death rate from strokes and diabetes for men 55 to 64 years old in the year 2000 /was/ three times higher for black than for white men; and 50 percent higher from cancer and heart disease."

Genes, see? Not quite. The same article quoted the Deputy Secretary of the U.S. Health and Human Services Department as stating that

> All those causes are preventable or treatable with great survivability...; the central task is improving access to health.... We should not be losing men because we have not provided access to care, treatment, information and education in a timely manner.

Moreover, although the economic element of the problem is greatest for <u>low</u>-income blacks, it exists as well for those blacks who <u>do</u> have financial access:

> The Institute of Medicine, on the basis of 100 studies, reports that "...even when African-Americans and other

> minorities have the same incomes, insurance coverage, and medical conditions as whites, they receive notably poorer care. Biases, prejudices and negative racial stereotypes... may be poisoning the reaction of doctors and other health providers." (ibid.)

As it does the reactions of police, teachers, employers, **boys and girls**.... In what follows the focus will be mostly on racism in the USA.

The dominating sets of institutions in U.S. history have been the "Big Four" of **nationalism, capitalism, imperialism,** and **militarism**. As noted above, racism existed millennia before any of those; however, racism has been much intensified by its interaction with those four social processes, the interaction itself greatly contributing to the strength and power of those same processes. How and why?

It is unnecessary to make that argument at any length regarding nationalism, imperialism and militarism; greed, envy, hatred, fear, and attitudes of superiority are the sine qua non of all three. Their success has always utilized and required force and violence, the recruiting for which is facilitated when those against whom it will be used are deemed "inferior" or "evil."

Less obviously but just as surely has this been so for the relationships between racism and capitalism. Nowadays in the USA, the term "class" refers to one's income group—high, middle, or low. In this age of **consumerism** people are generally identified by others and themselves in terms of their purchasing power, not the source of their incomes.

Before World War II, in contrast, one's "class" was usually identified by whether one was a worker or one who hired workers: working class or capitalist class (or in the latter's social circle).

The two classes were often in conscious conflict. But it was (and is) much mitigated in the capitalist world when workers' solidarity was weakened by the racism that pitted worker vs. worker. The mass starvation of the mid-19th century Irish "famine" (created by "free-market policies, not by "nature; WOODHAM-SMITH) led many thousands of poor Irish to seek work in England—and provided an early instance where racism pushed English workers toward self-harming irrationality. Its importance for British capitalism was noted by Marx, in 1870:

> All English industrial and commercial centers now possess

a working class <u>split</u> into two <u>hostile</u> camps: The ordinary
English worker hates the Irish worker because he sees in him a
competitor who lowers his standard of life.... He cherishes religious /i.e., anti-Catholic/, social and national prejudices against
the Irish worker. His attitude is much the same as that of the
"poor whites" towards the "niggers" in the former slave states of
the American Union. The Irishman pays him back with interest in his own money. He sees the English worker as both the
accomplice and the stupid tool of <u>English rule in Ireland</u>. (quoted in DELANY)

The same processes were already common in the urban U.S.
North in the early 19th century; they are the main concern of the
meticulous study <u>The Wages of Whiteness</u>:

> ...Working class formation and the systematic develop-
> ment of a sense of whiteness went hand in hand for the U.S.
> white working class...; race has at all times been a critical facto-
> ry in the history of U.S. class formation. (ROEDIGER)

Roediger's book concerns itself mostly with the two decades
before the Civil War. It delineates how the Irish in Boston, for
example, had difficulty finding even poor jobs, and were treated
shamefully both at work and also at pubs: "Micks and Dogs Not
Allowed." At the same time, the Irish workers "learned" to see the
pre-Civil War free blacks as competitors for jobs—in terms reflecting the ways in which themselves were seen.

> The crude, violent Know Nothing persecutions of Irish
> Catholics in the 1850's had been supplanted (especially but not
> only in the South) by social and class arrangements which
> achieved the same ends—"white, Anglo-Saxon, protestant
> (WASP) advantage in jobs, money, power, esteem—by more
> subtle, systematic discrimination. This was the post-Civil War
> period after the failure of "reconstruction" of southern slavery
> when WASP Americans improvised a caste-like social system:
> incorporating racist prejudices, discriminations, segregations
> and denial of civil rights against blacks and the Irish
> Catholics—a system which subsequently has been used against
> every people to immigrate to the U.S. (DELANY)

Ubiquitous over time and space, racism has of course taken on
diverse as well as similar ways and means over the globe. The USA,
however, stands alone as regards its racist history, Other societies
have been and remain racist; but, and much more easily than any

others, the USA <u>could</u> have risen above that blight. Why?

First, more than any other, the USA has drawn to itself peoples of every nationality, ethnicity, color, and religion to its shores. That <u>could</u> have served as an inexhaustible multicultural spring of social vitality; instead, the U.S. ideal for immigrants was for them to become part of the "melting pot." However, what is generally seen in the USA as a benign notion in fact has served as an imperative: You will be accepted—<u>despite</u> your origins—"so long as you become like us." The "us" came to mean the "WASPS"—wittingly or not.

<u>Of course</u> variety has persisted, and <u>of course</u> some significant percentage of immigrant families have risen to levels of comfort and dignity, my own included (on both the Irish Catholic and Russian Jewish sides). But. It is understandable that immigrants would serve mostly as endless supplies of cheap labor within an ongoing status quo. But each new group has been pitted against its relatively more assimilated predecessors: the once despised "Micks" (also derisively called "Paddy" and "Bridget") against the newly-arrived "Squareheads" and "Frogs" and "Wops" and "Polacks" and "Gooks" and...so on; <u>all</u> the former Europeans vs. the **"Indians,"** the "Niggers," the "Japs," the "Chinks," and the "Greasers." And then came 9/11. Now, it seems, both the despising and the despised "Americans" view those from the Muslim world—especially its Arab areas—with distrust, fear, and bottomless suspicion. A derogatory insulting name has yet to be settled upon, except for the Iraqis: "Hajis," an ugly echo of "gook" for the Vietnamese.

It hurts even to read those words; but for those against whom they were and are used, hurt feelings are but one part of a multidimensional and interacting set of "hurts"—economic, political, legal, cultural, physical, and emotional—as the long-poisoned multicultural springs dry up.

Second, just as the richness of our demographic mix <u>could</u> have led us to become the least racist of all societies, so too the richness of our natural resources <u>could</u> have led us to have the least fear of "the other." All other societies have emerged in a world of dire scarcities; the USA stands out as a unique opposite, a society without any <u>material</u> basis for racism, its abundance unmatched in past or present, with <u>always</u> plenty "to go around."

And then note that in the centuries before Pearl Harbor the vast oceans surrounding the USA meant that any basis for a fearful or militaristic population was nonexistent. (And even Pearl Harbor is 2,000 miles off our shores.) Despite all, we trod the path of an always spreading racism and persisting **militarism** from our beginnings to the present.

The continent was not, of course, "empty" when the first Europeans invaded; its settlement from Asia had begun thousands of years earlier. Although the hemisphere's original inhabitants were friendly and cooperative, an accelerating violence by the Europeans took hold. The consequences for the native peoples were genocidal in nature, matching the virtual extermination of the North American **buffalo**. It is estimated that there were 100 <u>million</u> "**Native Americans**" in our hemisphere at the time of the landing of Columbus; by 1900, there were only 10 million.

It needs adding that those 100 millions of "primitive" people, whatever the dangers and hardships of their existence, were very probably better fed, clothed, and housed—and with dignity—than their descendants have been for the past few centuries. (see **"Indians"** and MANDER /1992/; WRIGHT)

If there were any excuse at all for the murderous behavior of what became "the "Americans" before 1776, it would be a weak one: that they were merely part of the ferocious campaigns of the Spanish, French, and British. However, as the colonists took on their "American" identity and became a nation that ferocity heightened, as the new nation became dependent upon the simultaneous mistreatment of chattel slaves <u>and</u> the peoples native to the hemisphere.

The hard core of U.S. racist history is thus found in its centuries of subjugation, displacement, exploitation, and/or slaughter of both "Indians" and slaves. Racism served as a rationale for otherwise unspeakable behavior in those histories; and it set the stage for today's continuing, if usually less violent variations. (MARABLE)

In what follows, some of the past and current details of that sordid history's various dimensions will be examined summarily.

1. <u>Life and death</u>. First, the slave trade. The accepted estimates are that 20 million Africans were taken away from their homelands, but that only 4 million survived the months' long voyage. This says nothing of the horrors endured on the trip, or how the survivors' subsequent health was affected. (MINTZ; NORDHOLT; WILLIAMS, E. /1944/; GENOVESE)

Nor does it say anything about their health and life expectancies on the plantations. Because slaves were productive "assets," there was ample reason for the merchants and slaveowners to treat them with care, as with any "asset"; few slaves were lynched.

That the reason was not fully persuasive is suggested not only by the high death rates of the ocean passage, but also by abundantly documented materials concerning slaves' mistreatment on the plantations, and the numberless instances of institutionalized rape during and after slavery. Much more remains to be said (see **slavery**), and much may be easily imagined.

That is also true for the lives and deaths of "Indians" from the 17th century on; here we note only the decimation of their peoples—except that literal "decimation" would mean a 10 percent reduction of the tribal population from then to modern times; the actual reduction was closer to 90 percent (**"Indians"**).

That bitter history continued throughout the 19th century, only dwindling as the 20th century began. But new victims from Asia were beginning to fill the gap from the 1860s on: the Chinese, Japanese, and Filipinos. Chinese men were imported in vast quantities to build the railroads of the West; they worked and sweated and died prematurely for decades, indistinguishable from slaves, until, in the early 20th century, railroad construction—200,000 miles of it—was completed.

As they settled into towns and cities (mostly) along the Pacific Coast, they underwent persistent "racial" persecution and discrimination, up to and including many lynchings. Those took place all too often in San Francisco, then the largest city on the West Coast with, simultaneously, the greatest number of Chinese and the best-organized working class in the United States. Then as still, "white" workers allowed racism to direct their fears against the wrong target. (I. CHANG)

In the late 19th and early 20th centuries, Japanese began to arrive; by the late 1930s they numbered well over 100,000 (almost all on or near the Pacific Coast.)

The highest percentage of them, after working very hard <u>on</u> farms, were able to become small farmers themselves. Until Pearl Harbor. Then, soon after the attack, at least 150,000 Japanese men, women, and children were rounded up, placed in concentration camps and, without access to lawyers or visitors, left there until war's end; the precedent for **Camp X-ray**, Guantánamo.

Although there were no charges against any of them—except, because they were Japanese, being seen as a threat to our national security—neither was there any significant public opposition to their imprisonment. Indeed, quite the opposite; without exception, they lost their farmlands and homes to whites in their home region, with no recourse—except painfully, and not always successfully, well after the war. (WINANT)

2. <u>Socioeconomic conditions</u>. The malevolent treatments of the peoples of diverse national, ethnic, and religious origins in the USA have varied considerably in both degree and kind. Of the British, the English alone were essentially exempt; not so for the Scots, Welsh, and Irish: they were discriminated against mildly or strongly, the Scots very little, the Irish very much. Among European immigrants, those from the east were treated worse than those from the west; those from the south worse than those from the north. But none of the Europeans received the harsh treatment of Latin Americans and Asians; and that imposed upon "Native Americans" and "African Americans" was worst of all.

Of what did and does that treatment consist, in the realms of **jobs, health care, housing, and education**? (For a parallel discussion focused on close cousin gender, see **boys and girls, men and women**.)

<u>Jobs</u>. Who gets which **jobs** is commonly—if seldom admittedly—determined by racist considerations rather than the ability of the worker. In a given job, racism often means differential <u>wages</u> and chances for <u>promotion</u>. More subtly but not unimportantly, there is the matter of how workers are <u>treated</u> on the job. And of course whether or not one is qualified for a given job is much influenced by prior **education**—itself critically affected by one's "race." (See below.)

In all these respects conditions throughout the USA before World War II were on average more severe than today; since then, however, and despite numerous reforms, the incidence and seriousness of racial discrimination is still great, both for those harmed and for society as a whole. The results, among other miseries, include inescapable **poverty** and desperate lives for at least a sixth of the nation (measured conservatively), even during "best of times" of the 1990s. (MISHEL, et al.)

Among the abiding accompaniments of the stunted lives of racism's victims are the explanations offered by the comfortable for that plight: They are lazy, ignorant, immoral, <u>inferior</u>. This "blaming the victim" soothes racism's supporters while, at the same time, adding to the several vicious circles maintaining the ugly status quo. (PIVEN & CLOWARD; RYAN) <u>Education</u> is one of those "circles." Because the targets of racism rarely have full access to decent education and training, they have difficulty getting jobs with a living wage; thus they are doomed to live in poor **housing** in wretched neighborhoods; there the schools are understaffed, ill-equipped and overcrowded and, understandably, many of their teachers (some of whom are themselves prejudiced) and most of the students, suffer from demoralization.

Jonathan KOZOL, a dedicated young teacher, wrote a devastating book based on his own experiences in the 1960s. Its title was all too apt: <u>Death at an Early Age</u>. Kozol was teaching in Boston, a city seen as among the most civilized cities in the USA. Since then he has published several more books on the same subject; they too are devastating. (e.g., KOZOL, 1991)

Throughout our history, and up to the present, whatever has been wrong with our schools, and however severely affected others have been, it has been worst for blacks, and not only while enslaved.

After the Civil War, and until the early 20th century, most blacks lived in rural districts. Usually they had <u>no</u> schools—nor dentists, doctors, or lawyers. In parts of the rural South, that remained so for some decades <u>after</u> World War II. And, although there have almost always been schools for all in urban areas, in the slum districts the schools are as bad as the housing.

The recently introduced "voucher programs" do more to harm than to help the education of the poor and discriminated against. The original idea was to give a stipend of $2,500-$5,000 to parents of inner-city children to use toward private (including religious) school education; as passed, the legislation makes the grant available to <u>all</u>, rich and poor.

In thus subsidizing middle and upper income families, this drains a large number of students from public schools—further ravaging public education and further promoting private education. The average payment received by inner-city families is $2,500; it is insufficient to pay for tuition except at the lesser religious schools; at the same time, upper income families are subsidized to send <u>their</u> children to attend the best private schools.

About thirty years ago, the infamous "white flight" to the suburbs by the relatively affluent took hold, leaving the remaining largely upper middle and high income voters to become the basis for the "tax revolt" that has left public schools in always more desperate financial condition. The most recent development in that evolution is the spreading phenomenon of "gated communities."

And the vicious circles for poor people of color have become a noose.

Those who defend past and present status quos in these respects and who see the plight of the poor people of color as "their own fault" point to the existence of blacks in the past who "made it": A black doctor or judge or writer (etc.) personified the proof that opportunities exist for those who have sufficient strength, talent, and intelligence and who are willing to make the needed effort. More recently, the existence of a significant "black middle class" is cited to strengthen that argument.

Implicit in such arguments is that those who <u>are</u> well off <u>do</u> have the strength, and <u>did</u> make the effort, etc. As will be discussed at some length under **income distribution**, there is some truth in that but it is greatly outweighed by its untruth.

When such arguments refer to poor blacks, they neglect how very much was required of black individuals in the "pre-civil rights" past and, for presently achieving individuals, their efforts plus the relevant social reforms (which those who make such arguments seldom support), IF that significant percentage of blacks were to find their way out of poverty and maleducation and into a decent livelihood.

Before the 1960s, such individual achievement required amounts and kinds of effort rarely found in <u>any</u> of us, "regardless of race, creed, or color": a Paul Robeson or a Marian Anderson as singers, a Zora Houston or a James Baldwin as writers, a Thurgood Marshall as Supreme Court Justice, a W.E.B. DU BOIS as intellectual prodigy—or, on a humbler level, a Claude BROWN, born in the slums, a captive of poverty and imprisoned for petty crime, who, befriended by a prison counselor, struggled to get an education and wrote a stunning book on his saga: (<u>Manchild in the Promised Land</u>). Reading that, one learns how extraordinary a young black had to be in order to become "like us."

Few indeed of those of us who have been at worst only mildly afflicted by racism can even begin to imagine the ardours of such an effort—including, very probably, many blacks in the present generation who have "made it." The latter were much aided by the sociopolitical changes dating from the late 1960s—most importantly through **affirmative action** for education and anti-discrimination laws for jobs.

Terribly inadequate though such reforms have been and remain—and, now, are being lost—at least they lowered some of the barriers to equal opportunity and a decent existence. Nor is it unimportant to note that those mostly assisted in recent years were seldom among the worst off when they received that assistance. (FEAGIN & SYKES; DRAKE & CAYTON; LITWACK; OMI & WINANT)

And it is those worst off who have suffered the most from the legal injustices now to be noted.

<u>Racism and the law</u>. We pride ourselves on the glorious words of our Declaration of Independence that "All men are created equal," and on the twinned notion that in this nation all stand equally before the law. The reality blatantly violates that ideal, to the advantage of the rich and "white" and, regularly, to the harm of poor people of color—and, now, those from the Muslim world. They are arrested more frequently and on occasions when others would not be—for using or selling drugs, for "driving while black" (or in the Southwest, "brown") and for other assumed crimes and misdemeanors; once arrested, they are frequently represented badly (or not all) by lawyers, given higher prison sentences for a given crime **(crime and punishment)**, and subjected disproportionately to the **death penalty.**

Meanwhile, as those at the street level of crime—most notoriously drugs—are arrested and imprisoned for selling or use, their middle class white counterpart drug users and drug bosses are seldom even apprehended. More generally, if and when those higher up on the socioeconomic pyramid are arrested for, say, "white collar crimes," they are well-represented, and, if convicted, as with a Milken in the 1980s or, perhaps, a Grubman these days, they typically serve less or no time for crimes involving millions (even billions) of dollars than a young black caught and convicted for stealing $100 from a gas station. And as the number of prisoners has burgeoned in the past two decades or so, that has also provided "good arguments" for the rapidly growing **prison-industrial complex**—as already inadequate educational budgets are frozen or reduced.

To repeat, the ill-treatment of human beings is by no means confined to the USA; but, and quite apart from our ideals, we have gone farther quantitatively than any other democratic society with imprisonment: We have 2.3 million behind bars (with only China, with a population almost five times ours, coming even close). Those great numbers and the high percentage of poor and black among them are national disgraces that defy acceptable explanation.

Racism and dehumanization. In the Foreword, the social and economic devastation of the Irish by the English colonization was discussed. There were, of course, many differences between their treatment by the English, and the treatment of blacks and "Indians" in the USA; but there are also striking similarities, among which has been the impact of racism on the family.

It has been widely-noted that in the families of the Irish, of blacks and of "Native Americans," it has long been the women whose strength has held families together, and for essentially the same reasons (which, with variations, apply also to family survival in other groups victimized by racism).

Although the hardships facing the Irish family were due to the invasion and domination of their lands and lives by the Europeans (as also for the "Indians"), and the lives of the blacks by their subjection to slavery, in all cases the strength and dignity of the male as "head of the family" was crushed. Women were of course also deprived of any independence they might otherwise have had; not least when subjected to what has been termed "institutionalized rape."

Why then these differences between men and women? The answer is best found in the "division of labor" that took hold in prehistoric times and which, in numerous variations, has persisted: the male as hunter and warrior, the female as sustainer and nurturer. The latter qualities fall within the purview of what we think of as the "maternal instinct."

Doubtless there have always been, and are, men who have served happily and well as parents, and some women who have not. But it seems fair to assume that those men are very much in the minority, as would be so for the women who have not so served. (VEBLEN, 1899/1954)

For better and for worse, the prehistoric and, with important variations, the subsequent functions of men have typically been those based on "prowess": winning, whether vs. a wild animal, or in sports, business, sex or war; gaining and holding power, with whatever means are at hand.

Of course one finds a Joan of Arc in the past and a Margaret Thatcher in the present, Not only do they standout, but they have been seen as "acting like men" (of which, more under **boys and girls...**). Men are likely to think more of sexual conquest than love, of competition than cooperation, of using violence rather than persuasion to gain their ends. Of course there are exceptions; still....

All this is a way of saying that when Irish, "Indian" and black men were robbed of their abilities to serve their traditional functions, they were then deprived also of their pride, their dignity, their means of being <u>men</u>, of being self-respecting human beings.

The consequences for the Irish, "Indian," and black men were what might be expected under such conditions: to become misdirected, or undirected, to lose moral compass; to find ways of easing the pain, whether by drink or drugs or violence, among other ways of becoming self-destructive.

The loss of dignity for all these men began no later than the 17th century; with variations over time, it persisted into the modern period—much alleviated for the Irish both at home and abroad, considerably less so for blacks, and virtually not at all for "Indians."

The women were also under terrible pressure, of course; but in addition to noting that women have <u>always</u> been oppressed by men, everywhere, even in the best of times, the mere fact of their having the responsibility for the young and helpless has always made it less likely that they will, as the saying goes, go off the deep end. To repeat: Of course there have been exceptions for both men and women with respect to everything noted above. And it may be hoped that the exceptions favoring life and decency are in the ascendant, so long as social education and legislation provide those ways and means that make living a decent life feasible; up to now, the destructive ways and means still rule—in the USA, and elsewhere.

Such are some of the consequences of racism for those singled out as "inferior," or dangerous, or... something. But there have been grave consequences for the racists themselves, and for their societies, too, not least for the USA. The discussion of those consequences, as with all that has proceeded, must be desperately brief, all the more so because the individual and social damages will be treated in an overlapping fashion.

Whether it is "whites" treating people of color or each other badly, or men mistreating women, the dehumanizing consequences are not only suffered by the victims, but also by the perpetrators—and they are manifold. The poet John Donne, writing in the 17th century, the bloodiest ever until our own times, caught the essence of this when he wrote

> No man is an island, entire of itself;
> every man is a piece of the continent,
> a part of the main.
>   If a clod be washed away by the sea, Europe is the less; as well as if a promontory were, as well as if a manor of thy friends or of thine own were.
> Any man's death diminishes me,
> because I am involved in mankind.
>   And therefore never send to know for whom the bell tolls;
> it tolls for thee.

Or, as we put might put it today, we're all in the same boat.

When we are born, we are like soft clay; our lives at home and school and in the larger society shape us until, as adults, we become who and what we are; and although many further changes will occur, they are most likely to fit the shape already achieved; qualitative changes will depend upon extraordinary pressures or opportunities: a war, a happy or destructive marriage, a stimulating or crushing job, etc.

When we grow up in a pervasive racist society such as the USA, our "natural" feelings, thoughts, and behavior will be racist in one degree or another, depending upon time and place—which includes even those who have joined the struggles against racism: they too have "been taught to hate" (as the song in the show "South Pacific" put it), but with second thoughts.

It is generally accepted that our "human nature" has both a constructive and destructive side to it. VEBLEN, writing on the eve of World War I, saw these as, respectively, our "instinct of workmanship and our parental bent," and, wryly, as the "instinct of sportsmanship and the predatory bent," constantly struggling for dominance within us. And he saw the destructive side as winning, given the driving forces of capitalism and imperialism of our lives—which he called "imbecile institutions":

> But history records more frequent and more spectacular instances of the triumph of imbecile institutions over life and

culture than of peoples who have by force of instinctive insight saved themselves alive out of a desperately precarious institutional situation, such, for instance, as now faces the people of Christendom. (1914 /1946/)

Not just **capitalism** and **imperialism**, but racism is one of those "imbecile institutions"—and the three function in a mutually nourishing set of processes that damage all people, social wellbeing, and nature: workers divided by racism are vitally weakened in their essential struggles for trade unions as a means of balancing the otherwise unrestrained power of their employers; people caught up in capitalist **consumerism** diverted from their function as citizens, and thus allowing business to have its way in ravaging the **environment**; the forces for harmful geographic expansion—whether through **globalization** or war—having their path eased through racist fears and hates.

No species has ever survived except by mutual support, which, when applied to human beings, may be seen as "solidarity." That term need not connote affection or anything like it; it does connote a functional recognition of mutual interests.

The USA is the global leader today in acting so as to trample those mutual interests. Racism is one of the several elements of our society causing and allowing that set of tragedies—for all, everywhere.

Enough, already.

Reagan, Ronald/Reagonomics

As a performer in radio, film, and **TV**, Reagan was more than moderately successful; when he entered politics and combined his crooked smile and wisecracks with sneers, mixing hatred for blacks, the poor, and taxes into a vile stew, he was triumphantly so: the consummate con man for the rich and powerful—and the prejudiced. No president before Reagan had managed to be popular with the working class while openly seeking to weaken or break their unions; none had ever gained popular support for simultaneously lowering social expenditures benefiting the majority of taxpayers while, at the same time, lowering the taxes of the rich and raising those of the bottom 80 percent. (see **social security, taxes**)

Because of such domestic policies and a similarly heinous foreign policy, Reagan was a nightmare for New Deal liberals and those to their left; they saw him as the bottom of a pit of everything that was to be opposed and feared; we were wrong, that pit <u>has</u> no bottom; **Bush II** and his crew (many of whom were with Reagan) have plumbed new depths.

The gritty details of Reagan's role in carrying the USA from a faded New Deal era toward what is now spun as "compassionate conservatism" are told in full in Garry Wills' <u>Reagan's America</u>, upon which I have depended for much of what follows; for the rest I have taken the liberty of quoting myself. (DOWD, 1997a).

Born in small-town Illinois a few years before World War I, Reagan came to adulthood in the midst of the 1930s depression. He started work as a lifeguard, thence to radio sports announcer, thence, in 1937, to Hollywood. There he remained, making both successful and unsuccessful films throughout World War II.

He never left Hollywood during the war; however, when he went into politics he often gave the very strong impression that he had endured combat dangers. In that, as in other respects, Reagan moved easily back and forth from reality to make-believe, deceiving the public—and, quite possibly, himself.

Reagan was one of those few who, having performed in radio, shifted gears to work in film and then, as **TV** began to reach large audiences in the early 1950s, went to work there also (or as well). That evolution coincided with and help to explain his political shift from New Deal liberal to ultraconservative. What moved him from one side to the other were his years as a spokesman for **GE**—the most ideological and anti-union of giant corporations from the 1920s to the present.

He was a good enough actor for Hollywood; politically, with his "down home" sentimentality and optimism, he was even more than that for "Mr. and Mrs. America": he was a charmer; he became their "voice."

GE hired him first to give soft soap talks to its workers and later to give their speeches on the "rubber chicken circuit" (Rotary Clubs and the like) and to GE-organized meetings of corporate executives; then, for ten years after 1952, he became master of ceremonies for the General Electric Theater on TV.

In his years on the circuit for GE, Reagan's "role" was to give "The Speech." It became a comfortable role for him; he didn't so much learn his lines from GE as learn and recite them in a more persuasive way to make it <u>his</u> "Speech": pro-**big business**, anti-big government, anti-independent unionism, anti-liberal/left, anti-New Deal.

In his rhetoric and his attitudes—in his <u>style</u>—Reagan incarnated the illusions, ongoing disappointments, angers and fears and the adolescent dreams of much of the <u>voting</u> part of all segments of social spectrum. What **Nixon** had called the "silent majority" in the 1960s had become Reagan's <u>voting</u> majority by the 1980s.

That majority, which came to be called "the middle class," is comprised of small proprietors, blue <u>and</u> white collar workers, and farmers—many of whom would become stalwart members of the religious and militaristic right—happily joined by a large chunk of the not-so silent giants of industry and finance.

Reagan was the embodiment of what increasing numbers in the USA have become or are becoming: cold-hearted, substituting sentimentality for compassion; scornful or hateful of careful social analysis, but confident experts on a long list of complex social problems; quick to support wars, but unwilling to endure our casualties (while indifferent to others'); and, like Reagan himself, never having heard a shot fired in anger.

Like him, his enthusiasts attack the poor and profess belief in the "Puritan ethic" of hard and honest work while, at the same time, looking for a quick deal, some way to get something for nothing; and the more the merrier.

But Reagan differed in at least one very big way from the "middle class" whose hero he became; once "discovered," he was surrounded, financed, and guided by a group of experts at achieving cushy deals for him and for themselves on the very highest level; for which we—including most of his enthusiastic "middle class" supporters—will be paying for a long time, and paying again, now that his ways and means have been given a big jump by Bush II.

Reagan came to prominence when and how he did because his personality and talents fitted a society in which those who could rise most rapidly were those who had, as the saying goes, a different principle for every occasion. "America!" had become increasingly difficult to find by the 1970s; the era of giant business and cold war was one in which it was manna from heaven for those in power to find a "leader" who, seeming in his person to represent all that was precious of traditional "America" would pave the way toward acceptance of a very different reality in its name.

Reagan was not plucked from out of nowhere by those whose will he came to represent; the path from sports announcer to governor to president is easy to locate; it was not drawn for Reagan by a small group of conspirators; rather his pliant character and the slow but steady evolution of a consolidating power center found each other first about 1950, were joined in the Sixties, and took power in the Eighties. They have been there ever since, always growing stronger.

The details and the context of Reagan's ascent are expertly provided in WILLS (1988); here a few of them. Reagan the politician became a well-groomed set of <u>pretenses</u>, of images. The need for him to "learn his lines" appeared as preparations were being made for him to become Governor of California. He was prone to make "goofs" regarding social matters; after having committed particularly serious ones about welfare—exaggerating negative facts to a degree so alarming as to be self-defeating—the groomers were assigned to him.

His team hired BASICO (the Behavior Sciences Corporation of, naturally, Southern California) to create "the whole concept of the man." Here's a taste of it:

> The BASICO team assembled simple answers for Reagan, framed in terms of his theme, and arranged them into eight books of five-by-eight cards that would focus his and the voters' minds. From that time BASICO became the keepers of the candidate and his cards.... "We were with him every waking moment during the entire campaign... You'd follow him into the rest room before he goes onstage, giving him a last-minute bit of advice." (WILLS)

I don't know if BASICO is also doing Bush II, but the role played by Karl **Rove** and Andrew **Card** in his administration certainly has the same touch. Anyhow, Ronnie won the governorship of California in 1966 and was, of course, re-elected.

As has become customary for ultra-conservatives, Reagan consistently praised fiscal tightness while, at the same time, breaking the record for skyrocketing deficits. Along the way, as he was baiting the poor with sly but unmistakably racist wisecracks he made jokes as well about the other realms:

<u>Item</u>: **Vietnam**. "Pave it over and use it for a parking lot." As for protestors: "It's time for a little blood to flow." **Environment**: "See one redwood tree, and you've seen 'em all." Is that leadership, or what?

It was on Reagan's watch that "supply-side economics" was

born. The notion refers almost entirely to fiscal (taxing and spending) policies; they were (are) the Second Coming of pre-1930s policies and added up to something pretty simple: 1. Lower individual and corporate income (direct) taxes while increasing military expenditures. 2. There will be—surprise!—a budget deficit. 3. Lower social expenditures (whose nickname among his gang was "Starve the Beast." 4. Raise non-income (indirect) taxes—payroll taxes, sales taxes, diverse fees (national parks, etc.). Bush II's policy are a full copy. (see **deficits and surpluses, taxes/tax expenditures**)

How did it work? GDP grew, but never reached that of the Sixties (with its "Keynesian" policies); the rate of savings, supposed to rise, fell substantially; the rich, who received the lion's share of tax cuts, bought bigger yachts, while businesses "invested" in **mergers and acquisitions**; aggregate domestic **debt** (households, nonfinancial businesses, and government almost tripled; and, from having been the world's largest creditor in 1980, we had become its largest debtor in 1988 (from being owed $1 trillion to owing $1 trillion).

The fancy footwork of Reaganeconomics was especially dazzling for **milex**: "an extra $80 billion per year /emphasis in original/ in spending authority /for the military/ above and beyond what even conservative hard-liners had said was needed to restore U.S. military prowess." (HERTSGAARD)

It wasn't madness; it was large-scale thievery. David STOCKMAN, Reagan's Budget Chief, resigned in the midst of his tenure and wrote a book. In it he reveals that the aim of all those hi-jinks was just what you might have thought: 1. Enrich the rich. 2. Jack up **milex**. 3. Have an "acceptable" reason to cut social expenditures. (Today's news, again.)

Racing alongside that set of economic iniquities was another, the Savings and Loan (**S&L**) rip-off of the 1980s, with whose reverberations (and the taxes for which) we live still. For someone whose image was that of "the real America, the America of the little guy," Reagan's record in that scandal reveals just what a fraud he was. Why?

Because the S&Ls, usually called "thrifts," were organized in the Thirties, almost entirely as neighborhood banks designed to finance home mortgages for "the middle class." They got their funds from the savings of the same class of people to whom they made home loans; their rules placed a ceiling on what they could pay their depositors, and the interest cost of loans was kept low.

In those same depression years, the Federal Deposit Insurance Corporation (FDIC) was created. Its aim was to insure the deposits of that same middle class against the financial disasters that had wiped out small savers' deposits in the 1920s.

It was in Reagan's presidency that **financialization** of the economy was firming its grip, leading to ever-mounting **debt** and **speculation**. By the 1990s, industry had become secondary to finance, and corporations had come to be ruled over by **CEO**s whose specialty was large-scale gambling and theft. In the same process, the political power of **big business** rose accordingly. (GREIDER/1994/; PHILLIPS/2002/)

So, why leave those nice little S&Ls to themselves, all those unpicked cherries just waiting to be picked?

They weren't; in 1981, Reagan's first year, the Garn-St. Germain Bill for **deregulating** the thrifts was passed; it opened the door to reckless financial practices for households and all financial institutions, among them and leading the pack, the S&Ls.

Their ownership and control were soon taken over by sharpies, fools, and downright crooks: they got their capital every which way at always rising costs and made loans and investments of every which kind, including junk bonds (which are called "junk" because they are fool's gold). (PIZZO, et al.)

The mismanagement, stealing, and thievery led to countless bankruptcies—small, large, and gigantic. Meanwhile, the FDIC's rules had also been changed, to allow enormous-sized deposits to be insured. Between the bailouts and the payouts, and the $600/hour lawyers' fees for the Resolution Trust Corporation (created for the bailouts), the whole mess will cost the taxpayers a <u>minimum</u> of $200 <u>billion</u>.

Deeply involved in the **corruption** and failure of the S&Ls were and are still all levels of government—the bank regulators, Congress, the **FBI** and the **CIA**, bigwigs from business and finance and, of course Ronnie. Through it all he grinned and wisecracked. As his popularity rose. (SHERRILL /1995/)

Nothing has been said here about foreign policy under Reagan. It was wild, man, <u>wild</u>. And disgraceful. On his watch, and setting aside the "Star Wars" fiasco and related bumps up in **milex**, were the numerous military and non-military interventions here and there, all covert, all illegal: Twice in **Iran**, one noted in that entry, the other below; twice in Central America (**El Salvador, Nicaragua**);

once in **Grenada**.

The events leading up to our invasion of Grenada are recounted under its heading. Here we note only that it was one of several occasions in which **Reagan** not only badly exploited U.S. power for the shoddiest of reasons, but also got away with it. After overcoming a country whose total population was 100,000 max, he informed us in his State of the Union Address that "Our days of weakness are over. Our military forces are back on their feet and standing tall."

Even more revealing of Reagan's ways and means was what he said when it was shown that his gang had illegally made a deal with **Iran** to buy arms from them in order to give them to the U.S. organized and financed "contras" seeking to overthrow the Nicaraguan government. This was his public statement;

> I told the American people I did not trade arms for hostages. My heart and my best intention still tell me that is true, but the facts and the evidence tell me it is not. (DRAPER)

It seems fair to say that what **Bush II** has gotten away with on a larger scale in terms of unjust and dangerous fiscal policies are organically linked to those of Reagan; as is true for our ongoing aggressive foreign policies. Not quite a coincidence: some of Bush's advisers were Reagan's advisers in the 1980s (see **Bush II...His Team**). Nor is it surprising that Reagan's very expensive (and very profitable) and still unworkable "Star Wars" game has been brought back to life.

Ponder this: if for some reason Bush II were not to run again, and if Reagan, illness and all, were to run for President, what odds would you give for or against his winning? Especially if Arnold Schwarznegger would run as his Veep? Or vice versa?

Postscript: The foregoing was written in 2002; as I write now in June, 2004, Reagan has just died; what took place in the week or so after his death was a reprise of his political career: PR plumbing new depths—and, it seems, successfully so. Successfully for those who groomed him to be remembered as Mr. America Incarnate; successfully for those who have groomed Bush II and his obscene domestic and foreign policies and want some of Reagan's veneer to shine for him: "Starve the Beast" of badly-needed social policies at home while feeding monstrous military expenditures as we kill and ravish abroad.

Five years ago, responding to the change of name for Washington National Airport to Reagan..., David Corn wrote a piece for The Nation: "66 (Unflattering) Things About Ronald Reagan." If Bush II ever dies, he will certainly have broken that record—unless and until a sufficient number of us get seriously political. (see Afterword)

Red scare (see Sacco and Vanzetti)

rich and poor

Almost all of what might be expected to be dealt with under this heading is to be found under **big business, CEOs, jobs, inequality**, and **poverty**; here the intent is merely to clarify and dwell upon the meanings and confusions surrounding the words themselves.

The rich and poor were the focus of a wonderfully lively and provocative Broadway musical comedy—"Finian's Rainbow"—of the 1960s (made into a film in 1971 by Francis Ford Coppola: his first). The setting was the coal mining hills of the eastern USA in the Great Depression: ordinary hard-working and desperate people ruled over by tight-fisted owners. One of its many wonderful songs by Yip Harburg—sung by Fred Astaire in the film—was "When the idle poor become the idle rich."

The word "poor" in that context was used relatively; that is, the people were poor indeed relative to their bosses, but not so poor as to be starving. As discussed at length under **poverty**, the connotations of "rich" and "poor" are both relative and absolute. One is relatively poor in comparison with others; one is absolutely poor when life is shortened because of the absence of the food and shelter sufficient to keep one alive.

Almost all who read this are poor relative to Bill Gates (and many, many others); but it is doubtful if any who read this are starving to death. Also, the relatively very poor in the USA are relatively rich compared with the relatively poor in, say, India and Africa. Cold comfort to the poor in the USA who are "relatively well-off."

To which it may be added that when those from a poorer country emigrate to the USA in search of a better life, but are still classifiable as "poor," that designation is likely to mean that even though they have risen above the level of relative poverty of their country of origin, they may well have a more difficult life than earlier:

If, as is likely, they left a rural area in Latin America and are now in an urban area, their expenses will be greater (for water, heat, electricity, transportation, at least), and the remaining income may still leave them in a desperate and more complicated condition. Even worse, they have left their own culture and, all too often, their family, and are now surrounded by strangers, a foreign language and culture, and racist hostility.

This is another way of pointing to the fact that those in official relative poverty in the USA—more than twice the official estimates (see **poverty**)—are likely as not to be worse off than those in relative poverty in their own and poorer countries.

But that tangle of words need not be worked through when the focus is <u>absolute</u> poverty. That grips and kills at least one third of the world's people; that is, over two <u>billion</u> people. They do not have sufficient food to eat, sufficient water to drink or to cleanse themselves, sufficient clothing (if they are in cold climes), or sufficient access to the existing (but costly) medicines to prevent or cure a whole range of deadly diseases.

This happens in an era in which the richest nations are at their richest, the USA most of all. Let it be said that although not generous to a fault, the other rich nations do more than we to mitigate ongoing preventable disasters—in the realms of nutrition, shelter, availability of patented **pharmaceuticals** and **health care**, in their own and for poorer countries.

Nothing has been said about the rich. What does it mean, "rich"? It means people who have too much money to know what to do with it, who probably got it by dirty dealing and/or inheritance. There are, of course, exceptions to every rule. Which leaves the majority of the rich who <u>fit</u> the rule. Like George W. Bush.

Roosevelt, Franklin D. (FDR)

FDR was elected first in 1932 and for the fourth time in 1944. For the GOP that was a horror <u>never</u> to be repeated, so they legislated the two-term rule—much to their subsequent sorrow, when they wished to see **Reagan** become the permanent occupant of the White House.

FDR probably had the most mixed of all presidential records—mixed, that is, between awful and admirable policies, stubbornness and openness, being loved and hated. Although I was his critic as much as his admirer throughout his four terms, I see him as the best president of the USA, ever; indeed, when he died in April, 1945 (I was in the Army, overseas), I wept; nor was I alone in doing so.

The sorrow was in part personal, in part political, the latter mixed with anger at the fact that Truman became president; given why he had been anointed Vice President, it was clear that what was to come was much worse than what had preceded. (see **Truman**)

The awful and the admirable. FDR's administration came to be called "the New Deal" already in its first year. What had been seen as a recession in 1929 up through 1932 had by March of 1933 (when FDR was inaugurated) came to be understood as the worst depression in world history. That was more than symbolized by nationwide "runs" on all banks: Desperate depositors—a la' Argentina, 2002—sought hopelessly to get their (nonexistent) money. (Thus, the FDIC; see **financialization**)

FDR ruled that all banks be closed until the panic subsided; necessary, but not a cure. What he then did was awful: He established the National Recovery Administration (NRA). It was awful for at least two reasons: 1) It was a plan (first thought of in 1928 by then **CEO** of **GE** Gerard Swope) that effectively permitted **big business** to write a "code" for each of over 800 industries; the code set minimum prices, established geographic quotas, and got obedience through legal punishments. 2) It was just the opposite of what the economy needed: more production (and thus jobs) at lower prices.

To give you an idea of just how awful it was, Germany's Nazi government send over a delegation in 1934 to study the NRA, hoping it could be applied to their not very nice situation. In 1935 the Supreme Court, to the rage of FDR, declared the NRA unconstitutional. FDR then tried but failed, to "stack" the Court. (MITCHELL, B.)

In his first year, FDR also created the Agricultural Adjustment Administration (AAA), a variation on the NRA: set quotas to restrict output, keep prices up, favor mostly the big farmers, and walk away.

So it went from 1933 into 1935, FDR making nice speeches about the "ill-clothed, ill-fed, ill-housed" but doing nothing to clothe, feed, or house them.

Meanwhile, the political ground was shifting: strike after strike (on the waterfront, in autos, steel, etc.), left and right political groups growing: End Poverty in California (EPIC), headed by Upton

Sinclair and very popular; the Silver Shirts in Michigan, led by Father Coughlin (and very fascist); Huey Long's Share the Wealth Movement in Louisiana, the best-known, beginning left of center, ending right of center.

With the 1936 election looming, FDR's main advisors—Harry Hopkins and his wife Eleanor—counseled him to shift his emphasis away from bowing to business toward the direction of "clothing, food, and housing." Thus began what came to called "the Second New Deal"; limited, but admirable.

Its first major manifestation was the **Social Security** Act of 1935. Between then and 1938, when FDR's emphases turned sharply toward foreign policy, the following greatly overdue policies were enacted—all for the first time in our history: minimum-wage, maximum hour laws, the prohibition of child labor, the protection of workers' right not just to organize (long legal), but to strike (always illegal); adding the FDIC to protect depositors.

Then there were the Works Project and Public Works Administrations (WPA, PWA) and the Tennessee Valley Authority (TVA). WPA provided vital jobs and services in education, the arts, and entertainment, the latter building roads, bridges, dams, etc. ("infrastructure"). (see **deficits and surpluses**)

There were other programs in the "alphabet soup" of federal agencies that came to provide services and jobs that otherwise would have been nonexistent: the Civilian Conservation Corps (CCC), National Youth Administration (NYA) and others; all stimulated the economy while improving the society and the lives of its people: Good ideas for today. (See Afterword)

On the foreign front, FDR was similarly inclined toward the awful and the admirable. As noted under **fascism**, U.S. policies toward **Germany, Italy, Japan,** and **Spain** (see **Europe, Asia**)—the leading fascist powers of the 1930s—were seldom harmful and often helpful to those countries until after World War II was well underway: For example, we exported militarily applicable products (steel, oil, machinery) to both Germany and Italy when they were supplying airpower and ground troops to support Generalissimo Franco's fascist forces seeking to overthrow the Spanish Republic; meanwhile forbidding the Spanish government's freighter Mar Cantabrico even to enter New York Harbor to load goods (in 1938).

Not last but among the most awful of FDR's acts was when he

signed the law that forcibly rounded up 150,000 Japanese-Americans, took their lands away from them, and put them in concentration camps—in ways and with consequences more recently applied to hundreds of presumed "terrorists" now in Guantánamo: In neither case did the USA allow the prisoners to see lawyers, have visitors or <u>anything</u> provided by our and international laws.

It is pleasanter to turn to the "admirable." By 1938 German fascism's geographic expansion had begun into Austria and Czechoslovakia—in both cases without firing a shot (the rightwing Austrian government having acceded, the Czechs having been sold out by the British, French, and Italy at "Munich"). This constituted something of a wake-up call for FDR.

Step by step he began to lay the groundwork for U.S. involvement, beginning with the renewal of the draft in 1940 and the Lend-Lease provision of U.S. materiel to Britain. So apparent (and unpopular) were these and other steps that when Pearl Harbor was bombed by the Japanese in December of 1941, arguments spread that FDR had provoked the Japanese to do so and anticipated the bombing as a means of bringing the USA into the war.

Whatever the validity or invalidity of that argument, even for me—and I <u>hate</u> war—our entrance into World War II seemed essential at the time; however, U.S. behavior <u>after</u> the war provided many reasons to wonder whether our motive was to end fascism or "merely" to protect, even to enhance, our own power. (see **fascism**)

Be that as it may, during the war FDR behaved admirably. He sought to lessen Stalin's fears of undying U.S. hostility, he very much supported our creation of the United Nations and, not least (and unknown to almost all in the USA), during the war he arranged and supported our agreement with the Viet Minh to see to it that Vietnam would become independent after the war. (All this was turned on its head by Truman.) (YOUNG)

Saying all that, there was something more about him that brought me to tears when he died. FDR was an experienced and clever politician, skilled at mixing charm with deception. With him, as with **Reagan** and others, there may well have <u>been</u> a con game going on, but for me, his ongoing critic though I was (and remain), it seemed then and does still that the "con" was less important to him than that something good and necessary was being achieved.

I was born in 1919; Wilson was president; then Harding,

Coolidge, Hoover, FDR. Since then, Truman, Eisenhower, JFK, LBJ, Nixon, Ford, Carter, Reagan, Bush I. Clinton, Bush II. Stinkers, on balance, all of them; to one degree or another, all acquiescent or eager marchers in the parade that has taken and ever more takes "America!" down the tubes greased with an always broader and deeper **corruption**, joined by an always more aggressive global spread of U.S. power, largely acquiesced in by a population always easier to **spin** toward self-destruction, seemingly almost eager to fight the next war, if only the rationale can be swallowed (with the aid of a Coke or a Miller's).

FDR was part of that parade when he became president and initiated the first New Deal. But from 1935 on FDR began to drift away from his long-standing Rich Man's Club mentality. He didn't con the people into the Second New Deal; having convinced himself, he inspired us.

My many criticisms of FDR have always had an undertone of hope and the belief that he was one who was basically decent; that he could stop being a political pro and find the humanity in himself which was clearly there; and which, before he died, he had found. He was finally loved by most; finally, he deserved to be.

Rosenberg, Ethel and Julius

It was about 50 years ago (1953) that the Rosenbergs were executed in the electric chair. Their trial, their execution, and the behavior of those who brought that about and who cheered it constituted one of the ugliest and most disgraceful episodes in our history, even though it meant the killing of "only" two people.

The **Cold War** and **McCarthyism** had both begun well before the Rosenbergs were arrested and tried; they were the victims of both and their case added to the hysteria and social lunacy of both. What were the charges, and what served as "evidence" to convict them?

Julius and Ethel Rosenberg were charged with having conspired with Ethel's brother David Greenglass, a Soviet agent, to steal military secrets. That was the legal indictment. That came to be escalated in the public's mind as a conspiracy that had succeeded in stealing the secret of the Atom Bomb and placing our nation's very survival in jeopardy. When, after the guilty verdict, President Eisenhower denied clemency, he accused the Rosenberg's of "immeasurably increasing the chances of nuclear war."

It is relevant and necessary today to remind people in the USA that the **USSR** was our <u>ally</u> in World War II and, not irrelevantly, that it suffered more than any other single nation, with at least 28 million dead. (FRUMKIN)

Ethel and Julius Rosenberg were members of the Communist Party of the U.S.A.—a legal political party, it is also necessary to note. If the Rosenbergs were involved in any transfer of information to the Soviet Union it would not be remiss to point out that the USA had two allies in the war: the USSR and the UK. There were never charges made for shared information with British scientists. (see MEEROPOL)

The main "evidence" against the Rosenbergs was supplied by alleged co-conspirator David Greenglass, the <u>brother</u> of Ethel. He was a U.S. Army machinist stationed at Los Alamos.

> To justify the **death penalty**, which was invoked to press the Rosenbergs to confess and implicate others, the government left the impression that the couple had handed America's mightiest weapon to the Soviets and precipitated the Korean War.... But we now know the Soviet cables decoded before the trial provided no hard evidence of Ethel's complicity. (Sam Roberts, "Yes, They Were Guilty. But of What Exactly? /<u>NYT</u>, 6-15-03/) (see also ROBERTS)

Enter David Greenglass with the "necessary" evidence:

> He testified that his sister /Ethel/ had persuaded his wife to persuade him to steal atomic secrets from Los Alamos.... /However:/ Recently Mr. Greenglass has admitted that he lied about the most incriminating evidence against his sister." (ibid.)

And another "however": In return for his "full cooperation" with the government's prosecution of the Rosenbergs, the <u>wife</u> of Greenglass was <u>never</u> indicted, even though, according to the decoded Soviet cables she was a full-fledged agent, with her own code name (unlike Ethel Rosenberg).

In addition to those disgraceful governmental actions, an editorial of the <u>NYT</u>, "Remembering the Rosenbergs" pointed out that

> In imposing the death sentence, Judge Irving Kaufman held the Rosenbergs responsible not only for stealing atomic secrets but also for more than 50,000 deaths in the Korean war. **FBI** documents made public in the 1970s revealed that

/Kaufman/ had one-sided discussions with prosecutors about sentencing.... There is no reason to believe that either Rosenberg passed on secrets so valuable that they should have been blamed for tens of thousands of deaths. (6-19-03)

Judge Kaufman had violated court ethics in that respect; but he wasn't finished. The execution was set to occur at 11 p.m. on a Friday. Because there were to be two executions, "that would have pushed the executions well into the Jewish Sabbath.... Judge Kaufman said that the very idea of a Sabbath execution gave him 'considerable concern.'" The executions were conducted instead just at sunset.

The playwright Arthur Miller commented that "They were to be killed more quickly than planned to avoid any shadow of bad taste." (ibid.)

Sacco and Vanzetti

It is fitting that in this book the prosecutions of Sacco and Vanzetti and of the Rosenbergs are sequential. In different decades, both were products of a "witch hunt," the convictions in both cases depended upon "evidence" provided by dubious witnesses, the judges of both were clearly prejudiced from the onset; and all of the accused were electrocuted.

Niccolo Sacco and Bartolomeo Vanzetti were Italian-born anarchists. They were arrested in the spring of 1920 at the height of the "Red Scare" that had begun in 1919. That "scare" is said to have ended in 1921, but it had a second act in the 1930s, when the House Un-American Activities Committee was born, and a third in the era of **Cold War** and **McCarthyism**, Today's "homeland security" and "Patriotic Acts" threaten a reprise.

Why were they arrested? Or, more relevantly, what was the context for their arrest, and what was its pretext?

The context was the "Palmer Raids" marking post-Russian revolution and post-World War I USA. Woodrow Wilson was President, running for re-election in 1920; his Attorney General was A. Mitchell Palmer. What happened in the USA on 9/11/2001 had a uniqueness to it; up to a point. What followed 9/11 politically was all too reminiscent of—if also very different from—what happened with the Red Scare of 1919 and, after World War II, with the magnified fears of Soviet aggression and "Communists in the State Department."

Even before 1914 anti-immigrant sentiment in the USA was high, despite that all of us except **"Indians"** are immigrants, or their descendants. (see **racism**) Laws effectively cutting back or shutting off immigration began in 1917 and were in crescendo in the 1920s. Already in 1918 Congress had legislated deportation for aliens who opposed organized government or attached the institution of private property (that is, anarchists or socialists).

If the following reminds you of the present a bit too much, it's not your fault:

> In January, 1920, four thousand persons were rounded up all over the country, held in seclusion for long periods of time, brought into secret hearings, and ordered deported. In Boston, Department of Justice agents... arrested 600 people by raiding meeting halls or by invading their homes in the early morning.... In April... a typesetter and anarchist named Salsedo was arrested in New York by FBI agents, held for eight weeks in their offices on the 14th floor of the Park Row Building, not allowed family or friends or lawyers. Then his crushed body was found on the pavement below the building. The FBI said he had committed suicide. (ZINN, 2000)

That's the context; now the pretext. Sacco and Vanzetti lived and worked in Brockton, Mass. (a bit south of Boston). They were friends of Salsedo. In May, two weeks before they were arrested, there had been a robbery of a factory payroll truck, and the murder of its driver. Sacco and Vanzetti were charged with that crime, tried, found guilty, and sentenced to death. The principal witness for the prosecution, a man named Shaw, testified that he <u>knew</u> they were the killers because "he could tell the man (singular) he saw robbing the payroll truck was a foreigner by the way he ran; he was either Italian or Russian." (ibid.)

Their case aroused much protest in the USA and Europe; appeals went on for six years. They were executed in 1927. Fifty years later, in 1977, the Governor of Massachusetts issued a proclamation declaring the trial had been unfair. (see PALMER; ZINN, 2002)

In the USA it is normal for one who has been found guilty to make a statement to the court. My attention was first drawn to the Sacco and Vanzetti case when I was a young man and came across Vanzetti's "Last Speech to the Court" in a book of poetry. (ROD-MAN) It made a noteworthy difference to me; it might to you. I reprint it in its entirety (along with its grammatical errors):

I have talk a great deal of myself
but I even forgot to name Sacco.
Sacco too is a worker,
from his boyhood a skilled worker, lover of work,
with a good job and pay
a bank account, a good and lovely wife,
two beautiful children and a neat little home
at the verge of a wood, near a brook.
Sacco is a heart, a faith, a character, a man;
a man, lover of nature, and mankind:
a man who gave all, who sacrifice all
to the cause of liberty and to his love for mankind:
money, rest, mundane ambition,
his own wife, his children, himself
and his own life.
Sacco has never dreamt to steal, never to assassinate.
He and I have never brought a morsel
of bread to our mouths, from our childhood to today
which has not been gained by the sweat of our brows.
Never ...
Oh, yes, I may be more witful, as some have put it;
I am a better babbler than he is, but many, many times
in hearing his heartful voice ringing a faith
sublime, in considering his supreme sacrifice, remembering his heroism,
I felt small at the presence of his greatness
and found myself compelled to fight back
from my eyes the tears,
and quanch my heart
trobling to my throat to not weep before him;
this man called thief and assassin and doomed.
But Sacco's name will live in the hearts of the people
and in their gratitude when Katzmanns's bones
and yours will be dispersed by time;
when your name, his name, your laws, institutions,
and your false god are but a dim rememoring
of a cursed past in which man was wolf
to the man ...
*
If it had not been for these thing
I might have live out my life
talking at street corners to scorning men.
I might have die, unmarked, unknown, a failure.
Now we are not a failure.
This is our career and our triumph. Never

in our full life could we hope to do such work
for tolerance, for justice, for man's understanding
of man, as now we do by accident.
Our words, our lives, our pains—nothing!
The taking of our lives—lives of a good shoemaker and
a poor fishpeddler —
all! That last moment belongs to us —
that agony is our triumph.

S&L crisis (see financialization, Reagan....)

School of the Americas (see Latin America...)

SEC

The Securities and Exchange Commission was set up in the 1930s to supervise and regulate the issuance of new securities and the ongoing behavior of the stock and bond markets and their constituent companies. Its birth was prompted by the irresponsible to downright crooked behavior of the 1920s; all too similar to that which began to roil the financial sector from 2000 to the present—its symbol Enron—and which, then as now, became part and parcel of a stock market crack-up and a weakening economy.

Among many differences between then and now, however, is that the SEC's birth was followed by the "second" New Deal, with its suspicions of rampant big business, an increasingly strong union movement, a Congress more influenced by liberal than conservative (let alone right-wing) legislators, and, perhaps most pointedly, the virtual absence of **lobbyists**. (see **FDR**) Of lobbyists, much will be said in its place; here, and remembering how important the role of **stock options** has been recently, consider only this: Under the headline "Tighter Rules for Options Fall Victim to Lobbying," we read this:

> Long before the current wave of scandals, business interests have successfully protected stock options from attack in Congress. But last September (2001), an umbrella group calling itself the Stock Option Coalition was formed from high-technology companies, executives of the Fortune 500 companies, venture capitalist, biotechnology companies and the Nasdaq market—all sending out platoons of lobbyists, conducting sophisticated e-mail campaigns and reminding Congress of their

hefty campaign contributions.... For the moment, the legislation before Congress to overhaul securities and accounting laws makes no mention of stock options....

The article goes on to point out that Sen. McCain, who advocates putting strict limits on stock options complained loudly that "It's a bipartisan fix that's in." (NYT, 7-20-2) In that Sen. Daschle, the Democratic Senate leader, as the article points out, "helped to kill the stock options restrictions in the Senate," it seems that McCain is right.

On the same day, the NYT headlined its article on the SEC as "Suffering From Nonbenign Neglect," and went on to give jot and tittle to that assertion:

Item: "The agency's vital infrastructure has been sorely neglected, starved of adequate money and manpower by politicians."

Item: "In the 1990s, the agency got hollowed out, losing lots of experienced people."

Item: "In the 1980s, the agency reviewed all of a single company's major filings once every three years;...by the 1990s..., once every seven years."

Item: "...one investment house alone, Merrill Lynch, has more professionals in its legal and compliance departments than the lawyers, investigators and other professionals on the enforcement staff of the SEC." Item: "...its computer system was never sufficiently upgraded to make it useful for officials to manipulate data in useful ways. As a result the systems rival those of the **FBI** for being obsolete and all but unusable for performing some vital tasks and detecting problems. (Ibid.)

And then there is (or as will be seen later, was) its Chairman, Harvey L. Pitt. Appointed Chief Guard of the Chicken Coop, not long ago some of Mr. Pitt's best friends and employers were foxes—including Bushes I and II and Cheney, Enron and accounting giant and miscreant Arthur Andersen.

Mr. Pitt, evidently nostalgic for the large amounts of money he took in from his business friends—$3 million in the period just before becoming head of the SEC—on July 22, 2002 circulated a proposal to members of Congress (among others) 1)) that his salary be increased by $30,000 and 2) that his agency be elevated to cabinet level (as with Secretary of State, Treasury, Defense, etc.), above that of the CIA and the EPA. This, at the very moment when his dismissal was being proposed in the Senate.

For those who wish to know the meaning of the term chutzpah, Pitt's behavior fits the definition nicely; or if that isn't enough, there's this: Speaking of himself (in an interview with the NYT) he said "It is an enormous advantage to the public to have somebody who knows about the securities business and the securities law as I do, and it would be unthinkable to deprive people of my expertise." (7-29-02)

Which people would be thus deprived he did not specify, but a news story a few months later gives an inkling. Because of ongoing revelations of numerous accounting irregularities by Enron and others, Congress passed a package of modest laws in 2002 designed to protect the public. Among them was the creation of a board to oversee the accounting profession, whose presumed function that has been. The new board is to have a chair. Mr. Pitt appointed ex-**FBI** head William Webster to be that chair. Except for some complaints that heading the FBI was not the best qualification for supervising accounting hijinks, so far, so good.

Anyhow, Webster did have previous experience in the auditing world. Problem was that "he had headed the auditing committee of a company facing fraud accusations"—not as an SEC-type overseer, but as "participant." (NYT, 10-1-02, "SEC orders a probe of nomination.").

That's bad enough; somewhat worse is that Pitt made the appointment "after "Webster's disclosure" of that bothersome fact ".../and/ chose not to tell the other four /SEC/ commissioners who voted on Webster's nomination that day...," even though "the company /U.S. Technologies/ and its chief executive... are facing lawsuits by investors who say they were defrauded of millions of dollars."

It appears that Harvey Pitt just doesn't get it.

(That was written November 5, 2002; on November 7, bending to rising criticism, he submitted his resignation.) With the election triumphs of the GOP on that very day, it didn't seem likely that his replacement will be much different.

But it was. What hasn't changed, however, is the enduring conviction among those in economic and political power that those with economic and political power are, after all, to be trusted—if for no other reason that they are... ahem, in power.

slavery

Like its close relative **racism**, de facto slavery was probably common in prehistoric times. Because those times were prehistoric, there are of course no records to prove it, but VEBLEN was plausibly right in arguing that women captured in battles were the first slaves, and thus among the first instances of private property. (1898)

"Civilization" first took hold in Egypt and Mesopotamia; so did "history." It shows that slavery in Egypt was—"a product of force," wrote VEBLEN, "making possible an unproductive ruling class; in the case of Egypt, the priesthood." And pyramids.

The birthplace of western civilization, ancient Greece, was also a slave society. Although slavery is one of the most abominable of all social crimes, it seems to have escaped the condemnation of all but a very small minority of the citizens of the slaveholding nations or of their societies' admirers elsewhere: Neither Aristotle nor Jefferson—like four of our first five presidents, a slave owner—found Greece to be reprehensible; nor did many free Germans or many non-Germans (nor the US or UK governments: BREITMAN) express horror as numberless people were enslaved to work in German factories in the 1930s; nor, finally, does today's ongoing slave trade gain more than passing attention, and that from a few.

The relationship of the USA with slavery began when it was still a colony. Slaves were just another **commodity** but, by the 17th century the slave trade had already become a major economic factor for Britain, and its colonies in the western hemisphere.

Also, by then, enslavement had received the full support of the Church on the grounds that the merchant slavers were providing an opportunity for Africans to become Christians. That "opportunity" was denied most of them in the South; their masters vigorously opposed slaves learning anything, least of all the attachment of Jesus to equality.

By the next century, the trade was controlled by Britain. By then the gains from the slave trade and the plantations had become the prime source of profits and economic strength, providing the base for subsequent economic development in North America. In turn, that was a key element in the larger processes of the **colonialism** that provided the basis for the industrial capitalism in the 19th century:

The discovery of gold and silver in America, the extirpa-

tion, enslavement and entombment of the aboriginal population, the beginnings of the conquest and looting of the East
Indies, the turning of Africa into a warren for the hunting of
black-skins, signalized the rosy dawn of the era of capitalist production. These idyllic proceedings are the chief momenta of
primitive accumulation. (MARX, 1867 /1967/)

The manner in which the slaves were treated, whether upon
capture, on the deadly "middle passage," or after arrival, was anything but "Christian." In order to maximize their profits, the traders
typically overloaded the boats—e.g., carrying 600 slaves instead of
the maximum of 415 they were built to carry; the slaves were
chained hands to feet, effectively unable to move freely for most of
every day and night—for months. The horrible realities of eating
their few scraps of food, defecating, and sleeping are beyond our
comprehension:

Once landed, the slaves'—including children's— lives were
dominated by hard work for 12-16 hours, whether under hot sun or
freezing snow; were separated from families (even as infants); were
whipped and raped; were treated as though not human. When one
considers that the slaveowners were thus harming their own "investments," it is easy to infer that fear and hate were very much a constant in their thoughts. (NORDHOLDT; WILLIAMS, E.)

Withal, slavery as a sociopolitical (let alone ethical) issue, was
never a concern for more than a small minority of the white populations in either the North or the South, before or after the Civil
War. (MARABLE)

But what of the Underground Railroad? The Abolitionists? And
wasn't the Civil War fought to end slavery? We take them up in turn.

The "Railroad" and its "conductors" were people; they did not
of course involve locomotives. Beginning late in the 18th century,
its black and white volunteers assisted escaping slaves toward freedom with a pattern of secret routes that went into and through 14
northern states. Its volunteers went South, and to lead the way, they
provided food, shelter, and money to the escapees furnished in part
by northern supporters. Hiding by day, moving by night, it is estimated that about 50,000 escaped slaves ultimately gained freedom—
with deadly risks for all concerned. (ZINN, 2000)

That was a truly heroic chapter in our history, both for those
who escaped and those who helped them. But the volunteers and

conductors who helped were few in number: the peak estimate is for 3,000 in 1850. Congress showed what it thought of their principles and their courage when, in 1850, it passed the Fugitive Slave Act: Anyone caught helping a runaway slave was subject to a crippling fine and six months in prison. Slaves were, after all, property.

The Abolitionists undertook few physical risks, but they too were admirable. It was a small group and to be part of it before the Civil war was unpopular. It is pertinent in that regard to remember that the early 1960s civil rights struggles and the resistance to U.S. intervention in Vietnam were also carried on by small and initially very unpopular groups throughout the 1960s.

In all of those cases—as the 60s ended for civil rights and Vietnam and as the Civil War began for slavery—a significant element of public opinion had at least begun to "change sides": so much so in the case of the Civil War that it came to be and is still cited as a war to end slavery.

But there are many reasons for understanding that the Civil War was not fought to end slavery—most persuasively the words of President Lincoln to Horace Greeley, Editor of the New York Tribune, August, 1962:

> My paramount object in this struggle is to save the Union, and is not either to save or destroy Slavery. If I could save the Union without freeing any slave I would do it; and if I could save it by freeing all the slaves, I would do it; and if I could free it by freeing some and leaving others alone, I would also do it. (quoted in ZINN)

A month later Lincoln issued his preliminary Emancipation Proclamation. It gave the South four months to stop rebelling and threatened to emancipate their slaves if they continued to fight, while, however, promising to leave slavery untouched in states that came over to the North; indeed, still in 1863, the slave states occupied by northern troops—Delaware, Kentucky, Maryland, Missouri, and parts of Virginia and Louisiana—were able to retain their slaves. ZINN quotes the reaction of the London Spectator: "The principle is not that a human being cannot justly own another, but that he cannot own him unless he is loyal to the United States."

The war proceeded, always more violently, always more tragically for all concerned, with numberless shattered families and over 600,000 dead soldiers—equal to more than 5 million today. Our total dead from World Wars I plus II were also about 600,000 (for a population more many times larger).

After the war ended, a turbulent period ensued: northern troops occupied the South, the slaves were freed, and for a "brief period..., southern Negroes voted, elected blacks to state legislatures and to Congress, /and/ introduced free and racially mixed public education in the South": (ZINN) It seemed as though a new era had opened.

It had, but it closed shut violently a decade later, with the "**Compromise of 1877.**" Setting the Underground Railroaders and Abolitionists aside, there were two main viewpoints among the white people of the North: 1) Among the men who were to be drafted to fight the war, few wished to fight: those who could afford it bought their way out of the draft, and many of the others joined bloody riots to avoid duty—including riots against northern blacks; 2) however, the rich and the powerful <u>did</u> want the war, for "the Union" was necessary to retain the markets and enormous resource-rich territory for the rapidly industrializing USA.

In the infamous "Compromise," Congress agreed to allow the South to govern itself, thus bringing "reconstruction" to a halt and undoing it: it assured U.S. governmental indifference regarding the physical and social treatment of the freed slaves in exchange for unlimited access for northern capital to invest in and control the South's vast mineral and forest resources, its railroads, and the like. (WOODWARD)

Thus unleashed, the South set about to diminish the social, economic, and political conditions of black people down to their prewar levels—or worse: There had been no KKK before the war, then there was; nor, compared to post-1877, had lynchings been common. When enslaved, blacks, although badly treated, <u>were</u> assets, and to some extent protected; after 1877, as sharecroppers. They were of no concern, except as targets:

> ... The white South after Reconstruction... transformed lynching into a festival of racist violence.... Between 1880 and 1930, the number of black men, women, and children who died in ten Southern states "at the hands of persons unknown" almost certainly exceeded 2,500... /3,400 by 1945/ During that half century, a black person was murdered by a white mob nearly every week in every year. (LEWIS, D.L.; DRAY, P.)

The always increasing thousands of "poor white trash" who

were sharecroppers and, later, heavily exploited textile factory workers, were free to take their rage and frustration out on blacks, and did, with neither remorse nor interference. Thus, as the northern economy resumed its feeding off the South, the South turned its energies toward institutionalized racism—with very little or no interference, until the 1960s. (DOWD, 1956)

In seeking to understand the nature and ongoing consequences of slavery and racism to the USA, therefore, it is important to identify the role of the North in its existence and functioning. Quite apart from the fact that slavery was also practiced in the North until the late 1820s, perhaps most revealing is the role of slave trade in the economy of New England: our "City on the Hill," where the "land of the free and home of the brave" first spread its wings. (DAVIS, D.B.)

The South used and abused the slaves once arrived and sold, but the slave trade that made it possible was centered in New England. Here is VEBLEN's ironic comment on the home of U.S. Puritanism and freedom:

> The slave trade was never a "nice" occupation or an altogether unexceptionable investment—"balanced on the edge of the permissible." But even though it may have been distasteful to one and another of its New England men of affairs, and though there always was a suspicion of moral obliquity attached to the slave-trade, yet it had the good fortune to be drawn into the service of the greater good. In conjunction with its running-mate, the rum-trade, it laid the foundations of some very reputable fortunes at that focus of commercial enterprise that presently became the center of American culture, and so gave rise to some of the country's Best People. At least so they say.
>
> Perhaps also it was, in some part, in this early pursuit of gain in this moral penumbra that American business enterprise learned how not to let its right hand know what its left hand is doing; and there is always something to be done that is best done with the left hand. (1923)

Since then, the "moral penumbra" has enlarged beyond measure, and "American business enterprise" and our government have become magicians with that "left hand"—at home and abroad.

Whether in the deep past or the present, what became the USA was a slave society for more than half of its existence; the consequences of that for our nation's economic and noneconomic evolution cannot be measured with precision, but in both respects they were decisive. Slavery normally implies and requires, and especially did so in the USA, a slavery-dominated <u>society</u> as much as a society dominating slaves. In turn, this meant that whatever business considerations were needed for the continuation of the slave-cum-cotton system of the U.S. South, they were immeasurably reinforced by the social and political imperatives for maintaining a slave <u>society</u>.

Slavery was the functional core, of our always richer and more productive agricultural economy before the Civil War, going back to colonial times. It was therefore also the functional core of the always-strengthening trading and financial centers of the North. From the early colonial era into the early national decades, the always accelerating trade and finance of the northern (and, later, western) cities were critically dependent upon the growth of unfinished <u>exports</u> and finished <u>imports</u> of the South, as was the steady development of land and sea transportation. For the entire economy, until mid-19th century, the "growth point" (as economists put it) was the agricultural South, and <u>its</u> "growth point" was slavery. And everyone knew it. (CASH)

"Everyone" also knew that the slaveholding South usually controlled the entire government of the USA from 1789 to 1860: the White House 70 percent of those years, with similar or greater percentages for Congress and the Supreme Court. Those most concerned and disturbed by this were the rising industrialists of the North. They needed an interventionist State for protective tariffs, subsidized railroads (2/3 of whose construction costs were paid for by the government), and profitable access to mines and forests. (PHILLIPS)

Therefore, if the positive side of the slave South's role was to continue—that is, its contribution to economic growth and development—it also became essential to reduce its political power, even <u>if</u>, as Lincoln made clear, that required freeing the slaves. Even if, but <u>only</u> if.

The negative side is the mirror image of the positive: our people learned to see black people as "others" or, worse, not as people at all: more exactly, they were officially counted as 2/3 of a person for the voting purposes of their owners. The taking of the first steps of enslaving Africans and killing or mistreating "**Indians** allowed the rest to follow easily. But "the rest" did not end with the dehumanization of others; nor did it end with what was noted earlier under

racism: the dehumanization of one's self.

In learning to ignore or overlook what we as a people were doing to others, we learned to do something of the same regarding what was being done to ourselves, and in all corners of our lives: economic, social, cultural, political, military and environmental.

Abiding in or, worse, taking satisfaction in the making into creatures of other human beings, we lost our ability to note that we too were and are being made into creatures: creatures of **militarism**, of **nationalism**, of **exploitation**, of **consumerism** and of **debt**—creatures able to be manipulated by fear and hate and attitudes of superiority, greed and selfishness.

None of that is due <u>entirely</u> to slavery and the racism it depended upon and fed; of course not. But all were accomplished more easily because of them.

"Those whom the Gods would destroy, they first make mad."

Social Security

From the first moment the Social Security Act was passed in 1935 we were warned that it was the wrong thing to do. And it <u>was</u> done wrongly, but not in the sense that its critics mean it.

As "social security," it was compromised from the very start in that 1) it did not cover all the aged, and 2) both the contributions and the benefits were skewed to benefit those who needed it least and to provide less than a decent benefit for most. Now to the details.

The financing is by payroll deductions; that benefits are then determined by contribution sounds reasonable enough—until you think about it, to say nothing of when you look around the world where things are done differently and better. Thus, in all of Western Europe retirement is financed through generally progressive taxation and benefits are set at levels of reasonable comfort. Unsurprisingly, the USA also stands as a distant second in its social policies for **health care**, **unemployment** insurance, **children**, and **environmental** protection.

In 1935 the percentage of one's income deducted from the payroll (and matched by the employer) was one percent. In the Reagan years it began the sharp rise that now brings it to just under eight percent; except for another rotten egg in that kitchen.

Deductions are made up to a level of about $87,000 annual

income: anything up to $87,000 you pay the going percentage; anything over that? You still pay only the normal percentage of $87,000. So let's suppose you are a WorldCom executive and you get (note I did not say "earn") $8,700,000. You still pay only eight percent of $87,000 = $6,425. Moreover, from 1973 to 2000, income taxes rose by 21 percent but the Social Security deduction by 82 percent.

There is much talk of a crisis in the Social Security Trust Fund. On that, only two points: 1) The "crisis" in that Fund would not became real, if at all, for another 30 years or so. Before then, it could be alleviated simply enough within the present unfair framework by just raising the monthly deduction by a percentage point or so. Much better than that, however, is that it could be entirely taken care of simply by having the percentage monthly deduction be taken from incomes all the way up to the top, and leave the richest still the richest. Fair's fair, no? (BRITTAIN)

Then, 2) until the 1960s, Social Security was not part of the government's budget, nor should it be; **LBJ** changed that in order to disguise the money costs of the Vietnam war. How? By including Social Security benefit payments under government expenditures (which they are not) he thus falsely raised total expenditures and thus reduced the percentage of **military expenditures** to the total. This despite the fact that the Fund's holdings are due entirely to payroll deductions, and are not part of the tax fund. All's fair in cold war....

That deception continues to have its dire effects today in the many arguments for the **privatization** of social security; those who push those arguments most, as always, are the insurance companies and Wall Streeters. Why? 1) The insurance companies would surely love to have more customers, and they would have, from those who could afford it; keep social insurance a **commodity**, not a need. 2) Then some—only some—of those now having deductions made from their pay would feel able or inclined or foolish enough to put money into stocks or mutual funds.

If those trying to privatize have their way, one day we will be required to have some of our monthly income go into one form of stock or security or another. That would of course constitute a nice runup for the stock market. That is, the average working stiff would be creating jobs and raising incomes for Wall Streeters.

Any person of moderate income who supports such changes hasn't paid much attention to what's happened to the stock averages in recent years.

In addition to Social Security, up until the 1980s most workers had "defined pension" plans, provided and financed by their employers; now with the much-touted 401ks, they have instead "defined contribution plans. " That is, plans where it is the worker who makes most or all of the "contribution"; or, when the employer also contributes, more often than not it is in the form of stock. And, when the employee leaves the company, that's it for the company: the company has no commitments beyond the worker's retirement.

But what's good for the company has not been good for their employees. Recent research has shown that for the median 401(k) account (that is, half above and half below) the amount due the retired worker in 1999 was $15,246, but only $13,493 in 2000: after which, the market entered its long swoon. (WOLMAN; COLAMOSCA) The large numbers of those who put their money into those slot machines in the glistening 1990s now find themselves moving toward quiet desperation, many wishing they'd never heard of such programs:

> Item: (Between 1983 and 2001) the average net worth of an older household grew 44 percent, adjusted for inflation.... But much of that growth was in the accounts of the richest households, which pushed the averages up. For the net worth of the median older household—the one at the midpoint of the economic ladder, a better indicator of what is typical—the picture changed. That figure declined by 2.2 percent, or $4,000, to $199,000... The advent of self-directed retirement plans... is giving rise to an elite minority who are well-prepared for retirement... (M.W. Walsh, "Healthier and Wiser? Sure, But Not Wealthier: As Pensions Slip Away Retirees May Take a Fall," NYT, 6-13-04)

And if they knew about it, all would wonder why they can't have what those in the military and Congress have been granted (by that self-same Congress) in the way of old age security, both generous—in some cases too generous; as for Congress. Item: When Rep. James Trafficant (D-Ohio) was expelled from Congress and sent to prison for bribery and corruption, July 26, 2002, it was announced that he would still receive his congressional life pension of $37,120 a year which, over the course of his life, is likely to exceed more than $1,000,000. Paid for by our taxes.

Item: Rep. Trafficant is but one beneficiary among what will ultimately amount to many thousands in the same lovely boat;

namely the boat for both Senators and Representatives. It is they who decide on legislation (president signing), and they who wrote their own pension plans; and what they decided on was not bad: they get the same pay after they retire (or are voted out), year after year until death does them part from us. Not bad.

Setting such essentially dirty tricks aside, for those who still think that Social Security should be privatized rather than restructured and strengthened in order to meet social needs, consider the information concerning privately financed and administered pensions (i.e., by companies). Such pensions are "guaranteed" by the Pension Benefit Guaranty Corporation (counterpart of the Federal Deposit Insurance Corporation) a federal corporation that "guarantees" pensions for 44 million people. The reason for the "..." is that as of July 2002, <u>unfunded</u> pension liabilities (the difference between assets and liabilities) were $111 <u>billion</u>, four times those of 2001— and this with the market still plunging. By December, 2002, the gap was $300 billion. ("U.S. pension agency is sinking," <u>IHT</u>, 1-27-03)

The reason that company-administered pension funds administered them so as to allow obligations to exceed the assets to pay them off is—of course—because they have typically **speculated** the pension funds in the stock market, expecting 10 percent returns. But not getting them. (<u>SFC</u>, 7-29-2, <u>BW</u>, 8-5-2)

Thus, as <u>BW</u> shows, GM (for example) has had to put up $2.2 <u>billion</u> in cash for 2002 to make up for its investment losses; subsequently, if its investment returns are "only" 5 percent (instead of the once expected 10 percent), they will have to find $3 billion; if their investment returns are <u>minus</u> 5 percent, they'll have to find $4.5 billion. And so it goes (if not with such large amounts) for who knows how many other corporations?

But hanky-panky is not the only or even the main problem with employer-financed and administered pensions; it is, rather, their <u>stinginess</u> (as also with their health care systems):

<u>Item</u>: A recently retired employee from Bank of America in San Francisco, after working there for 20 years, has a monthly check due her of $191. But she only receives $48. The rest is deducted by the bank for medical and dental benefits. Moreover, as health insurance costs rise for the company (and everyone else: see **health care**), that will be taken out of her pension, the Bank of America declares. In contrast, when former BofA President Coulgter recently left the com-

pany (at age 51), "he got parting gifts worth more than $30 million, plus a $5 million annual pension and free medical and dental benefits for life." ("Rank-and-file pensioners struggle." SFC, 9-22-02)

Is there no way out of this mess? Indeed there is., IF we were to design a social security system in terms a) of need, and b) ability to pay, whether using payroll deductions or a truly progressive income tax, the fiscal and the human problems would be resolved; and only the rich would have reason to complain. They'd still be living high on the hog, but at least it could be good for their character.

Spanish Civil War (see Europe... Spain)

speculation

The speculative fervor that took hold in the 1980s and whose bubble began to pop as the 1990s ended has been treated in factual detail under **financialization, debt, Reagan,** and **CEOs**. The intent of what follows is to probe the nature and predictable consequences of those not only recurring but spreading and deepening processes.

Widespread speculation has not been confined to the immediate past, of course; its birth coincided with that of **capitalism**. The first major speculative drama occurred in 17th century Holland, also the first society to show the signs of what would become modern capitalism. The Dutch speculation was almost "pure"; it had nothing to do with production, or even with finance; it had to do with making money out of timing. In that case the timing had to do with what today would be called "buy and sell orders." For what? Unless you already know the answer, you'd never guess: tulips. It was called "the tulip mania" and it really shook things up. (BOXER; BOWDEN, et al.)

The next major development occurred in what was the first full-fledged capitalist society, Great Britain; it was speculation in the shares of the South Sea Company (of England); when it collapsed it provided us with the term that has been pertinent many times since: "bubble." (KINDLEBERGER)

Now an enormous time-jump to the USA in the 1920s, and what was called its "new economy" (not for the last time, you will have noted). There were many resemblance's between what happened then and there with here and now (and with the 17th and 18th century bubbles): The postwar years were full of technological and product change (in **cars**, electrical products, **farming**...). A maximum of a fifth of the population had income to spare (while the bottom two-thirds languished in one degree or another of difficulty. (SOULE)

As all other economies wobbled after World War I, the USA was well on its way to becoming the financial and industrial leader of the world. By 1925 or so, all this was having dramatic effects on Wall Street: up, up, and beyond went share prices. So euphoric was the mood by 1928 that the then leading U.S. economist (Prof. Irving Fisher of Harvard) famously stated that "the economy is on a high and rising plateau," and went on to observe that recessions were a thing of the past. (GALBRAITH)

As he spoke, even the stars of the economy—cars, steel, and housing construction—were already showing signs of softness; but Wall Street continued to soar.

In 1929, even after "the market" began to break wide open on October's "black Thursday," optimism continued. There was a small upturn in early 1930; however, another big drop to even lower levels in 1931. That roller coaster ride was repeated in 1932, with another little up and bigger down—despite President Hoover's now classic remark that "prosperity is just around the corner." The bottom was not reached until March of 1933. (MITCHELL)

The British economist KEYNES saw things for what they were; understandably so, for <u>his</u> economy (only a few years earlier the showplace of the capitalist world) had been in serious recession throughout the entire decade of the 1920s, <u>averaging</u> 10 percent unemployment. By the time he came out with his <u>General Theory of Employment, Interest and Money</u> (1936), he had come to see the dangers of succumbing to the lure of easy money:

> Speculators may do no harm as bubbles on a steady stream of enterprise. But the position is serious when enterprise becomes the bubble on a whirlpool of speculation. When the capital development of a country becomes the by-product of the activities of a casino, the job is likely to be ill-done. The measure of success of Wall Street, regarded as an institution of which the proper social purpose is to direct new investment into the most profitable channels in terms of future yield, cannot be claimed as one of the outstanding triumphs of <u>laissez-faire</u> capitalism—which is not surprising, if I am right in thinking that the best brains of Wall Street have been in fact directed towards a different object. (1936)

Those warnings were issued in an era whose "casino" technology was, compared to today's, what Franklin's kite was to an F-16. By the standards of Keynes's time, speculation was rampant; they were as nothing compared to today, whether in terms of the number of participants, geographic scope, speed, frequency or volume:

1. Participants. The reference is both to individuals and companies. The "who" until about the 1980s referred to individuals and funds representing them, where the individuals were almost always upper middle class in status and income, and the funds the composite representative for others (if also for some of those individuals).

Speculation had not yet become the game of a good half of the population or, in terms of funds, as much as two-thirds: All company retirement funds are in the market, with, recently, devastating effect. Now you and your neighbors are likely to be dabbling or more, whether they know it or not. (In my own case, for example, my private pension fund—the largest in the world—"dabbles" without my knowledge or say in whatever it wishes to; what it wished to and did in the recent past has led my monthly income from that fund to fall by 25 percent.)

As for participant companies, in the earlier period many businesses of one size, type, or sector, might have been "in the market"; today what is unusual—especially for big and giant companies—is not to be speculating in stocks and bonds and/or foreign exchange: the casino is open, and filled by all. (MINSKY)

2. Geographic scope/speed and frequency. If you are under 35-40, you might have difficulty imagining a world in which the instruments of communication were telephones and telegrams, whether for individuals or businesses. Contemporary communications and transportation have made it possible to compress the world into one economy; **globalization** has done it.

To be sure, the largest share of global business is done by 1,000 or so giant companies; but their shares can be speculated in by almost everyone, everywhere, 24/7.

The **MNC**s and **TNC**s must be involved in foreign exchange speculation: they are buying and selling, paying and being paid all over the globe daily. Speculation for them is keeping ahead of the curve; not to speculate means foregoing profit or enduring loss—just because the exchange rates have changed and you hadn't covered yourself. Pretty strong motivations there.

Thus it is that those who own the shares of those companies, like it or not, are indirectly speculating along with them. We all go together when they go.

And so it is, also, for almost all of us in terms of our retirement funds, our own speculating, whatever: We've all got a tiger by the tail, like it or not. Which takes us to the next dimension of today's speculative doings.

3. <u>Volume</u>. Some will remember the witty comment of Senator Dirksen (Rep. Ill.) in the early 1950s: "A billion here and a billion there, and pretty soon we're talking big money."

I thought of that when, in 1986, looking over the annual report of the Bank of International Settlements (the Swiss clearing house for all currency transactions). It reported that in 1986 the average <u>daily</u> foreign currency transactions were over $180 <u>billion</u>; and that <u>only</u> 10 percent of that was for trade and business investment, the rest speculative.

Hallucinating! But by the mid-1990s the <u>daily</u> level was about $800 <u>billion</u>, only three percent for trade and investment; now the figure is regularly over $1.5 <u>trillion</u> daily, 99 percent of it speculation. (LEWIS, M.)

This is not just Keynes's gambling casino; this approaches economic insanity, a set of frenzied activities resembling a kid's pinball, except that all the kids are trying to play on one machine and they're all high on something—and, to repeat, the biggest speculators, the biggest companies <u>must</u> "play the game." I have said nothing here about the wildest and recently most popular madness of all: <u>derivatives</u>. A good $2 <u>trillion</u> is invested in them. I don't understand how they work; it would be pleasant to think that someone else really does. Now hear this: The LTCM derivative whizzers who lost a couple of <u>billion</u> a few years ago (and came within a hair of taking many financial giants down with them), were advised by two economists who, because of their theories in <u>this</u> realm, had received the Nobel Prize in Economics. They were forced to admit—how could they otherwise?—that they hadn't quite understood the whole game. Get it?

The **bolded** discussions noted earlier suggest not only how reckless all of this has become and continues to be so, but also that its dangers are multiple and enormous. More's the worse, if there is a plausible means by which these speculative processes could be contained and reversed, I am not aware of them, except by total disaster—e.g. **Enron**.

Item: In the Western States in 2000-01—most disastrously in California, costing a minimum of $8 billion dollars in electricity bills and seemingly endless troubles arising from breakdowns. The power-provider was Enron, a company whose main source of income was 24/7 speculation—and manipulation; able to do so because of the recent deregulation allowing hands-off behavior in energy markets. Enron's CEO and, at the same time Bush II's closest buddy, was Ken Lay (who gave W. $100,000 just for the inaugural ceremonies).

In the months from January 2000 to June 2001, the monthly per hour wholesale megawatt price of electricity rose from around $40 to $317. Why? Who dunnit? And how?

At the top of the scam were the chiefs: Ken Lay, Jeffrey Skilling, Andrew Fastow, and Richard Causey, all now in deep-doo legal problems. But their dirty work was done by a small army of scamps who did the 24/7 speculating. Now, as revealed in June, 2004, we know just how responsible those unregulated rascals were. Here some quotes from newly-released documents (SFC, "New Evidence of Enron Schemes," 6-15-04).

Fasten your seat belts.

> Kevin: (Speaking of demands for refunds) "So the rumor's true? They're (expeltive) takin' all the money back you guys stole from those poor grandmothers in California?"
> Bob: "Yeah, Grandma Millie, man. But she's the one who could-n't figure out how to (expletive) vote on the butterfly ballot."

> Tim: (On profit-taking from California) "He steals money from California to the tune of about a million..."
> Person 2: "Will you rephrase that?"
> Tim: "OK, he, um, arbitages the California market to the tune of a million bucks or two a day."

> Matt: (On their hopes that Bush would be elected President) "Tell you what—you heard this here first: When Bush wins—"
> Tom: "Caps are gone."
> Matt: "Ken Lay's going to be Secretary of Energy."

Make up your own "expletives."

As pursued under **debt**, the massive accumulation of debt of all kinds in the past two or three decades has been essential for that same period's rates of growth (or absence of stagnation). The debt is integrally related to <u>all</u> the financial—and thus productive—activities in the USA and globally; it <u>must</u> continue to rise or consumer and business and governmental expenditures <u>will</u> fall.

The sorcerer's apprentice is in charge and there's no place to hide.

spin

The word signifies the use of language to transform what, if written or spoken straightforwardly, would provoke opposition; to make words into what will provide, instead, support or indifference.

Take, for instance, "compassionate conservatism," **Bush II's** campaign slogan. First, ask what difference it would have made had he campaigned as, simply, a conservative. He would have lost many of the moderate centrists who voted for him. Or, suppose he had run simply as "compassionate." He would have lost much of the immoderate center/right. So it goes.

Or take the great spin of 1947, when what had been called the Department of War since 1789 had its name changed to the Department of Defense while, at the same time, its nicely spun companion "military" expenditures were listed thenceforth in the budget as "defense" expenditures.

But spinning is not confined to words; it is also used effectively with images, the honing of both of which having been carried out for decades in commercial advertising.

<u>Item</u>: In his campaign for the presidency in 1988, it is generally agreed that Reagan's then V.P. **Bush I's** decisive ploy was the **TV** political ad against Gov. Dukakis (D. Mass). The ad showed a revolving prison gate while, in the background, a voice went on about Willie Horton, a black man in prison for murder. The clear implication was that if Dukakis were elected prison gates over the nation would open wide. The Dukakis campaign just fell apart.

Would that spin had been or will be confined to the likes of the Bushies. Far from it. It has been a vital accompaniment of political democracy. The first Queen Elizabeth didn't need to spin, nor did Louis XIV. The need began when the people began to have a say in government. The say was never much, limited as it was to the voting booth; but for those with power, even a little is too much.

In the USA the need for spinning became apparent in the late

19th century, when the Populist movement began to cause shudders in the halls of power. That need was met best in the early 20th century, for Woodrow Wilson: In the election campaign of 1916 (war raging in Europe) he ran on a platform of keeping us out of war while his PR man Edward L. Bernays spun us into war. (TYE; more generally, see **media**, **advertising**; CHOMSKY/HERMAN; ENSENZBERGER; EWEN)

In 1948, George ORWELL's <u>1984</u> stood as a warning against Big Brother and mind management. In his fictional society "Oceania," control from the top was achieved through "doublespeak" and "doublethink." We have gone both beyond and beneath that; now we live by muddlespeak and muddlethink.

Star Wars (see milex, Reagan)

SUVs (see cars)

Taft-Hartley Act (see Truman, unions)

Taiwan (see China)

taxes/"tax expenditures"

"Taxes" are one side of what is called governmental "fiscal policy"; "expenditures" are the other side. "Tax expenditures" are the <u>increased</u> taxes for some (usually those in the bottom 90 percent of incomes) resulting from the <u>decreased</u> taxes of those in the top 10 percent without a corresponding <u>decrease</u> of expenditures.

Taxes we have always had with us; tax expenditures, a 20th century invention, became common and conscious policy under **Reagan.** Under **Bush II** they should have become the name of the game.

This is important stuff and very easy to get confused about, especially when, as is now customary, discussions of these matters by legislators, governors, presidents, and selected "experts" combine misinformation with disinformation—intentionally or not.

The following brief discussion of taxes plus that contained in **deficits and surpluses** can serve as only an introduction; better than nothing, it is to be hoped.

First, note the vital difference between the conduct of fiscal policies on the federal level as compared with those of cities and states. The federal government can legally spend more than it taxes, run a deficit, and take care of it by increasing its debt; states and localities must finance their expenditures either through current taxes and/or legislatively or electorally approved bonds, the interest and principal for which are paid through taxation. That is, the federal government can legally manipulate taxes and expenditures for good or ill considerably more than the states and cities.

In the past century or so, that ability and its usage have grown always greater; presently, as will be seen below, with always more devastating socioeconomic effects on states and localities.

Second, in order to have a useful perspective on what is happening in the USA now it is important to understand something of taxation's origins, its variations over time and, especially, how drastic those variations have become in the past quarter century or so.

The system of taxes and expenditures is one of several manifestations of modern societies' structures of **power** that determine which socioeconomic policies will—and will not—be enacted, who will benefit from them, and who will pay.

When the USA began as a nation, one of the principles of the Constitution was that Congress had the specific power "to lay and to collect taxes." Even though Jefferson was rich, he argued (to general acceptance) that taxes should be levied in terms of "ability to pay." (He also proposed the abolition of **slavery**, even though he was a slaveowner: Where is he now that we need him?)

Ability to pay as a taxing principle is the basis for a "progressive" tax structure. It means that as one's income rises, not only does the amount of tax rise, but always more so, for the rate also rises.

In the USA, the only period in which that principle even nudged toward realization was during and for a few years after World War II. Hot war and **cold war** provided the political setting, and the enormous **military expenditures** of both wars and their associated increased average levels of income provided for a broad economic base, accompanied by the continuing politics of the New Deal and **Truman**'s "Fair Deal."

The result was a certain progressivity in the taxation of both individual incomes and corporate profits—with, however, a slow but sure increase in indirect taxes and fees (sales taxes and fees, and payroll deductions). (PECHMAN)

The individual income tax reached its progressive highs in the 1950s; in the Kennedy/Johnson years those rates started to go down; in the 1970s the decline went further; in the Reagan years, progressive taxes were given the heave-ho.

Under Clinton some ground was regained for low-income working families when the Earned Income Tax Credit (EITC: a tax rebate) was somewhat expanded. That political hiccough was followed by the gargantuan steps backward into regressivity produced by Bush II's three tax cuts (of which, more below).

Here some representative data on the past half-century or so:

1. The top individual income tax rate and maximum progressivity were reached during World War II: 91 percent; brought down to 77 percent by **JFK** in 1963. That was the "surtax" rate, which, as successively higher income levels are reached, brings about a higher "marginal" rate. Contain your fears for the Very Rich: given innumerable loopholes, the top rate is never paid (nor anything close to it); but it keeps the top 10 percenters' blood boiling.

2. In the giddy 1980s, the tax code was lowered repeatedly for both individual and corporate rates, along with countless provisions (including a newly enacted extravagant depreciation allowance which, when not usable by a given company, could be sold to other companies).

3. In 1983, a presidential commission headed by Alan **Greenspan** declared that because corporate and individual tax rates were going down, it would be necessary to raise Social Security and Medicare (payroll) taxes. That done, it is now normal for lower and middle income families to pay always more in payroll than in income taxes. (see **social security**); and for the rich to pay less.

4. The "Tax Reform Act of 1986 dropped the highest individual rate to 28 percent; and that was the "nominal" rate, opening the door wider for **lobbyists** and lawyers to create and find loopholes. (PHILLIPS, 2002)

"Loopholes." They are said to be more popular than sex among the very rich. One among many loopholes is that concerning "tax shelters." They are intricately arranged devices, with domestic and foreign "shelters" that enable high-income individuals to avoid taxes altogether.

That one and others are aided and abetted by a related cut in the

IRS budgets, substantially reducing the numbers of government audi-
tors, tax collectors, and special agents whose job it is to investigate and
report on "high-profile tax advisers and individuals." ("IRS Taking
Aim at Big Tax Shelter Business," NYT, 7-6-03). Now a sketch and
table of how tax burdens have been turned upside down recently:

> Since 1973 corporate income taxes have risen only 75
> percent as much as corporate profits....; Social Security taxes,
> which apply /only/ to the first $87,000 of pay, grew 82 percent
> faster than incomes...; the number of tax investigations fell 37
> percent from 1992 to 2002." ("Tax Inquiries Fall as Cheating
> Increases," NYT, 4-14-03)

Changing sources of federal tax receipts

	1960	1998
Individual income tax	49%	49%
Corporate income tax	23%	11%
Social Security	16%	33%
Other (Excise, etc.)	12%	7%

(HEINTZ, et al.)

In addition, we all pay state and local taxes. Note that the lowest incomes pay a higher overall percentage of their incomes than
the very rich—who now have a larger after-tax income than the bottom half of the U.S. population put together: (HEINTZ, et al.)

U.S. average state and local taxes in 1995 as a share of family income (for non-older married couples)

Income Group	Lowest 20%	Top 1%
Sales and Excise taxes	6.7%	1.1%
Property taxes	4.5%	1.9%
Income taxes	1.3%	5.0%
Total	12.5%	8.0%

Third, we now resume with the Bush II tax cuts and associated
tax expenditures, with their very pleasant probabilities for the few
and their very ugly realities for most. As a point of departure, keep
in mind that the grand favoritism for the rich of Bush II's fiscal policies—as with **Social Security** and **health care**—also provides favors
for those who are making those policies: not least the P. and V.P.;

both of them (among many others in the Administration and in Congress) have already benefited nicely from Tax Cuts I and II, and their pockets will bulge even more after III.

How rich? Well, Bush II and Cheney and most who surround them are in the top one percent group. They are not as rich as the fabled "Forbes 400," of course, but as things are going, they might even get to the bottom ring of that hard-working bunch. Just how much hard working was in fact responsible for their fortunes has been detailed for the Top 400 by Forbes, no friend of the workingman:

> Parents did not have great wealth or own a business: 31%. Family was upper-class but had less than $1 million /aw!/, or received some start-up capital from a family member: 14%. Inherited a medium-size business, wealth of more than $1 million, or substantial start-up capital: 7%. Inherited wealth in excess of $50 million or a large company: 6%. Inheritance alone was enough to qualify for the 400: 41% (HEINTZ, et al.; from FORBES, 7-5-99, 7-6-9)

Note that 55% inherited $1 million or more: No wonder they want to get rid of the estate tax! But that's wealth; how about the 400 biggest income receivers? Those two groups certainly overlap, but they deserve a separate look (and are getting it from the tax cut). Control your envy genes as you find that:

> The 400 wealthiest taxpayers accounted for more than 1 percent of all the income in the United States in 2000, more than double their share eight years earlier, according to the Internal Revenue Service. But their tax burden plummeted over the same period...: The average income of the 400... was almost $174 million (up from $64.8 million in 1992).... In 2000, the top 400 on average paid 23.3 percent of their income in federal income tax, down from 26.4 in 1992 and 29.9 percent in 1995. Two factors explain the drop: reduced capital gains taxes—which account for 64 percent of their income—from 28 to 20 percent, and bigger gifts to charity.... This year's capital gains tax cut was down to 15 percent.... The figures do not include the incomes of the many wealthy Americans who use tax shelters /see "Postscript"/ to reduce their reported incomes. A second report shows that in 2002 there were 2,022 Americans with incomes above $200,000 who paid no taxes anywhere in the world (up from 37 in 1977). ("Very Richest's Share of Income Grew Even Bigger, Data Show," (NYT, 6-26-03) (emphasis added)

Back to the present. First, a look at what has been done to the tax structure; 2) then what it means on the expenditure side (which includes the impact on states and localities); and what all this is likely to mean for the socioeconomy.

1. <u>Who gets what cuts?</u>. Bush II arranged two massive tax cuts before that of 2003—"One a year, folks; bring 'em on!" The latest is by far the biggest of all, and was initially meant to be twice that which Congress passed in June, 2003. Initially proposed to amount to over $800 billion in cuts, it ended up with only $320 <u>billion</u>.

Its size, as will be seen later, is but one of its large defects; the other is how blatantly it goes about making the very rich even richer. That becomes clear if we note what happens to two different families with two children apiece on two different income levels;

> The family with $41,000/year /which is near the median income in the USA; half above and half below/ now pays $1,303 in income taxes and will pay $323 less; the other family is in the top one percent, with $530,000/year /more than ten times as much; with half of the top one-ers getting more/; it now pays $138,000 and will pay $12,772 less—assuming it doesn't have the sense to hire a lawyer to find all those loopholes (which can reduce their taxes to zero. ("A Tax Cut Without End," <u>NYT</u>, 5-23-03)

Then there are the cuts in both capital gains and dividend taxes, down to 15 percent (about half of their previous levels). Naturally, almost all the income from capital gains and dividends accrue to those in the top income brackets. And that rate is only a bit more than half of the individual income tax. So far so good.

Did I mention the estate tax? The estate tax currently affects only millionaires—people with the richest 2 percent of estates. Nearly half of <u>all</u> estate taxes are paid by the wealthiest <u>one-tenth</u> of one percent of the U.S. population, 2-3,000 families. Consider this:

> The estate tax is a transfer tax on the unearned inheritance of large amounts of wealth, the bulk of the largest estates are appreciated assets, which have never been taxed. If we tax wages, it is only fair to tax capital gains.

Who said that, some anarchist? Nope. Chuck Collins who, along with William Gates Sr. (Bill's dad) is co-author with Gates Sr. of "Wealth and Our Commonwealth: Why America Should Tax Accumulated Fortunes." (http://www.responsiblewealth.org)

Nor was billionaire Warren Buffett an anarchist, last I heard. This is how he views the latest tax cuts:

> The taxes I pay to the federal government... are roughly the same proportion of my income—about 30 percent—as that paid by the receptionist in my office... But she pays a far higher portion of her income in payroll /social security/ taxes than I do.... Now the Senate says that dividends should be tax-free to recipients. /Were/ this measure to go through, and the directors of Berkshire Hathaway (which does not now pay a dividend) therefore decide to pay $1 billion in dividends next year, /then/ owning 31 percent of Berkshire, I would receive $310 million in additional income, owe not another dime in federal tax, and see my tax rate plunge to 3 percent. And /my/ receptionist would still be paying 30 percent..., ten times /my/ proportion.... (WP, "Dividend Voodoo," 5-20-2003)

A traitor to his class, that one; but not to his country. Like PHILLIPS, Buffett has fears for unbridled capitalism. When appointed Arnold Schwarznegger's financial adviser when Arnold ran for Governor of California in the dignified recall election of 2003, he immediately proposed a repeal of Prop. 13—immediately rejected by Arnold, with loud support from the entire conservative community. Why?

Because Prop. 13, although the "middle class" believed it was in their interest, was mostly beneficial for businesses properties. And, because of the loss of state revenues, that has meant severe pains for education and health care; something that selfsame "middle class" has learned not to care about. (see Paul Krugman, Op-ed, NYT, 8-22-03, "Conan The Deceiver.")

2. Expenditures and consequences. When Bush II entered the White House, the government was running a sizeable surplus, and it was expected that in his four years a fiscal surplus over several trillion might accumulate. His first and second cuts have instead produced a two trillion deficit, with more expected. Bush II expects the latest cuts to add $320 billion to the debt; period. The general consensus is that it will be well over $400 billion annually for ten years (that's $4 trillion)—assuming he is not allowed to rob from Social Security and Medicare and assuming the economy expands at an average rate of 3-3.5 percent annually. (Edmund L. Andrews, Op-ed, NYT, 8-24-03, "For Budget Shortfalls, Choose Grim or Grimmer.") Don't bet on those assumptions. Why not?

Bush's tax cuts are put forth as stimuli to the economy, the reasoning being that the recipients of rebates will rush out and buy, buy, buy. That might well be true, were the rebates going mostly to the two-thirds of the population; but at least <u>half</u> of them are going to the top 10 percent.

> <u>Item</u>: "88 percent of Americans will save less than $100 on their 2006 federal tax cuts as a result of this year's tax cut; and the average will be $4. ("Harper's Index," in <u>Harper's Magazine</u>, May 2003)

The Top 10-ers have been living high on the hog for some time already; they have to really <u>concentrate</u> to think of more things to buy. Even more worrisome is that the cuts in taxes and the rising deficit have given the Administration just the argument it wants to "starve the beast" (i.e., social expenditures) <u>and</u> to reduce the federal government's usual contributions to the 50 states and localities for <u>their</u> social expenditures (on education, health, housing, prisons, fire departments, infrastructure). <u>All</u> of those, unlike tax cuts for the rich, are both socially necessary <u>and</u> job creating, directly and, through the wages received, indirectly. (see **deficits and surpluses**)

In short, although the economy is already in a weak spot, <u>this</u> fiscal policy is the opposite of what's needed, both economically stupid and ethically reprehensible. (LINDERT)

The economic stupidity is that if, as is Bush's argument, the tax cuts are to stimulate the economy, it is the wrong path; as will be pursued in the <u>Afterword</u>, the very government expenditures that are being cut are those which, were they to be increased would, provide two or three times the stimuli. (see, for example, Jeff Madrick, "Economic Scene," <u>NYT</u>, 7-19-03).

All the foregoing has been put together from a combination of ongoing reports and my own humble musings. What about someone less humble, say, Prof. Paul Krugman? If we were to time warp ourselves back no more than five years, we would find that virtually all references to Krugman saw him as one of the top <u>mainstream</u> economists; with all the leading universities hot on his trail to add his illustrious name to their faculties.

Compare his present writings with those of, say five years ago, and there are two large differences: 1) he wrote very little for popular consumption; 2) what he wrote, popular or professional, was square in the middle, if also more intelligently than most. He began to change just a few years ago and then became the Op-ed economist for the New York Times; note the title of his most recent book: The Great Unraveling.... It is the USA we'd like to think well of that Krugman sees as "unraveling." Right on; or, better, on to the left.

So then, what does Prof. Krugman have to say about current tax policy? The title of a relevant article tells it all: The Tax-Cut Con. (NYT Magazine, 9-14-03) Here some representative excerpts, both repetitive of and in addition to mine above:

> "... Modern American politics has been dominated for 25 years by a crusade against taxes."
> Critically quoting Tom DeLay (House majority leader) in 2003: "Nothing is more important in the face of a war than cutting taxes." /Tell that to the Marines./
> "A result of the tax-cut crusade is that there is now a fundamental mismatch between the benefits Americans expect to receive from the government and the revenues government collect."
> "Still, aren't taxes much higher than they used to be? Not if we're looking back over the past 30 years. As a percent of GDP federal taxes are currently at their low point since the Eisenhower administration /1950s/...; with families in the middle of the income distribution... paying about 26 percent of their income in taxes today... not much changed since 1970."
> "Meanwhile wealthy Americans have seen a sharp drop in their tax burden... /to/ the lowest rate since 1932."
> "When fully phased in, the 2001 tax cut will deliver 42 percent of its benefits to the top 1 percent..., that is, families with more than $330,000 per year."
> "The 2003 tax cut... concentrates its benefits on the really, really rich. Families with incomes over $1 million a year— 0.13 percent /that's thirteen one-hundredths of one percent, folks/—of the population."
> /From the 2003 tax cut/"... about half of American families received less than $100; a great majority... less than $500."

Welcome aboard, Prof. Krugman (and also Prof. Stiglitz /see **IMF**, et al./).

In addition to whatever else the Bush tax cuts mean, most

important for the society will be the <u>increased</u> taxes for the bottom 80 percent of the people—most notably, but not only payroll taxes for Social Security and Social Security "deductions" for Medicare. Ugly though those increased taxes will be, also cruelly damaging will be the jobs lost due to social expenditure cutbacks in all 50 states, all now in deficit, and unable to maintain expenditures except by <u>raising</u> their taxes—both very difficult politically and stupid economically. Compassionate conservatism at work; more accurately, raw **capitalism** at work. (JOHNSTON)

The political power associated with concentrated economic power insures that a capitalist democracy is necessarily a <u>limited</u> democracy. However, there are great differences in the degrees and realms of those limitations, and they are amply manifested in patterns of taxes and expenditures.

Thus, all the Scandinavian countries are capitalist as are, for example, Germany and Austria; but <u>all</u> of them are more democratic than we as represented in their patterns of benefits and payments: essentially free health care, cheaper or free access to university education (with a stronger K-12 system) and abundant child care, widespread and good public housing, more and longer paid vacations, shorter work hours; you name it. <u>Item</u>: I still remember my first visit to Copenhagen 40 years ago. As the tourist bus was passing an attractive housing area the driver wryly remarked "This is where the poor people live."

Those and other western European countries also have very rich people and giant companies who would probably prefer the U.S. system; perhaps some of those companies are wise enough (as well as politically unable) not to try. In any case, their political systems are such that the benefits just noted have been voted in by the beneficiaries without having to overcome tens of thousands of **lobbyists**: Their countries are "social democracies."

The USA has neither that name nor those practices; Jefferson's "ability to pay" has receded into a blurred history. Only part of the reason, as suggested earlier, is that the largest percentage of those in the Senate and the House are themselves very well off, as are the White House and Cabinet biggies: The aggregated year 2000 incomes of "the president, vice-president, and of the secretaries of state, treasury, defense, and commerce ranged from $130 to $191 <u>million</u> and their wealth from $185 to 624 <u>million</u>." (PHILLIPS,2002)

The other part has to do with the ways in which the corporate giants in industry, finance, and agriculture utilize **lobbyists** to see that their felt needs and wishes are understood and acted upon:

> Between 1995-2000, House and Senate members of tax-writing committees received $45.7 <u>million</u>" (ibid.) to assist them in understanding what would be best for the nation." (ibid.)

In some sense, 'twas ever thus. Until the 20th century, members of the Senate were elected not by the people but by their state legislatures—themselves almost always corrupted from their toes up. When a closer approximation to democracy took hold, and senators had to be popularly elected, time and technology (mostly, now, **TV**) made the process of money buying all a bit more complex; but only a bit more.

Economic power is not focussed only on taxes and expenditures, of course; but under that heading fall so many different taxes and so many different expenditures that when summed up leave very little of the socio-economic process unaffected or not given direction by those processes.

If any or all of that is to change, the energy for it to do so must rise from the bottom and middle levels of the USA; it will not descend from the top dogs who benefit and strive to maintain—or worsen—the status quo. Concerning which, see the <u>Afterword</u>.

<u>Postscript on tax shelters</u>. A tax shelter is something in which individuals and companies can invest. Their essence is a set of deceptions allowing the investor to conceal income and/or to posit false losses. There are many and complex variations, all of them permitted by tax laws written specifically to allow such legal chicanery—accomplished through **lobbyists**, of course. (A reminder: Such <u>non</u>-payment of taxes by the rich raises the taxes of all others, for a given the level of governmental expenditures.)

So, in July of 2003, a tax shelter case was taken up in Federal Court. It was a dramatic verbal contest between the accused, a Nobel Laureate (Myron S. Scholes) and a Justice Department lawyer (Charles P. Hurley). Scholes received his Nobel prize in econ along with a colleague at the University of Free Markets—oops! 'scuze me, University of Chicago—for his contributions to mathematical **economics**, with specific reference to speculative processes. (see **speculation**)

He and his associate became the principal advisors (and partners) in a hedge fund specializing in derivatives: Long Term Capital

Management (LTCM). Its subsequent 1998 collapse required govern-mental intervention to avert a global financial panic. (<u>NYT</u>, "Partner Testifies That Tax Shelter of Hedge Fund Was Legitimate," 7-9-03; also, next day, "Economist Questioned on Tax Shelter Role.")

In the many hours of questioning, one indication of the limits of the Nobelist's integrity was provided when Hurley sought to "impeach Scholes's earlier testimony in which he minimized his expertise about taxes.... 'I am not an expert on taxes'" had said the author of a book later displayed: <u>Tax and Business Strategy</u>. It is used as a text (cost: $130!) at the Stanford Graduate School of Business, Scholes its pri-mary author. Sort of a stupid fib for such an intelligent man.

So what's the fuss? The fuss is that Scholes organized a tax shel-ter which would provide $375 <u>million</u> in tax benefits for its partici-pants (including, of course, LTCM), at the cost of $4 million. Cool. Just as cool, however, is that though it is nice to see the government tracking this down, and even when it wins the case, it is asking only $40 million in taxes and $9 million in fines. I am no Nobel Laureate in Economics (or anything else), but I can add and subtract, dammit: $375 million minus $49 million = $326 <u>million</u> in taxes saved. Sort of sounds like an <u>incentive</u> to create lots more shelters, no?

Maybe Congress is stupid? Or, is it possible that **corruption** has snuck into their ranks? You're paying your money; take your choice.

technology

In 1917, as war ripped Europe apart, Einstein wrote to a friend that "Our much-praised technological progress, and civilization gen-erally, could be compared to an axe in the hands of a pathological criminal." (FOLSING) Although he didn't know it at the time (1905), in having demonstrated that E=MC2, that lifelong pacifist helped pave the way for making the most destructive "axe" ever, which would be used at **Hiroshima/Nagasaki** by what increasingly seems to be a pathological society.

Ever since knives and spears, technology has been used both constructively and destructively. When, how, where, and why it will be used—and, in consequence, who will benefit and who and what will be harmed—finds its answer in the structure of **power**, at whose center now sit capitalism and its State—with some "collateral ben-efits" for the less powerful, too; of course. <u>But</u>.

It is a very large <u>but</u> that broadens, deepens, and becomes more multi-dimensional over time. It has been common to think of the production of <u>things</u> when technology is mentioned. Now, however, its use and misuse shape and permeate all goods and services, and all of human, social, and environmental existence.

When technology took its first big leaps in England in the eighteenth century, the harm done was almost entirely to farmers and pre-industrial workers, and the gains went almost entirely to what became large landowners (who, by 1790, a century later, owned 80 percent of the cultivable land of England). (MANTOUX)

Thus was laid the basis for the industrial **capitalism** of the nineteenth century. The earlier "progress," in obliterating the fabled "yeomanry" and cottage industry, gave birth to what became a powerless working class—inspiring, in 1770, Goldsmith's epic poem "The Deserted Village" and its "Ill fares the land, to hastening ills a prey/ Where wealth accumulates, and men decay."

Those exploited were the "fuel" of industrial capitalism, and their lives burned out quickly. As (HOBSBAWM, 1968) has shown, between 1821 and 1851, the very years of the most dramatic technological improvements of the industrial revolution, the life span of the average working person in Britain declined substantially—from 37 to 46 percent who died by age 19 (remembering that the new technology utilized children in mines and mills, without stint).

Worker exploitation became less lethal as Britannia came to rule the waves (much enabled by steamships), allowing workers' real incomes to rise by the 1880s—but only because they were able to organize into **unions** as, however, exploitation spread over the globe to the weaker and imperialized societies. Sound familiar?

In recent decades the advancing technologies of transportation, communications, and transportable productive equipment have allowed transnational corporations (**TNCs**) to deepen and tighten their hold on the human and other resources of the whole globe, supported by both the rich and poor nations' easily-corrupted governments in the USA, Europe, Japan and in the "emerging market economies" of Latin America, Asia, and Africa.

Once again, peasants are swept off their lands to allow the new technologies and agribusinesses to have their way. (see **Archer... ADM**) In consequence, small farmers have plummeted from a life that was merely difficult to one that is harrowing, have lost their culture and their history, and have been forced into the exploding cities of their own country or those of richer societies, where most confront hatred and a squalid existence.

"Ah!" economists have said for over two hundred years and still say, "but in the **long run**, all these changes are for the good of all. Those in the poorer countries need only be patient: Behold the levels of real income of industrial workers in the strongest countries!" There is much wrong with such observations: KEYNES remarked: "In the long run we're dead." Here we look at only some of the fallacies.

First, there is no chance whatsoever that more than a small percentage of the people of the poorer countries will ever reach the average levels of material comfort in the leading industrial economies of today, if only because there is no other set of countries which they can "imperialize." Nor will they—except, perhaps and alas! **China**—ever have access to the relative military might that cleared the path for the now rich societies. They are already or soon will be ruled not by their own governments but by the new Holy Family: **TNCs, WTO, IMF**.

Second, in the richest countries, led by the USA, exploitation is very much on the rise, and much facilitated by "technological progress." In the 1990s, as U.S. growth and wealth broke records, the majority of workers were harmed more than benefited. Not only did real wages fall or remain stagnant from 1973 until the late 1990s, but the average worker (not just the poorest) put in 260 more hours of work in 1999—that is six weeks of extra work—than in 1989, with little or no wage increases. (BW, 12-6-99) And this says nothing about unreported data, such as the spreading practice of having workers "punch out" and then continue to work (for which Wal-Mart is being sued), or the diverse "overwork" practices of home workers and pat-time temps: "beloved by many employers, because they're cheaper and more flexible than those you put on the payroll." (Fortune Small Business, 4/2000)

Such phenomena are but part of a long list of dire outcomes resulting from the combination of the most concentrated **big business** sector ever, the uses to which new technologies can be put, the intimidating effects of **consumerism** and **debt**. A key part of the framework within which that has been happening has been **downsizing and outsourcing**; it much weakened already weak unions. If you are part of the average working family, your monthly income is less than your household **debt**: you are unlikely to risk losing your job by militancy.

Already in the eighteenth century workers were rioting against the new technology, famously so with the "machine-breakers" (called "Luddites") early in the next century. Those who protested were not protesting technology as such, but the ways it was or was not used. (HOBSBAWM, 1964). Similarly, today's workers are not protesting "free trade" but the ways in which the freedom of capital harms workers in both the rich and the poor nations—despite economists' and politicians' hype to the contrary.

As technology has sped up, so has **waste**, much of it destructive; not technology's "fault" as such, of course. Be that as it may, any kind of waste is obscene in the face of the inadequate to fatally low levels of income for at least two-thirds of the world's people. Over 2 <u>billion</u> struggle to stay alive on less than $2 a day as, each year, as more than 15 <u>million</u> children die of malnutrition-related illnesses.

There are grounds for seeing social criminality in the possibilities that have been foregone through the massive waste of human and non-human resources and possibilities. Consider what could have been done in the past century with the technology, knowledge, and resources of the globe; set that next to the perils, tragedies, and irrational economies confronting us every day. Moderate estimates see <u>half</u> of GDP as sheer waste, useless to people and society; and such estimates ignore the common practices in durable consumer goods (**cars**, computers) of "deliberate obsolescence," and the gross wastes of **military expenditures**.

The foregoing is not merely or mostly an expression of annoyance and outrage. It points to an ongoing calamity whose effects have already been drastic on a large scale and which threaten to expand always further, and beyond control. Of the abuse and misuse of technology there will be no end, so long as it is profits, not human needs and possibilities, that guide its use. Marx put it forcefully long ago:

> Within the capitalist system all methods for raising the social productiveness of labour are brought about at the cost of the individual labourer; all means for the development of production transform themselves into means of domination over, and exploitation of producers; they mutilate the labourer into a fragment of a man, degrade him to the level of an appendage of a machine, destroy every remnant of charm in his work and turn it into a hated toil. (MARX, 1867)

teenagers and the young

As an old geezer, I know how very easy it is to be scornful of youngsters as the memory of one's own youth dims; but contemporary adolescents and young people must be seen as something more than just the latest generation, in ways both frightening and hopeful. First, their scary side.

We have all been adolescent and young and gone through those simultaneously difficult and exciting years of quiet and noisy desperation and wonderment, whether enticing or fearful. All that is still there—although if one is <u>not</u> young the noisy part seems more prominent; and, if one <u>is</u> young, the desperation may well outweigh the wonderment.

For those who reached adolescence in the 1950s or, even more so, those who did so from the 1960s to the present, the new shaping socioeconomic elements went well beyond anything earlier. Film was important <u>before</u> World War II, and has remained so, but in sharply different ways since then. But **TV** has become the most powerful and pervasive shaping force of the **media** since the 1950s; in the past 25 years, increasingly it has been <u>MTV</u> that has done the shaping for the young, in ways leaving other social forces behind—and gasping. (BANKS, BARBER)

Conformity was a hallmark of the USA as far back as the early 19th century, when DE TOCQUEVILLE wrote and pointed to its astonishing presence in the USA—well before the advent of mass media. By the early 20th century, when passage through at least grade school and literacy had become common, newspapers and magazines tended at least as much to increase as to decrease that conformity; as was true with even greater strength with film and radio in the interwar years.

But the quantum jump toward what we have today was provided by **TV**. Although invented in the 1920s, it could only become a mass product when enabled to be so by the higher average incomes of post-World War II USA—just in time to become a prime mover in the emergence of **consumerism**, now our dominant social characteristic.

When TV first took off, the programs and the **advertising** were directed mostly to an adult audience. That began to change as the 70s opened, but all too slowly for youngsters. For them, TV became an increasingly <u>boring</u> way of spending time. All that changed in

1981, and continues to do so at an accelerating rate.

As some—now no longer "young"—will remember, one midnight in August of 1981 a NASA rocket was launched and a countdown started whose purpose was to prepare viewers for a blank screen, a series of moon shots and, then, the image of Neil Armstrong placing an MTV flag in the dusty soil of the moon as a loud voice announced "Ladies and Gentlemen, Rock and Roll." At that moment the Buggles's song <u>Video Killed the Radio Star</u> became the first music video to appear on the home screen.

It was the birth of a new and frightening era, for MTV from its beginning appealed to some combination of the most trivial and the worst in us; over time it has done so always more intensely and cleverly, and for a powerful reason: It sells. (MAZZOCCO)

In his important study of MTV, BANKS asks "where does the ad end and the video begin?" He answers his own question by showing that the resemblance between commercials and music videos is such that there is finally <u>no</u> dividing line. In his <u>Jihad vs. McWorld</u>, BARBER took that point further, when he showed the consequences of the organic relationships between the various elements of the media and of what they sell:

> McWorld is an entertainment shopping experience that brings together malls, multiple movie theatres, theme parks, spectator sport arenas, fast food chains and television into a single vast enterprise that, on the way to maximizing its profits, transforms human beings...

MTV is increasingly the focus of attention for the young, promoting a popular culture of fast music, fast computers, and fast food; as such, given its great and rising popularity among children and adolescents, it represents a risk for the future.

Teenagers who may not "hear" or understand lyrics cannot avoid the often-disturbing images that characterize a rising number of videos containing an excess of violence, substance abuse, suicides, and sexual behavior that combines inanity, recklessness, and brutality. This transformation of the very meaning of **entertainment** and its resulting debasement fits all too smoothly into the ongoing spread of **corruption** and **decadence** into every nook and cranny of our lives, from top to bottom. (FINNEGAN)

The probability is high that a large majority of those in their early teens to those in their late twenties are adherents of all that is awful in the "infotainment" world, not least that of MTV. Nonetheless, I am convinced that a significant minority of the young, whether or not they are fans of MTV, have another and encouraging inner life as well. Here a brief impressionistic note on that hopeful development.

The basis for the generalizations to follow depends largely upon my having taught young people from 1949 to the present in universities in the USA and in Italy. That experience is something less than a random sample, of course; but it can stand as an important element of such a sample. The young have changed a <u>lot</u>.

I am encouraged. This from one whose tastes are drastically different from the young of today, not least in the realm of music (MTV's core). I have always loved music, from Bach and Casals to blues and Bix, and it is a struggle for me not to be appalled at the musical tastes of today's teenagers (to say nothing about ways of speech and dress). So what's to be encouraged about?

First and foremost, and despite their almost desperate conformity in the realms of taste, the young I know now strike me as the most <u>skeptical</u> young people I have <u>ever</u> known; a moment's reflection suggests why.

What almost all their parents and grandparents think and feel and value was shaped by the socialization processes going back as far as the 1920s; or, even if the parents were born in the 1950s, they would have had half a century of such socialization: In what?

Well, to begin with what is vital: In "learning" to accept certain institutions and, yes, slogans, more or less without reflection; for example, the "principles" of the **Cold War**, the "principles" of **globalization**; the pervasive existence and functioning of a bought and paid for political system—bought and paid for not just by expensive election campaigns, but by the crucial role of **lobbyists**; the widespread existence and functional effectiveness of **poverty** and **racism**. There is much more, of course; see the Table of Contents.

Suffice it to say here that although we adults might well be upset about some or all of that, we have come to <u>accept</u> it as a set of givens. However, the very definition of a "young" person usually—not always—includes a decent share of idealism, not least those attached to the "America!" they are taught to sing about and whose flag they must salute in grade school.

To say that is to say something else: It is not just that most of the young's families and teachers and the politicians of the day are all in some degree, phonies; it is, also, that whatever was wrong with the USA when their parents were kids has gotten wronger: We are a <u>more</u> belligerent nation than ever, there is <u>more</u> poverty, <u>more</u> inequality, <u>more</u> corruption, <u>more</u> school deterioration, <u>more</u> environmental damage, <u>higher</u> costs for <u>less</u> health care—you name it; all <u>worse</u>, to repeat, than when their parents were kids.

The adults are doing damned little about it; all too often, indeed, they seem to <u>want</u> to believe the Orwellian lies and deceptions that now fill the air. It is harder to convince the youngies—a good strong minority of them, at least—that the rotten smell in the air is a delectable gorgonzola. Thus the substantial and noisy preponderance of the young at the No-Global and anti-war demonstrations.

The addiction of youngsters today to ways of being and living that may seem to us elders to combine stupidity with bad taste with self-destruction, whatever else it might be, is at least for some a way of criticizing their society and us elders; of "giving us the finger," as they might put it.

So: Some comparisons between the young of earlier decades and now. The 1960s was a time during which young people were in protest and even revolt to one degree or another, and considerably more so than any of their predecessors (or, until just now, those today).

I worked closely with them in all those years, and my impression was that the protest and the revolt were energized by <u>disillusionment</u>: the failure of the USA to live up to its ideals, whether as regards **poverty, racism,** and/or the war in **Vietnam.** And today?

Today, I am increasingly convinced, a sizeable minority of the young are not <u>disillusioned</u>, but <u>without</u> illusions. They see our society for what it is, and react with their patterns of often-bizarre behavior; and/or, for a goodly number of them, with political efforts.

Like the young who behaved with political vigor and responsibility in earlier generations those today are in a minority (as were those who built **unions** and those who fought against **racism** and against the war in Vietnam); such people, over time and space and age, are <u>always</u> in the minority, often a tiny one.

Moreover, as regards today's young, my impression grows that there are many on the sideline who, if and when the social process becomes still uglier, will be surprised to see themselves enlarging that tiny minority. I am encouraged. FINNEGAN's <u>Cold New World...</u> speaks well to this point, as well to their desperation.

As for the rest of us, like the young, we must learn as much as we can if we are to move toward a decent society; but we who are <u>not</u> young have much indeed to <u>unlearn</u>; more than those "kids" do.

terrorism

The **Middle East** is high on the list of the many areas wracked by terrorism; in discussing **Israel/Palestine**, I pointed out that "like beauty, terrorism is in the eye of the beholder." When the beholder is the USA, there is a distinct lack of perspective concerning our own terrorist history.

If "terrorism" refers to the use of deadly means in order to weaken an opponent through bottomless fear and demoralization, then we have consciously used it with the greatest damage of all: with **nukes** on **Hiroshima/Nagasaki**, with **carpet bombing** and **napalm** in **Vietnam** and the fire bombing of Dresden, Tokyo, or Formosa (in which I participated); etc. The explicit aim of all of that was to demoralize the civilian population and intimidate their governments. The victims <u>were</u> terrorized, but not always demoralized; and we have seen who did <u>our</u> terrorizing as heroes.

None of that makes it easier to accept the tragedy of 9/11. Quantitatively the number of deaths was small when compared with our own terrorist actions. But for the USA it was the first time in our history when we had suffered death and destruction from abroad in our land—except for Pearl Harbor (2,000 miles distant, and in 1941 still a colony).

Pearl Harbor and 9/11 were quite dissimilar in both origin and intent, but very much the same in terms of some of what followed. In 1941 the USA was essentially indifferent to Japanese criminality in Asia and Nazi expansionism in Europe; Pearl Harbor instantly and zealously drew us into those wars (although even then, our war with Germany began when <u>they</u> declared war on <u>us</u>).

What followed the horrendous destruction of 9/11 was very different in detail, but very similar in one key respect; it allowed the ongoing administration leeway to enact a set of both domestic and foreign policies which before 9/11 would quite simply have been unlikely—and whose reversal will be difficult indeed.

It is well to recall that the presidency of **Bush II** was limping as summer ended in 2001; substantial doubts about the validity of his victory were current, the "new economy's" splendor was dimming by the day, scandals were rife about numerous giant companies **CEOs**, among them some of Bush and Cheney's friends and, by and large, things were looking up for the Demos.

The catastrophic attack of 9/11 turned all of that around; within six months Bush II and his administration were riding high—so much so and so quickly that rumors began to circulate that 9/11 was a plot of the Bush II circle: 2 + 2 = 4.

That is very much to be doubted; what is not to be doubted is that 9/11 was political manna from heaven and seen as being so by Bush II's advisory circle (most importantly, **Rove** and **Cheney**). Terrorism soon came to serve the political aims of the GOP's rightwing in much the same ways (with variations, of course) as the **Cold War** had for social conservatives and militarists in preceding decades.

Sitting presidents <u>always</u> gain popularity in wartime; moreover, war enables the stifling of dissent, narrowly limits the content of political opposition by the party <u>out</u> of power and is a boon to that large handful of giant companies of the **military-industrial complex**—whether the "war" is real or imagined.

The cultivated and exacerbated fears of communism, the Soviet Union, and China came to have a deleterious impact on all quarters of society—in education, entertainment, politics, industrial relations, and foreign policy and its "cold" wars in **Korea**, **Vietnam**, **Latin America** and **Europe**, with brutal political consequences in **Africa**; put together, they constituted a tidal wave of damage and destruction, from whose effects we are unlikely ever fully to recover.

It would be pleasant to believe that the post-9/11 world will <u>not</u> produce such a "tidal wave"; pleasant, but naive; both at home and abroad, steps already taken are more than ominous; and it needs reminding that they are piled atop the lasting heap of damage done in the cold war decades, from **Truman** through **JFK** and **LBJ**, **Nixon** through **Reagan** and **Bush I** and Clinton.

Societies are organic in nature; when they have undergone important changes, next steps are unavoidably conditioned by what then exists. The USA has never been a humble nation; in the past half century or so, it has become **arrogant**, and behaved accordingly, whether as regards the **environment**, the world economy, or foreign affairs.

That set of malign policies has been little contested. The associated political atmosphere in that same half century has discouraged or punished protest, has caused it to be seen not as legitimate and desirable dissent but as a form of insanity, stupidity, naivete' or, as now, <u>Treason</u>, the title of a recent and popular best seller by Ann COULTER: those she sees as traitors were once called "liberals."

Those who carried out the attack against the Twin Towers were, by any reasonable definition, "terrorists."

Such a definition would emphasize that such tactics are not expected to defeat an enemy, but to frighten or terrify, to demoralize; they are the tactics of those who seek change but whose cause— be it national, or religious, or ideological—lacks the means to go beyond what are, usually, suicidal attacks.

As such, there have been terrorists who have gained—and deserved—admiration: The **Israelis** look with admiration on those in Palestine in 1947 (and later) who attacked the then resident British power—and who were called "terrorists" by the British; it would not be inaccurate to see as "terrorists" those colonists who took singular action against the British, whether in relatively mild actions such as the "Boston Tea Party" or more bloody ones that ensued; and also those in South Africa who won out against the Afrikaaner and were jailed, and executed for their "terrorism." And so it has gone.

If the terrorists who blew up the Twin Towers are different from those just noted (among others), it does not follow that the means we now adopt in the name of defeating them are acceptable, let alone likely to succeed. The Bush administration has cleverly chosen to portray the 9/11 attackers as "hating America" and the freedom and democracy for which we stand. Hate us, they do; but their focus is not upon our freedom nor our democracy, but our dominating power over the globe.

To accept the Bush administration's premise is to generate <u>more</u> anger and attacks against us while, at the same time, imperiling what freedom and democracy we do possess.

There is little or no understanding in the USA, least of all in the White House, of why there is so much resentment against us; little or no comprehension that the ways and means we have used over the globe which we see as emblems of our superiority are seen by its victims as demolishing their cultures, their economies, their lives.

The eminent judicial scholar Ronald Dworkin, reflecting on the dangers of anti-terrorist practices and policies—not least at Guantánamo—already extant in 2003, after summarizing the precariousness of our ongoing operations went on to say what all must consider seriously; he is worth quoting at length:

> Rights would be worthless—and the idea of a right incomprehensible—unless respecting rights meant taking some risk. We can and must try to limit those risks, but some risk will remain. It may be that we would be marginally more secure if we decided to care nothing for the human rights of anyone else. That is true in domestic policy as well. We run a marginally increased risk of violent death at the hands of murderers every day by insisting on rights for accused criminals in order to keep faith with our own humanity. For the same reason we must run a marginally increased risk of terrorism as well. Of course we must sharpen our vigilance, but we must also discipline our fear. The government says that only our own safety matters. That is a counsel of shame: we are braver than that, and have more self-respect. ("Terror and the Attack on Civil Liberties. NYRB, 11 -6-03)

Lest we become our own worst enemy. (COLE)

Postscript: In our world of ugly surprises, the latest one has to do with false alarms and their opposite: phoney good news. We learned to become accustomed to the shifting up of colored "alerts" from 9/11 on, not a single one of which was followed by a terrorist attack. OK, already, we are not surprsied to see the White House trying to keep our fears high; good for what ails them. But, of a sudden, a different kind of surprise in mid-June, 2004.

Then it was revealed that "A State Department report that incorrectly showed a decline last year in terrorism worldwide (for which the White House repeatedly took credit) was a 'big mistake,' Secretary of State Colin Powell said Sunday." And he went on to say, "it's not a political judgement that said 'let's see if we can cook the books. We can't get away with that *now*.'" (italics added) ("Powell calls faulty U.S. terror report 'big mistake,'" SFC, 6-14-04)

"Now?" Say again?

Three Mile Island/Chernobyl (see nukes)

TIPS

Operation TIPS—Terrorism Information and Preventive System—was one of five component programs of the Citizen Corps, to be administered by the Department of Justice, under Attorney General **Ashcroft**. It was scheduled to go into effect in August of 2002.

A public and congressional outcry led the Bush administration first to postpone, then to abandon the program.

"Abandon" TIPS it did but, at the same time, it put into effect something in the nature of "sheep's clothing." It is useful to examine the original, for on the basis of their relatively straightforward original program "shall ye know them." Here its official description when announced by the Department of Justice:

> TIPS is meant to be a national system for reporting suspicious, and potentially terrorist-related activity. It is meant to involve millions of U.S. workers who, in the daily course of their work, are in a unique position to see potentially unusual or suspicious activity in public places... All it will take to volunteer is a telephone or access to the Internet as tips can be reported on the toll-free hotline or online. Information received will be entered into the national database and referred electronically to point of contact in each state as appropriate.... (<https//www.citizencorps.gov/tips.html>)

The workers expected to serve included truck and bus drivers, train conductors, mail carriers, utility readers, ship captains, and cabbies. In a <u>NYT</u> essay of 7-21-2), "Citizen Snoops Wanted (Call Toll-Free")" the reporter interviewed several such workers and quoted these (among other) responses:

> A deliveryman said, "he had noticed that some Arab store owners in Bay Ridge signed a different name every time they received a package from him." He also said he was struck by the increased number of satellite dishes he was delivering to Arabs after Sept. 11.
> An immigrant Russian truck driver said "A terrorist could move in front of my truck and I don't know who he is. But if I see anything, I call. It's 100 percent. I love the United States."

Another trucker from New Jersey who delivers janitorial supplies said that people in immigrant neighborhoods seem to stare at him. "They stare more than anybody else," he said before launching an unprintable tirade against Indians.

It began to fall apart when the U.S. Postal Service announced in 2002 that their postal workers will not participate. Since then it has come together again, piece by piece. See **Ashcroft**, under **Bush II**)

tobacco

History is rife with injustice, from its beginnings to the present. There is one realm of injustice which, especially in a democracy, should rankle more than others; that which permits massive crimes to go unpunished (or to get away with a slap on the wrist), while much lesser crimes draw relatively strong punishment.

Beginning only with the modern world, such unequal outcomes were common as the groundwork for modern industrial **capitalism** was being established; most notably in the treatment of workers in the mines and the "dark satanic mills" of Britain, and in the slave trade. Most revealing of all is that in neither case was the fatal damage done to the victims even <u>seen</u> as a crime; "After all...." After all <u>what</u>? After the life expectancy of the average British workers <u>fell</u> by 20 percent in 30 years? (HOBSBAWM, 1968) After of the 20 million Africans sent to "America" only 4 million survived (and then as slaves)? (WILLIAMS, E.)

That is, the very definition of what <u>constitutes</u> a crime in modern society is a function principally of property relations—as is, therefore, its definition of "justice."

Much else is very relevant here—the whys and wherefores of the 2 million + inhabitants of our prisons, the relationship between the prison sentence given to one who has been caught selling marijuana or stealing a car (etc.) as compared with a Michael Milken, who stole millions. And so on. (**crime and punishment**) Here we turn to focus on tobacco and its crimes.

Crimes? It is only with great difficulty that even the "no-smoking" people in our society can see the advertising and sale of tobacco products as a crime—even though, as will be noted soon, the results have been and always more are, death, serious injury, and disablement for <u>millions</u>. All along, in full knowledge of all this, the tobacco industry has done everything it can to <u>increase</u> its sales, most especially among the understandably most prized and most susceptible: kids. As we proceed, just to clear the terminological air, let it be said that although there has been no <u>law</u> against making and selling of tobacco products, the companies that have been doing that, <u>knowing</u> the deadly consequences of smoking, will be seen as criminals here, in the hope that one day the law might be adjusted to function in favor of human rights, not property rights.

So: Let us count (only a few of) the ways of the tobacco industry's criminality: 1. Some data on the harm done and expected. 2. The past and present behavior with respect to tobacco's dangers, at home and abroad of those who market the tobacco, and of those who do their **advertising** and, as in the case of **TV** and film, their "public relations."

1. <u>Is</u> smoking dangerous to your health? If you're one of the lucky ones, perhaps not; but "luck" by definition points to exceptions. The rule is, you'll live long enough to suffer, and then die early.

The World Health Organization estimates that the global death toll from smoking is <u>five million</u> smokers a <u>year</u>, and that over the next decade that amount will double to 10 million. In the USA itself, the Centers for Disease Control and Prevention estimate the annual toll to be 440,000. ("Cigarettes Cost U.S. $7 Per Pack Sold, Study Says," <u>NYT</u>, 4-12-02) The "$7 per pack" costs referred to by that headline are the sum of medical costs of $3.45 per pack, and the loss of job productivity from smoking.

These casualties do not include smoking's consequences as found by WHO's agency for Research on Cancer study, where "newly-identified causes of death not hitherto attributed to smoking have been identified: cancers of the stomach, liver, cervix, uterus, kidney, nasal sinus, and myeloid leukemia." ("Smoking even more deadly than believed, scientists say." <u>IHT</u>, 6-29-02)

The Centers for Disease Control has another way of pointing to just how dangerous cigs are: "The Centers expect smoking to cause more deaths than AIDS, malaria, TB, automobile crashes, homicides, and suicides <u>combined</u>." ("Death in the Ashes," <u>NYT</u>, Op-ed, 7-26-01) Gotta light? Know a funeral director?

The immediately foregoing information is new; but tobacco has been known to be deadly for a very long time: when I started smoking in the 1930s we thought it was cute when we called our cigs "coffin nails," and the term "smoker's cough" was common.

Now anyone who does not know about its dangers is either caught up in self-deception or, as the companies know, are part of the most promising market: that is, in "the developing countries."

2. Those countries are home to the billions of the world's poorest and most ignorant; the industry's behavior there goes beyond obscenity:

> Developing countries are a particular concern because the industry, facing constraints in industrialized nations, is expected to market aggressively there.... A global convention that would greatly restrict the marketing of tobacco products... is moving toward final approval despite objections by the United States and a few other tobacco-exporting nations.... /The pact/ commits all signing countries to ban all tobacco advertising and sponsorships.... American negotiators object... to provisions /re: advertising/ that they believe conflict with constitutional protections of commercial speech. (IHT, ibid.)

Philip Morris, the world's largest tobacco company (newly spun name: Altria Group) took in $19 billion in profits in the past year; it "sees the treaty as a potential catastrophe for their business." But help is on its way: The article noting that also has as its headline "Bush is working to undermine strong terms of tobacco pact." (SFC, 4-30-03) There we learn that "the United States wants signatories to be able to ignore any provision of the treaty they disagree with." After all, a treaty is just a scrap of paper, nezpa?

Then there is the industry's means of stirring up business in the poor countries and, as well, in the films that are global. In 2001, they began a program of "Enticing Third World Youth." (NYT, 8-24-2001) The subheads tell the tale: "The First Pack is Free." "Big Tobacco Is Accused of Crossing an Age Line."

> A new study of schoolchildren 13 to 15 in 68 countries, conducted by the WHO and the Centers for Disease Control and Prevention, found that about 11 percent of the children in Latin America and the Caribbean were offered free cigarettes by a tobacco company representative in 1999 and 2000...; /in Russia, 17 percent, in Jordan, 25 percent/. Sugar and honey can be found in some of the cigarettes. (emphasis added)

Nothing criminal about giving kids something sweet, is there? Especially not, if one wishes to "lure children who might otherwise shy away from the acrid taste of cigarettes." (ibid.) Good thinking!

As for films, oldies will never forget Paul Henreid lighting up two cigarettes at one time, one for Bette Davis, the other for himself. Wow. Or old Bogie, always with a smoke going, on and off screen: He died of lung cancer in his fifties; as, even younger, did the first "cowboy" on those Marlboro billboards.

Just to show how rotten we can get, theaters now presume to keep kids out from R-rated films (where they smoke a lot and other naughty things); so now the film companies—under no encouragement or rewards from the tobacco industry, none; perish the thought!—now see to it that smoking is common in movies rated G, PG, and PG 13: Two out of three tobacco shots in the Top 50 movies from April 2000-March 2001 were in such films; and much the same (or worse) holds for videos. (Full page ad in NYT, 6-10-2002), from "Smoke Free Movies.")

The tobacco companies need have nothing to fear from the amiable Bush administration; but what about those in Congress and in state legislatures? Can't be too careful; and there are always **lobbyists** eager to give help where it's needed. May we allow one example to suffice?

> The tobacco industry has spent $1.7 billion lobbying /only/ the Maryland legislature since 1997. Philip Morris paid the most for lobbying, $649,000.... (NYT, "Maryland: The Tobacco Lobby," 7-903)

Multiply that by 50 states, times 10 for NY and CA, divide by 2 for ND and ME, and pretty soon, as Sen. Dirksen once put it, "Pretty soon you're talking big money."

But surely the tobacco companies only just found out that their product was harmful, like, yesterday? That's what they've been saying for years now, adding some variation on "the butler did it." Except that we now know that they knew all along, and they are not just criminals but—I know this is hard to believe—liars. "Shredding of Smoking Data Is Ruled Deliberate," (NYT, 4-12-02)

The case in which that was the finding was in Australia, but it had to do with Brown & Williamson, a U.S. company (and a subsidiary of British American Tobacco). (emphasis added)

> The destruction began in 1985...; by 1992 the company decided this was not giving them enough protection.... The order went out that "There is an urgent need to introduce a

comprehensive and consistent records management program in all operating companies.... Records should be maintained only for so long as they are needed and no longer." A former chief executive of the industry research group has admitted to overseeing the destruction of close to one <u>million</u> pages of documents from 1990 to 1997. (<u>NYT</u>, ibid.)

But the crookedness had still other depths to plumb: 1. "Tobacco Industry Fought Drugs' Marketing." Which drugs? "The nicotine gum and skin patches that help people to quit smoking, according to a new study of tobacco industry documents—published in today's issue of the <u>Journal of the American Medical Association</u>." The article describes how Philip Morris... exerted financial leverage over the pharmaceutical divisions of giant chemical companies by threatening to cut off purchases from the companies' agricultural divisions.

> The drug companies then toned down their marketing strategies..., focusing on smokers who had already decided to quit rather than making broader appeals based on the health benefits of quitting. What otherwise might be considered merely hardball business tactics was unethical in this case because the tobacco companies knew the health risks of smoking, said Dr. Lisa Bero, a professor of clinical pharmacy and health policy..., senior author of the study.

2. We close shop with this delightful little prank of Philip Morris (oops! the nice Altria Group): "The Philip Morris Companies officially apologized yesterday for a study commissioned last month by an international affiliate that found that the Czech Republic benefited financially from the premature deaths of smokers." Say again? It seems that the study concluded that "cigarettes were not a drain on the country's budget, in part because the government saved money on health care, pensions and housing when smokers died prematurely."

Nobody's perfect. They apologized, didn't they? They did. And this is what they said:

> For one of our tobacco companies to commission that was not just a terrible mistake, it was wrong. All of us at Philip Morris, no matter where we work, are extremely sorry for this. No one benefits from the very real, serious and significant diseases caused by smoking. (<u>IHT</u>, 2-9-04)

Postscript: "Tobacco Smuggling Deal," NYT, 4-6-04: Philip Morris International, part of the Altria Group, has agreed to pay about $1 billion over 12 years to settle European Union charges that it aids cigarette smuggling that costs governments billions in tax revenue...

Naughty, naughty, Phil; gotta be more careful with your next boost for the good ole bottom line.

Who's kidding whom? I want know two things: When are we going to classify as a premeditated crime selling stuff you know kills people?

And how many of the execs and staff of these companies still smoke?

torture and abuse

The outrage and horror that spread and deepened after the revelations concerning Abu Ghraib prison in the spring of 2004 were fully justified, as was the revulsion at Nicholas Berg's beheading and, earlier, the mutliation of U.S. personnel at Fallujah.

Also outrageous, horrifying and repellent, however, were the innumerable responses from members of Congress and the White House, epitomized in Bush's "This is not the America I know." Ignorance for most is due to lack of opportunity; in Bush's case, as with so many others in the USA, such ignorance is a consequence of **arrogance**, indifference, disdain and even contempt for the plight of others. However, that the widespread ignorance of the realities of our past and present is "understandable" does not make it less deplorable or less tragic—or less dangerous— in its consequences. For all too long, these traits of Uncle Sam have provided the basis for our virtual addiction to the **double standard** both at home and abroad.

Such attitudes and behavior virtually scream out for comment and condemnation. What follows here is but a truncated noting of examples from the distant and recent past (with references to fuller entries such as **slavery**; and see ZINN/2000/for much else).

1. Torture and abuse began when we as a society began, with our arrival on this continent and our murderous treatment first of "**Indians**" and then of **slaves**. The reference here is not to the major crimes of stealing the native tribes' lands and "**Indian removal**" nor to slavery itself, but only to the accompanying and enduring system-

atic torture, abuse and murder, including its rampant, institutionalized, and large-scale rape of girls and women.

What was born in the 17th century in what became the first 13 states had by the 18th century evolved into a raging epidemic that would go on for two centuries. Today's mistreatment of "**Indians**" and "African-Americans" (among others) is considerably more subdued and subtler than earlier; the harm done to its victims measured more in sociopsychological and economic than in raw physical terms.

2. Then there is lynching. It began well before it was so named, most famously with the "witches of Salem" (and other women and places). During **slavery**, the murder of slaves was restrained; after all they were a vital form of private property; most of the lynching was, so to speak, indiscriminate. But after the infamous **Compromise of 1877** lynching became wildly common against free blacks. Both before and after that, lynching was also all too common for others than blacks—and continued to be applied in the truly "Wild West." It was still going on against the Chinese in "the city that cares"—my home town of San Francisco—in the 20th century.

Lynching usually meant being hanged; it almost always meant torture before and during the murder. Long ago? In some sense, yes; except that between 1890 and 1940 there were several <u>thousand</u> lynchings, and some after that—for example, one that is not so classified the execution of **Ethel and Julius Rosenberg** (which see), and some that are: the 1955 lynching of 14-year-old Emmett Till (accused of whistling at a girl), and the recent dragging to death behind a car of a gay man.

It needs adding that the photos from Abu Ghraib showing laughing abusers are as nothing whe set against the numberless photos of lynchings where crowds are laughing, cherring, and jumping with joy as black men are hanging and writhing.

3. Then there is the matter of **prisons** and the **death penalty**—overlapping but separable for present purposes. It is striking and shocking that the USA leads the world in its rate of imprisonment and the use of the death penalty, jailing "people at eight times the rate of France and six times the rate of Canada," (<u>NYT</u> editorial 5-17-04), as it does in the **death penalty**.

Prisons everywhere and always have provided conditions making torture and abuse easy and common—by prison guards and, with the guards' acquiescence, by prisoners against other prisoners.

Violence is a normal part of life, whether in men's or women's prisons, and rape is pervasive, systematic, and continuous—to the point where the victims are driven insane or are murdered. Rape is not confined to but is especially practiced mostly against young men and women by their fellow prisoners and by prison guards. It is joined by other and common forms of mistreatment that fall under the headings of abuse and even torture—whether the prisons are in the East, West, North or South.

The foregoing says nothing about whether those who are imprisoned have been justly tried or sentenced. (see **crime and punishment**). But something must be said about those who suffer the **death penalty**. Among the leading countries in the world, only three use that penalty: ourselves, Russia and China. (The European Union will not admit membership to such a nation). In all cases, it is known (through DNA tests, generally) that a significant percentage of those sentenced and executed have been innocent of the charges against them. In the USA this crime itself has been most common because of **racism**—long as applied to blacks, but also and increasingly to other minorities; especially, in the Southwest, to Latinos. (Bush's adopted state of Texas leads the country in executions: one of fifty states, it presently has more than 20 percent of all those on death row.)

So what's all the fuss about Abu Graib, Mr. and Mrs. America? Doesn't look good, that's what. And anyway, it was only a few guys and gals screwing around, representing themselves not "America!"

Most people may or may not have believed that. And many really <u>wanted</u> to believe it. The news in June—and who knows what's next?—took care of that. <u>NYT</u>, 6-8-04: "Lawyers Decided Bans on Torture Didn't Bind Bush: A Pentagon Memo in 2003...Cited the President's 'Inherent' Authority in a Military Campaign." The headline is not as bad as the story under it. Here only a few excerpts, mostly referring to a March 3, 2003 legal memorandum:

> ...Bush was not bound by either an international treaty or by a federal anti-torture law because he had the authority as commender-in-chief to approve any technique needed to protect the nation's security.
>
> The memo showed that not only lawyers from the Defense and Justice Departments and the White House approved of this policy but also the counsel to Vice President Cheney was involved in the negotiations. The State Department lawyer, William H. Taft IV, dissented, warning that such a position

would weaken the protections of the Geneva Conventions for American troops.

The March 6 document provides tightly constructed definitions of torture. For example, if an interrogator "knows that severe pain will result from his actions, if causing such harm is not his objective, he lacks the requisite specific intent even though the defendant/ the torturer/ did not act in good faith...; instead he is guilty of torture only if he acts with the express purpose of inflicting severe pain or suffering on a person within his control." (My emphasis; and one supposes that in order to know if the torturer was thus breaking the law, we simply ask him: Mr. T., were you trying to hurt that captive, which is illegal, or were you just trying to protect our nation's security?)

As for who knew what and when did he/ she/ they know it: As indicated above, that memo was sent to the Defense and Justice Departments and the White House. After the news surfaced, **Ashcroft**, in an appearance before a Senate committee, "refused to provide several of the memorandums, saying that they amounted to confidential legal advice given to the president and did not have to be shared with Congress." (NYT, 6-9-04: "Ashcroft Says the White House Never Authorized Tactics Breaking Laws on Torture.")

Liar! Liar! Hair's on Fire!

transnational corporations (TNCs) (see nig business)

Truman, Harry S.

Not all of our presidents have been seen as "American as apple pie," but Harry Truman is surely one of them. Those so designated have had certain shared characteristics (if also important differences): "country boys" rather than "city slickers," brash and plain-spoken, "one of the boys"—a phrase with several linked connotations: ethical "flexibility," not an "egghead," and (not least) "quick on the draw."

There have been more than a few much-loved presidents who were not reminiscent of apple pie, some of them—not least **FDR**—one would like to see in the White House again. But Truman was almost perfect for the role: He was chosen for the job precisely because he fitted the above-noted characteristics to a "T."

It is necessary to add here that the Democratic Party until the 1960s was riven into two (if overlapping) factions: the relatively

New Deal-ish North and the unrepentant "Solid South." (Now Solid GOP)

What was "solid" about the Democratic Party in the South was a) that it couldn't be beaten, b) that it was a still lively residue of the **Compromise of 1877**, which allowed the white South to continue to treat ex-slaves and their descendants as though they were <u>not</u> "ex": they had no right to <u>register</u> to vote, let alone to vote; usually no access to <u>any</u> education or <u>any</u> health care; nothing.

Truman's state, Missouri, was functionally part of the Solid South; although formally it had been with the Union during the Civil War, in outlook it was not; its legislature had sought to secede. The "St. Louis Blues" resonates with that Missouri reality.

It was out of that context that Harry S. Truman had arisen—or was plucked up—to become FDR's running mate in the 1944 election. It was known then that FDR would die within a year; his V.P. would become President. The powers-that-were in the Democratic Party wanted anyone except FDR's then V.P. Henry Wallace to be the new V.P. Although a U.S. Senator when selected by the inside claque, Truman was virtually unknown beyond Missouri. Henry Wallace was very well known by 1944, and widely admired for good reasons; good for us, wrong reasons in the judgment of the Democratic bigwigs.

Wallace was Secretary of Agriculture, 1933-40, and was another kind of "apple pie American," except that his "Americanism" was more Jeffersonian than Jacksonian: He was a successful farmer and editor of a farm journal, and although not a city slicker, neither was he one of the boys: he was an <u>anti</u>-militarist and soft-spoken. During World War II, as V.P., he had emphasized that the USA should seek remedies for the world's poor and organize for a peaceful "one world." He was decent, well informed, and compassionate; in short, dangerous.

Truman was the beneficiary. The only other reasonable contender for V.P. was James Byrnes; however, although Wallace was too "radical" for the Solid South, Byrnes was too conservative for the relatively liberal North.

The "compromise of 1944" was Harry. His political career had begun when he was chosen by the notorious Pendergast machine of St. Louis to become Missouri's senator in 1934. Before that he had served as an artillery officer in World War I, had run a haberdashery, and had been a local judge. Just right.

Truman became President when FDR died, in April of 1945. Neither before nor after that had he been either entirely admirable or entirely despicable; but he got off to a very bad start: it was he who authorized the atomic bombing of **Hiroshima/Nagasaki**. Consonant with that quite unwarranted massive destruction, "the first shot of the **Cold War**," he went along all too easily with **McCarthyism**—until its weapons were turned upon his own administration. (ALPEROVITZ; FREELAND)

It was Truman who stood approvingly beside Winston Churchill in Fulton, Missouri in March of 1946, less than a year after FDR's death, as Churchill pronounced that

> the United States stands at this time at the pinnacle of world power.... Opportunity is here now, clear and shining, for both our countries.... America should not ignore or fritter it away..., for it faces a peril to Christian civilization.... From the Baltic to the Adriatic, an iron curtain has descended across the European continent. (quoted in FREELAND)

All that, at the very moment when the **USSR** didn't have enough iron to repair its rail system or food to feed its people, let alone to represent a "peril to 'Christian civilization.'" Good ole boy that he was, already as 1947 ended 1) Truman's administration had announced the "Truman (Greece-Turkey) Doctrine," 2) the War Department had been renamed the Defense Department, 3) the National Security Administration had been created, and 4) foundations had been laid for the Marshall Plan/North Atlantic Treaty Organization (to be member of one was to be a member of both).

What issued from the White House in subsequent administrations—whether of **JFK**, **LBJ**, **Nixon**, **Reagan**, **Clinton**, or **Bushes I and II**—had their organic beginnings in the policies initiated in Truman's two administrations.

That is the good ole boy side of Truman (or part of it). He had a better side: 1) In 1947, Harry unsuccessfully vetoed the anti-**union** Taft-Hartley Act, passed by a conservative-controlled Congress in the name of anti-Communism—a major enabling step in the ensuing processes that have critically reduced membership in trade unions and their strength. 2) In 1950, Truman proposed a national health care system (voted down);

3) Later he took the first, albeit timid, steps aimed at reducing **racism**. And 4) as noted above, he did stand against McCarthy him-

self belatedly, while also going along with a vigorous anti-Communism, thereby feeding McCarthyism.

In sum, domestically, with his "Fair Deal," he was a "sort-of" New Dealer. But it was his "Give 'em Hell Harry" foreign policies that opened the doors to the Korean war and its continuing horrors; and before that (see **Vietnam**) it was he, in <u>1945</u> who facilitated the French wish to re-occupy Vietnam by sending ships with newly-released British and Dutch prisoners to "hold the fort" for the French until they could get there (transported from Europe in 13 U.S. merchant ships).

I was no fan of Harry; but when compared with **Bush II**, he looks pretty good. However, if that's not damning with faint praise, I don't know what would be.

TV

<u>Introduction</u>. If the world was going to come to end "apocalyptically," as foreseen in the Bible, there was still a long way to go as the 19th century ended—despite the valiant efforts of the Four Horsemen: famine, pestilence, destruction, and death.

The Big Four needed <u>help</u>; then—as though by a miracle!—in the blink of an eye, the new century provided us with the ability to destroy each other and the rest of life on earth—easily.

The first leap was in the 1890s, with the invention of **cars**, and its fabulous contribution to global warming; soon after, in the 1920s, came the invention of TV which, when the mass market for it came into being after World War II, was invaluable in assisting us to distance ourselves from our humanity and to anaesthetize us to the irrationality and dangers of our personal and social lives. But, vital though they were, cars and TV were insufficient to provide the nails for our coffin; then, who says the age of miracles is over?—voila'! <u>another</u> miracle!—the best and brightest invented **nukes**. Hip, Hip, Hooray!

Taken separately, no one of that lethal gang could turn the trick; it is the ways in which they, like the four horsemen, mutually support and transform each other that have given Apocalypse its needed boost. If current tendencies persist—and they are in fact accelerating—the Big Apoc could have its day in this very century. Hey! If you're not already too old, it could even come in your lifetime.

In a society very different from ours any one of the three might be safely absorbed; not in this one. A sane society would produce goods and services to meet human and social **needs** and possibilities while, at the same time, seeking the means to lessen rather than exacerbate to exploit racial, ethnic, and national rivalries. **Cars** and **nukes** have been discussed at length elsewhere; here we consider the nature and behavior of TV and the ways in which it has contributed to the social and military afflictions of our era.

Amusing Ourselves to Death. That is the title of the probing book by Neil POSTMAN. **Advertising** has always been central to the very existence of the **media**; TV is now the most powerful of the media, and the principal source of advertising's income; and always more so.

Among the media, TV has had the most powerful impact on thoughts and feelings and behavior. It does so by what is being screened—a sports event, a film, MTV, a talk/game show, or a political ad; how the "what" is portrayed; and the intent of what is being seen and heard. From its very beginnings, it became first a part of and then the dominant member of "the consciousness industry." (ENSENZBERGER).

When TV became common in households in the 1950s more often than not its programs were shallow, boring, sentimental and unrealistic with a minority a bit better: news and sports programs were generally straightforward and less inundated with ads than now, and there were always some reasonably worthy dramas to be seen (even when, as on **GE** Theater, introduced by **Reagan**).

Recently, in contrast—MTV well in the lead—what is virtually unavoidable is a mixture of prurience and puritanism, raw sex and violence, real sentimentality and insipidity, with the ads often equaling the "show" or, increasingly, with "infomercials" integrated with what has become "infotainment." (BARBER, BANKS)

Who watches all this, and for how much time? The group that grows most rapidly and ominously and that already watches most are the young. In a 1999 survey conducted by the Kaiser HMO of 3,000 youngsters ages 1 through 18 in the USA, these were the findings (and you may be sure the numbers are even higher today):

> Children on average spend 5 hours, 29 minutes every day, seven days a week, with media for recreation. /For those/ 8 years and older, the total is significantly higher, 6 hours 43 minutes a day, more than the equivalent of an adult work week. Much of

that time is spent alone. (WP, "The Media Generation: Multitask Children....," 11-19=99)

Plus, it's even worse for the youngest children; a new study of 2,500 children aged 1-3 (reported in the journal *Pediatrics*, April, 2004) found that

> They watched an average of 2.2 hours a day at age 1 and 3.6 hours a day at age 3; some watched 12 hours or more...increasing the risk of attention deficit disorder by age 7. (NYT, 4-6-04, "Children's TV Habits are Linked to Attention Issues.")

And elsewhere?

> A 1996 survey of teenagers in TV-owning households in 41 nations finds that they watch an average six hours of TV per day, and nowhere in the survey is the figure under five house. (HERMAN/MCCHESNEY)

"Watching" is the key word. It is in the very nature of TV (and much of "online") that its audience is a passive consumer of its images. Jerry MANDER, one-time star of the TV/advertising complex, has explained that among the many dangers of TV is that its technology requires its programs to hold each scene to a desired maximum length of 2-3 seconds, in order to prevent "watcher boredom." (MANDER /1978/)

The associated short attention span becomes habitual—and not only for TV—as watchers become "fast consumers" of what is seen and heard; and the content that best fits that technology consists of melodramatic versions of life; its always broad limits continue to expand to the point of delirium, with predictable effects.

Reading, whether of philosophy or thrillers, can also be merely a form of consumption, just as TV watchers can be reflective of what they are seeing. But the probabilities lie elsewhere. Writing in 1985, POSTMAN observed:

> We are now well into the second /in 2004 the third/ generation of children for whom television has been their first and most accessible teacher and, for many, their most reliable companion and friend.... There is no audience so young that it is barred from television. There is no poverty so abject that it must forego television. There is no education so exalted that it is not modified by television. And most important of all, there is no subject of public interest—politics, news, education, religion,

science, sports—that does not find its way to television. Which means that all public understanding of these subjects is shaped by the biases of television.

For better and for worse, we are an emotional species. The emotions aroused in us by "infotainment" and "infomercials" are quite the opposite of what may be seen as the best in us: our possibilities for compassion, for reflection and reason, for enlightened self-interest.

Whatever positive marvels science may have brought, techniques of persuasion have successfully acted to turn our lives as consumers to purposes that qualify as harmful, often to the point of social and self-destruction—as with cars and nuclear energy, as with TV itself, as with that large and growing bundle of goods and services the sale of which is useful to the sellers, but not to the buyers; as noted more than once in this work, "we have been taught to want what we don't need, and not to want what we do." (BARAN/1969/

The Iceman Cometh. Almost a century ago (in 1907), Albert Einstein—simultaneously a humanist and pacifist who would, however, provide the theoretical basis for **nukes**—glimpsed what the past had already revealed and what was lying in wait over time:

> Our entire much-praised technological progress, and civilization generally, could be compared to an axe in the hand of a pathological criminal. (FOLSING)

Which takes us back to the Three Henchmen of the Apocalyptic Four. Of the three, both cars and TV could serve a useful and harmless set of functions in a reasonable society; they have not. In the past half-century we have gone in the opposite direction, accelerating and whooping it up all the way.

What we have become is the outcome of two centuries or so of the mutually transforming relationships of **capitalism**, industrial **technology**, **imperialism**, and **nationalism**, and their offspring modern **militarism**. As the 19th century ended, their combined effects had already been disastrous for most of the people in the world. That world badly needed to search for and find the ways and means to bring about peace and comfort for all; instead it soon produced two world wars, accompanied by destruction, convulsions, and chaos.

That done, it nevertheless was possible for a new path to be taken after World War II. During the war itself numerous arguments for such a world were being made, most helpfully from the White

House of FDR and Henry Wallace. (see FREELAND; **Truman**).

Instead, the main social tendencies promoted by the USA became the **Cold War** and **consumerism**. Both required substantial support by the **media**, most especially by TV. Sitting in the hot center of the consumerist stage were **cars**: relentless dramatic advertising on TV made very little of their use as transportation and very much of their function as image—"You are what you drive; drive what you want others to think you are."

We mortals can be good and awful, sane and mad, peaceful and violent; TV has had several triumphs which, taken together, have made us more awful than good, more nutty than sane, more violent than peaceful; in succeeding at that, TV has made us ever more likely to become oblivious to and acquiescent in decisions that might well culminate in blowing up the world. (RAMPTON/STAUBER, 2004)

Think of it this way: at least you won't have to worry about your credit card balances anymore.

unemployment/unemployment compensation

Economics began with Adam Smith in the 18th century, and the systematic collection of economic data had begun to become common in Britain by the 1860s. However, it is revealing that the economic data put together in the USA did not cover either unemployment or **poverty** until much later: for the jobless, during the depression of the 1930s; for poverty, not until the 1960s (as **LBJ** sought to create his "Great Society").

Earlier, whatever information was available was in the form of estimates, such as those having joblessness fluctuate between 5 and 13 percent in the "prosperity decade" of the USA. (SOULE)

Now a closer look at the measurement process; after that, what is and is not done in the way of assistance to the jobless; then, what seems to be forthcoming for jobs and related governmental policy.

Through a glass darkly. Inadequate though earlier estimates may have been, they may have been more telling than the "official" measures adopted in the 1930s, and which last to this day. Why? Because the official unemployment rate is not just a number; it is a number which, when announced, has economic and political reverberations. Thus <u>how</u> it is measured is less a matter of statistics and more one of politics and power.

How is it measured? The starting-point is the definition of "the labor force": Only those who are in the labor force are seen as either employed or unemployed. And one is in the labor force if and only if one has a full- or part-time paid job, or is known to be seeking one.

The resulting numbers of official jobless are determined by "sampling." Trying to find out anything for a large population—polls are another example—usually requires sampling; but who designs the "sample" and why is the question.

So, let's get on with it. Say you lost your job five years ago, sought a job for two years, became discouraged and stopped looking. You are in "the hard-core jobless," but you are not unemployed. Scoot! Or, you have a part-time job, so you are statistically employed even though a) you lost a full-time job and need another one to keep you and your family going—preferably at the previous wage and skill level—and/or you are only working one hour a week. Sound ridiculous to you? You're right.

Those definitions are either made in Congress or approved by Congress—a group of people (a majority of whom are lawyers) few if any of whom have had direct experience with being "hard-core" or involuntary part-time. The USA is virtually unique in this way of measuring joblessness and, as will be seen, in related matters.

In late 1993, as the leading economies still struggled with recession or its strong traces, the American Express Company had its London Branch look more closely into the measurement matter. The company, after all, is one of the big lenders in the world and, unsurprisingly, prefers to have debts repaid rather than not, as happens with a good portion of the unemployed. So they commissioned a study. They discovered that if the German means of measurement were applied the unemployment rate rose as follows for the countries noted: France, from 12.0 to 13.7 percent; UK, from 9.8 to 12.3 percent; Japan (which follows our way), from 2.7 to 9.6 percent; USA, from 6.4 to 9.3 percent. (IHT, "Unemployment measures misleading," 1-25-94)

So: Take the two leading economies in the worked, Japan and the USA. Japan now sees its unemployment as close to 6 percent; should that be tripled? The USA (as this is written) has 6.4 percent; should that go to 9.3 percent? No, it should be higher, for both long-term unemployment and forced part-time job are considerably higher now than in the early 90s (see below). A reasonable guess would be in the area of 11-12 percent.

Before going on, and in support of the foregoing "guess," it is relevant to report that in 2003, the Bureau of Labor Statistics (BLS) of the Department of Labor for the first time began to report publicly their best guess as to the relevant numbers—in a footnote, with no further discussion or announcement. When their reasoning was publicized, the "unofficial/official rate was over 10 percent. (NYT, "Changes...." 1-13-04)

Why have the hard-core and forced part-timers increased substantially? Because what is good for the TNCs and those at the top levels of the income distribution is, for the same reasons, bad for the people who used to work for them here. The two major factors are 1) that because of new production techniques, many jobs have been permanently lost; 2) statistically greater are the jobs now in far-off and much cheaper places—most importantly, but by no means only, in Mexico, China, and India, They are jobs producing **cars**, textiles, computers, steel, shoes..., anything in industry, and lots in the once best-paid services—all of that facilitated by **downsizing and outsourcing, NAFTA, globalization**, and the **free market**.

Between 1999 and 2001, 9.9 million lost their jobs; those "permanent layoffs, due to downsizing, no longer dip as sharply in the expansion period between recessions." (NYT, "Data Show Growing Trend Toward Permanent Layoffs," 8-22-01).

Losing a job is really hard; but it's not just a matter of money. Say you have worked hard and well for 15-25 years as a skilled steelworker or on an auto assembly line. You will have had "middle class" wages, bought a house and a car, maybe sent your kids to college, received health care and pension benefits, enjoyed a certain camaraderie with your fellow workers—had some dignity.

What's it like to have to accept, finally, that you are never going back to that, you are now one of that large group of badly-paid (or jobless) bunch of people you once scorned? Maybe you've lost your house; maybe your family is giving you a hard time. What's that like? (Especially, if as is probable, you are sitting on a mountain of debt?) You quietly become demoralized. Meanwhile the White House acts:

> Item: "The Bush Administration, under fire for its handling of the economy, has quietly killed off /the BLS/ Labor Department Program that tracked mass layoffs by U.S. companies." (SFC, 1-3-03)

Good thinking, Prez.

Brother, Can You Spare a Dime? That was another song of the depression, when the official rate was at 25 percent in 1933 (and still at 10 percent in 1941). It was really tough to be unemployed in those years, until the late 1930s, when the "second New Deal" kicked in with its Fair Labor Standards Act (and related socioeconomic policies: see **FDR**).

Only then, along with the 8-hour day and the minimum wage, did unemployment compensation begin in the USA: nothing grandiose, indeed nothing close to allowing one to pay the bills. Out of work, you received only 50 percent of your wage, and that for only 26 weeks—with, once in a while, an extension of 13 weeks if granted by a "compassionate" Congress—which does not apply to the Congress of 2003-2004; they've decided <u>not</u> to extend.

Then your second year of no job comes at you, You've already lost your house because you couldn't make the mortgage payment. Doing so, if you knew about it (and most in the USA definitely do not) you might make a little less fun of the French: They pay 75 percent of your wage, for <u>60 months</u>. (<u>IHT</u>, "Walking papers: How to make the best of losing a job," 3-17/18-02)

Your former employer is less unhappy than you; he not only doesn't have to pay you, his remaining workforce—with a weak or <u>no</u> **union**—is a wee bit more careful of being uppity, and not at all likely to complain about working overtime without pay: Already in the late 90s, the average worker in the USA—facing downsizing, etc.—was working 260 hours more a year without pay than earlier. (<u>BW</u>, 12-6-99)

Bush II, whose memory is poor about all that "compassionate" stuff, is trying to amend the Fair Labor Standards Act to be "more flexible" regarding overtime pay. With the GOP dominated-Congress, it's just a matter of time. Presently, about 80 percent of workers are in jobs qualifying them for time-and-a-half overtime pay. The legislation proposed would "make it easier for employers to exempt many of those workers from overtime protection by classifying them as administrative, professional, or executive personnel." (<u>NYT</u>, "Picking Workers' Pockets," Op-ed, 7-11-93) "Look, Ma: I'm an Executive!"

The foregoing is more threatening than the mere numbers suggest. The structure of employment in the past 10-15 years has changed dramatically, both as regards who seeks jobs and the structure of those jobs. With the advent of **consumerism** and its concomitant rise not just in spending but, necessarily, in borrowing, more than half of all married women with children now work or seek work; they have to. At the same time, the best jobs have diminished severely, so the average income of the full-working family has increased less than it would have 25 years ago—as **profits** have gone up nicely:

> While profits have shot up as a percentage of national income, reaching their highest level since the mid-1950s, labor's share is shrinking. /Meanwhile/ the average hourly wage for office or factory jobs below the rank of supervisor or manager is up only 3 cents since July /2003/...; "in the 40 years of /our/ hourly wage survey, wage growth has never been this slow,"...reports the economist at the Center for Economic and Policy Research." (NYT, "A Recovery for Profits, but Not for Workers," 12-21-03)

In 2001—before 9/11—the economy had begun to slow, and, despite repeated public statements that (in effect) "prosperity is just around the corner" and the inability to call a recession by its name, the process we are now in is called a "jobless recovery": something new.

As recently as 1990, economists generally agreed that for the economy to be "healthy," it had to be growing at 3 to 3.5 percent. We have been at 1 to 2 percent for three years as this is written. It is worth adding that in the 1980s, the fabled Alan Greenspan declared that the "natural" rate of unemployment was 6 percent, meaning: no inflation, and lots of "flexibility" (no upward wage pressures) in the economy. Paradise for business—unless you remember that business has to sell its goods and services to people with jobs.

For an idea of what's going on in the job market as the new century proceeds, note these successive headlines from the NYT: "Long-Term Jobless Rose by 50 Percent Over Last Year" (9-9-02); "Jobless Claims for Benefits Reach a High Set in 1983" (7-11-03); "Teenagers Facing Hard Competition for Summer Jobs; Worst Market in Years; Economy and Older Workers Reduce the Opportunities for Youth Employment" (7-12-03) Get it? Several articles of in-depth analysis on these matters may be found in the April, 2004 "Jobs Crunch" issue of *Monthly Review*.

What's to be done? Certainly not what the Bush people are doing—which is, cutting **taxes**, but mostly of the very rich: 80 percent of families will receive less than a $100 tax cut; the rich, upwards of

$12,000. Enriching the rich is supposed stimulate the economy and thus create jobs. The high probability is very much the opposite.

As discussed under **taxes** and **deficits and surpluses**, the best way to create jobs is not by cutting taxes but by increasing governmental social expenditures: it is generally agreed that each added $1 of governmental expenditures produces $3 times that in ultimate expenditures and accompanying increases in jobs—while at the same time improving the socioeconomy (via education, transport, health care, public services, etc.). (LINDERT)

Tax cuts going principally to the rich—the top 10 percent get more than half of the tax rebates—are unlikely to increase their already extraordinary consumption and will go instead into savings and speculation—while, at the same time, jobs continue to be lost and **unions** weakened in consequence of "successful" globalization.

The number of officially unemployed is now 9 million and rising; the more realistic number would probably come close to double that. Let's say it's "only" 15 million or so now, with another 15 million rightfully scared out of their wits. If you are one of those, or even if not, this would seem to be a time for raising hell—some of which is best raised where you work: see the next entry.

unions

As a **capitalist** society, indeed the capitalist society, the history of the USA has of course been marked by class conflict between capital and labor; but awareness of that struggle more often than not has been from the top down rather than from the bottom up. Gabriel KOLKO points to part of the explanation:

> American society /has had/ a class structure without decisive class conflict; a society that has had conflict limited to smaller issues that were not crucial to the existing order, and on which the price of satisfying opposition was relatively modest from the viewpoint of continuation of the social system. In brief, a static class structure, serving class ends might be frozen into American society even if the interest and values served were those of a ruling class. (KOLKO, 1970)

A closely related reason why U.S. workers have been less class conscious than workers elsewhere is that they have been so swayed by **racism**; have been "paid the wages of whiteness." (ROEDIGER)

Those "wages" are the "inner reward" from acting on attitudes of pre-sumed superiority, accompanied by cultivated fear and hatred; they have been pervasive throughout our history. The result has been a U.S. socialization process which, in poisoning the relationships among workers, has enhanced the strength of their employers. Of course.

From their beginnings, almost all U.S. unions have been liberal/centrist rather than liberal/radical, seeking to do better within the capitalist system; as such their efforts came to be called "business unionism" by themselves, and without irony.

There have been some exceptions over time for some unions, and a few unions that have been radical from beginning to end, most notably the "Wobblies" (the (Industrial Workers of the World, IWW). The Wobblies first became significant about a century ago; their radicalism brought down the wrath of all parties: conservative unionists (who engaged in lynchings), employers (with spies and violence), and the government (with imprisonment). (DUBOVSKY; KORNBLUH; HUBERMAN /1937/)

Whatever unions' aims and nature, business opposition to unionism has never faltered. Almost universally, businesses have brought every tactic to bear to keep workers from achieving any kind or degree of power: the law, raw economic power (firing organizers), subversion through infiltration, and violence (up to and including murder). (see DU BOFF; HUBERMAN /1937/; ZINN /2000/)

The harsh depression of the 1930s altered that picture somewhat, at least for a few decades. There were many bitter struggles as workers sought to organize (or re-organize) unions in industry (steel, cars, electrical products, etc.). Most vividly was this so on the waterfront in San Francisco in 1934. The dockworkers produced the nation's first and only—and bloody—general strike. (On the East Coast, a related but different and failing struggle was going on within the corrupted union, vividly portrayed in the epic film "On the Waterfront.")

Those and related efforts were instrumental in pushing the USA into a period that constrained the "rugged individualism" of U.S. capitalism, replacing it—in part—with the liberalism of the "second" New Deal in 1935 and subsequently. (see **FDR)**

However, from the 1970s on unions began the continuing descent toward weakness, as business directly benefited from anti-union policies such as those of **Reagan** in the 1980s. Those policies reflected the growing economic and political power of **big business:**

In the 1950s, 35 percent of workers were in unions; now it is less then 13 percent (and only about 8 percent for the private sector). That decline was made easier for business by the erosion of workers' solidarity and tenacity, also facilitated by the associated rise of **consumerism**, and the politics of the **Cold War**

The latter, in bringing higher employment levels and higher wages to organized workers reduced their militancy while encouraging **corruption** to take hold in union politics. The first steps in that set of processes began but did not end with the Taft-Hartley Act of 1947 and the **McCarthyism** that soon followed. In the next decade or so, it became easier for companies to resist and even to break increasingly demoralized unions—aided no little by **Reagan,** when he was head of the Screen Actors' Guild, and by others—including Walt Disney—who took it upon themselves to "name names." (NAVASKY)

In the larger continuity from the late 19th century until World War II, the AFL was the bedrock of U.S. unionism, assured when the onset of World War I and the subsequent **Red scare** laid waste the one-third of union members who were also members of the American Socialist Party (led by Eugene Debs). (GINGER) It was in those years that the Socialists and the IWW combined to bring out a glorious moment for organized labor, never yet repeated: They opposed U.S. involvement in the war. For their efforts, their leader (Eugene Debs) and, as well, IWW members were imprisoned, and some—like Emma Goldman—deported. (ZINN, 2002)

Throughout, the AFL's position and strategy has always been centrist, and explicitly anti-radical. It faced its greatest threat in the 1930s, not from business but from the newly formed Congress of Industrial Organizations (CIO). The CIO had to be relatively radical as it sought to organize workers in mass-production industries such as steel, autos, and rubber. Any union members in those industries had belonged to AFL craft unions (electricians, carpenters, etc.), leaving most workers out in the unorganized cold.

In this most capitalist of all nations, bereft of non-modern traditions, the institution of private property has had—still has—an almost sacred aura, especially in the courts. Unions had been "legal" since the late 19th century; but it was a toothless legality: unions could exist, but the courts ruled that they could not strike, for to do so constituted an invasion of the rights of private property. That was not changed until the Wagner Act of 1935.

That legislation made it easier—if still difficult—for workers to strike and thus to achieve their aims, and it also set up a National Labor Relations Board to make it more difficult for employers to interfere with efforts to organize. "Easier" for workers; "more difficult" for employers? Like all laws this was written on paper; how and even whether it would be enforced changed as the structure of power changed.

By the 1970s the changes that bring us to the present had taken hold. Although the decline in union density had begun as early as the 1950s, with the election and administration of Reagan changes for the worse became full-throated: unions being busted, workers intimidated to <u>not</u> work with, <u>not</u> to try to organize a union, elections for/against unions easier to contaminate for the benefit of business. We were on our way back to the 1920s.

In the 1980s, as Reagan's popularity rose, the popularity of unions fell; although there shouldn't have been a causal connection, there was: it was to be found in the political air of the 1980s.

It was an air polluted by an encouraged recurrence of racism and the slandering of the poor, and all the more so as both the tone and the content of Reaganism, in touting the virtues of "private enterprise," was at the same time demeaning the value of cooperative social efforts. (see WILLS, 1988)

By the 1990s, given all that <u>and</u> the worker-destabilizing effects of **downsizing..../globalization**, the percentage of unionized workers in the private sector had dropped from its (not very) high of the 1950s to its dangerousl low of today. In a probing discussion by Kate BRONFENBRENNER, we learn that

> Between 1997 and 2001, there was a drop in employment in the manufacturing sector of 9.2 percent.../and/ an increase in the service sector of 10.9 percent.... The biggest factor in decline in union density is the loss of union <u>jobs</u>. Union jobs are contracted out or moved out of the country.... There is a whole economy that is dependent upon /union jobs/. When the manufacturing plant in a community leaves, the retail stores also tend to leave, the restaurants close down, the housing market falls out..., pushing wages down for all workers, which then once again lowers the demand for all products, and the economy starts to spiral downward. (BRONFENBRENNER)

The decline just noted between 1997-2001 was on top of what

had been going on for 20 years or so; it must be seen as a vital factor in the recession that began in 2001. While the "new economy" was having its praises sung to the skies, the structure of the labor force was steadily being re-arranged toward a diminution of the skilled and a rising percentage of unskilled and semi-skilled workers—with lower wages, higher hours, and less or no benefits.

Nor did it help that many unions, as with the political power structure, had by the 1990s come to be ruled by and for their "leaders"—well-symbolized by the AFL-CIO conventions, where the union leaders could be seen parading in their business suits and puffing their cigars—with seldom heard an encouraging word for the average worker. (see Jim Smith, "The Corporatization of Unions," in Z Magazine, 7/8, 2002)

The decline in trade union membership in the private sector began to be countered in some degree with its growth in the public sector from the 1960s on; more recently, the noteworthy growth of the service workers' union (SEIU) and, it may be added, its spirit, have been setting an example for others in the private sector.

Better than nothing, but much less than what is needed, given the existing weakness of organized labor, in the face of the policies of the **Bush II** administration. Their most recent attempt—in the name of "homeland security"—has been to "re-classify" hundreds of thousands of public workers who now receive overtime; re-classify them how? So they won't be unionized and won't get overtime, silly.

In 1848, Marx and Engels ended their Manifesto with the soaring words "Working Men of All Countries Unite!" (Make that "Working Men, Women and Children of All Countries Unite!") It was necessary way back then, but virtually impossible. It is even more necessary today, still extraordinarily difficult, but not as impossible. **Globalization** is doing its damages on every continent, to the best-off as well as the worst-off workers. Some workers in some countries have already come to see that all workers—indeed all the world's people—are in the same boat. If today's globalization has any positive side to it at all, that's it.

Joe Hill, an organizer for the IWW, was executed by a federal firing squad in 1915; just before that, he wrote a note to his comrade Big Bill Haywood (of the mine workers' union). This is what it said: "Don't waste any time mourning: organize!"

Joe was speaking to us, too; today.

Unocal (see Asia: Afghanistan)

U.S. Senate and House/Supreme Court

As two-thirds of our much-lauded "checks and balance" system, Congress and the Court are two of the most cherished of the institutions of the USA. What the Constitution designed them to do was to protect our democracy from what might otherwise evolve into a White House with overweening power. Have the checks and balances done their job?

The first response is that in giving the nation a set of principles to which it must abide, the Constitution was for the USA (and for others) an excellent idea; an idea, however, like much else in the Constitution, that has required and received many amendments; but not as many as are needed if our fabled democracy is ever to become real.

One amendment it needs badly but has not received would set down provisions explicitly designed to minimize the **corruption** that has infected all three "thirds" from our beginnings; instead, all along the way, corrupting processes have managed to find always new ways and heights. Make that depths.

The only way in which a democracy can come into existence and thrive is when a majority of its citizens think and feel and <u>live</u> democratically—which means considerably more than voting periodically, especially when that voting is merely choosing between Tweedledee or Tweedledum, both bought and paid for, a little or a lot. But that anything like a majority of our people has or would think, feel, and live democratically has never been likely. Consider first that many of the Constitution's framers were slaveholders, and all of them were men and that our history has been splotched throughout by the fundamentally <u>anti</u>-democratic processes of **racism** and sexism (see **boys and girls...**).

Then, add in the theme song of U.S. politics: "Money makes the world go around, the world go around....". In the capitalist era, money has everywhere influenced politics everywhere, if in different degrees and combinations; it has done so most effectively in the USA, especially in the past 20 years or so.

Before examining some of the representative consequences of what was to become our plutocracy, it is useful to note some relevant facts about how our government is s'posed to work.

1. The President appoints the members of the Supreme Court and all other Federal judges—all with lifelong terms—on approval of the Senate.

2. Each state has two senators, irrespective of population; they serve for six years.

3. Each member of the House is popularly elected in terms of the number of its eligible voters; they serve for two years.

Looks pretty good, until you examine the realities From their start, from 1789 on, the path toward democracy led up a steep and slippery hill, made so by the long-standing influence of **slavery** and **racism** and, importantly, the disproportionate influence of the South in the composition of the Senate, the Court, and the White House. We look first at the Senate.

Each state is allowed two Senators, irrespective of population. Until 1913, they were chosen not by popular elections, but by the decisions of state legislators: big trouble for democracy right there, in both respects. The Senate's members, quite apart from all else, in allowing two for each state irrespective of population, is automatically at best "partially" democratic—and "partially" is too generous.

No legislation can pass without majority approval of both House and Senate; and the majority approval of the Senate, though it requires 51 or more senators, neither necessarily nor usually means 51 percent or more of the population's representation.

This has been especially relevant in terms of the "southern bloc" votes, which has enabled the South, in dominating the Senate more often than not, to have a disproportionate say on both U.S. domestic and foreign policy.

This was true before the Civil War and, aided and abetted by the **Compromise of 1877**, came to be so again from the 1870s and until shortly after World War II; then, since the 1970s, the South has been able to regain its political potency in the Senate, the Court, and the White House—made all the more disturbing by the influence of the militant Christian Right on the South.

In principle, the House hears the people's voice.

But House or Senate, South, North, East, or West, money has had the loudest voice, from 1789 to 2003. Behold:

Item: One of the myths concerning our past and present is that our economic development was a consequence first and foremost of energetic business leaders using the **free market** to make their own and our nation's fortune. There has been and there is some truth in that; but for almost all major economic achievements, whether in agriculture, mining, manufacture, forestry, transportation, technology, chemistry, physics, the Internet—you name it—governmental intervention from 1789 to this morning has been vital. It has been brought about and accompanied by convivial relationships between businessmen and the federal and state governments of their time.

That conviviality began with canals and roads and tariffs and banking and the subsidizing of technological change, from Alexander Hamilton on—the best-known instance being that of the "employment" of Eli Whitney and his "invention" of interchangeable parts, first for muskets and the War of 1812, then with the cotton gin. But it went on and on, spectacularly again with the railroads of the 19th century. Two-thirds of their construction costs were paid for by the USA; it did so with the seriously questionable method of giving "land-grants" to the railroaders—that is, giving them free possession of millions of valuable acres which, whether sold or kept (for their use in mining, forestry, etc.) enhanced the wealth of the already wealthy. (SCHEIBER; DU BOFF; PHILLIPS /2002/)

All that marked the entire 19th and 20th centuries, up to and including the governmental payment for what became the computer and Internet world, nuclear physics, bombs, and energy.

The point is that all this had to have governmental approval, and the latter had to have congressional approval. The latter was achieved through one sort of pressure or another, not least of which was financial.

Item: The U.S. Senate was decisive in that entire history, both because it was one of the two legislative houses that had to approve, the other because its members up to 1913, were themselves more often than not individually involved on the business side. Thus,

> there was the extreme example of corporations and wealth seizing one level of government to control another. This was the takeover of state legislatures by corporations, railroads, and mining companies, partly to dominate their legislatures but just as important, to get a lock on the U.S. Senate, the members of which (until 1913) were chosen by those very legislatures. (PHILLIPS, 2002)

After 1913, senators had to undergo "direct election," that is, by the voters, not the state legislatures. Until then, the Senate was aptly called "the rich man's club." PHILLIPS quotes Mark Twain as saying, "I think I can say with pride that we have legislatures that bring higher prices than any in the world." He might have added that the Senators were in and of themselves a pretty "pricey" bunch. PHILLIPS provides a list of 22 Senators who were millionaires, 1902-3, their fortunes from railroads, mining, public utilities, ranching, etc. Today those millionaires would be on the same level as centimillionaires, or even billionaires.

Item: Since 1913, therefore, the Senate has become immune to money. Say what? Just joking. Although there are a few rich senators now, their relationship with money is still intimate, but more indirectly so; whether you become and remain a senator depends on your relationship to **lobbyists** and related **campaign finance**. Lately, it is true, there have been a few very rich men who, as multimillionaires (or more), have been able to run a successful (or even an unsuccessful) campaign for either House or Senate (or for mayor or governor) with their own money. That misses the point, which is: one cannot get into office without a lot of money; or stay in office unless the sources of the money are satisfied.

And although some small fraction of political money comes from workers, old people, teachers, and the like, more than 90 percent is from the business world. (PHILLIPS, 1994) (see **lobbyists**)

What has been said of the Senate of course applies as well to the House. Only rarely does anyone even stand for election, let alone win one, without spending a million, or many millions (depending upon the location).

It is a commonplace now that very promising possibilities for Congress (and state legislatures) have become fewer and fewer in number. Part of the reason is a general disgust with the degrees of corruption involved; another part, of at least as much importance, is that it has become virtually impossible to get the financial strength to run for office without becoming part of that corruption. So, the race goeth to the dirty.

As for Supreme Court: The Justices have always been appointed by the White House and approved by the Senate. Merit has seldom been the decisive, if even a relevant, factor. It is hard to stomach, but the highest court in the land has been thoroughly politicized—not always, for all, but more often than not, for most.

More recently, the scandals of the past have come to seem moments of relative purity, when set against our having to contemplate the insult to decency and honesty represented by Justice Thomas—who, as things go, may one day become our Chief Justice.

USSR (see Europe...)

Wall Street
(see financialization, SEC, Glass-Steagall)

war crimes (see carpet bombing...)

waste

Introduction. The 20th century combined waste with destruction in ways and degrees surpassing all previous periods; and its first half was outdone by the second. If that seems an outrageous statement, consider only this:

1) There has not been a year without wars since World War II, large and small, on some continent. Although no single war has yet matched the 60 million European deaths during World War II, the total for all the "small" wars (in the Middle East, Central Asia, Central and South America, and Africa) and the larger wars of Korea and Vietnam (at least 3 million in both), is a large multiple of that of World War I. Those deaths are appalling in themselves; add to that the socioeconomic damage, displacement, demoralization, and social paralysis—etc.—accompanying and following those wars, and the human, physical and social waste is staggering.

2. But the wars' wastes neither stopped nor started there. They must include the extraordinary wastefulness systematically created by the **military-industrial complex** (detailed under that heading) and, less obviously and unquantifiable, what is lost to societies when a significant amount of their people's efforts and skills and creative possibilities are siphoned off into **militarism** and the ugly politics associated with it—a politics that inexorably pits military against human and social needs, a politics brought to a fine polish by

Reagan, for whom to increase **milex** and reduce social spending—
"the Beast"—provided a double satisfaction—as was subsequently
detailed by his Budget Director. (STOCKMAN)

3. Nevertheless, the "honors" for massive waste and destruction
of resources, equipment, and lives do not go only to war and militarism. Setting aside our <u>trillions</u> of **milex** since 1945, and the wars
accompanying them, the "peaceful" functioning of the socioeconomy has itself been responsible for at least as much waste and destruction, always accelerating.

That is a large generalization; to support it even partially
requires a large discussion. (Much of will be said of course also
applies to other societies; which only accentuates the problem.)

In the many parts of the ensuing discussion it will useful if the
reader keeps in mind several related questions:

1. <u>What</u> is produced, and what is <u>not</u> produced, ` and <u>why</u>?
<u>How</u> are they produced, within what structures of control?

2. What is <u>consumed</u>, by <u>whom</u>?

3. How well are <u>human</u> and <u>natural</u> resources used, as measured
in terms of satisfaction, stability, safety, the environment, time,
needs and possibilities?

4. How much of our wastes are <u>destructive</u>?

Implicitly or explicitly, those are the questions directing what
follows, with one degree or another of "answer." We begin with what
may seem to be a terminological matter, but is much more than that.

<u>Efficiency and waste</u>. The USA and its people waste so much
in so many ways it is hard to know where to begin this discussion.
But because we <u>do</u> waste so much and also declare ourselves to be
the very most efficient economy in the world, it is best to start off
with something like a definition of "waste," and its costly, deadly,
and simply foolish components and consequences—beginning with
what's wrong with the comfortable view that the USA is #1 in economic efficiency when in fact we are the most wasteful of all
nations. (DOWD, 1989)

That otherwise reasonable people can accept such a contradiction is rooted in the confusion between <u>plant</u> efficiency and <u>eco-
nomic</u> efficiency: "plant" refers to the processes taking place <u>within</u>
a company, "economic" to the socioeconomy as a whole.

The USA was long seem as the world's leader in plant efficiency, whether for **cars**, electronic goods, steel, textiles—almost every-

thing. That was reasonably accurate up to about 1960; since then it has often been considerably less so: the Japanese and Germans produce better cars than our Big Three with greater efficiency; many countries—even India!—produce steel more cheaply than we, and over time that has been so as well for a broad range of manufactures, even in the realms of TVs and various ingredients of the computer world—especially and increasingly, now, by China. (see **globalization**)

Ah, but aren't other countries' wages a little or a lot lower? They are indeed obscenely lower in the "emerging economies" of the world, with wages and conditions matching or even worse than those of the industrial revolution in Britain; but there we are referring not to efficiency but to wage slavery.

In the leading industrial countries, money wages are higher as often as lower than in the USA: For example, higher in Germany, Canada and Norway; lower in France, Britain, and Japan (as is also true for the purchasing power of those money wages. (PHILLIPS, 2002.

Nor does that take into account the considerably lower "social wage" in the USA: the health insurance, pensions, paid vacations, public education and housing of <u>all</u> the other rich societies are much higher than ours (for those who receive them at all).

Moreover, if the great efficiency of the U.S. economy is the focus, it is difficult to explain why the average hours worked by U.S. workers are so much higher than, for example in Japan, Britain, Germany and France—in that all of had higher hours worked than we from 1950 through the 1980s; but the honors for that went to the USA in the 90s. (see below) The reasons for that unhappy reversal are to be found in the realm of <u>political</u> economy more than in narrow economic considerations. (PHILLIPS, 2002; and see **Reaganomics**).

There is another relevant and vital difference between the USA and others, little noted or discussed; namely, the costs of what David GORDON calls "bloated management." Recently, much attention has rightfully been paid to the exorbitant incomes of **CEOs**, functioning as though presiding over a gambling casino; large sums of money rewarding their **greed** and guile, often with great harm done to the productive health of their companies. To those costly practices must be added the greatly rising bureaucratic—that is, non-production—costs in the largest companies, due to 1) the inflation of managerial staffs (thus enlarging the "empire" of the top officers), and, 2) the enormous increase in the number of "supervisors" who are, in effect, "patrolling" the workers.

The foregoing developments began to be substantial in the 1970s, a decade of simultaneously rising prices <u>and</u> rising unemployment ("stagflation"), of increased foreign competition, of "deindustrialization"—"**downsizing** and **outsourcing**"—and the related beginnings of the **financialization** of the U.S. and global economies.

All that taken together with the most numerous and largest ever **mergers and acquisitions**—and the market and political power thereby gained—made life more difficult for industrial workers. Their unions' membership and bargaining power declined sharply: from about a third of the labor force in strong unions in the 1950s, to less than a tenth today, in weak unions; from the 1970s to the late 1990s, their real wages and social benefits fell; they were beleaguered by a process where "good jobs" were lost, probably permanently. Meanwhile, their CEOs were doing very well indeed: In the early 1990s, the ratio of CEOs incomes to those of production workers, which were already exceptionally high at 140: 1, rose to 209: 1; now they are over 450:1. (Compare that with a ratio of 7:1 in Japan in the same years.) (GORDON)

To top things off, also in the 90s, the intensity and hours of work increased for the average worker (<u>Item</u>: In 1999, the average worker put in 260 more hours of overtime—without pay—than ten years earlier; which equals six extra weeks of work. <u>BW</u>, 12-6-99).

All this led to what management saw as a discipline problem with disgruntled workers, if also as an opportunity for worker exploitation to rise. So, in those years companies hired always-greater numbers of those supervisors to watch and control the behavior of workers on the job. Already by the mid-90s, this was one result:

> ... Between 15 and 20 percent of private nonfarm employees in the United States /1996/ work as managers and supervisors. In 1994 we spent $1.3 <u>trillion</u> on the salaries and benefits of <u>non</u>production and supervisory workers, almost one-fifth of total gross domestic product, almost exactly the size of the revenues absorbed by the entire federal government. (D. GORDON)

The foregoing response of U.S. companies to the developments of the past quarter century were, for a while, unique, whether as regards the outrageous incomes of CEOs, money and social wages, or, and among other matters, the numbers of supervisors. No longer: **globalization**, which has "americanization" written all over it, has taught the other industrial countries that they too must introduce more "flexibility" in the labor force. Read: weakened unions, lowered unemployment compensation, health care benefits and pensions, and, soon, "supervisors"—all of this (from capital's point of view) made more urgent by a staggering world economy. So much for the vaunted <u>plant</u> efficiency of the USA. For sake of argument, however, let us assume that the USA is still in the lead (even though it is not). It is in the even more vital realm of <u>socioeconomic</u> efficiency that we have been and remain the world's undisputed chump: we have the most wasteful productive system in history; here two examples from a long list, one trivial the other important, toothpaste and cars.

Plant efficiency in both industries is measured by the difference between the unit cost of production and its market price: The latter embodies the non-productive costs (advertising, marketing, and useless product variations), and profits—which, in turn, are due to the market power of the giant companies in both areas, allowing them and their rivals to set agreed-upon profitable prices (see **big business**).

The cost of <u>production</u> of a typical tube of toothpaste is under 10 percent of its price; the rest is for non-production. And much the same is true for cars. On the one occasion in which **GM** was forced to come up with data on its costs and revenues, before the FTC in 1939—a <u>very</u> different agency from today's—GM's own figures showed that production costs were less than 20 percent of market price; the other 80 percent was for marketing, for annual style changes and related "planned obsolescence" (which accounted for one-third of production cost), and for profits. (FTC)

Such contributions to <u>in</u>efficiency, wasting both human and nonhuman resources, are not only widespread in the industrial sector, but elsewhere too—of course. Most disgustingly, because so clearly harmful, is the waste in our system of **health care**. It is worth repeating some ugly facts quoted there:

> We spend over $209 <u>billion</u> each year on <u>paperwork</u> in the offices of insurance companies, hospitals, and doctors—at least half of which could be saved through national health insurance. We spend $150 billion on medications, on prices 50% higher than Canadians pay for the same drugs. By slashing bureaucracy and drug prices we could save enough to cover <u>all</u> of the uninsured and improve coverage for the rest of us." (HIMMEL-STEIN) (emphasis added)

There are at least 1,500 separate "for profit" health insurers in the USA; their <u>administrative</u> costs amount to 25-35 percent of <u>total</u> health care costs in the USA; Canada has but one insurer: the government.

Its costs are lower than <u>one</u> of many insurers (Blue Cross) in just <u>one</u> of our states, Massachusetts.

All that unproductive effort may (or may not) be done with great "efficiency" <u>within</u> a particular company or those who do its advertising, etc. However, and although the foregoing contributes a large chunk of <u>economic</u> inefficiency, it is but a glimpse into the considerably larger economic and social realms of waste—and destructive waste. (see **environment**)

<u>The large and growing family of waste</u>. Here a mere listing of the most alarming of such realms, pursued further below and/or in indicated references:

1)   The waste of human beings and resources destroyed and crippled from war.

2)   The waste of human beings—to them and the society—who could be having interesting and socially-needed productive jobs, but whose lack of education and health and opportunity sticks them in mind-numbing or useless jobs—or in joblessness.

3)   The waste of resources, time and, energy involved in traffic jams and TV watching, and shopping 'til dropping.

4)   The waste, and what is lost to people and society because of the ways things are done (see environment)

5)   what is done (see military expenditures,

6)   those "things" that are not done at all

7)   are done badly, as in the realms of education, health care, housing, and

8)   the actual as compared with the possible and desirable structures of consumption, production, and related jobs, as suggested by the pertinent comment (in education) of the late scientist Stephen Jay GOULD, where he points to the most enduring and tragic waste of all:

> I am somehow less interested in the weight and convolutions of Einstein's brain than in the near certainty that people of equal talent have lived and died in the cotton fields and sweatshops.

<u>The tragedies of waste</u>. The realities of our reckless and destructive ways have meant long-standing and always worsening tragedy, both in what they have wrought and in the possibilities they have foregone or denied. To repeat an observation made elsewhere in this book, nature, current technology, and existing and easily achievable productive capacities taken together in the recent past and in the foreseeable future could provide everything needed by <u>all</u> the world's peoples for their health and comfort, and for their realization of decent and safe lives.

Instead, at least 80 percent of the world's population—over 4 <u>billion</u> people—go without adequate food, clothing, shelter, medical care, or education, their lives cruelly and needlessly shortened, cramped, and miserable, as millions die every year from starvation or malnutrition-related diseases—15 million of them being children. (UNICEF).

And this says nothing of the lives of the remaining relatively well-off (or <u>very</u> well-off) 20 percent. All too many of us are involved in mind-numbing jobs providing all too many unnecessary or trivial goods and services that we buy—and borrow to buy—because "We have been taught to want what we don't need, and not to want what we do." (BARAN, 1969) Some of those jobs are well-paid, but many more are badly underpaid; in both cases, more often than not they are jobs that waste the untapped abilities of a large majority of the people.

The stark contrast between that dreary, painful, and wasteful world and what <u>could</u> be has existed throughout history—going back to the Pharoahs (and, among other wastes, their pyramids) and up to this moment. From its slow beginnings with spears and fire, technological advance has always accelerated and broadened its reach—from tools and machines to medicine and culture, to everything, everywhere.

As it has done so, the gap between reality and possibility has always widened, producing what have seemed like, but were not, inevitable wars and unavoidable **environmental** damage; both of which have deepened and spread in their dangers and disasters.

To suggest that both military and environmental disasters were and are avoidable is, however, to say something else: they are avoidable if and only with substantial changes in the structure of **power** and in our guiding socioeconomic principles.

In the <u>Afterword</u>, the kinds of desirable, necessary, and possible changes in those respects will be outlined, with further reading.

The dirty laundry list of waste. We conclude with brief suggestions pointing to other subject headings that reveal how systematic we are in our ways wasting of wasting of producing destructive wastes— beginning with the most directly destructive processes of all, war.

Waste, militarism, and war. The years since World War II have been the most wasteful and destructively wasteful of all history, consequent upon the separate and interacting damages to the **environment** and the separate but related waste and destruction issuing from our omnipresent and politically omnipotent **militarism/ military industrial complex/milex** and the **Cold War**. Under the latter headings, the justifications given for our historic and, since World War II, accelerating militarism and addiction to military spending are seen as supported not by any threats to our wellbeing, let alone to our survival, but as responses to ideology and the political power of relevant **big business**.

Those militarized activities provide a clear and obvious representation of their "price." Less obvious but at least as substantial are the great wastes resulting from the ways and means of **farming, racism** and oppression (see **boys and girls...**) and from **consumerism**. In addition to what is discussed in those sections, here an additional comment.

Agricultural waste. There is much waste in agriculture, some of it destructive (**environment**), some of it not. The focus here is upon the indirect, but not therefore less harmful, consequences of a particular source of waste. The reference is to our (and other rich countries') agricultural subsidies and what they mean to the poorest people in the rest of the world. They have two dimensions:

a) The subsidies for U.S. and other rich countries' farmers producing staple crops (e.g., cotton, corn, and sugar), allow U.S. farmers to sell at 20 percent below the actual cost of production, and to do so in the poorer countries, where the same products have much lower costs because of their cheaper land and cheaper labor. The result?

America subsidizes its farmers so heavily that they can undersell poor competitors abroad. And just to make sure, it has tariff barriers in place that make it extremely hard for many Third World farmers to sell in the United States. The same is true for their efforts to sell in Europe and Japan. The world's

farming system is rigged in favor of the rich... The developed
world pays out more than $300 billion a year in farm subsidies,
seven times what it gives in development aid. (<u>NYT</u>, Editorial,
"Down with farm subsidies," 12-3-02)

b) What this means today is what it has meant throughout the
past century; namely, that in the poorer and the <u>very</u> poor countries
of the world, where the small—often tiny—farmers depend upon
farming for their own food and for supplemental income, they have
been pushed off by the land and into joblessness, despair and often
problematic and dangerous emigration by **globalization**—while, at
the same time, foreign agribusinesses (see **Archer Daniels Midland**)
come in to their lands with capital, modern techniques, and large-
scale farming, and export tomatoes and fruits (etc.) to the rich countries. These "export platforms" are springboards for profits outside
the producing country.

The net result for the poorer societies is always more unequal
income structures, their people subject always more to malnutrition,
starvation, and social unrest, their lives and lands misused and wasted. In the name of progress.

<u>Racial and gender oppression</u>. Oppression is not by any means
practiced only in the USA; but given our ideals and our vision of
ourselves and our nation, we have considerably less excuse for its
ubiquity than, say, the Chinese or the French. In both types of injustice, and whatever else is terrible about them, human possibilities
are thwarted and wasted.

Advantages there may or may not be to the racists and sexists,
of course; but they are minimal concerned with what is lost to the
victims and, though seldom noted, minimal also when consideration
is given to what is lost to the oppressors and to the society as a
whole. (ROEDIGER)

What is lost to the victims is simple to state: a full and dignified
existence in which their possibilities as human beings can be realized;
that they are not is an enormous waste to their society. But, to be
"realistic," is not that offset by the gains to the oppressors? It is not.

The basis for saying that is not mostly a matter of ethics or
morality, unethical and immoral though oppression is. It is not a way
of saying "do unto others as you would have them do unto you," if
you wish to be a "nice person"; rather, it is to recognize that in
demeaning others we also demean ourselves, as we also deprive our-

selves of the richness of what those others could have meant not just for themselves, but ourselves as individuals and as members of a decent rather than an indecent society.

The Beatles used to sing: "Imagine!" Imagine what it would be like to be in a high school classroom, half boys and half girls, half "white" and half "people of color," with none in the room having been impoverished because of racism, with none of the girls having been socialized to see themselves as only future wives and mothers, with undignified and lowpaid jobs before marriage, and after (or while) the kids grow up. Imagine what it would be like as a child to have parents both of whom are self-assured as regards their talents and education, neither more privileged than the other in terms of opportunity or reward; in a family in which sisters and brothers were equal in esteem, and both looked upon their economic and personal lives with the same level of freedom and dignity.

Imagine a society in which all that was so, and much, much more; in which hate was a four-letter word; in which slums had ceased to exist, because there had never been any reason for them except as by-products of racism and the **inequality** it has institutionalized.

Imagine how much better off everyone would be in such a society—economically, politically, culturally and emotionally.

And then tote up the real waste to this society of not being that society.

Consumptionitis and economic propaganda. In the 20th century the world first became accustomed to being propagandized by politicians, high and low, right, middle, and left. In the same century, if a bit later, we also became accustomed to being propagandized by one company after another: but we didn't call it that, we called it **advertising**. Its aim and result was **consumerism**, now spreading like a giant oil spill over the world.

Interestingly enough, the advertising techniques that came to be used in the first swirl of modern advertising in the 1920s for **tobacco** and **cars** had their beginnings in the USA during World War I, in the hands of one individual in particular, Edward L. Bernays—who also happened to be the nephew of Sigmund Freud. (TYE) Bernays was hired by the Wilson Administration to begin the drumbeat for U.S. involvement in Europe's first world war—Wilson, not so uninterestingly, having campaigned for re-election in that same year on a platform that included keeping the U.S. out of that war: In today's

Orwellianisms, he was a "compassionate militarist." World War I saw the use of radio for the first time, as means of military communication; as it did also, of large posters touting patriotism.

Bernays combined radio and those posters most popularly and successfully for the American Tobacco Company with his famous campaign "Reach for a Lucky Instead of a Sweet," as the nation was going on its first, but not its last "Slim is beautiful" campaign—now become "Skinny is beautiful-". (TYE)

But consumerism's acknowledged birth came in 1923 when **GM**, faced with a market-wide leveling off in the demand for **cars**, introduced the "planned obsolescence" of the annual model change, consumer credit, and massive advertising campaigns: the Holy Family of consumerism. (Concerning all of which, see the relevant subjects elsewhere.) Here we are concerned only with the waste of it all; the very <u>great</u> waste.

"Planned obsolescence" is by definition the deliberate use of waste in order to make profits. An automotive executive friend of mine in Italy, whose company makes parts (everything but the chassis and the motor), when asked why he sold his parts all over the world but not in the USA, said "It's very simple, our parts are guaranteed to last for 10 years; they don't want them there." Go figure.

The same strategy has clearly become part of the computer industry for both software and hardware—as it has in all industries where they can get away with it. "Getting away with it" in this connection means facing a public which is more concerned with appearances and keeping up with or surpassing the Joneses than with the function performed by the product; and "the Joneses came to be effective focus of buyers in the 1920s. As is discussed more fully under **consumerism**, such did not become a deep-seated inclination until the general public could pay for it, and that was after World War II, when a) average real family incomes were considerably higher than earlier, and b) when consumer credit became common—and then, from the 1960s on, took the form of credit cards: now, given **advertising** and **TV**, the cards are the heart of the matter. Hard to believe, but until then, although the well-off could "charge" purchases at the local department store, gas station, or corner grocery, that was <u>it</u>.

Now all can borrow, and almost all are foolish enough not to ask what it costs to do so until too late (**debt**); now we all watch TV a <u>lot</u>; now TV commercials and "infomercials" are more watched more and longer than what used to be thought of as regular programs (BARBER); now MORE! is the national anthem, shopping as recreation and borrowing to buy are a major source of wasteful production, wasteful consumption; and now the wasteful constructs of giant and pervasive malls have become a second home, as often as not more inviting than what was once called "home sweet home."

In her fine novel <u>Tar Baby</u>, Toni MORRISON provides a soliloquy on waste in the USA that sums it up:

> That was the sole lesson of their world: how to make waste, how to make machines that make more waste, how to make wasteful products, how to talk waste, how to study waste, how to design waste, how to cure people who were sickened by waste so they could be well enough to endure it, how to mobilize waste, legalize waste.... And it would drown them one day, they would all sink into their own waste and the waste they had made of the world and then, finally, they would know true peace and the happiness they had been looking for all along....

And so? What began in the USA and took hold after World War II now spreads to all of the richer countries and to many of the poorer ones. The spread and deepening of the foregoing litany of wasteful practices has now taken on the dimensions of a global culture, nourished by and nourishing the ideology of the **free market** and the **globalization** that have—so far—assiduously and successfully neutralized the popular movements seeking to curtail the waste and social damages intrinsic to the entire set of processes. (BARBER)

If resistant political movements do not spread and strengthen, so as to move toward success, the awful developments described above and in the essay on the **environment** are likely within a century or so to bring life on earth as we know it toward its end.

SUV, anyone?

welfare (see poverty)

Wilson, Charles

He deserves a note, but a very brief one. Just as President Coolidge entered the history books mostly because of his remark that "The business of America is business," so now does Charlie (that's what he was called) Wilson—if this may be seen as a history book. As both head of GM and Secretary of Defense after World War II, and with a narrower perspective than Silent Cal, Charlie informed us that "What's Good for General Motors is good for America." Tell that to the thousands of GM retirees who are now having to wonder whether their pensions are going to be paid and, if so, in what percentage. Or, for that matter, the dozens of thousands of workers who were globalized out.

But Charlie was outdone by Lawrence Summers (now Harvard's head) who, when he was with the World Bank wrote, in an internal memo,

> Just between you and me, shouldn't the World Bank be encouraging more migration of the dirty industries to the LDCs /less-developed countries/? I think the economic logic behind dumping a load of toxic waste in the lowest wage countries is impeccable and we should face up to that... I've always thought that underpopulated countries in Africa are vastly under-polluted.... (quoted in MM, 5/2003).

Summers went on from the World Bank to become Clinton's Treasury Secretary. When confronted with this story, he says he was kidding. Funny guy, the President of Harvard.

youth (see teenagers/young)

zoos

This isn't here because I couldn't think of anything else that starts with a "z"—although that may have spurred me on; no, its because I detest zoos and cherish animals.

The rationale for zoos has been that it is through them that we, especially our children, can learn about and learn to care for animals. A lofty aim, but a self-defeating means. It could be argued that in the dark past when we didn't have film or **TV** that if we were to know any animals other than cats and dogs and canaries, zoos were the only answer That's a terrible answer; if you don't believe me, just <u>watch</u> the animals.

Now we have TV and film, so that excuse no longer holds. Of course it is only the documentaries that teach; most of TV and film do the opposite of teaching; they present animals as targets, or enemies or, in cartoons, as... icky poo.

What zoos teach is something else again: In a world bursting with cruelties of all sorts, zoos let us believe that if the end is positive the means are acceptable; if <u>we</u> do it—and "we" by definition are good souls—it's gotta be OK.

There are essentially two kinds of zoos: the old-fashioned kind, with cages and bars, and those that let the animals "run free." The latter are surely better than the former. However.

A major difference is that in the caged-animal zoos, you can hardly escape noticing that the animals have become insane: madly pacing back and forth, madly staring, madly complaining. As who wouldn't. The "natural environment" zoos also warp the animals' lives and emotions, but more subtly, and often as not out of view. The difference between the two types is akin to that between maximum and minimum-security **prisons**.

We may well have to lock up some people to protect ourselves and, for that matter, them from themselves; but there is no need at all for maximum security prisons; that being so, it is conceivable that some day we'll not have them; only those of <u>minimum</u> security—most of the inhabitants of which wouldn't be there either, had we a socially decent and caring society.

That comparison is made to point to this: We—in the USA and elsewhere—are perhaps on the way to getting rid of the old-fashioned cage-'em-up zoos; that makes us feel better about the "minimum security" zoos. What we adults have learned from zoos, and that our children still learn, is that it's alright to imprison animals, to take them away from their natural lives so that <u>we</u> can have—what?—something that teaches rotten lessons, one of them being that prisons are a one-fits all solution.

If you listen carefully in the night, you can hear the animals howling: "SPCA, where are you? Hey! Fellow animals! We <u>need</u> you!"

Afterword

The quintessential "American" poet Carl SANDBURG, in his The People, Yes, lamented that "America was promises." Although that was written in the first half of the 20th century, it was already appropriate. Since then, even the promises are well on their way to being forgotten.

In more than one of the essays of this book, it has been argued that the tragedy began as "America!" began. "Tragedy" because ours might have become an entirely marvelous society.

Except for the millions of Africans who were stolen from their lands and enslaved, almost all of those who came to the USA did so for two overlapping reasons: 1) to escape from hopelessness, pogroms, oppression, poverty, or starvation in their home countries; 2) to go to a mythical new nation holding forth the promises of well-being, of freedom, of safety, of peace—one or all of those, and more.

And when, after their arrival and attempts to settle, conditions were difficult and even dangerous, almost always the "promises" continued to resonate.

Some of those hopes were to be met in their own lives or those of their children, some were forgotten, some were never met at all,

This book has been concerned with the latter and, just as important, the ways in which some of them—those having to do with money—in being met in one degree or another have at the same time allowed or required that the other promises be violated:

1) "Wellbeing"? To be sure, most became materially comfortable and some became rich. Meanwhile, inexcusable poverty was created or worsened for always more than a tenth of the people with unnecessary hardship for another third—all that in the midst of dazzling plenty for a small minority.

2) Freedom? Yes and no, where the no has been at least as important as the yes. The inequality of "freedom" is kin to the inequality of income and wealth; what has been denied to some has been allowed to others, all too often at the expense of others—in the economic, cultural, and political realms, and often as cause and effect.

3) Safety? The USA is a very safe place, compared with, say, Africa and the Middle East. But—and setting aside that we have made others outside the USA very unsafe—there is very little safety indeed in terms of our air, our water, and our health, to say nothing of our tendency toward war—which takes us to,

4. Peace? We are simultaneously the strongest and most warlike of all nations. "Peace through strength" is a tried but not always true epigram; especially if those uttering it are looking for reasons to "defend" us from enemies in other continents. The always high and presently rising militarism of the USA has taken a terrible toll in the past, and it is likely to rise in the near future.

That toll is not measured only in the trillions of dollars spent and wasted, or even in the lives lost and wasted, however serious that has been. It must also be measured by the damage done by militarism to the social framework: to our politics, our economy, our culture, our <u>character</u> as a people.

As already related in many of these essays our history has always been marked by an inclination toward violence, on all levels. Over time it has contaminated our lives, our outlook, and our ways of being so much so as to be taken for granted: <u>normal</u>.

What has been put forth in this book and now here is of course a far cry from what we have been taught—and would wish to—admire and love about our country; but it will not come as "news" for what may be seen as a rising and significant minority in the USA. They—we—are people who are uneasily aware of the inappropriate and unacceptable behavior of the USA both at home and abroad that makes a sad mockery of the "American dream."

It is highly probable that the numbers of our minority are a large multiple of the protest marchers against globalization, discrimination, inadequate social policies, and war. We not only seek answers to <u>why</u> our country seems bent upon ravaging its ideals of decency, freedom, and peace but, at least as important, <u>what</u> can be done to halt present economic, social, and military processes and to begin to move in a saner, safer, decent direction.

To get a good grip on the answers to either question is not easy; of course. In the hurly-burly and high pressures of daily existence at work and at home it is understandable that most can find neither the time nor the energy to "study out the land" (Walt Whitman) and think through the ugly realities of our past and present.

Our general dependence upon newspapers, weeklies, and most of all, upon TV for information and understanding generally makes matters worse; those sources tend to deal with complicated processes either not at all, in snippets, or in Orwellian ways, spinning already sparse information into disinformation.

This book's intent has been to make it more <u>practical</u> for over-ly busy and distracted people to strengthen their grasp on key ele-ments of the USA's disturbing and dangerous realities and, ideally, to energize its readers to probe deeply on their own—assisted in part by the book's many references and its bibliography.

Assume for a moment that the book's aims have been at least partially realized; that's the easy part. The hard part is to know what can be done and to set about doing it. The answers to that are at least as complex as the problems needing resolution.

Suppose further that my many gloomy discussions are valid, including those regarding political corruption and its deliberate or unintentional allies in the media; and recognize that people like our-selves lack access to either the money or the media resources of the powerful. How then can we engage the ongoing power structure effectively? And, an equally large and separate question, in order to seek what? That is, what <u>can</u> and what <u>should</u> be our political means and ends?

<u>Means</u>. As I seek now to respond to those questions be assured that I do not see my response as definitive for others, or as settled even for myself. Other valid responses can be and are being put forth; the most important matter is to get going; having done that, aims and means can and should be high on the agenda of discussion. I start this way.

Our strength inheres in our numbers and our principles; but for them to have meaning both must be dealt with carefully and ener-getically: How can we make the most of our numbers? It is not easy. The people of the USA are among the least politically minded and active of any of the leading nations. Politics for most of us has been and remains passive; usually it means <u>only</u> voting—for or against someone or some policy, both placed before us like a meal in a cheap boarding house.

We vote for a Tweedledee or a Tweedledum, selected in tightly controlled conventions by a few dozen pros; we vote for or against some proposal in which we have had little or no input. <u>Of course</u>, it is sometimes true that the "dee" is somewhat less unsatisfactory than the "dum"—but their long-run tendencies tend to resemble family quarrels more than a fight over principle. The two major parties have <u>never</u> been seriously representative of ordinary people; nowadays both are considerably less so. Thus, and only by way of example (see **health** care), although Clinton may be seen as a very much more desirable president than Bush II, Clinton's directions admittedly came first and foremost from giant industrial and financial companies.

Thus it was that when Clinton announced he would attempt a badly-needed national health care system, from the first moment he compromised fatally when he ruled out <u>any</u> discussion of national health insurance, thus assuring that the "health-for-profit" **HMOs** would have their way. Unsurprisingly, the HMOs are now stronger than ever and, predictably, the costs of health care for patients soar <u>as</u> treatment declines.

That "in his heart" Bill Clinton might have wished for universal health care only makes it worse; he gave in to the moneyed interests without a blink or a word of explanation to the public—a "word" that would have required at least a muted reference to national health insurance.

There are of course some in both houses of Congress who do something admirable from time to time; but even at the best of times, they have been in a tiny minority. It is easy to blame Congress, for they deserve it; but the blame also falls on us for our passive resistance.

The Congress is under very practical pressures to "go along"; otherwise it is almost impossible to be elected. We, on the other hand, have been socialized to accept both the big lie that free market capitalism takes care of our socioeconomic needs and its corollary that government cannot be trusted to do so.

Despite some qualms, a large majority of our people see no need for <u>us</u> to be involved political beings. Those with wealth and power know better than to allow that dictum to apply to them: they pay out tens of billions of dollars annually for tens of thousands of **lobbyists**, institutional advertising, and bought-and-paid-for candidates' campaigns. They know that "the free market" doesn't take care of <u>their</u> needs and possibilities. It is worth repeating the cautionary words of Adam SMITH, the unwitting father of today's free market ideology:

> Businessmen are an order of men whose interest is never exactly the same with that of the public, who have generally an interest to deceive and even to oppress the public, and who accordingly have, upon many occasions, both deceived and oppressed it.

So we must do more than vote. That has both short-run and long-run meanings; it means undertaking the difficult and time-consuming work of organizing from the ground up—while, always, also deciding how and when and where to <u>use</u> our organized power.

Does it mean a third party? Perhaps; probably, now or later. If so, does that mean functioning on local, state, <u>and/or</u> national levels? And whether third party or not, what else must be discussed and decided upon in terms of organization? Plenty.

Whatever else is required, surely all of us must become involved on the <u>local</u> level. That's where we live and can relatively easily contact and regularly work with our fellow citizens. Nor is <u>that</u> as easy as it sounds.

In my own political experience it has always been more difficult for me to speak on politics to my neighbors than to strangers. There is a certain hesitancy that arises from wishing to stay on good terms with one's neighbors, both despite and because of political differences. How one deals with that has to be decided on a one-to-one basis; although, also in my experience, there are can be many pleasant surprises.

The local level is in any case where one <u>must</u> work politically; but we also <u>must</u> work with statewide and national groups, understanding that one's effect is greater the closer to home—while, at the same time, never forgetting that progress in any locality is easily drowned out by regress on the state and national levels. In short, we must work on <u>all</u> levels; to do so, we must change our way of life: serious political work differs from intermittent voting as humming to oneself in the shower does from being a professional singer.

And there is much more to think through and discuss.

But now, and in addition to working to de-militarize our nation, what do we want?

<u>Goals</u>. First, it seems clear that for both fundamental human <u>and</u> political reasons, we must work for what is most <u>needed</u> by our people and our society. In addition, the power and the enormous riches of the USA endow us with both the ability and the obligation to assist those badly off to become better off; that is, as we work for the betterment of our own people and society, decency and safety require that at the same time we work to construct a world in which *all* people's <u>basic needs</u> are met.

That is a moral and a political imperative for both the near and the distant future; a matter of enlightened self-interest as well as decency. It cannot be repeated too often: We are all in the same boat, as regards war and peace—and, not least, the environment.

What is <u>most</u> needed? Where to begin? Here a distinction must be made between the needs of people in a rich society such as ours, and those of the poorer nations; <u>and</u> to see them as harmonious, not conflicting. Among many distinctions, most obvious is that in a society such as ours it would be politically difficult but <u>economically</u> simple—and it will be argued, beneficial for the economy—for <u>everyone's</u> basic needs to be met. But for the non-rich nations, and all the more so for the poorest among them (where more than half of the world's people live), it is <u>both</u> economically <u>and</u> politically difficult to meet that aim without substantial assistance from the rich nations—assistance, however, that must not be a cloak for further exploitation.

As has been argued in many elements of this book—most clearly as regards the **Cold War** and **globalization**—the USA has—of course—hitherto functioned in sharp contrast with what is desirable and necessary.

That said, and irrespective of rich or poor societies, what are the "basic needs"? They are the same for all human beings: nutrition, health, shelter, education—and water. "Water"? Simple lack of access to clean water is a lethal and spreading problem for over a <u>billion</u> poor people already; with more than 2 million children dying yearly because of that alone.

Listing the just-noted five needs immediately points to complexities <u>within</u> as well as between societies. In the very rich USA, although looked upon enviously by most of the peoples of the world, many millions eat badly in both quantitative and qualitative terms; they must depend upon always fewer emergency hospitals for what little health care they receive; they live in squalid, dangerous, and cramped housing; they are educated little and badly; and even in the USA, although there is not yet a shortage of water, its price is rising, and shortages are well on their way in a few rural and urban areas.

Lacking sufficient quantities and qualities of the "Basic 5," a large minority in the USA also lacks something else: the socioeconomic <u>opportunity</u> to move out of poverty, the ability to have a political voice in the shaping of our society and thus of their lives.

So basic needs should also include equal opportunity and the

right to participate. (Look into DALY & COBB, SEN, STRET-
TON, and also—this is not a typo—STREETEN for excellent dis-
cussions of these complexities; and the UN Human Development
Report and its "Human Development Index.")

For basic needs to be met in the USA and elsewhere we must
move toward a genuinely democratic society, one in which the structure of power always moves away from its triangularly-shaped plutocracy toward equality. (See PHILLIPS, 2002).

It may reasonably be argued that anything like full democracy
is impossible in a capitalist society. I believe that is so, but in the
USA (but not always elsewhere) it is my conviction that it is politically self-defeating to work successfully for any "ism," by whatever
name. Angry calls for "revolution" are understandable; for the foreseeable future, however, if we are to make steady and substantial
progress politically we must recognize that neither verbal nor physical violence ever make sense to more than a very few while, at the
same time, they turn away those who might otherwise participate in
the struggles for necessary and desirable social change.

Those who criticize the basic needs approach as "reformism"
are right as regards the work for a particular reform (e.g., housing, or
social security, or...); the apparent achievement of a single reform is
almost always followed by a decline of political effort by its direct
beneficiaries, a strengthening of its opponents, and retrogression.

On the other hand, working persistently and effectively for the
satisfaction the basic needs program with multiple and interdependent components can and likely would unavoidably eat away at the
uglier realities of capitalism while also moving toward a "non-capitalist" society. What kind of society would that be?

A non-capitalist society. The term is meant to suggest an economy always more popularly controlled, with a thought-through mixture of public and private ownership. There is nothing wrong with
private ownership as such; it is a matter of power: Small farms are
fine, agribusiness is deadly; small shops and factories (and the like),
when workers are legally guaranteed the meeting of their basic needs
and a living wage, are both attractive and economically wise.

What has been and is wrong about the private ownership of the
means of production has been the inordinate power of capital, and
the systemic misuse accompanying it: the power to exploit workers,
to control the government and to "manage minds."

In a society that meets the basic needs of all, worker exploitation would come to an end; workers have always been exploitable only because they have no way to survive except on their employers' terms. But the non-capitalist society suggested here is one which would also disallow <u>giant</u> companies.

It needs saying immediately that efficient production often entails production on a large-scale; however, when that is so, the production must be under public ownership and control, and /or in some circumstances under the control of its workers.

Also, and, among other matters needing discussion, modern economies require some significant degree of economic <u>planning</u>. Planning as such can be harmful and as well as helpful; if, as, and when a political movement toward a truly democratic society evolves, what could and would evolve alongside would be the kind of social and political consciousness that could guarantee sane and desirable economic planning.

Nor is it irrelevant to note that we have <u>had</u> "economic planning" for some time now, but the planning has been done by a congeries of giant companies, whose plans have as their aim the enhancement of the profits and power of the few, and let the pieces fall where they may.

In sum, it is not working for reform as such that is self-defeating over the longer term, but the illusion that any one or two reforms can be attained and sustained in and of themselves—as distinct from a program of linked reforms, linked both in their political creation and in their supportive interactions.

Working for such a linked program would accomplish something else that is vital: in working together for common aims, what have been diverse and competing groups, will not only be stronger as a many-sided group, but will also cease fighting among themselves for what, once attained, soon become crumbs.

To the degree that this approach would succeed, the resistance from those now accustomed to rule would also rise, moving toward a flash point. But in the processes of our creating that resistance, U.S. politics for all would have been changing; we would no longer <u>only</u> vote, we would also have strengthened our social and political understanding and our self-respect; and our ability to forge ahead <u>and</u> to defend our rights would intensify. Nor can we forget that in recent years, even without a movement to repress, the USA (in the phrasing of Yeats) has been "slouching towards" a postmodern form of fascism: one depending more upon the techniques of advertising and religious zeal than jackboots and death camps; with or without a strong political movement, we face a grim future; only if we strengthen ourselves politically is there any hope for a safe and sane future. But is it economically <u>practical</u> to seek to fulfill basic needs here at home and, as well, for the rest of the world? It is more than practical; it is an economic and environmental, political—and moral—necessity. A serious look at such **A to Zs** as **cars, consumerism** and **advertising** and **media, environment** and **waste, inequality, poverty, globalization** and many others treated in this study informs that the present system has already failed in many ways, is failing in still others, and is doomed to commit suicide through its always more potent destruction of the environment.

I take the liberty of sending the reader back to the discussions just noted, and here make only a summary assertive statement.

First, when, back in the Sixties, the Beatles—or was it the Stones?— sang "Can't get no satisfaction," they were pointing at the way of life now enfolding us all—working and borrowing always more for an always more frenzied life. (see SCITOVSKY, <u>Joyless Economy</u>) But the Sixties were just the beginning of something now approaching social idiocy, perhaps best symbolized by the frenzied desires of virtually all to have at least one (and, better, two or three) cars, costing more and lasting less, in order to get stuck in traffic and spend all too much time to find all too few parking spaces. (The statistical reality is that "the average household now has 1.75 drivers but 1.9 personal vehicles." <u>NYT</u>, 8-30-03)

Meanwhile, along with the whiz-bang economy of the Nineties, poverty and inequality both rose rapidly, as did hours of (usually unpaid) work (see **jobs**); and along with always rising health care costs, health care on the average diminished.

The globalization that was supposed to mean a better life for all has already meant a loss of millions of good jobs for some and not enough even bad jobs for all—to say nothing of the terrible damage done to the poorer countries. Official + actual **unemployment** is over 10 percent and unlikely to fall.

Moreover, in addition to the blue collar jobs of autos and steel and textiles (etc.) being "downsized and outsource," a significant number of the zippy jobs in the New Economy have now disappeared for a minimum of 10 percent, with worse to come. Within 5 years, if not already, India and China (with the help of their millions of desperately exploited workers) will be the place where an always rising percentage of almost all jobs are going—causing the $2 a day maquiladora workers to lose their jobs. With much more than just those jobs at stake.

Globalization, sold as "a rising tide that lifts all boats," is a sham and a disaster for most, beneficial largely for those who manage to keep their capital moving with where the game is being played. But that leaves out the devastation wrought on the poorer economies in the world: that's where those poor people at the Mexican border came from, after their agriculture was "export-platformed" out from under them.

In short, the big booms of the past few decades have turned out to be warning guns. New ways of using human and natural and technological resources must be developed; putting all those together to meet human needs and possibilities has a future; what we're doing now promises only more economic and social disasters. (DALY & COBB)

When Adam Smith wrote of the tendency of businessmen to "deceive and oppress" he had no idea of the numbers of people who would be harmed or the dimensions of the harm when their power reached today's heights; nor could he have foreseen that the majority peoples of democratic societies would acquiesce in such disasters.

The ways and means of those in power that have brought us to what must be seen as a major socioeconomic crisis are continually fortified, and the pace of change toward disaster accelerates accordingly. Only we can assist our nation and our world to a safer harbor.

* * *

In the early 1970s I began work on a book prompted by the oncoming bicentennial celebrations of the Declaration of Independence and "The American Dream." Its title was The Twisted Dream. The notion of "twisted" had reference to the difficulty of reconciling "All men are created equal" with the mute acceptance of slavery; more deeply, I saw that "dream" as having become inordinately subverted by our subsequent history.

The 1970s were troubling enough at home, with its managed

deterioration for the bottom half of the population; but the policies and the consequences of the 1980s pushed bad to worse, both at home and abroad.

The administrations of Nixon and Reagan were among the most disgraceful in our history; yet Nixon, who committed major crimes both at home and abroad, had been "rehabilitated" in the public mind by the time he died, while Reagan, despite his carefree militarism and cruel social policies, remains one of the most popular presidents in our entire history.

And the 1990s? Generally viewed as the most wondrous decade ever, like the 1920s those were years of inordinate gains for the rich, widespread corruption at the highest levels of business and politics, and a striking callousness on the part of the USA toward its own and other nations' needs and peoples.

Fittingly enough, the 90s ended with the installation of a president made possible by a suspect election in a state controlled by his brother and a Supreme Court at least one of whose key members attained his position under dubious conditions.

There was nothing secret about any of that; what deserves serious attention is that it could happen and its negative aspects intensify with so very little comment or resistance in our country; as though the general public had become anesthetized.

As the Civil War in the USA was approaching, Abraham Lincoln declared "We must disenthrall ourselves." Carl Sandburg (noted in the Preface) was his most loving biographer in Abraham Lincoln: The Prairie Years.

In Sandburg's collection of poems, The People, Yes, one had to do with needs, from which a few lines are pertinent:

> Who can make a poem of the depths of weariness
> bringing meaning to those never in the depths?
> Those who order what they please when they choose to
> have it—
> can they understand the many down under who come
> home to their wives and children at night and night after night
> as yet too brave and unbroken
> to say, "I ache all over"?
> How can a poem deal with production cost
> and leave out definite misery paying a permanent price in
> shattered health and early old age?
> When will the efficiency engineers and the poets

get together on a program?
Will that be a cold day? Will that be a special hour?
Will somebody be coocoo then?
And if so, who?

The broken promises lamented by Sandburg continue to be shattered with each passing day, taking us closer to the edge of a socioeconomic, military, and environmental abyss. The promises of "America!" must be redeemed if we are to move back from that abyss; they can be and will be, if, as, and only when we study out our common interests and work together to achieve them.

If not now, when?

Bibliography

An Introductory Note

The aim of this small encyclopedia is to provide readers with brief discussions of many important matters generally treated blandly or misleadingly in the media, most books, and in schools—when they are not ignored.

It is hoped that those who read this will take it upon themselves to deepen their understanding by going on to other books more conventional in <u>form</u> that can be found in the following listing.

Some of those books can serve as a set of substantial introductions for more sustained study; to assist in that, the following few books are now singled out. All of them provide broad perspectives on areas of vital relevance; in their own turn they might send readers to still more books. If such efforts are made by those who read book, its main hope will be fulfilled.

1. The most useful and, happily, most readable of all histories of the USA is Howard Zinn's <u>A People's History of the United States</u>.

2. Kevin Phillips, a self-styled Republican conservative, has in recent years written several books exploring what he sees as the dangerous depths to which political corruption and economic autocracy have gone, so far as now to threaten the society he wishes to see "conserved." See especially his <u>Arrogant Capital</u> and <u>Wealth and Democracy in the United States</u>.

3. The scope, penetration, and consequences of U.S. economic, military, political, and cultural dominance over the globe are well-treated in Noam Chomsky, <u>Year 501: The Conquest Continues</u>, William Greider, <u>One World, Ready or Not</u>, and Benjamin Barber, <u>Jihad vs. McWorld</u>.

4. In the past century, the media and advertising in newspapers and magazines, radio, TV, and film have gained always more importance and sway in the entirety of our existence; that being so, those with already substantial power outside the media world have acted so as to gain control over and increase the concentration of media ownership. See Edward S. Herman and Robert McChesney, <u>Global Media</u> and Ben Bagdikian, <u>Media Monopoly</u>.

5. All of the foregoing developments have emerged within the always strengthening socioeconomic, cultural and political frame-

work of capitalism, with the early and continuing assistance of the economics profession that came into existence as it did. My Capitalism and Its Economics seeks to illuminate their mutually supportive interactions, from Adam Smith and the industrial revolution to the present.

All of the just noted books and the hundreds that follow (both new and used) are to be found for sale easily and, often, cheaply on the Internet, with listings of relevant used book shops over the country and ways of ordering. See, for example, <www.abebooks.com>, or <www.google.com>. On the Web site for my community classes in the San Francisco area are also many suggested articles: <www.dougdowd.org>. Now the books used and cited for this work.

* * *

ADAMS, N.S., MCCOY, A.W. (eds.) 1970. *Laos: War and Revolution*. New York: Harper & Row.

ADAMS, W., BROCK, J. 1986. *The Bigness Complex: Industry, Labor, and Government in the American Economy*. New York: Pantheon.

AGEE, P. 1975. *Inside the Company: CIA Diary*. New York: Bantam.

ALBELDA, R. DRAGO, R., SHULMAN, S. 2001. *Unlevel Playing Fields: Understanding Wage Inequality and Discrimination*. Cambridge, MA: Dollars & Sense.

____WITHORN, A., (eds.). 2002. *Lost Ground: Welfare Reform, Poverty, and Beyond*. Cambridge, MA: South End Press.

ALLEN, G.C. 1946. *A Short Economic History of Modern Japan: 1867-1937*. London: Macmillan.

ALPEROVITZ, G. 1965. *Atomic Diplomacy: Hiroshima and Potsdam*. New York: Vintage Books.

ALTERMAN, E. 2003. *What Liberal Media?* New York: The Nation.

ALTMAN, D. 2002. "Ensuring Competition for Military Contracts," *NYT*, 9-15-02.

ANDERSON, S., CAVANAGH, J., LEE, T. 2000. *Field Guide to the Global Economy*. New York: The New Press.

ARONSON, J. 1970. *The Press and Cold War*. Indianapolis: Bobbs-Merrill.

ASHWORTH. W. 1987. *A Short History of the World Economy Since 1950*. London: Longman.

AUDEN, W.H. (see RODMAN, *Modern Poetry*)

AUSTIN, J. 1990. FOCUS: *America's Growing Correctional-Industrial Complex* (San Francisco: National Council on Crime and Delinquency.

____IRWIN, J. 1990. *Who Goes to Prison?* San Francisco: NCCD.

BAGDIKIAN, B. 1983. *The Media Monopoly*. Boston: Beacon Press.

BALIBAR, E., WALLERSTEIN, I. 1991. *Race, Nation, Class: Ambiguous Identities*. New York: Verso.

BANKS, J. 1996. *Monopoly Television: MTV's Quest to Control the Music*. Boulder, CO: Westview Press.

BANNER, S. 2002. *The Death Penalty: An American History*. Cambridge: Harvard Univ. Press.

BARAN, P., SWEEZY, P. 1966. *Monopoly Capital: An Essay on the American Economic and Social Order*. New York: Monthly Review Press.

____1957. *The Political Economy of Growth*. New York: Monthly Review Press.

____1969 "Theses on Advertising," in *The Longer View*. New York: Monthly Review Press.

BARBER, B. 1996. *Jihad vs. McWorld: How Globalism and Tribalism Are Reshaping the World*. New York; Ballantine.

BARITZ, L. (ed.) 1977. *The Culture of the Twenties*. New York: Bobbs-Merrill.

BARNET, R. 1970. *The Economy of Death: A Hard Look at the Defense Budget and the Military-Industrial Complex*. New York: Atheneum.

BARNET, R., CAVANAGH, J. 1994. *Global Dreams: Imperial Corporations and the New World Order*. New York: Simon and Shuster.

BEARD, C. 1969. *The Devil Theory of War*. Westport, Conn.: Greenwood.

BECKLES, H. 1989. *White Servitude and Black Slavery in Barbados, 1627-1715*. Knoxville: Univ. of Tenn. Press.

BENERIA, L., FELDMAN, S. 1992. *Unequal Burden: Economic Crises, Persistent Poverty, and Women's Work*. Boulder, CO: Westview Press.

BERLE, A.A., MEANS, G. 1932. *The Modern Corporation and Private Property*. New York: Macmillan.

BERNAYS, E. 1952. *Public Relations*. Norman, OK: University of Oklahoma Press.

BERRY, W. 1977. *The Unsettling of America: Culture and Agriculture*. New York: Avon.

BIERCE, A. 1911/2000. *The Devil's Dictionary*. New York: Devon.

BIRD, K., LIFSCHULTZ, L. (eds.) 1998. *Hiroshima's Shadow: Writings on the Denial of History and the Smithsonian Controversy*.

BLACKBURN, R. (ed.) 1973. *Ideology in Social Science: Readings in Critical Social Theory*. New York: Vintage.

BLAIR, J.M. 1978. *The Control of Oil*. New York: Vintage.

BLIX, H. 2004. *Disarming Iraq*. New York: Pantheon Books.

BLOCK, F. 1977. *The Origins of International Economic Disorder*. Berkeley: Univ. of California Press.

BLUESTONE, B., HARRISON, B. 1982 *Deindustrialization of America*. New York: Basic Books.

____1988. *The Great U-Turn: Corporate Restructuring and the Polarizing of America*. New York: Basic Books.

BLUM, W. 2000. *Rogue State: A Guide to the World's Only Superpower*. Monroe, ME: Common Courage Press.

____2004. *Killing Hope: U.S. Military and CIA Interventions Since World War II*. Monroe, ME: Common Courage Press.

BOGGS, C. 1971. *Gramsci's Marxism*. London: Pluto Press.

BOIES, J.L. 1994, *Buying for Armageddon: Business, Society, and Military Spending Since the Cuban Missile Crisis.* New Brunswick, NJ: Rutgers Univ. Press.

BOK, D. 2003. *Universities in the Marketplace: The Commercialization of Higher Education.* Princeton: Princeton University Press.

BONNER, R. 1984. *Weakness and Deceit: U.S. Policy and El Salvador.* New York: New York Times Books.

BONNIFIELD, P. 1987. *The Dust Bowl, Men, Dirt and Depression.* Albuquerque: Univ. of New Mexico Press.

BORCHER, W. 1949/1971. *The Man Outside.* New York: New Directions.

BOUCHER, D. (ed.) 1999. *The Paradox of Plenty: Hunger in a Bountiful World.* Oakland, CA: Food First Books.

BOVARD, J. 1995. *Shakedown: How the Government Screws You From A to Z.* New York: Viking.

BOWDEN, W. et al. 1937. *Economic History of Europe Since 1750.* New York: H. Fertig.

BOWLES, S. 1991. What Markets Can—and Cannot—Do. *Challenge Magazine* July-August.

BOXER, C.R. 1965. *The Dutch Seaborne Empire.* New York: Knopf.

BRADY, R.A. 1933. *The Rationalization Movement in German Industry.* Berkeley: Univ. of California Press.

____1937. *The Spirit and Structure of German Fascism.* New York: Viking Press.

____1943/1999. *Business as a System of Power.* New York: Columbia Univ. Press/ Piscataway, NJ: Transaction Publishers.

BRANCH, E. D., 1929. *The Hunting of the Buffalo.* New York: Appleton Co.

BRANDS, H.W. 1993. *The Devil We Knew: America and the Cold War.* Oxford: Oxford University Press.

BRANFMAN, F. 1972. *Voices from the Plain of Jars.* New York: Harper Colophon.

BRAUDEL, F. 1979/1992. *The Structures of Everyday Life, Vol. I.* Berkeley: University of California Press.

BRAVERMAN, H. 1974. *Labor and Monopoly Capital: The Degradation of Work in the Twentieth Century.* New York: Monthly Review Press.

BREITMAN, R. 1998. *What the Nazis Planned, What the British and the Americans Knew.* New York: Hill & Wang.

BRESLOW, M. (et al.). 1999. *The Environment in Crisis.* Cambridge, MA: Dollars & Sense.

BRITTAIN, J. 1972. *The Payroll Tax for Social Security.* Washington: The Brookings Institution.

BRENAN, G. 1943. *The Spanish Labyrinth: An Account of the Social and Political Background of the Spanish Civil War.* New York: Cambridge University Press.

BRONFENBRENNER, K. 2003. "Declining Unionization, Rising Inequality," *Multinational Monitor,* May.

BROWN, Claire. *American Standards of Living, 1918-1988.* New York: Blackwell.

BROWN, Claude. 1965. *Manchild in the Promised Land.* New York: Macmillan.

BRYANT, H. 2002. *SHUT OUT: A Story of Race and Baseball in Boston.* New York: Routledge.

BUNDY, MCG. 1988. *Danger and Survival: Choices About the Bomb in the First*

Fifty Years. New York: Random House.

BusinessWeek. (various issues)

CAHILL, T. 1995. *How the Irish Saved Civilization*. New York; Doubleday.

CAHN, B. (ed.). 2002. *The Affirmative Action Debate*. New York: Routledge.

CALLENBACH, E. 1996. *Bring Back the Buffalo: A sustainable future for America's Great Plains*. Berkeley: Univ. of California Press.

CAMPEN, J. (et al.). 1999. *Real World Banking*. Cambridge, MA: Dollars & Sense.

CAREY, a. 1997. *Taking the Risk Out of Democracy*. Sydney: New South Wales Press.

CARMICHAEL, V. 1993. *Framing History: The Rosenberg Story and the Cold War*. Minneapolis: Univ. of Minnesota Press.

CARSON, R. 1962. *Silent Spring*. Greenwich, Conn.: Fawcett Press.

CASH, W. 1941. *The Mind of the South*. New York: Knopf.

CATO INSTITUTE. Policy Analysis No. 241: Archer Daniels Midland: A Study in Corporate Welfare (James Bovard), 9-26-1995

CAUTE, D. 1978. *The Great Fear: The Anti-Communist Purge Under Eisenhower and Truman*. New York: Simon & Schuster.

CHANG, I. 2003. *The Chinese in America: A Narrative History*. New York: Viking.

CHANG, L., KORNBUHL, P. (ed.) 1992. *The Cuban Missile Crisis*. New York: New Press.

CHILDE, V.G. 1951. *Man Makes Himself*. New York: Mentor Books.

CHOMSKY, N. 1969. *American Power and the New Mandarins*. New York: Pantheon.

____1970. *At War with Asia*. New York: Vintage.

____1991. *Deterring Democracy*. London: Verso.

____1993. *Year 501: The Conquest Continues*. Boston: South End Press.

CHOMSKY, N., HERMAN, E.S. 1988. *Manufacturing Consent: The Political Economy of the Mass Media*. New York: Pantheon.

CHURCHILL, W. 1997. *A Little Matter of Genocide*. San Francisco: City Lights Books.

CIRINO, R. 1971. *Don't Blame the People*. New York: Random House.

CLARK, G.N. 1947. *The Seventeenth Century*. London: Oxford University Press.

CLARKE, R.A. 2004. *Against All Enemies: Inside America's War on Terror*. New York: The Free Press.

CLOGG, R. (ed.) 2002. *Greece, 1940-1949: Occupation, Resistance, Civil War*. London: Palgrave Macmillan.

COCKROFT, J., FRANK, A.G., JOHNSON, D.L. 1972. *Dependence and Underdevelopment*, New York: Doubleday.

COLE, D. 2003. *Enemy Aliens: Double Standards and Constitutional Freedoms in the War on Terrorism*. New York: The New Press.

COLL, S. 2003. *Ghost Wars: The Secret History of the CIA, Afghanistan and Bin Laden, From the Soviet Invasion to September 10, 2001*. New York: The Penguin Press.

COLLINS, C., LEONDAR-WRIGHT, B. SKLAR, H. 1999. *Shifting Fortunes: The Perils of the Growing American Wealth Gap*. Boston: United for a Fair

Economy.

CONASON, JOE. 2004. *Big Lies: The Right-Wing Propaganda Machine and How It Distorts the Truth.* New York: Thomas Dunne/ St. Martin's.

COOK, B.W. 1981. *The Declassified Eisenhower: A Divided Legacy.* New York: Doubleday.

COULTER, A. 2003. *Treason: Liberal Treachery From the Cold War to the War on Terrorism.* New York: Crown Forum.

CRILE, G. 2003. *Charlie Wilson's War: The Extraordinary History of the Largest Covert Operation in History.* New York: Atlantic Monthly Press.

CUMINGS, B. 1981. *The Origins of the Korean War,* Two vols. Princeton: Princeton University Press.

____, HALLIDAY, J. 1988. *Korea: The Unkown War.* New York: Pantheon.

CYPHER, J. 1987. "Military Spending, Technical Change, and Economic Growth," *Journal of Economic Issues* (March).

____1991. "The War Dividend," *Dollars & Sense,* May.

____1998. "Financial Domination in the US Economy," in Fayasmanesh, S. and Tool, M. (ed.) *Institutionalist Theory and Practices.* (Cheltenham, UK: Edward Elgar.

____2001. "Nafta's Lessons: From Economic Mythology to Current Realities," *Labor Studies Journal,* Spring.

____2002. "Return of The Iron Triangle," *Dollars & Sense,* Jan./Feb.

____2002. "A Prop, Not a Burden: The U.S. Economy Relies on Militarism," *Dollars & Sense,* July/August.

CZECH, B. 2003. *Shoveling Fuel for a Runaway Train.* Berkeley: University of California Press.

DALY, H.E., COBB, J.B., Jr. 1989. *For the Common Good: Redirecting the Economy toward Community, the Environment, and a Sustainable Future.* Boston: Beacon Press.

DALY, H. 1996. *Beyond Growth: The Economics of Sustainable Development.* Boston: Beacon Press.

DANNER, M. 1994. *The Massacre at El Mozote: A Parable of the Cold War.* New York: Vintage.

DAVIS, D.B. 1988. *The Problem of Slavery in Western Culture.* New York: Oxford University Press.

DAVIS, M. 1998. *Ecology of Fear: Los Angeles and the Imagination of Disaster.* New York: Henry Holt

DE CASTRO, J. 1950. *The Geography of Hunger.* New York: Monthly Review Press. (republished as *The Geopolitics of Hunger,* 1990)

DENNISON, G. 1969. *The Lives of Children.* New York:; Random House.

DELANY, W. 2001. *The Green and the Red: Revolutionary Republicanism and Socialism in Irish History, 1848-1923.* New York: Writer's Showcase.

DE TOCQUEVILLE, A. 1846. *Democracy in America.* New York: Macmillan.

DE ZENGOTITA, T. "The Numbing of the American Mind," *Harper's* Magazine, April, 2002.

DOBB, M. 1937. *Political Economy and Capitalism.* London: Routledge and Kegan Paul.

_____1966. *Soviet Economic Development Since 1917*. London: Routledge and Kegan Paul,

DOBSON, A. (ed.) 1991. *The Green Reader: Essays Toward A Sustainable Society*. San Francisco: Mercury House.

DOMANICK, J. 2003. *Cruel Justice: Three Strikes and the Politics of Crime in America's Golden State*. Berkeley, CA: University of California Press.

DOMHOFF, W. 1998. *Power and Politics in the Year 2000*. New York: Oxford Univ. Press.

DONOVAN, J.A. 1970. *Militarism, U.S.A.* New York: Scribner's.

DORFMAN, J. 1934. *Thorstein Veblen and His America*. New York: Viking.

DOWD, D. 1950. "Two-Thirds of the World," *Antioch Review*, Fall.

_____1956. "A Comparative Analysis of Economic Development in the American West and South," *Journal of Economic History*, December.

_____1964/2000. *Thorstein Veblen*. New Brunswick, NJ: Transaction Publishers.

_____1965, *Step by Step*. New York: W.W. Norton.

_____1967. "An End to Alibis: America Fouls Its Dream," *The Nation*, February.

_____1978. "The CIA's Laotian Colony," in Adams, N.S. and McCoy, A.W., *Laos: War and Revolution*. New York: Harpers.

_____1982. "Militarized Economy, Brutalized Society," *Economic Forum* (Summer)

_____1989. *The Waste of Nations*. Boulder, Col.: Westview Press.

_____1993. *U.S. Capitalist Development Since 1775: Of, By, and For Which People*. Armonk, NY: M.E.Sharpe.

_____1997a. *Blues for America: A Critique, A Lament, and Some Memories*. New York: Monthly Review Press.

_____1997b. *Against the Conventional Wisdom: A Primer for Current Economic Controversies and Proposals*. Boulder, Col.: Westview Press.

_____2000/2004. *Capitalism and Its Economics: A Critical History*. London: Pluto Press.

_____2001. *And It's Each for Himself and God For All: Once More, U.S. Capitalism on a Rampage*. (Pacifica, CA: Vai Vecchio Press.

_____(ed,) 2002. *Understanding Capitalism: Critical Analysis, from Karl Marx to Amartya Sen*. London: Pluto Press.

DRAKE, S. & CAYTON, H. 1992 (1945). *Black Metropolis: A Study of Negro Life in a Northern City*. Chicago: Univ. of Chicago Press.

DRAPER, T. 1991. *A Very Thin Line: The Iran-Contra Affairs*. New York: Hill & Wang.

DRAY. P. 2002. *At the Hands of Persons Unknown: The Lynching of Black America*. New York: Random House.

DREW, E. 2002. "War Games in the Senate." *New York Review of Books*, 12-5-02.

DU BOFF, R. 1989. *Accumulation and Power: An Economic History of the United States*. Armonk, NY: M.E.Sharpe.

DUBOFSKY, M. 1974. *We Shall Be All: A History of the Industrial Workers of the World*. New York: Quadrangle.

DU BOIS, W.E.B. 1989 (1903) *The Souls of Black Fools*. New York: Penguin.

DUUS, P. 1976. *The Rise of Modern Japan*. Boston: Houghton Mifflin.

DWORKIN, R. "The Threat to Patriotism," *NYRB*, 2-28-02.

EHRENREICH, B. 1990. *Fear of Falling: The Inner Life of the Middle Class*. New York: Harper Perennial.

_____2001. *Nickel and Dimed: On (Not) Getting By in America*. New York: Henry Holt.

_____B, & J. 1971. *The American Health Empire*. New York: Random House.

EISENBERG, C.1996. *Drawing the Line: The American Decision to Divide Germany, 1944-49*. New York: Cambridge Univ. Press

ELIOT, T.S. 1937. *Collected Poems: 1909-1935*. London: Faber & Faber Limited.

ELLIS, R. 2003. *The Empty Ocean: Plundering the World's Marine Life*. Washington: Island Press/Shearwater Books.

ELON, A. 2004. "A Very Special Relationship," *NYRB*, 1-15.

ELLSBERG, D. 1972. *Papers on the War*. New York: Simon & Schuster.

_____2002. *Secrets: A Memoir on Vietnam and the Pentagon Papers*. New York: Viking Penguin.

ENGLER, R. 1961. *The Politics of Oil*. Chicago: Univ. of Chicago Press.

ENSENZBERGER, H. 1974. *The Consciousness Industry*. New York: Seabury Press.

EVEREST, L. 2004. *Oil, Power and Empire: Iraq and the U.S. Global Agenda*. Monroe, ME: Common Courage Press.

EWEN, S. 1976. *Advertising and the Social Roots of the Consumer Culture*. New York: McGraw-Hill.

_____1996. *PR! A Social History of Spin*. New York: Basic Books.

FALL, B. 1967. *Last Reflections on a War*. Garden City, NY: Doubleday.

FANON, F. 1963. *The Wretched of the Earth*. New York: Grove Press.

FAULKNER, H. 1947. *The Decline of Laissez-faire: 1897-1917*. New York: Rinehart.

FEAGIN, J. & SYKES, M. 1994. *Living with Racism: The Black Middle Class Experience*. Boston: Beacon Press.

Federal Trade Commission. 1939. *Report on the Automobile Industry*. Washington, D.C.: USGPO

FEIS, H. 1930. *Europe, the World's Banker: 1870-1914*. New York: A.M. Kelley

FINNEGAN, W. 1998. *Cold New World: Growing up in a Harder Country*. New York: Random House.

FITZGERALD, F. 1972. *Fire in the Lake: The Vietnamese and the Americans in Vietnam*. New York: Random House.

_____2000. *Way Out There in the Blue*. New York: Simon & Schuster.

FOLBRE, N., et al. 1995. *The New Field Guide to the U.S. Economy: A Compact and Irreverent Guide*. New York: The New Press.

FOLBRE, N. 1996. *The War on the Poor: A Defense Manual*. New York: The New Press.

Fortune Magazine (various issues)

FOSTER, J.B. 1999. *The Vulnerable Planet*. New York: Monthly Review Press.

_____2000. *Marx's Ecology*. New York: Monthly Review Press.

_____2002. *Ecology vs. Capitalism*. New York: Monthly Review Press.

FRANK, A.G. 1979. *Dependent Accumulation and Underdevelopment*. New York: Monthly Review Press.

FRANKLIN, M. 1988. *Rich Man's Farming: The Crisis in Agriculture*. London:

Routledge.

FREELAND, R. 1972. *The Truman Doctrine and the Origins of McCarthyism: Foreign Policy, Domestic Politics, and Internal Security, 1946-1948*. New York: Knopf.

FRIED, A. 1997. *McCarthyism: The Great American Red Scare*. New York: Oxford University Press.

FREUD, S. 1930. *Civilization and Its Discontents*. New York: Knopf.

FROMM, E. 1941. *Escape from Freedom*. New York: Holt & Company.

FRUMKIN, G. 1951. *Population Changes in Europe Since 1939*. New York: United Nations.

GALBRAITH, J.K. 1955. *The Great Crash, 1929*. Boston: Houghton Mifflin.

GALLETTI, M. 2001. "Le relazione tra Italia e Kurdistan," (Collected Essays), in Quaderni di ORIENTE MODERNO.

GANS, H. 1995. *The War Against the Poor: The Underclass and Antipoverty Policy*. New York: Basic Books.

GARDNER. L. 1995. *Pay Any Price: Lyndon Johnson and the Wars for Vietnam*. Chicago: J.R. Dee.

GATTO, J.T. 1992. *Dumbing Us Down: The Hidden Curriculum of Compulsory Schooling*. Philadelphia: New Society Publishers.

GENOVESE, E. 1967. *The Political Economy of Slavery*. New York: Vintage Books.

GEORGE, S. 1976. *How the Other Half Dies*. London: Penguin.

_____1979. *Feeding the Few: Corporate Control of Food*. Washington, D.C.: Institute for Policy Studies.

_____1994. (with Fabrizio Sabelli) *Faith and Credit: The World's Secular Empire*. Boulder, Colo.: Westview Press.

GERSCHENKRON, A. 1943, *Bread and Democracy in Germany*. Berkeley: Univ. of California Press.

GERVASI, T. 1986. *The Myth of Soviet Military Superiority*. New York: Harper & Row.

GINGER, R. 1969. *The Bending Cross: A Biography of Eugene Victor Debs*. New Brunswick: Rutgers Univ. Press.

GINZBERG, E. 1964. *The House of Adam Smith*. New York: Octagon Books.

GLUCKMAN, A. (et al.) 2003. *Current Economic Issues*. Cambridge, MA: Dollars & Sense.

GOODWIN, Doris Kearns. 1973. *Lyndon Johnson and the American Dream*. New York: Harper & Row.

GORDON, C. 1994. *The Clinton Health Care Plan: Dead on Arrival*. Westfield, NJ: Open Magazine Series (P.O. Box 2726, 07091)

GORDON, D.M. 1996. *Fat and Mean: The Corporate Squeeze of Working Americans and the Myth of Managerial Downsizing*. New York: Free Press.

GOULD, S. 2003. *The Hedgehog and the Fox, and the Magister's Pox: Mending the Gap Between Science and Humanities*. New York: Three Rivers Press.

GRAMSCI, A. 1967. *The Modern Prince and Other Writings*. New York: New World Paperbacks.

GREGORY, J. 1989. *American Exodus: The Dust Bowl Migration and Okie Culture in California*. New York: Oxford Univ. Press.

GREIDER, K. 2003. *The Big Fix: How the Pharmaceutical Industry Rips Off American Consumers.* New York: Public Affairs Reports.

GREIDER, W. 1994. *Who Will Tell the People?* New York: Simon & Schuster.

____1997. *One World, Ready or Not: The Manic Logic of Global Capitalism.* New York: Simon and Schuster.

____1998. *Fortress America: The American Military and the Consequences of Peace.* New York: Public Affairs.

____2003. *The Soul of Capitalism: Opening Paths to a Moral Economy.* New York: Simon & Schuster.

GRIFFITH, R.W. 1971. *The Politics of Fear: Joseph McCarthy and the Senate.* Rochelle Park, NJ: Hayden.

GROSS, B. 1980. *Friendly Fascism: The New Face of Power in America.* New York: M. Evans.

GURLEY, J. 1979, *Challengers to Capitalism: Marx, Lenin, Stalin, and Mao.* New York: W.W. Norton, Inc.

HACK, R. 2004. *Puppetmaster: The Secret Life of J. Edgar Hoover.* New York: New Millenium Press & Audio.

HAHNEL, R. 1999. *Panic Rules: Everything you Need to Know About the Global Economy.* Cambridge, MA: South End Press.

HALBERSTAM, D. 1965. *The Making of a Quagmire.* New York: Random House.

HALDEMAN, H.R. 1994. *The Haldeman Diaries: Inside the Nixon White House.* New York: Putnam.

HALLINAN, A. 2001. *Going Up the River: Travels in a Prison Nation.* New York: Random House.

HALPERIN, M., et al. 1976. *The Lawless State: The Crimes of the U.S. Intelligence Agencies.* New York: Penguin Books.

HAMMOND, J., B. 1911. *The Village Labourer.* London: Guild Books.

____1924. *The Rise of Modern Industry.* New York: Harcourt, Brace.

HANDLIN, O. 1981, *The Uprooted.* Boston: Atlantic Monthly Press.

HARRINGTON, M. 1962. *The Other America.* Baltimore: Penguin.

HARTMAN, C. 1983. *America's Housing Crisis: What is to be Done?* London: Methuen.

HAYEK, F. 1952/1999. *The Road to Serfdom.* London: Routledge.

HAYNES, H,P. 1989. *The Recurring Silent Spring.* New York: Pergamon Press.

HECKSCHER, E. 1935. *Mercantilism.* (2 vols.) New York: Macmillan.

HEINTZ, J, FOLBRE, N. 2000. *Field Guide to the U.S. Economy.* New York: The New Press.

HENWOOD, D. 1997. *Wall Street: How it Works and for Whom.* New York: Verso.

HERIVEL, T. WRIGHT, P (eds.) 2003. *Prison Nation: The Warehousing of America's Poor.* New York: Routledge.

HERMAN, E.S. 1981. *Corporate Control, Corporate Power.* New York: Cambridge Univ. Press.

____1999. *The Myth of the Liberal Media.* New York: Peter Lang.

____2003. "From Guatemala to Iraq." *Z Magazine*, January.

___WUERKER, M. 1992. *Beyond Hypocrisy: Decoding the News in an Age of Propaganda* (including The Doublespeak Dictionary). Boston: South End Press.

____MCCHESNEY, R. 1999. *The Global Media: The New Missionaries of Global Capitalism*. London: Cassell.

HERSEY, J. 1946/1989. *Hiroshima*. New York: Vintage Books.

HERSH, B. 1992. *The Old Boys: The American Elite and the Origins of the CIA*. New York: Scribner's.

HERSH, S. 1970. *My Lai 4: A Report on the Massacre and Its Aftermath*. New York: Random House.

____1983. *The Price of Power: Kissinger in the Nixon White House*. New York: Summit Books.

HERTSGAARD, M. 1988. *On Bended Knee: The Press and the Reagan Presidency*. New York: Farrar, Straus and Giroux.

HIGBEE, E. 1963. *Farms and Farmers in an Urban Age*. New York: Twentieth Century Fund

HIMMELSTEIN, D., WOOLHANDLER, S., "We Pay for National Insurance But Don't Get It," *Journal of Health Affairs* (7-10-02)

HISS, T. 1999. *The View from Alger's Window: A Son's Memoir*. New York: Knopf.

HOARE, Q., SMITH, G.N. (eds.) 1971. *Selections from the Prison Notebooks of Antonio Gramsci*. London: Lawrence & Wishart.

HOBSBAWM, E.J. 1964. *Labouring Men: Studies in the History of Labour*. London: Weidenfeld and Nicolson.

____1968. *Industry and Empire*. New York: Pantheon.

____1984. *Further Studies in the History of Labour*. London: Weidenfeld and Nicolson.

____1990. *Nations and Nationalism Since 1780*. New York: Cambridge University Press.

HOBSON, J.A. 1902. *Imperialism*. London: Allen & Unwin.

HOCHSCHILD, A. 1999. *King Leopold's Ghost: A Story of Greed, Terror and Heroism in Colonial Africa*. London: Macmillan.

HOCHSCHILD, A.R. 2004. *The Commercialization of Intimate Life: Notes from Home and Work*. Berkeley: University of California Press.

HOFFMAN, R.J.S. 1933. *Great Britain and the German Trade Rivalry*. Philadelphia: Univ. of Pennsylvania Press.

HUBERMAN, L. 1937. *The Labor Spy Racket*. New York: Modern Age.

____1937/1955. *We, the People*. New York: Monthly Review Press.

____1940. *America, Incorporated*. New York: Viking.

HUNT, E.K. 1979. *History of Economic Thought: A Critical Perspective*. Belmont, CA: Wadsworth.

HUXLEY, A. 1931. *Brave New World*. New York: Harper & Bros.

IGNATIEFF, M. 1984. *The Needs of Strangers*. London: Chatto & Windus, Hogarth Press.

ISHERWOOD, C. 1931. *The Berlin Stories*. New York: New Directions.

IVINS, M., DUBOSE, L. 2000. *Shrub: The Short but Happy Political Life of George W. Bush*. New York: Random House.

____2004. *Bushwacker: Life in George W. Bush's America*. New York: Random House.

JACKSON, K., ed. 1989. *Cambodia: 1975-1978. Rendezvous with Death.*

Princeton: Princeton University Press.

JEFFERS, R. 1925. "Shine Perishing Republic," from *Selected Poems*. New York: Random House.

JOHNSON, C. 2000. *Blowback: The Costs and Consequences of American Empire*. New York: Henry Holt & Co.

JOHNSTON, D.C. 2003. *Perfectly Legal: The Covert Campaign to Rig Our Tax System to Benefit the Super Rich—and Cheat Everybody Else*. New York: Viking.

JONAS, S. 1991. *The Battle for Guatemala: Rebels, Death Squads, and U.S. Power*. Boulder, CO: Westview Press.

JOSEPHSON, M. 1934. *The Robber Barons*. New York: Harcourt Brace Jovanovich

JUNGK, R. 1958. *Brighter Than a Thousand Suns: A Personal History of the Atomic Scientists*. New York: Harcourt Brace

KAHIN, G. 1968. *The United States in Vietnam*. New York: Harper & Row.

____1986. *Intervention: How America Became Involved in Vietnam*. New York: Knopf.

KAPP, K.W. 1950. *The Social Costs of Private Enterprise*. Cambridge, MA: Harvard University Press.

KEANEY, M. 2002. "Unhealthy Accumulation: the Globalization of Health Care Privatization," *Review of Social Economy*, September.

KEMP, T. 1967. *Theories of Imperialism*. London: Dobson.

KESSLER, R. 2002. *The Secret History of the FBI*. New York: St. Martin's Press.

KEYNES, J.M. 1919. *The Economic Consequences of the Peace*. London: Macmillan.

____1931. *Essays in Persuasion*. London: Macmillan.

____1936, *The General Theory of Employment, Interest and Money*. New York: Harcourt and Brace.

KINDLEBERGER, C. 1978. *Manias, Panics, and Crashes: A History of Financial Crises*. New York: Wiley.

KINZER, S. 2003. *All the Shahs's Men: An American Coup and the Roots of Middle East Terror*. Hoboken, NJ: Wiley.

KLARE, M. 2001. Resource Wars: The New Landscape of Global Conflict. New York: Henry Holt.

KLEIN, C. 2001. "Coverage for Low Earners Dwindles," <editors@plansponsor.com>

KLEIN, N. 1999. *No Logo*. New York: Picador.

____2002 *Fences and Windows: Dispatches from the Front Lines of the Globalization Debate*. New York: HarperCollins

KOFSKY, F. 1987. *Harry S. Truman and the War Scare of 1948*. New York: St. Martin's Press.

KOHN, A. 1986. *No Contest: The Case Against Competition; Why we lose in our race to win*. Boston: Houghton Mifflin.

KOLKO, G. 1969. *The Roots of American Foreign* Policy. Boston: Beacon.

____1970. "The Decline of American Radicalism in the Twentieth Cemetery," in WEINSTEIN/EAKINS.

KOLKO, J. 1988. *Restructuring the World Economy*. New York: Pantheon.

KORNBUHL, P., BYRNE, m. (eds.) 1993. *The Iran-Contra Scandal: The Declassified History*. New York: New Press.

KORNBLUH, J. (ed.) 1964. *Rebel Voices: An I.W.W. Anthology*. Ann Arbor: University of Michigan Press.

KOZOL, J. 1967. *Death at an Early Age*. New York: Bantam Books.

_____1991. Savage Inequalities: Children in America's Schools. New York: Crown Publishers.

KRUGMAN, P. 2002. "For Richer." *New York Times Magazine*, October 20.

_____2003. *The Great Unraveling: Losing Our Way in the New Century*. New York: Norton.

KUTTNER, R. 1996. *Everything for Sale: The Virtues and Limitations of Markets*. New York: Knopf.

LA FEBER, W. 1976. *America, Russia and the Cold War*. New York: Wiley.

LANE, F. 1973. *Venice, A Maritime Republic*. Baltimore: Johns Hopkins Univ. Press.

LAPHAM, L. 1989. *Money and Class in America*. New York: Harper & Row.

LAPPE', F. et. al. 1998. *World Hunger: 12 Myths*. New York: Grove Press.

_____F. & A. 2003. *Hope's Edge: The Next Diet for a Small Planet*. New York: Tarcher/Putnam.

LASKI, H. 1936. *The Rise of European Liberalism*. London: Allen & Unwin.

LEBOW, N., STEIN, J.G. 1994. *We All Lost the Cold War*. (Princeton: Princeton Univ. Pres..

LE CARRE', J. 1995. *Our Game*. New York: Knopf.

LEFFLER, M. 1992. *A Preponderance of Power: National Security, the Truman Administration, and the Cold War*. Stanford, CA: Stanford Univ. Press.

Left Business Observer (various issues)

LEIGH, J.P. 1995. *Causes of Death in the Workplace*. Westport, Ct. Greenwood Publishing Group.

_____et. al. 2000. *Causes of Occupational Injuries and Illnesses*. Ann Arbor: Univ. of Michigan Press.

LEKACHMAN, R. 1982. *Greed is not Enough*. 1982. New York: Pantheon.

LEWIS, D.L. 2002. "An American Pastime," *New York Review of Books*, November 21.

LEWIS, M. 1989. *Liar's Poker*. New York: W.W. Norton.

LEWIS, S. 1920. *Main Street*. New York: Dover Publications.

LEWIS, W.A. 1949. *Economic Survey, 1919-1939*. London: Allen and Unwin.

LICHTMAN, R. 1982. *The Production of Desire. The Integration of Psychoanalysis into Marxist Theory*. New York: Free Press.

LIEBLING, A.J. 1961. *The Press*. New York: Ballantine.

LINDERT, P. 2004. *Growing Public*. Cambridge: Cambridge University Press.

LITWACK, L. 1980. *Been in the Storm So Long: The Aftermath of Slavery*. New York: Random House.

LIVELY, P. 1987. *The Moon Tiger*. London: Andre Deutsch.

LOCKWOOD, W. 1964. *The Economic Development of Modern Japan*. Princeton: Princeton Univ. Press.

LYND, R. and H. 1937. *Middletown: A Study in Cultural Conflicts.* New York: Harcourt, Brace & Co.

MCCAFFERTY, K. 2002. *Testimony of an Irish Slave Girl.* New York: Viking.

MCCHESNEY, R. 1999. *Rich Media, Poor Democracy: Communication Politics in Dubious Times.* Champaign, Ill.: Univ. of Illinois Press.

____FOSTER, J.B. 2003. "The Left-Wing Media?" *Monthly Review*, June.

____2004. *The Problem of the Media: U.S. Communication Politics in the Twenty-First Century.* New York: Monthly Review Press.

MCCOY, A.W. 1972. *The Politics of Heroin in Southeast Asia.* New York: Harper.

MCLOUGHLIN, W.G. 1984. *The Cherokee Ghost Dance.* Macon, Ga: Mercer Univ. Press.

MCGINNIS, J. 1969. The Selling of the President. New York: The Trident Press.

MCNAMARA, R. 1995. *In Retrospect: The Tragedy and Lessons of Vietnam.* New York: Times Books..

MADRICK, J. 1995. *The End of Affluence: The Causes and Consequences of America's Economic Dilemma.* New York: Random House.

MAGDOFF, F., FOSTER, J., BETTEL, F. 2000. *Hungry for Profit: The Agribusiness Threat to Farmers, Food and the Environment.* New York: Monthly Review Press.

MAGDOFF, H. 1968. *The Age of Imperialism: The Economics of U.S. Foreign Policy.* New York: Monthly Review Press.

____2003. *Imperialism Without Colonies.* New York: Monthly Review Press.

MALKIN, M. 2002. "Ethanol is a big fraud on consumers," (SFC, 8-28-02)

MALTHUS, T. 1798/1970. *An Essay on the Principle of Population.* Baltimore: Penguin.

MALRAUX, A. 1927. *Man's Fate.* New York: Vintage.

MANDER, J. 1978. *Four Arguments for the Elimination of Television.* New York: Morrow.

____1992. *In the Absence of the Sacred: The Failure of Technology and the Survival of the Indian Nations.* San Francisco: Sierra Club.

MANGOLD, T. 1991. *Cold Warrior: James Jesus Angleton, The CIA's Master Spy Hunter.* New York: Simon & Schuster.

MANNING, R. 2004. *Against the Grain: How Agriculture Has Hijacked Civilization.* San Francisco: North Point Press.

MANTOUX, P. 1906. *The Industrial Revolution in the Eighteenth Century.* London: Cape.

MARABLE, M. 2002. *The Great Wells of Democracy: The Meaning of Race in American Life.* New York: Basic Civitas Books.

MARCUSE, H. 1964. *One-Dimensional Man.* Boston: Beacon Press.

MARKUSEN, A., YUDKEN, J. 1992. *Dismantling the Cold War Economy.* New York: Basic Books.

MARSHALL, A. 1890. *Principles of Economics.* London: Macmillan.

MARTINEZ, E. 2003. "Don't Call This Country America," *Z Magazine*, July/August.

MARX, K. 1844/1963. *Early Writings.* (translated and edited by T.B. Bottomore. New York: McGraw-Hill.

_____1867/1967. *Capital, Vol. I.* New York: International Publishers.

_____and ENGELS, F. 1845-46/1970. *The German Ideology.* New York: International Publishers.

_____1967. *Selected Works.* New York: International Publishers.

MATRAY, J.I. (ed.) 1991. *Historical Dictionary of the Korean War.* New York: Greenwood Press.

MAZZOCCO, S. 2003. "The Americanization of Youth Through MTV." Research Paper, University of Modena, Italy.

MAYER, M. 2002. ""Banking's Future Lies in the Past," *NYT*, 8-25-02

MEEROPOL, M. 2003. *An Execution in the Family: One Son's Journey.* New York: St. Martin's Press.

MELMAN, S. 1965. *Our Depleted Society.* New York: Holt, Rinehart & Winston.

_____1970. *Pentagon Capitalism.* New York: McGraw-Hill.

_____1974, *The Permanent War Economy.* New York: McGraw-Hill.

MERWIN, W.S. 1997. *The Vixen.* New York: Alfred A. Knopf.

MESZAROS, I. 1998. "The Uncontrollability of Globalizing Capital," *Monthly Review*, February.

MEYER, C. 1980. *Facing Reality.* New York: Harper & Row.

MILLER, D. NOWAK, M. 1977. *The Fifties: The Way We Really Were.* New York: Doubleday.

MILLER, H. 1971. *Rich Man, Poor Man.* New York: Crowell.

MILLER, J. (et al.). 2003. *Real World Macro.* Cambridge, MA: Dollars & Sense.

MILLER, M.C. 2001. *The Bush Dyslexicon.* New York: Norton.

MILLS, C.W. 1951. *White Collar.* New York: Oxford University Press.

_____1956. *The Power Elite.* New York: Oxford University Press.

_____1967. *The Sociological Imagination.* New York: Oxford Univ. Press.

MINSKY, H. 1996. *Stabilizing an Unstable Economy.* New Haven: Yale University Press.

MINTZ, S. 1986. *Sweetness and Power: The Place of Sugar in Modern History.* New York: Penguin.

MISHEL, L., BERNSTEIN, J., BOUSHEY, H. 2003. *The State of Working America, 2002/2003. An Economic Policy Institute Book.* Ithaca, NY: ILR Press. an imprint of Cornell University Press.

MITCHELL, B. 1947. *Depression Decade: From New Era through New Deal, 1920-1941.* New York: Rinehart.

MOISE, E. 1986. *Tonkin Gulf and the Escalation of the War in Vietnam.* Chapel Hill: University of North Carolina Press.

MOORE, M. 2002. *Stupid White Men.* New York: HarperCollins.

MORISON, S.E. 1965. *Oxford History of the American People, Vol 3.* New York: New American Library.

MORRISON, T. 1982. *Tar Baby.* New York: Penguin Plume.

NATIONAL RESOURCES COMMITTEE. 1939. *The Structure of the American Economy.* Washington, D.C.: U.S. Government Printing Office.

NAVARRO, V. 2002. *The Political Economy of Social Inequalities: Consequences for Health and Quality of Life.* Amityville, NY: Baywood Press.

NAVASKY, V. 1980. *Naming Names.* New York: Viking.

NAYLOR, R.T. 1987. *Hot Money and the Politics of Debt*. New York: Simon and Schuster.

NELSON, C. 1999. *Manifesto of a Tenured Radical: Higher Education Under Fire*. Evanston: U. of Ill. Press.

NEUMANN, F. 1942/1963. *Behemoth: The Structure and Practice of National Socialism*. New York: Harper.

NEWMAN, K. 1993. *Declining Fortunes: The Withering of the American Dream*. New York: Basic Books.

NEWMAN, N. 2002. "'Homeland Security as Union Busting," Progressive Populist (6-15-02) <www.populist.com>

NEW YORK TIMES. 1971. *The Pentagon Papers*. Chicago: Quadrangle Books.

NORDHAUS, W.D. 2004. "The Story of a Bubble," NYRB, 1-15.

NORDHOLDT, W.S. 1970. *The People That Walk in Darkness*. New York: Ballantine.

OFFNER, A. (et al.). 2003. *Real World Micro*. Cambridge, MA: Dollars & Sense.

O'FLAHERTY, L. 1984. *Famine*. Dublin: Wolfhound Press.

OGLESBY, C., SHAULL, R. 1967. *Containment and Change*. London: Macmillan.

OLLMAN, B. 1976. *Alienation: Marx's Conception of Man in Capitalist Society*. Cambridge: Cambridge Univ. Press.

OMI, M., WINANT, H. 1994. *Racial Formation in the United States: From the 1960s to the 1990s*. New York: Routledge.

O'NEILL, J.R. 2000. *Something New Under the Sun: An Environmental History of the Twentieth-Century World*. New York: W.W. Norton.

ORWELL, G. 1938/1962 *Homage to Catalonia*. New York: Harcourt Brace.

____1846. *Animal Farm*. New York: Harcourt & Brace.

____1949/2003. *Nineteen Eighty-Four* (1984). New York: Plume/Harcourt Brace.

OSBERG, L. (ed.) 1991. *Inequality and Poverty: International Perspectives*. Armonk, NY: M.E.Sharpe.

PALERMO, J. 2001. *In His Own Right: The Political Odyssey of Senator Robert F. Kennedy*. New York: Columbia University Press.

PALMER, A. 1979. *The Penguin Dictionary of Twentieth Century History*. New York: Penguin.

PARRY, J.H. 1965. *The Spanish Seaborne Empire*. New York: Knopf.

PECHMAN, J. 1989. *Tax Reform, The Rich and the Poor*. Washington: The Brookings Institution.

PHILLIPS, K. 1991. *The Politics of Rich and Poor: Wealth and the American Electorate in the Reagan Aftermath*. New York: Harper Perennial.

____1994. *Arrogant Capital: Washington, Wall Street, and the Frustration of American Politics*. New York: Harper Perennial.

____2002. *Wealth and Democracy: A Political History of the American Rich*. New York: Broadway.

____2004. "Bush Family Values: War, Wealth, Oil." *Los Angeles Times*, Feb. 8.

____2004. *American Dynasty*. New York: Viking.

PILGER, J. 2003. *The New Rulers of the World*. London: Verso.

PITT, W.R./RITTER, S. 2002. *War on Iraq: What Team Bush Doesn't Want You To Know*. New York: Context Books.

PIVEN, F., CLOWARD, R. 1971. *Regulating the Poor*. New York: Pantheon.

PIZZO, S., et al. 1989. *Inside Job: The Looting of America's Savings and Loans*. New York: McGraw-Hill.

POSTMAN, N. 1985. *Amusing Ourselves to Death: Public Discourse in the Age of Show Business.*. New York: Viking Penguin.

POTTER, D. 1958. *People of Plenty*. Chicago: Univ. of Chicago Press.

POWELL, C. 1995. *My American Journey*. New York: Random House.

POWERS, T. 1979. *The Man Who Kept the Secrets; Richard Helms and the CIA*. New York: Knopf.

_____2002. *Intelligence Wars: American Secret History from Hitler to Al-Qaeda*. New York: New York Review of Books.

RAMPTON, S., STAUBER, J. 2003. *Weapons of Mass Deception: The Uses of Propaganda in Bush's War on Iraq*. New York: Taucher/Penguin.

_____2004. *Banana Republicans: How the Right Wing is Turning America Into a One-Party State*. New York: Tarcher/ Penguin.

RASSELL, E. "A Bad Bargain: Why U.S. Health Care Costs So Much and Covers So Few," *D&S*, May 1993.

RAVENSCRAFT, D., SCHERER, F.M. 1987. *Mergers, Sell-Offs, and Economic Efficiency*. Washington: The Brookings Institution.

REED, J. 1917/1877. *Ten Days That Shook the World*. New York: Penguin.

REUSS, A. (et al.). 2002. *Real World Globalization*. Cambridge, MA: Dollars & Sense.

RIDGEWAY, J. 1973. *The Last Play: The Struggle to Monopolize the World's Energy Resources*. New York: Dutton.

ROBERTS, S. 2001. *The Untold Story of Atomic Spy David Greenglass, and How He Sent His Sister Ethel Rosenberg to the Electric Chair*. New York: Random House.

ROBINS, N. 1992. *The FBI's War on Freedom of Expression*. New York: Morrow.

ROBINSON, J. 1962. *Economic Philosophy*. Chicago: Aldine.

RODMAN, S. 1939. *A New Anthology of Modern Poetry*. New York: Modern Library.

ROEDIGER, D. 1991. *The Wages of Whiteness: Race and the Making of the American Working Class*. New York: Verso.

ROGIN, L. 1956. *The Meaning and Validity of Economic Theory*. New York: Harper.

ROVERE, R. 1959. *Senator Joe McCarthy*. New York: Harper.

RYAN, W. 1976. *Blaming the Victim*. New York: Random House.

SACKREY, C. 1973. *The Political Economy of Urban Poverty*. New York: W.W. Norton.

_____(et al.). 2002. *Introduction to Political Economy*. Cambridge, MA: Dollars & Sense.

SALVEMINI, G. 1936. *Under the Axe of Fascism*. New York: H. Fertig.

SAMPSON, A. 1975. *The Seven Sisters*. New York: Viking.

SANDBURG, C. 1936. *The People, Yes*. New York: Harcourt Brace Jovanovich.

SAUNDERS, F.S. 1999. *The Cultural Cold War: The CIA and the World of Arts and Letters*. New York: New Press

SCHEIBER, H.N. 1964. *United States Economic History: Selected Readings*. New

York: Knopf.

SCHILLER, H. 1971. *Mass Communications and American Empire.* Boston: Beacon Press.

____1973. *The Mind Managers.* Boston: Beacon Press.

____1976. *Communications and Cultural Domination.* Boston: Beacon Press.

____1989. *Culture, Inc.: The Corporate Takeover of Public Expression.* New York: Oxford University Press.

SCHLESINGER, S., KINZER, S. 1982. *Bitter Fruit: The Untold Story of the U.S. Coup in Guatemala.* New York: Doubleday.

SCHMIDT, C. 1939. *The Corporate State in Action.* New York: Columbia University Press.

SCHOR, J. 1991. *The Overworked American.* New York: Basic Books.

____1998. *The Overspent American.* New York: Basic Books.

SCHULTZ, B. & R. 1989. *It Did Happen Here: Recollections of Political Repression in America.* Berkeley: Univ. of Calif. Press.

SCOTT, P. 1972. *The War Conspiracy: The Secret Road to the Second Indochina War.* Indianapolis: Bobbs-Merrill.

SCITOVSKY, T. 1976. *The Joyless Economy,* New York: Oxford Univ. Press.

SEN, A. 1981. *Poverty and Famine: An Essay on Entitlement and Deprivation.* Oxford: Clarenden Press.

____*Development as Freedom.* New York: Knopf.

SENDER, R. 1936. *Seven Red Sundays.* New York: Liverright.

SENNETT, W. & COBB, J. 1973. *The Hidden Injuries of Class.* New York: Vintage.

SHAWCROSS, W. 1979. *Sideshow: Kissinger, Nixon and the Destruction of Cambodia.* New York: Pocket Books.

SHERMAN, H. 1977. *Stagflation.* New York: Harper.

SHERRILL, R. 1968. *The Accidental President.* New York: Pyramid Books.

____1995. "The Madness of the Market: Dangerous to Your Health," *The Nation* 1-9/16.

SHERWIN, M.J. 1987. *A World Destroyed: Hiroshima and the Origins of the Arms Race.* New York: Vintage.

SILONE, I. 1934. *Fontamara.* New York: Macmillan.

SIMPSON, C. 1993. *Blowback: America's Recruitment of Nazis and Its Effects on the Cold War.* New York: Weidenfeld & Nicolson.

SINCLAIR, U. 1906/2001. *The Jungle.* New York/Mineola, NY: Doubleday/Dover.

____1920. *The Brass Check* Pasadena, CA: Self-published.

____1926. *Oil!* London: Werner Laurie.

SINGER, D. 1999. *Whose Millennium? Theirs or Ours?* New York: Monthly Review Press.

SINGER, P.W. 2003. *Corporate Warriors: The Rise of the Privatized Military Industry.* Ithaca: Cornell University Press.

SLATER, P. 1971/1990, *The Pursuit of Loneliness.* Boston: Beacon Press.

SMITH, A. 1776/1937. *An Inquiry into the Nature and Causes of the Wealth of Nations.* New York: Modern Library.

SMITH, R., EMSHWILLER, J.R. 2003. *24 Days.* New York: Harper Business.

SNOW, E. 1972. *The Long Revolution.* New York: Random House.

SOULE, G. 1947. *Prosperity Decade: From War to Depression*. New York: Rinehart.

STAMPP, K. 1956. *The Peculiar Institution: Slavery in the Ante-Bellum South*. New York: Vintage.

STARR, P. 1982. *The Social Transformation of American Medicine: The Rise of a Sovereign Profession and the Making of a Vast Industry*. New York: Basic Books.

STAVRIANOS, L.S. 1989. *Lifelines From Our Past: A New World History*. Armonk, NY: M.E. Sharpe.

STEFFENS, L. 1904-1957. *The Shame of the Cities*. New York: Sagamore Press.

STEINBECK, J. 1939. *The Grapes of Wrath*. New York: Viking.

STEINBERG, S. 1981. *The Ethnic Myth: Race, Ethnicity, and Class in America*. Boston: Beacon Press.

STIGLITZ, J. 2002. *Globalization and Its Discontents*. New York: W.W. Norton.

____2003. *The Roaring Nineties: A New History of the World's Most Prosperous Decade*. New York: Norton.

STOCKDALE, J. and S, 1984. *Love and War*. New York: Harper & Row.

STOCKMAN, D. 1987. *The Triumph of Politics*. New York: Harper.

STONE, I.F. 1952/1958. *The Hidden History of the Korean War, 1950-51*. Boston: Little, Brown.

____1967. *In a Time of Torment*. New York: Random House.

STREETEN, P. 1984. "Basic Needs: Some Unsettled Questions," *World Development*, Vol. 12, No. 9.

STRETTON, H. 1999. *Economics: A New Introduction*. London: Pluto Press.

SUMMERS, A. 1993. *The Secret Life of J. Edgar Hoover*. New York: Putnam.

SWARD, K. 1948. *The Legend of Henry Ford*. New York: Rinehart.

SWEDBERG, R. (ed.) 1991. *Joseph A. Schumpeter: The Economics and Sociology of Capitalism*. Princeton: Princeton Univ. Press.

SWEEZY, P. 1938. *Monopoly and Competition in the English Coal Trade: 1550-1850*. Cambridge: Harvard Univ. Press.

____1939. "Interest Groupings in the American Economy." (see NATIONAL RESOURCES COMMITTEE)

____1941. *The Theory of Capitalist Development*. New York: Oxford.

____1949. *Socialism*. New York: Macmillan.

____1972. *Modern Capitalism and Other Essays*. New York: Monthly Review Press.

SWOPE, G. 1931. *The Swope Plan for Stabilizing Business*. New York: The Business Bourse.

TACITUS. 98 A.D. *Agricola*. Cambridge: Loeb Classical Library, No.5; Harvard University Press.

TAKAKI, R. 1995. *Hiroshima: Why America Dropped the Bomb*. Boston: Little, Brown & Company.

TAIARA, C. 2002. "All Quiet in the Classroom," *San Francisco Bay Guardian*

TANZER, M. 1969. *The Political Economy of Oil and the Underdeveloped Countries*. Boston: Beacon Press.

____1974. *The Energy Crisis: World Struggle for Power and Wealth*. New York: Monthly Review Press.

TAWNEY, R.H. 1920. *The Acquisitive Society*. New York: Harcourt Brace.

____1926. *Religion and the Rise of Capitalism*. New York: Harcourt Brace.

TERKEL, S. 1974. *Working: People Talk About What They Do All Day and How They Feel About What They Do.* New York: Pantheon.

____1982. *Hard Times: An Oral History of the Great Depression.* New York: Pantheon.

____1984. *The Good War: An Oral History of World War Two.* New York: The New Press.

TUCKER, R.C. 1978, *The Marx-Engels Reader.* New York: Norton.

TURGEON, L. 1996. *Bastard Keynesianism: The Evolution of Economic Thinking and Policymaking since World War II.* Westport, Conn: Greenwood Press.

TYE, L. 1998. *The Father of Spin: Edward L. Bernays and the Birth of Public Relations.* New York: Crown.

UNICEF. 1986. *Report on the State of the World's Children.* New York: UNICEF.

UNITED NATIONS. 1990. *Human Development Report.* New York: United Nations.

UPDIKE, J. "Glad Rags," *New Yorker* (3-1-1993)

ULLMAN, J. (ed.) 1983. *Social Costs in Modern Society.* Westport, Conn.: Quorum Books.

URIBE, A. 1975. *The Black Book of American Intervention in Chile.* Boston: Beacon Press.

U.S. DEPARTMENT OF AGRICULTURE. 1999. *Advanced Report on Household Security in the United States, 1993-1999.* Washington, D.C: USGPO.

U.S. DEPARTMENT OF EDUCATION. 1999. *National Center for Educational Statistics.* Washington, D.C.

U.S. FEDERAL TRADE COMMISSION. 1940. *Report on the Automotive Industry.* Washington: USGPO.

USGPO. 2002. *Economic Report of the President.*

U.S. Senate Intelligence Committee. 1975. Alleged Assassination Plots Involving Foreign Leaders (November); *Covert Action in Chile,1963-73.* U.S.G.P.O.

VEBLEN, T. 1898. "The Beginnings of Ownership," and "The Barbarian Status of Women," in *American Journal of Sociology,* September and November, 1898. (Reprinted in Ardzrooni, L. /Ed./. 1934. (Veblen's) *Essays in Our Changing Order.* New York: Viking.

____1899. *The Theory of the Leisure Class.* New York: Macmillan.

____1904. *The Theory of Business Enterprise.* New York: Scribner's.

____1914/1946. *The Instinct of Workmanship.* New York: Huebsch.

____1915/1946. *Imperial Germany and the Industrial Revolution.* New York: Macmillan.

____1917/1945 *An Inquiry Into the Nature of Peace.* New York: Macmillan/Viking.

____1918. *The Higher Learning in America: A Memorandum on the Conduct of Universities by Businessmen.* New York: Huebsch.

____1919. *The Place of Science in Modern Civilization.* New York: Huebsch.

____1923. *Absentee Ownership and Business Enterprise in Recent Times.* Huebsch.

____1925/1994 *The Laxdaela Saga* New York: Routledge.

____1934, *Essays in Our Changing Order.* New York: Viking. (Edited by Ardzrooni, L.)

WEALE, A. (ed.) 1995. *Eye-Witness Hiroshima.* New York: Carroll & Graf.

WEINSTEIN, J., EAKINS, D. 1970. *Toward a New America*. New York: Vintage.

WILCOX, C. 1969. *Toward Social Welfare*. Homewood, Ill: Irwin.

WILLIAMS, E. 1944. *Capitalism and Slavery*. Chapel Hill, NC: Univ. of North Carolina Press.

_____1984 (1970). *From Columbus to Castro: The History of the Caribbean 1492-1969*. New York: Vintage Books.

WILLIAMS, W.A. 1959. *The Tragedy of American Diplomacy*. New York: Dell.

_____1966. *The Contours of American History*. Chicago: Quadrangle.

_____1969 *The Roots of the Modern American Empire*. New York: Random House.

_____1980. *Empire as a Way of Life*. New York: Oxford Univ. Press.

WILLIAMSON, T. (et al.). 2002. *Making a Place for Community*. Cambridge, MA: Dollars & Sense.

WILLS, G. 1969. *Nixon Agonistes: The Crisis of the Self-Made Man*. New York: Houghton Mifflin.

_____1988. *Reagan's America*. New York: Penguin.

WINANT, H. 2001. *The World Is A Ghetto: Race and Democracy Since World War II*. New York: Basic Books.

WITTNER, L. 1978. *Cold War America: From Hiroshima to Watergate*. New York: Holt, Rinehart and Winston.

WOLFF, E. 1987. *Growth, Accumulation and Unproductive Activity*. New York: Cambridge Univ. Press.

_____1995. *Top Heavy: A Study of Increasing Inequality of Wealth in America*. New York: Twentieth Century.

WOLMAN, W., COLAMOSCA, A. 2002. *The Great 401(k) Hoax: Why Your Family's Financial Security Is at Risk and What You Can Do About It*. New York: Perseus Publishing.

WOODHAM-SMITH, C. 1962. *The Great Hunger*. New York: Harper

WOODHOUSE, C.M. 1990. *The Rise and Fall of the Greek Colonels*. London: Granada.

WOODWARD, C. V. 1956. *Reunion and Reaction*. New York: Doubleday; Anchor.

_____1963. *Tom Watson: Agrarian Rebel*. New York: Oxford University Press.

_____1966. *The Strange Career of Jim Crow*. New York: Oxford University Press.

WRIGHT, J. 1995. *Competing Solutions: American Health Care Proposals and International Experience*. Washington, D.C.: The Brookings Institution.

WRIGHT, M.I. 2003. *YOU: Back the Attack! WE"LL Bomb Whoever We Want!*. New York: Seven Stories Press.

WRIGHT, R. 1992. *Stolen Continents: The Americas Through Indian Eyes Since 1492*. Boston: Houghton Mifflin.

YATES, M. 1994. *Longer House, Fewer Jobs: Employment and Unemployment in the United States*. New York: Monthly Review Press.

_____1998. *Why Unions Matter*. New York: Monthly Review Press.

_____2003. *Naming the System: Inequality and Work in the Global Economy*. New York: Monthly Review Press.

YOUNG, M.B. 1991. *The Vietnam Wars: 1945-1990*. New York: HarperCollins.

ZAROULIS, N. & SULLIVAN, G. 1984. *Who Spoke Up? American Protests Against the War in Vietnam*. New York: Harper & Row.

ZEPEZAUER, M., NAIMAN, A. 1996. *Take the Rich Off Welfare*. Tucson, AZ: Odonian Press.

ZINN, H. 1973. *Postwar America: 1945-1971*. Indianapolis: Bobbs-Merrill.

1986/2002. *Emma: A Play*. Boston: South End Press.

____1999. *You Can't Be Neutral on a Moving Train*. Boston: Houghton Mifflin.

____2000. *A People's History of the United States*. New York: The New Press.

Z Nagazine. (various issues) + Web site: <www.zmag.org>

ZWEIG, M. 2000. *The Working Class Majority: America's Best Kept Secret*. Ithaca, NY: Cornell University Press.

About the Author

Douglas F. Dowd has been teaching and writing socioeconomic history for more than 50 years, beginning at U.C. Berkeley (where he had done his studies), and then leaving to teach at Cornell University for almost 20 years. He returned to the San Francisco Bay Area to teach again at Berkeley, U.C. Santa Cruz, and at the California State Universities at San Jose and San Francisco.

In the 1950s his research in medieval and early modern Italian economic history gained him a Guggenheim Research Fellowship, followed by a Fulbright fellowship for teaching in Italy in 1966-67. He returned in 1986 to teach there in alternate semesters for ten more years, and resumed doing so a few years ago. In addition to his university teaching, for over 30 years he has offered weekly free community classes in the San Francisco Bay Area (for which there is a web site: www.dougdowd.org)

A professor of economic history at Johns Hopkins University in Italy and also at the University of California, Douglas F. Dowd has written over 10 books critical of capitalism, including *Capitalism and Its Economics: A Critical History*, *The Twisted Dream: Capitalist Development in the United States Since 1776*, and *Understanding Capitalism: Critical Analysis From Karl Marx to Amartya Sen*.